NEUROCOGNITIVE DISORDERS IN AGING

*To my mother, Julie Aron, and to the
memory of my friend and mentor, Liz Bates.*

NEUROCOGNITIVE DISORDERS IN AGING

Daniel Kempler
Emerson College

SAGE Publications
Thousand Oaks ■ London ■ New Delhi

For information:

 Sage Publications, Inc.
2455 Teller Road
Thousand Oaks, California 91320
E-mail: order@sagepub.com

Sage Publications Ltd.
1 Oliver's Yard
55 City Road
London EC1Y 1SP
United Kingdom

Sage Publications India Pvt. Ltd.
B-42, Panchsheel Enclave
Post Box 4109
New Delhi 110 017 India

Printed in the United States of America

Library of Congress Cataloging-in-Publication data

Kempler, Daniel.
Neurocognitive disorders in aging / Daniel Kempler.
     p. cm.
Includes bibliographical references and index.
ISBN 0-7619-2162-1 (cloth) — ISBN 0-7619-2163-X (pbk.)
   1. Cognition disorders in old age. 2. Geriatric neuropsychiatry. I. Title.
RC553.C64K45 2005
618.97′689—dc22   2004005706

04   05   06   07   08   10   9   8   7   6   5   4   3   2   1

Acquiring Editor:	Jim Brace-Thompson
Editorial Assistant:	Karen Ehrmann
Production Editor:	Sanford Robinson
Typesetter:	C&M Digitals (P) Ltd.
Copy Editor:	Gillian Dickens
Indexer:	Julie Grayson
Cover Designer:	Janet Foulger

CONTENTS

INTRODUCTION

It is now common knowledge that the elderly are the fastest growing segment of the population. The number of people in the United States age 65 years or older is expected to grow from 35 million in 2000 to 70.3 million in 2030. It is also well known that the elderly have more medical problems than any other age group:

- More than 80% of those older than 65 have at least one chronic medical illness.
- The elderly are hospitalized more than twice as often as younger adults.
- Between 33% and 66% of the patients in acute care wards are elderly.
- Ninety percent of the long-term beds (i.e., nursing homes) are occupied by the elderly.
- The elderly account for 33% of all health care expenditures.
- The elderly receive 25% of all prescriptions.

Some of the most common disorders in the elderly result in focal neurological deficits, dementia, and/or movement disorders. This book is an introduction to the common disorders that cause cognitive and related behavioral disturbances in older people. The book emphasizes the links between brain dysfunction, cognitive impairment, diagnosis, and treatment. The book is organized along the following lines.

Chapter 1 reviews in some detail differences between younger and older adults that affect the evaluation and treatment of older patients. Because the process of healthy aging is associated with changes in thinking and behavior, it is important that these typical and healthy changes not be confused with, or identified as, disorders. To put it another way, without an understanding of how the young and old differ, it is impossible to know (a) whether there is something wrong with an older person and/or (b) how to help. Chapter 2 presents basic neuroanatomy important to understanding the relationship between brain damage and behavior, and Chapter 3 introduces the anatomy and physiology of stroke, one of the most common causes of brain dysfunction in aging. The next 10 chapters present cognitive and behavioral disorders in a consistent manner. Each chapter introduces areas of normal function, changes in healthy aging, and common behavioral symptoms of disease, followed by diagnostic and treatment issues. Chapters 4 through 9 focus on cognitive dysfunctions that arise after injury to relatively localized regions of the brain. Chapters 10, 11, and 12 address the more global issues of memory, dementia, delirium, and depression. Chapter 13 introduces several common movement disorders that are associated with aging and cognitive dysfunction, with a focus on Parkinson's disease. The final chapter summarizes current work on successful aging.

This book is written to be a suitable introduction for students and professionals with no prior background in gerontology, medicine, or related fields, as well as those who have a general knowledge and/or exposure to these topics but wish to learn more about specific disorders. I have written this to be practical and helpful. My goal is that the book will serve as a reference for people who have contact with the elderly on a frequent or infrequent basis—including those who work in day care and nursing homes, social workers, psychologists, rehabilitation specialists, physicians, nurses, and family members of older people with cognitive, behavioral, and motor disturbances. I hope that it provides answers to common questions about the behavior of older adults: Is it normal or not? If not, what could be causing it? And what can be done about it? If this book answers some of these difficult questions some of the time, it will have succeeded.

ACKNOWLEDGMENTS

Wittingly or not, many people contributed time, ideas, and emotional support to this project over many years. The partial list of colleagues and friends below is inadequate—it is incomplete and a meager way to thank important people. To those listed here and to all those omitted (you know who you are), thank you for helping me through the process of writing a book. I could not have done it without you.

Although the book covers much broader topics and themes than my own work, my research is included here where appropriate, and it influenced my perspective on all related topics discussed. My research and my thinking has been greatly influenced and facilitated by teachers, colleagues, and friends over the years. Susie Curtiss and Jeff Cummings, very early on, encouraged me to look at the effects of brain damage on behavior. Jeff Metter, who was instrumental in the early revolution investigating focal brain disorders such as aphasia through functional neuroimaging, gave me my start in academics. Amit Almor, Elaine Andersen, Victor Henderson, Maryellen MacDonald, and Mark Seidenberg made my years of research on language deficits in Alzheimer's interesting, enjoyable, and productive. Many people inspired me to continue with research and writing through my years at the USC School of Medicine, including Mickie Welsh, Evelyn Teng, and particularly Barbara Cone-Wesson, whose positive attitude and boundless energy have been a source of strength for many years. Dave Peterson and Liz Zelinski at the USC School of Gerontology gave me the opportunity and freedom to develop a course on neurocognitive disorders in aging, which eventually led to this book. Diana Sidtis, friend and colleague for the past 25 years, taught me about the value and synergy of collaboration. Collaboration with her and others has made my work much more interesting than it would have been on my own. Finally, like so many others, I am indebted to the extreme generosity and brilliance of Liz Bates, who should be credited with any professional success I may have. She introduced me to ideas, people, and places I would never have known without her.

I am also lucky to have so many good friends outside of my profession. Without them, I am lost. In particular, I want to acknowledge Brenda Mallory, Galust Mardirussian, and Harvey Segalove, who have sustained me over the past quarter century with their insights, love, and wit. Wally Aron is the best model of intellect and kindness I can imagine, not to mention being one of the best writers on the planet. During the past year, several others made it possible for me to finish the manuscript while transitioning to a new life, cajoling and entertaining me through difficult times, including Liz Anker, Cindy Bartlett, Mira Goral, Karl Johnson, Marye Tharp, and Jenny Tripp.

The final form of this manuscript was improved by several people: My friend and colleague Zoë Hunter helped set a clear tone by severely editing early chapters; an anonymous reviewer provided detailed and helpful suggestions at several important junctures; Teresa Seeman and Melissa Tabbarah were kind enough to contribute a chapter on successful aging, an area outside of my expertise; and the book would have taken even longer to complete without the superb assistance of Alex Burnham.

Finally, I would not have had the guts to undertake writing a book or the perseverance to complete it without the strength, inspiration, and enduring friendships of two amazing women: my mother, Julie Aron, and my mentor, Liz Bates. I could not have done this, or much at all, without them.

DXK
Boston
March 2004

1

How Do Younger and Older Patients Differ?

Chapter Preview

To begin our exploration of neurocognitive disorders in aging, we will explore five key questions:

1. How does the age of the patient shape a clinical evaluation?

Many people age successfully. That is, they remain relatively healthy through much of the aging process. However, even successful aging is accompanied by inevitable changes in mental and physical functions. Disease in older adults is superimposed on these usual effects of aging. The overlay of disease on top of the healthy aging process changes the way diseases are manifested, assessed, and treated. Therefore, understanding healthy aging is a prerequisite to evaluating and treating age-related diseases. To know if any particular change in an older adult is abnormal, worrisome, or constitutes a disease process, we must first distinguish between the effects of healthy aging versus disease. A brief warning: This is not always easy and sometimes not even possible.

2. How do we interpret data from older patients?

We can determine if a change in cognitive function or behavior is likely due to disease by the combined use of age-appropriate norms, comparison with younger cohorts, and comparison with a patient's own performance over time.

3. What is special about arriving at a diagnosis for older adults?

The diagnosis is crucial for many reasons, including the importance of determining whether the cause of the problem is reversible.

4. How is a prognosis special for older adults?

The prognosis informs all who have contact with the patient about how the patient will fare under various conditions and, importantly, the likelihood of spontaneous recovery, if therapy is warranted, and the predicted outcome of specific treatments. Certain prognostic indicators are more likely to play a role in establishing the prognosis for older than younger adults, including the role of medication, disease chronicity, and irreversibility.

(Continued)

(Continued)

5. How do recovery and treatment plans differ for younger versus older patients?

Although older patients may recover more slowly and less completely than younger patients with the same type of injury, they are often excellent candidates for treatment if the goals and mechanics of treatment are sensitive to the differences between younger and older patients.

Primary aging refers to the typical age-related decrements that are the usual and natural losses of function. These include hair loss, skin wrinkles, difficulty seeing close up, word-finding difficulty, and some loss of short-term memory. These changes are natural, expected, and nearly universal aspects of healthy, even successful, aging. **Secondary aging** refers to the declines in function due to abuse, disuse, or disease that increase in risk or severity with age. For example, long-term exposure of sun puts older people at increased risk for skin cancer, the flexibility of blood vessels declines with age and increases the risk of stroke, and neurochemical and anatomical changes in the brain that accompany aging increase the risk of dementia. Although primary versus secondary aging is a convenient distinction, it is not always clear where primary aging ends and secondary aging begins, particularly in the area of cognition, which is the primary focus of this book. For instance, as we age, we have greater and greater difficulty finding the right words—and occasionally, mid-thought or mid-sentence, we may forget what we were saying altogether. This is a typical part of healthy aging. However, word-finding difficulty and short-term memory lapses are also two signs of early dementia. How do we know if these problems are typical changes associated with aging or signs of a disease? In fact, in the very earliest stages of dementia, if mild to moderate word-finding problems are the only symptom, they could easily be mistaken for normal age-related word-finding difficulty. This overlap between the signs of primary and secondary aging makes distinguishing the two difficult but not impossible. Remember as you read this book that although there is often no easy or foolproof test to decide whether a particular behavior is the result of primary or

secondary aging, with enough information and careful evaluation, the task is usually possible.

Each chapter in this book reviews cognitive and behavioral changes seen in healthy aging as a background to discussing the signs and symptoms of common disorders. This first chapter reviews general changes in aging that affect clinical work with older patients regardless of specific disorders, divided into five important areas: conducting the evaluation, interpreting data gathered in an evaluation, determining the diagnosis, estimating the prognosis, and planning treatment.

EVALUATION

Evaluation is the process of gathering the crucial information to decide what, if anything, is wrong. It is the first step toward developing a diagnosis, which forms the basis for creating a treatment plan.

Evaluations take many forms. Some evaluations are informal and consist of observations made by watching or having a conversation with a patient. Some evaluations are formal, meaning that they use structured test protocols, frequently administered and interpreted in a standard way. Test protocols often yield quantitative data. Evaluations can be performed by a wide range of health care providers.

This section reviews the most important and universal aspects of evaluations, including preparing for an evaluation, collecting the patient history, developing a symptom list, and eliciting clinical signs.

The evaluation begins before the patient is seen. Typically, initial contact between the patient, caregiver, and clinician will provide helpful information in planning the clinical visit. With all patients, this will consist of a reason for the visit and basic demographic information, including age. This, in turn, prompts the clinician to ask certain other questions and prepare for the visit. Even at this point, before the clinic visit, age can be a crucial factor in appropriate preparation. Evaluations of older patients must take many particular issues into consideration, including the following:

• *Transportation and reminders.* Declining independence, mobility, memory, and sensory systems in the elderly make it essential that, prior to the interview, transportation is arranged and patients and caregivers are reminded to bring medical records, glasses, hearing aids, dentures, and a person who knows the patient well to the evaluation.

• *Time of interview.* Although the time of an evaluation for younger patients is typically considered vis-à-vis the work schedule, with older patients, mobility and alertness are primary considerations. Mornings are usually better because older people are typically more alert early in the day, but if transportation and mobility are issues, they may need extra time to get to the clinic, so very early appointments may be difficult. Morning is usually better than later in the day for older people to be evaluated. They tend to be more alert and less confused early in the day, although some elders require increased time to get somewhere, so it should not be too early.

• *Length of interview.* Evaluations of older patients take longer than comparable evaluations with younger patients, so it is wise to allow plenty of time, sometimes even extra appointments.

• *Review of medical records.* Older people typically have large medical records, which take more time to review.

• *Social history.* Include, if not emphasize, family and social support systems, including durable power of attorney for health care, wills, attitudes toward death and dying, and hospice care when appropriate.

• *Nutrition.* Ask about dentures, the presence of a kitchen in the home, transportation to grocery store, and so on.

• *Psychiatric/emotional.* Include a discussion of possible depression.

• *Medication.* This is usually a long list, and it should cover all of the medications taken, not just those prescribed. This may include over-the-counter medication and prescription medications prescribed for the patient and for others. If appropriate, investigate the possibility of polypharmacy. Be aware that dosages often differ for younger versus older patients due to changes in metabolic rates as we age.

• *Primary Symptoms.* Older patients may underreport important symptoms, explaining them away as typical of aging. Some symptoms may not appear in older patients due to altered physical exertion patterns and other lifestyle change. For instance, if the patient is not very physically active, typical warning symptoms that only occur with exertion may not appear at all.

The first element of an evaluation is usually the **history,** which refers to everything that might have contributed to or affected the problems that brought the patient to the health care provider. Historical information can be gathered by direct conversation with the patient, an interview with a friend or caregiver, review of prior medical records, or a combination of these and any other reliable information source. Certain issues are considered important no matter what the age of the client, including medical history, social support, and primary symptoms. For older patients, medical histories are likely to be longer and more complicated than for younger patients and therefore may take more time to review. Social history for older patients, as with anyone, is likely to include living situation but will also often emphasize family and social support systems, durable power of attorney for health care, wills, attitudes toward death and dying, and hospice care when appropriate. Nutritional status, frequently a minor issue with younger patients, is often compromised in older patients by practical considerations, including dentures, availability of transportation to a grocery store, and lack of cooking facilities. Another area that needs to be emphasized in the history of older patients is medication. Older patients typically take more medications than younger patients. Both prescription and over-the-counter drugs should be documented because of the frequent and sometimes negative effects of medications on cognition. These effects include delirium, depression, hallucinations, psychomotor slowing, memory impairment, and dementia, which can be caused by relatively common drugs used to treat everything from swelling and depression to hypertension, epilepsy, and Parkinson's disease (Jain, 2000). Because of the multiple medications taken by many older people, they are very susceptible to the risk of **polypharmacy**—that is, the problems that occur when a patient is taking more over-the-counter and/or prescription medications than are actually needed (Hohl, 2001; Larsen & Martin, 1999). Dosages often differ for younger and older patients due to changes in metabolic rates as we age (Spina & Scordo, 2002). The possibility of depression, particularly because of its effect on thinking and frequency in older patients, should be carefully investigated (see Chapter 12).

The precise content and focus of the history will vary with setting, type of health care provider, and the patient's primary concern but will always include the primary reason the patient is being evaluated. This is sometimes called the *chief complaint*—an unfortunate term because patients may in fact not complain about anything, even very important health concerns. **Symptom** is the technical term referring to any abnormality described by the patient. Symptoms are the patient's subjective experience and can be a simple description of a problem (e.g., "I can no longer get out of a chair without help") or more vague (e.g., "Sometimes when I go up stairs, my legs feel funny"). It may be difficult to elicit a clear picture of the problem from some patient reports (e.g., "Nothing's wrong" or "My daughter just wants to put me in a home"). Sometimes, patients describe a conclusion about what has caused their problem (e.g., "I had a heart attack"), which, of course, should be verified rather than believed for the simple reason that terms are not used in the same way by all people. For instance, many people do not distinguish between a heart attack and a stroke, a difference that can be crucial in diagnosis and treatment. If the patient does not offer sufficient information, every lead should be pursued either by direct questions (e.g., When did it start? Precisely when does it happen? Is it getting worse? Does it feel like numbness?) or by asking other individuals who know the patient well. Older patients may underreport important symptoms, explaining them away as typical of aging. Some symptoms that are expected in younger people may not appear in older patients at all. For example, with decreased physical activity, typical warning symptoms such as chest pain that occur only with exertion may not appear at all. Other symptoms common in younger people present differently in older patients. To take one concrete example, pneumonia, a single diagnosis, can cause very different symptoms and disabilities in older versus younger patients. In younger people, pneumonia typically causes a fever and fatigue. In older people, pneumonia rarely causes a fever but does cause confusion (Rowe & Besdine, 1988). Finally, symptoms in the elderly are likely to be multiple. It is crucial not to stop probing for symptoms after only one has been revealed.

Following a history, an actual examination often takes place to follow up and find the causes of relevant symptoms. This might be a physical examination, a psychiatric examination, a neuropsychological evaluation, and so forth, again depending on the setting and the expertise of the health care provider. Through this examination, the clinician identifies **clinical signs**—objective abnormalities. Signs may be the same as the symptoms described by the patient but will often be more technical in nature, using jargon of the specialty. For instance, a patient may describe her symptom as "trouble walking," and the corresponding clinical sign, referring to the same phenomenon observed by the examiner, might be "slow, wide-based, unsteady gait." Clinical signs often also include observations not noticed by the patient, such as slowed reflexes, loss of balance when pushed, reduced hearing sensitivity, or slurred speech.

INTERPRETATION OF DATA

An evaluation yields data. To reach a diagnosis, the clinician must interpret these data to determine if an individual patient is experiencing a decline in function and, if so, whether it is part of the healthy aging process. This is typically done by comparing the patient's data with (a) published norms, (b) younger people, or (c) the patient's own prior level of functioning. Each of these types of comparisons has its advantages and disadvantages.

Standardized Tests and Published Norms: Risks and Benefits

Many disciplines have standardized tests that can be administered to patients in the same manner in different locations and at different times. These include everything from blood and urine analyses, to tests of strength and range of movement, to tests of higher cognitive function such as problem solving and reading comprehension. The beauty of standardized tests is that clinicians at different sites can compare the performance of an individual patient to a large number of healthy and/or impaired individuals on the same test. Standardized tests allow the clinician to derive a set of numbers representing a particular patient's performance (i.e., test scores). These scores allow comparison between this patient and the performance of others of comparable age, sex, and sometimes even educational and cultural background. From this comparison, the clinician can see if a particular patient's performance fits into the normal range or the range of people with particular disorders. This, in turn, helps to determine the diagnosis, the likelihood of recovery, and the type of treatment that is most appropriate. Test results are also helpful in conveying to the patient and caregivers what is going on; caregivers often want to know "how does she compare with others?" and "have you ever seen anyone like her before?" Standardized performance scores allow clinicians to say with some assurance how the patient fits into a range (e.g., "She performed in the middle of the range for healthy people in her age group" vs. "She is below the normal range but in the top 10% of a comparison group of people with Alzheimer's-type dementia"). Test scores can be helpful in several ways: (a) They highlight for the clinician which, if any, areas of function are in need of improvement, thereby guiding treatment recommendations; (b) they can be obtained repeatedly over time to monitor decline and/or improvement; and (c) they are a very helpful tool to demonstrate the degree of impairment and improvement to patients, caregivers, and health insurance agencies.

There are also disadvantages inherent in the use and interpretation of standardized tests. One pitfall of using standardized tests is that there is always a considerable amount of information that cannot be determined by standardized tests. For instance, standardized tests cannot by themselves tell the clinician or family member how much of a decrement a patient has experienced unless there is sequential information on that particular patient on the same test. Being in the 60th percentile might represent a decline in function for one person and not for another, depending on that person's prior level of functioning. Therefore, standardized tests often leave open whether there has been a decline in performance. Second, there can be surprisingly little relationship between performance on a test in the clinic and hypothetically related functional abilities at home. For instance, a patient may not be able to manipulate small objects or read numbers well in the clinic but be able to work a push-button telephone perfectly well at home. Third, and a crucial consideration in working with older patients, many standardized tests are not normed adequately for older people or people with particular disorders, having no or very small appropriate comparison groups. This is particularly important because older adults, just by virtue of being older, have different performance characteristics than younger adults due to many factors, including a lack of exposure to various facts and events (cohort effects; see below), slower responses, and expected changes in particular mental functions. Appropriate age norms compensate for these differences between younger and older adults and thereby reduce the danger of misinterpreting a behavior typical of older adults as an indication of disease. Fourth, tests vary greatly in their **sensitivity** (the probability of accurately identifying patients with disease) and **specificity** (the probability of accurately identifying patients without disease)—that is, their ability to distinguish healthy from impaired patients. Importantly, the sensitivity and specificity of particular tests vary depending on particular patient characteristics. For instance, the Mini-Mental Status Examination (Folstein, Folstein, & McHugh, 1975), a commonly used screening instrument for dementia in the elderly, is more sensitive to dementia in those with relatively high levels of education (e.g., Grigoletto, Zappala, Anderson, & Lebowitz, 1999). Finally, test scores often do not capture qualitative information about symptoms; that is, they do not tell you what specific behavior or problem is responsible for a particular rating. For instance, two patients can obtain the same score on a particular test for very different reasons, some germane to the test, such as poor memory on a memory test, and some less central, such as off-task behavior or poor vision. For these and other reasons, reliance on published norms may be inappropriate or difficult for certain individuals on certain tests.

Direct Comparison With Younger People: The Effects of Cohort, Age, and Disease

We are sometimes faced with only younger groups for comparison. This happens in at least two particular and relatively common circumstances: (a) when we use standardized tests that are developed for and normed on children or younger adults or (b) when we use data generated from cross-sectional as opposed to longitudinal research (Schaie, 1996). There are good reasons for both.

Tests that are developed and normed on only younger adults are frequently the newer tests that use unique and interesting methods.

Data from older adults, when we are lucky enough to find them, come from either longitudinal or cross-sectional research. Longitudinal research accumulates data by following individuals over time (e.g., Schaie, 2000). The participants are typically given the same tests or questions multiple times over a period of years. This is probably the most reliable way to obtain data on the effects of early development and aging. However, longitudinal research is difficult, time-consuming, and expensive. It is difficult to rely on people being available for testing over a long period of time. Obviously, if we want to know the effects on aging over several

decades, an appropriate longitudinal study could take 30 or 40 years to complete. Finally, due to these difficulties, they are very expensive to perform.

The most common alternative is a cross-sectional research design. Cross-sectional studies sample individuals at various ages, comparing, for instance, a group of people in their 50s with a group in their 70s. On the basis of these data, we draw conclusions about the effects of aging between ages 50 and 70 without having to follow any individuals over a period of 20 years. Cross-sectional data are often available because cross-sectional research is quicker and, for that reason, much more cost-effective than longitudinal research. However, in all cross-sectional research results, we draw conclusions about aging based on a comparison of the performance of older adults with younger adults. One problem with such comparisons is the risk of mistakenly attributing a difference between younger and older adults to aging or disease when in fact it may be due to generational or cohort effects (Hofer & Sliwinski, 2001; Schaie & Willis, 2002).

A **cohort** is a particular group of people, often defined by age or generation. Cohorts are defined by age bands (e.g., 39–59) and shared experience (e.g., male veterans of World War II or adult women who work outside of the home). Research studies often define their cohorts differently, using different age bands and other distinct criteria. A **cohort effect** refers to the fact that different groups have different life experiences and therefore different knowledge and skills. Cohort effects are particularly important in studies of aging and disease, in which it is essential that we distinguish between effects of early and midlife life experiences versus a typical decline in function with age versus the effects of disease. A concrete example will illustrate. People born in the 1920s and 1930s differ from people born in the 1950s and 1960s in many ways. For instance, the younger, more recent, generation is more likely to be exposed to computers (U.S. Bureau of the Census, 2000), and younger women are more likely to be involved in work outside the home than prior generations (U.S. Department of Labor, 2001). Although a cross-sectional comparison of a computer-based typing or visual pattern resolution might show better performance by people in their 40s than people in their 80s, this does not necessarily mean that we lose the ability to do these tasks as we age. In this case, these "age differences" may simply be due to life experiences (i.e., cohort effects); specifically, the older generation did not have the same amount of practice doing similar tasks throughout their lives. Many early life circumstances can contribute to cohort differences, including the type of work performed during one's life; the availability of health care; childbirth and child care practices; exposure to television, video, movies, and computers; pollutants; and cultural phenomena such as fads in exercise, food, and medication. Several powerful influences on cohorts are mentioned below.

One particularly powerful influence on cohorts is education. The extent of formal education and the closely related accomplishmen of literacy, usually accomplished early in life and practiced throughout life, are strong predictors of cognitive function and test performance later in life. In general, older people have less education than younger people (see Figure 1.1). Urban versus rural locale, socioeconomic class, and race interact with education such that older, rural, and poorer people and non-Whites tend to have had less access to educational opportunities than younger, urban, and economically privileged groups. Literacy plays an obvious role in performance on tests that require reading and writing. Literacy also affects spoken/auditory language performance because the exposure to print is strongly related to vocabulary (Cunningham & Stanovich, 1997), which in turn affects performance on any verbal test. In addition, because literacy is in many cases closely correlated with education, they are both correlated with other cognitive performance, including world knowledge and problem solving.

Another important variable in interpreting test results is cultural background. The ethnic makeup of the U.S. population is changing dramatically and rapidly. Patients who are not North American Caucasians present the obvious challenge of communication across languages, which immediately renders useless many of the tests developed and normed only in English. Moreover, cultures differ in many aspects relevant to test/evaluation performance, including familiarity with test-taking skills, familiarity with actual content (e.g., color terms, animal terms), and familiarity with and attitudes toward health care in general (Dick, Teng, Kempler, Davis, & Taussig, 2002; Salas-Provance, Erickson, & Reed, 2002). Translation of a test into another language does not necessarily solve these problems, in part because the languages themselves have different properties that affect performance. For example, Kempler, Teng, et al. (1998) found significantly different performance across cultures in a test of animal name generation (name as many animals as you can in 60 seconds) that was attributed to the fact that animal names are significantly longer in some languages than others (e.g., Spanish animal names are two and three syllables, whereas Vietnamese animal names are all one syllable).

Another important effect on performance of older individuals stems from their life experience in later years and the ways in which

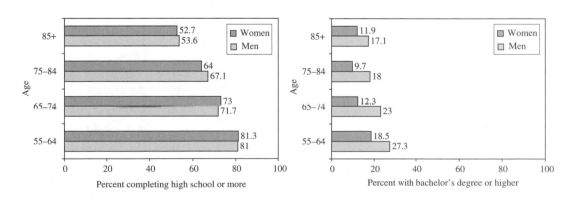

Figure 1.1   Percentage of People 55 Years and Older by Educational Attainment, Age, and Sex: 1999.

the everyday lives of older people, particularly after retirement, differ from younger people. Older people, whether they are retired and living independently or residing in a residential facility where there may be few opportunities for activity, have different cognitive demands placed on them than younger people in the workforce and/or raising a family. Diminished cognitive demands placed on older adults may involve learning fewer new procedures; performing fewer complex, speeded tasks; and functioning with less cognitive effort overall. Therefore, when faced with cognitive batteries in a testing situation and asked to perform novel tasks, they may be at a disadvantage compared to younger cohorts. This may be due to their relatively recent lack of practice and recent change in level of cognitive activity rather than either natural aging or disease (La Rue, 1992; Labouvie-Vief & Lawrence, 1985; McKhann & Albert, 2002).

A combination of cross-sectional and longitudinal research designs alleviates many of the problems associated with purely longitudinal and cross-sectional studies (see Schaie, 1996). In one combination approach, researchers start with a cross-sectional design but, after a certain number of years, (a) retest at least some of the original respondents, yielding valuable longitudinal data, and (b) test a new group of respondents from the same age groups, yielding cross-sectional data. For instance, say in 1990, three cohorts (40-, 50-, and 60-year-olds) are tested. In 2000, some of those same people are tested again, yielding longitudinal data from those ages 40 to 50, 50 to 60, and 60 to 70, and four new groups are tested (40-, 50-, 60-, and 70-year-olds), providing cross-sectional data from matched groups for the original set (some of whom are now age 70).

Comparison of Patients With Themselves Over Time

One way to overcome the difficulties inherent in standardized tests and cross-sectional data is to look at an individual's current function vis-à-vis his or her prior level of functioning. Decrements in function seen this way may be due to healthy aging or disease, but this method eliminates cohort effects and erroneous comparisons with inappropriate groups or data. To compar

a patient with his or her own prior level of performance, clinicians need to obtain performance data at regular intervals through the patient's life span. In some areas of medicine, this is done through regular blood, urine, and other tests, which allow long-term tracking of various health indicators such as cholesterol and blood pressure. In the area of cognitive function, however, we rarely have appropriate test data collected over a long period of time. Therefore, we often rely on either patient or caregiver reports. For instance, if the family is concerned that a patient has gotten lost while driving, and this is a new behavior, we can ask for an estimate of the number of times the individual has gotten lost while driving this year versus last year versus the year before. This is easier with some notable events such as getting lost than it is for more frequent and less obvious mental events such as forgetting a word. In addition, recall, particularly about oneself or a loved one, is extremely selective and at times unreliable. To overcome the inherent difficulty and subjectivity in recalling the frequency of recent events, researchers have developed several standardized methods to aid in this task. One such scale, the Adult Functional Adaptive Behavior Scale (Spirrison & Pierce, 1992), asks the clinician to rate a patient's current performance in a number of different skills and behaviors on a 4-point scale. This scale helps the professional to assess a person's skills in

- eating,
- ambulation,
- toileting,
- dressing,
- grooming,
- managing personal area,
- socialization,
- environmental orientation,
- reality orientation,
- receptive speech comprehension,
- expressive communication,
- memory,
- managing money, and
- managing health needs.

Each of the 4 ratings in a particular category (1.5 = *independent,* 1.0 = *mild impairment,* 0.5 = *moderate impairment,* and 0.0 = *severe impairment*) is accompanied by a statement that describes a typical patient at that level. For example, the point scales for "eating" and "managing money" are given as follows:

Eating

0.0—Unable to feed self

0.5—Eats with assistance

1.0—Feeds self

1.5—Buys and prepares own food

Managing money

0.0—Unable to manage money

0.5—Manages small sums of money appropriately

1.0—Manages savings account

1.5—Manages checking account and pays bills regularly

DETERMINING A DIAGNOSIS

Ideally, an evaluation will determine a **diagnosis,** the nature of a disease. A **clinical diagnosis** is one made from the study of signs and symptoms, as opposed to a **pathological diagnosis,** which might be based on blood tests or biopsy results. A **differential diagnosis** is an educated guess of two or more diseases that fit the patient's symptoms. A differential diagnosis is useful when the diagnosis is not clear or when test results are pending or not definitive. Diagnoses range in specificity. They can be the same as a sign (e.g., word-finding difficulties, memory problems). A diagnosis can also be a **syndrome,** a label for a group of signs and symptoms (e.g., Alzheimer's disease). In all cases, the diagnosis serves as a label to foster communication with patients, families, caregivers, other health care professionals, and insurance companies.

A diagnosis is optimally informative when it specifies the **etiology**—the cause of the signs and symptoms. The etiology for any single disease can vary in level and detail. For instance, to a neurologist, the etiology of a stroke might include whether the stroke was hemorrhagic or thromboembolic (see Chapter 3) and the location

(e.g., "The cause of the patient's language problems is a hemorrhagic stroke affecting the left frontal lobe"). An epidemiologist might describe the cause of the same stroke in terms of the risk factors of a poor diet, family history, and a sedentary lifestyle. A cardiovascular scientist could describe the cause of the same incident in terms of cellular changes in arteries that transport blood to the brain. Two specific etiologies that are useful in describing a range of symptoms are (a) **iatrogenic,** which describes problems that are caused by medical intervention (Greek: *iatros* = physician; *gen* = producing), and (b) **idiopathic,** which describes problems with unclear causes (Greek: *idios* = one's own; *pathos* = suffering).

A diagnosis may also include the severity, as well as anything else relevant to a particular patient. For instance, a relatively uninformative diagnosis might be "dementia," whereas a more specific diagnosis for the same patient might be "mild dementia affecting primarily memory and language comprehension that is probably hereditary given numerous family members with the same history." Of course, the type of diagnosis given will depend on the extent of information available, the purpose of the diagnosis (e.g., therapy, pharmaceutical prescription, insurance reimbursement, communication), and the audience (e.g., caregiver vs. physician vs. other health care provider).

Most diagnostic testing is aimed at identifying and labeling the anatomic, physiologic, mental, and psychological impairment. This information then helps health care providers develop appropriate treatment. However, prior to entertaining treatment, it is also crucial to understand the functional consequences of the disease process—that is, how the impairments affect real-life activities (e.g., walking, reading), and impede participation in real-life roles (e.g., inability for a student to attend school) (World Health Organization [WHO], 2000). In some literature, the terms **disability** and **handicap** are used to refer to how changes in body structures and function (i.e., impairments) affect activities and roles, respectively (WHO, 1990). It is important to remember that the consequences of a disease may include (1) restrictions in daily activities such as toileting, ambulation, performing household chores, and job duties, as well as

(2) social disadvantages such as the stigma or restrictions imposed by society when an individual looks or acts differently from the social norm or is treated differently because he or she carries a particular diagnostic label (Granger & Granger, 1986).

There are many reasons to look beyond a particular diagnostic label at the disabilities and handicaps. First, there is not a one-to-one correspondence between disease and associated disabilities or handicaps. The same disease can produce qualitatively and quantitatively different disabilities in different individuals. A single disorder may cause a disability for one patient and not for another. Therefore, when dealing with any individual, it is crucial to know what disabilities are present in each case prior to initiating treatment. One concrete example would be the effect of diseases such as Parkinson's and stroke on driving ability. The diagnoses of Parkinson's disease or stroke do not carry any straightforward implications for driving ability. Some patients with early to moderate Parkinson's disease can drive safely; the impairments associated with the disease may not affect vision, voluntary movement, or reaction time sufficiently to interfere. However, for others, either the early effects of tremor and hypokinesia or the side effects of medication (see Chapter 13) will prevent them from driving, thus creating a very clear disability in this area. Likewise, after stroke, many patients with paralysis will not be able to drive, whereas others with aphasia (see Chapter 4) but no paralysis will be able to drive safely.

Second, if the focus is solely on the disease, and the disability is minimized or ignored, it is entirely possible that the disease can be "cured" but disability will remain. This can happen, for instance, with surgical treatment of brain tumors. In this case, the surgical "cure," or removal of the tumor, can leave untreated or actually create muscle weakness, paralysis, and speech and cognitive problems. These impairments, in turn, create significant disabilities in walking, talking, and thinking, which interfere with many daily activities, and all require treatment following surgery. In some cases, a focus on the diagnosis or disease, without appreciation for the disability or handicap, will prevent a clinician from recommending appropriate or sufficient intervention.

The concepts of **disability** and **handicap** are particularly important in treating the elderly because of the chronicity of their diseases. In younger patients, diseases are frequently acute, and it is often possible and sufficient to find and treat the disease, with the expectation that the disability and/or handicap will resolve. However, with chronic diseases common in older patients, including Parkinson's disease, stroke, and many dementias, the goal of treatment is often not a cure at all but rather successful management of the disease to ameliorate any disability or handicap. For this reason, it is important to use tests of functional ability, assessing both basic tasks of feeding, dressing, toileting, and mobility and how much the current impairment interferes with function in their daily lives.

DETERMINING A PROGNOSIS

Based on the diagnosis, etiology, and degree of disability and handicap, health care providers formulate a **prognosis**—the likelihood of recovery (Greek: *pro* = before; *gnosis* = knowing). Prognoses can be vague (e.g., "good" vs. "poor") or provided in helpful detail (e.g., "The prognosis for recovery of language function to the level where the patient will be able to independently order food in a restaurant within the next 6 months is excellent if the patient engages in intensive daily speech therapy"). Obviously, the more specific clinicians can be, the more informed the patient and the caregivers will be. Unfortunately, no one can see the future, so prognoses tend to be more vague than we might like. Many factors affect a prognosis and are common to almost any disorder or age group. For instance, patients with mild impairments, high motivation, and good access to quality treatment have a better prognosis than those with severe impairments, poor motivation, and no access to treatment. One unfortunate tendency has been to assume that age itself is a negative prognostic indicator. However, despite the inaccuracy of such a blanket statement, which is too general to be helpful, it is true that certain common characteristics of older patients do affect the likelihood of recovery (Rowe & Besdine, 1988). These include the following:

- *Reversibility and chronicity of disease.* Many diseases associated with aging, such as Parkinson's and Alzheimer's diseases, are irreversible. In other cases, the impairments associated with, for instance, a stroke, may not be progressive but can be chronic. With irreversible and/or chronic diseases, the goal is not to cure but rather to manage the effects of the disease over time.

- *Multiple health problems.* Older adults, more frequently than younger adults, have multiple problems (also called *comorbidity*), such as diabetes, tremor, and dementia, which can all cause their own difficulties and exacerbate the disabilities caused by one another. The mere presence of multiple problems and the treatment(s) associated with each also reduce the patients' physiologic reserve and energy that they can devote toward rehabilitation.

- *Chronicity.* Chronic illnesses that will not be cured are frequent in the elderly. The goal for chronic diseases is to manage effects over a long period of time.

- *Family and social support.* Many older patients live alone or in nursing homes. Their close friends and family members may have died and/or moved away. In short, they may be without an immediate close social support network. Consequently, they may have difficulty with basic and necessary activities, such as obtaining adequate nutrition, medication refills, and transportation to therapy sessions. All of these facts can affect prognosis.

- *Economics.* Older people often live on a fixed income, and health insurance often limits the covered treatments. Frequently, health insurance only provides a fixed number of sessions per year, no matter what the problem or the potential benefit of treatment. This will limit the access to appropriate treatment.

- *Medications.* Older patients often do not tolerate medication as well as younger patients due to changed metabolism, nutrition, and risk of interaction with other medications.

- *Physiologic reserve.* Physiologic aging, multiple health concerns, multiple treatments,

depression, and lack of social support combine to further reduce older patients' physiologic reserve and energy that they can devote toward rehabilitation.

- *Sensory impairments.* Age-associated vision changes (presbyopia) and hearing impairment (presbycusis) can interfere with basic elements of communicating on the telephone, driving, reading instructions, participating in treatment, and taking medications.

- *Attitude.* Many of the above-mentioned issues combine in a negative way to create a negative attitude (e.g., "One more thing is going wrong; why should I even try?"), even frank depression, resulting in memory problems and lack of desire to participate. This, in turn, leads to its own treatment challenges and can have a predictably negative effect on self-care as well as specific treatments (e.g., Backman & Hentinen, 1999).

How Do Recovery and Treatment Plans Differ for Younger Versus Older Patients?

Recovery from neurological damage is not well understood. We do know that after an initial insult to the brain, there is often substantial spontaneous recovery. There are probably many mechanisms underlying spontaneous recovery, including resolution of edema (swelling) and return of blood flow to damaged regions, either directly or indirectly through alternate paths. One common theory of neurologic recovery, the notion of *diaschisis* (Greek: "shocked throughout"), originally discussed by Von Monakow (1914), refers to dysfunction of distinct brain regions, connected to but distant from the site of damage. Initially after brain damage, edema and shock interrupt transynaptic and blood flow communication between many distinct and distant brain structures. These distant regions, although not structurally damaged, function poorly. With reduction of edema and recovery from the initial shock, much of the interrupted neuronal transmission and blood flow is restored, and these distant regions can recover from their temporarily diminished level of functioning.

After the initial several weeks following the onset of an acute brain injury such as stroke, neurological recovery continues, probably through different mechanisms—most likely compensation by other brain regions taking over functions that were previously accomplished by the now-damaged areas (e.g., Stein, 2000). Of course, not all neurological and cognitive function returns spontaneously. That is where treatment comes in.

Who Is a Candidate for Treatment?

One early and important decision to make is whether any given patient is a candidate for treatment. Ideally, a diagnosis and etiology can be established before treatment is considered. This helps to guide treatment by informing the clinician of the likelihood of recovery and the type of treatment that is most apt to help. The health care provider uses the signs, symptoms, disabilities, handicaps, diagnosis, prognosis, and individual patient characteristics combined with what is known about available treatments to determine if treatment would be beneficial for a particular patient. Then, of course, the patient and her or his family/caregivers make the final decision of whether to follow the recommendations. There are three relatively common outcomes from this imprecise formula: (a) The patient has no impairment and therapy is not recommended or obtained, (b) the patient has deficits but therapy is either not recommended or not obtained, and (c) the patient has measurable problems and therapy is recommended and obtained. A few examples will illustrate.

Not every person who is evaluated is impaired. Some patients **malinger.** This means they feign an illness or impairment, generally to obtain a "secondary gain," sometimes to get out of work, acquire money from insurance companies, or obtain other less concrete benefits such as attention (e.g., Nies & Sweet, 1994). It takes clinical expertise and sufficient experience with disorders to determine that a patient is faking an impairment such as a hearing loss or memory impairment (Iverson, 1995; Martin, Champlin, & McCreery, 2001).

Other unimpaired patients are evaluated only because they are worried. Some older clients show the typical signs of aging but otherwise do not have measurable or notable impairments.

They may want assurance that they are OK, but they may not want or need ongoing treatment. This is particularly true for anomia and short-term memory problems, which worry otherwise well older individuals, often because of the association of these common aspects of primary aging with well-publicized and serious diseases such Alzheimer's. This category of patients is often referred to as the "worried well."

Other clients have measurable and notable impairments but, nonetheless, are not candidates for treatment because they do not need it, do not want it, cannot practically obtain it, have religious/cultural reasons not to participate in it, or have a diagnosis and prognosis so bleak that it just does not make sense. One example may be a patient who has trouble remembering phone numbers as well as she used to but has compensated perfectly on her own by using a phone book. She may have a measurable memory deficit on testing but no disability or handicap, and without other reasons to engage in treatment, given the time and expense of ongoing behavioral treatment and the potential side effects of drugs, it may not be worth her time, expense, or risk.

Others with impairment who could potentially benefit from treatment may not want it. For instance, some patients have obvious problems that are creating disabilities and handicaps such as chronic hoarseness from long-term smoking or significant memory lapses from a mild head injury or stroke. However, they may want from the clinician only one thing: assurance that they do not have a feared disease—in these cases, laryngeal cancer and Alzheimer's disease, respectively. Once reassured, they decline or do not show up for what could be very effective treatment to relieve their symptoms.

In addition, there are people who could probably be helped by Western health care intervention but have cultural and/or religious reasons against using it. Christian Scientists, Seventh Day Adventists, and traditional societies all have their own belief systems, which sometimes come into conflict with Western medical approaches (e.g., Salas-Provance et al., 2002). Some of the most common examples of this are the prohibitions for Jehovah's Witnesses against genetic counseling, prolongation of life by artificial means, removal of body parts at autopsy, and blood transfusion. These prohibitions are often not absolute and change over time. For instance, although Jehovah's Witnesses have had a longstanding ban on receiving human blood transfusions, the use of calf's blood and blood components (e.g., plasma expanders) has become more acceptable in recent years. In many cases, these groups are disproportionately older because it is generally the older generations in the United States who are less assimilated into the Western medical model (e.g., Salas-Provance et al., 2002). One of the most frustrating groups of patients are those who have measurable and notable impairments that interfere with function and who want treatment but, for some practical reason, cannot obtain it. This is too frequently true of elders who live rurally without ready transportation, those who reside in a nursing home without access to therapists, and those who cannot afford treatment.

Finally, there are those patients who can benefit from treatment, want treatment, and can get it. In that case, the specific goals and modalities of a treatment plan can be carried out.

What Is the Goal of Treatment?

Rehabilitation is a general term for treatment to regain lost function. Rehabilitation is generally directed toward (a) **restoration of function** and/or (b) **compensation for lost function** (Almli & Finger, 1992).

Restoration of function refers to treatment aimed at regaining the ability to accomplish a goal in the same manner and with the same efficiency as before the injury. For instance, some injuries result in muscle weakness and slow movements of the legs, arms, or tongue. These have predictable consequences, generally impairing the speed and coordination needed for walking, writing, chewing, and speaking, among other activities. If the cause of the impairment(s) is nonprogressive, the disability is relatively mild, and the patient is motivated to regain the function and has the wherewithal to participate in therapy, then rehabilitation aimed at restoration may be appropriate. In these cases, well-planned and diligently practiced exercises to regain strength and coordination can help the patient regain the same or similar facility with these activities as before the accident or disease: The patient will be able to ambulate, perform dexterously with his or her hands, and speak without any obvious observable difference than before the onset. Of course, there may be subtle residual difficulties, such as increased effort, particularly when tired, that may persist.

In contrast, a compensatory approach to rehabilitation is aimed at developing the ability to accomplish a particular goal by a different means than prior to the injury. For instance, if an injury results in severe and permanent muscle weakness (i.e., paralysis) of the arms, legs, or tongue, the patient will not realistically be able to walk, write, or communicate in the way she or he did prior to the injury, no matter how motivated the patient may be and how many times exercises are performed. In this case, the goal is not to restore the ability to perform the same activities in the same way but rather to perform the same function in an alternative way. In the case of walking, the solution might be learning to use a cane or a leg brace, to use a wheelchair instead of walking, or some combination of these and other strategies. In the case of communicating with severely and permanently impaired oral movements, the function of "speaking" may be accomplished via anything from a relatively low-tech and inexpensive alternative such as writing to the use of a computer-generated voice, activated by typing on a keyboard. All prosthetic devices, whether as common as eyeglasses and hearing aids or less common, such as wheelchairs, computer-assisted communication devices, and feeding tubes, are considered compensatory techniques. Other aspects of compensatory rehabilitation involve counseling, instructing caregivers, and altering the environment. Caregivers can often change their behavior to compensate for the impairment. For example, for a patient with hearing or comprehension difficulties, caregivers may speak more loudly or slowly to make the auditory signal easier to process. Likewise, the environment can be altered to make life easier on someone with an impairment. This might include, for instance, using clothing with Velcro closures and eliminating carpets to help people with certain mobility problems, as well as using color-coded and written signs to remind people with memory problems to lock doors, turn off cooking appliances, and so forth.

An important consideration, particularly when working with older patients, is the relationship between a poor prognosis and treatment planning. Poor prognoses are associated with slowly progressive diseases such as Alzheimer's, short life expectancy due to terminal cancer, and other disease characteristics. When patients are not likely to regain much function or for very long, or if they are likely to decline in function despite rehabilitative efforts, treatment planning is often centered on planning for the future and emotional adjustment. Of course, planning for the future and emotional adjustment are part of any complete therapy program but take on particular importance when return of function is unlikely. Certainly, some traditional treatments, particularly compensatory techniques of altering the environment to improve function, can also be used. But much of the treatment, often subsumed under the term *counseling,* revolves around practical issues of realistic planning for help in the home, discussion of nursing homes, feeding tubes, and emotional issues surrounding realistic expectations, acceptance, and grieving.

Treatment for neurological damage in adults includes many modalities, the most prominent being medication, surgery, and behavioral treatment (a.k.a. "therapy"). Optimal treatment will often consider and use more than one modality. For instance, for many, the first approach and mainstay of treatment for Parkinson's disease is medication. However, behavioral therapy for improving balance, movement, and speech is also a valuable and recognized adjunct to medical treatment. In some severe or advanced cases of Parkinson's, in which medical and behavioral treatments are insufficient, surgery may also be considered (see Chapter 13). In other diagnoses, the order and emphasis of treatment modalities may be different: Brain aneurysms require primary surgical repair but may require medication in the aftermath of surgery to control seizures, as well as behavioral therapy to address the cognitive impairments that often result from brain surgery. To complicate matters, some diseases can be treated in any one of several ways, and experts often disagree about the effectiveness of various treatments. For example, medications to slow the progress of Alzheimer's disease or aid the recovery from stroke are in initial phases of being tested with difficult-to-interpret results (Whitehouse, 1999). Surgical intervention for Parkinson's disease, although popular in the 1950s, is now viewed by some as too risky for many patients (Rascol, Goetz, Koller, Poewe, & Sampaio, 2002). Behavioral therapy is constantly challenged to provide proof that it works, perhaps because it tends to work slowly and without mystery in an age when medication and surgery often appear to provide relatively quick and effortless cures.

Because there are typically many options for treatment, one of the most difficult clinical jobs is selecting, combining, and dosing treatments for the best possible outcome. Providers can be selected and combined from a wide range of professions and can include the following, to name a few: general practitioners; geriatricians; surgeons; occupational, physical, and speech-language therapists; social workers; pharmacists; and nontraditional healers (e.g., chiropractic, acupuncturists, herbalists). Health insurance, which often determines whether services will be paid for and provided, can make obtaining optimal health care very complicated because the decision about if, who, and how to treat is usually not in the hands of any one person or entity. Therefore, clients, their caregivers, and their various consultants and health care providers must be diligent and careful in monitoring each step of the rehabilitation process. To give one simple example: Some insurance companies pay for a limited number of rehabilitation sessions, which can include occupational, physical, and speech therapy. If no one is monitoring how many sessions of each have been used, the therapy "benefit" may have been exhausted by one modality (e.g., physical therapy) while the patient is still on a waiting list to receive another (e.g., speech therapy), leaving the patient with the choice of paying cash for or not receiving the latter at all. Of course, the same is true for medication, with insurance companies covering the cost of certain medications and not others, putting patients and physicians in the difficult position of having to weigh the advantages and disadvantages of financial costs and medical benefits, resulting in rationed doses or inadequate treatment.

Another potential barrier to carrying out a treatment plan, particularly with older patients, is the location of treatment. Younger adults are typically treated in a hospital or outpatient clinic, but older patients, due to limited mobility, transportation challenges, illness, and other reasons, may not be able to access either of these locations. Clinicians may have to make special arrangements for home care and contend with limited staff, space, and transportation available at convalescent and other residential facilities. In some cases, when reaching the patient is difficult, treatment can be managed creatively, for instance, by using assistants, training family members, and maintaining close follow-ups by telephone with the patients, nursing home staff, and caregivers.

Many other therapeutic decisions will be made by each clinician. These will include when, over the course of recovery, is the best time to provide treatment In some cases (e.g., in the course of progressive disorders), early intervention may help to delay the onset of symptoms. In the case of acute disorders (e.g., stroke), early intervention may help to maximize spontaneous recovery. On the other hand, it may be advisable to provide some treatments only after the patient is medically and psychologically stable and can therefore participate fully in treatment.

The question of therapeutic "dosing"—how much treatment is appropriate—also varies tremendously. In some cases (e.g., with medication), the minimum effective dose to control symptoms with fewest side effects is often a wise approach. However, in some cases, as with some antibiotics, the strongest tolerable dose may serve to eliminate disease early and prevent worsening and recurrence. Related to dosing is the question of when it is the right time to end treatment. There are often multiple and distinct short-term and long-term goals within any treatment. Each particular goal may carry different criteria for the cessation of treatment. For instance, chemotherapy can be provided to cure or control tumor growth. If cure is the goal, criteria for ending the treatment may be a clear test result (which could be a cure or a clear failure to cure) or any indication that there is no clear benefit from continuing the current treatment. For other chemotherapies, the goal is not to cure but to control a tumor, and treatment may continue indefinitely and possibly increase in dosage over time. All treatments have criteria for ending, generally driven by a cost-benefit analysis, which compares the amount of improvement that can be expected from any given treatment with the cost, side effects, and inconvenience of that treatment. In addition, treatment duration is always affected by patient characteristics, including everything from stamina and availability of transportation to religious beliefs and prejudice about certain disciplines.

With this background in working with elderly, we can now proceed to learn about specific disorders of the brain that affect thinking and behavior and what we can do about them. The chapters that follow provide examples and discussion of specific treatment approaches for particular impairments.

2

Brain Basics

Chapter Preview

To understand how brain damage affects behavior, we must understand a bit about the brain itself. This chapter introduces three aspects of the brain:

1. the structures of the brain;

2. neuropsychology, the relationship between brain structures and specific behaviors; and

3. brain imaging—how we take and interpret pictures of the brain.

This chapter is a reference section for the rest of the book. Throughout this book, you will read about patients with impaired behavior due to brain damage. The location of that brain damage is not incidental—it is crucial to our understanding of why one patient acts one way and another patient acts differently. To most efficiently talk about the location of brain damage, we need to label and, in some cases, visualize the size and location of particular regions of the brain, where they are in relation to other regions, and how they interact, both through nerve impulses and chemicals. This chapter, perhaps a bit dry and technical, should help the reader develop a vocabulary to talk about brain damage and be a resource when looking back from other chapters as particular patients and syndromes are discussed.

TERMINOLOGY

Before introducing brain structures, a note about terminology is in order. The terminology used to describe the brain is a minefield of English and foreign words (mostly Latin and Greek), some used interchangeably and some used inconsistently. As scientists learn more about the brain structures and how they interact with one another, new terms for structures and groups of structures are coined, and the older terms remain in use as well. This creates a situation in which there are many terms to describe any given brain structure. The term we use depends on the background of the speaker, the sophistication of the listener or reader, the level of precision needed, the emphasis, and the specific data that are being discussed. This is not surprising because this is the way language works: Just as we have many different ways to describe common elements in our daily life (*car, auto, wheels, Chevy, sport utility vehicle, SUV, transportation*), many different terms can also be used to describe any particular brain structure, depending on the era, purpose, and emphasis. Although this may help us to understand why different terms are used, it will not eliminate the inherent frustration of trying to learn the names of brain structures. Be patient and accept the ambiguities and inconsistencies.

In addition to the names of structures themselves, we often use terms to identify the position of one structure relative to another. These terms only help locate objects and brain or body parts in relationship to other objects and brain or body parts. Many terms are familiar and can apply to everything in the physical world: **Superior** means *above* or *on top* of something, **inferior** means *below* something, **medial** means *toward the center,* and **lateral** means *toward the side.* Note the relativity of these terms: It is not helpful to say that something is lateral unless you have an anchor point and know that is toward the side relative to something else. *Lateral* by itself does not tell you in any absolute terms where an object or brain or body part is.

Some common terms have unfamiliar-sounding synonyms that are used more often to talk about nonhumans than humans. **Anterior** is the common term to locate something *in front of* something else, but **ventral,** which refers to the *underside* or *belly* of an animal on all fours, and **rostral,** which means *toward the nose,* can both mean *toward the front,* depending on the point of reference. **Posterior** and **dorsal** both mean *toward the back.* Terms such as *ventral* and *dorsal,* which are commonly used to talk about animals, can be confusing when applied to humans. For instance, in humans, *dorsal* and *posterior* both mean *in back of,* and although a shark's dorsal fin is on its back, it is likely to be superior, not posterior, to most other elements of the fish. **Ipsilateral** means *on the same side,* **contralateral** means *on the opposite side,* and **bilateral** means *on both sides.* Confused yet? In this case, a picture really is worth a thousand words (see Figure 2.1).

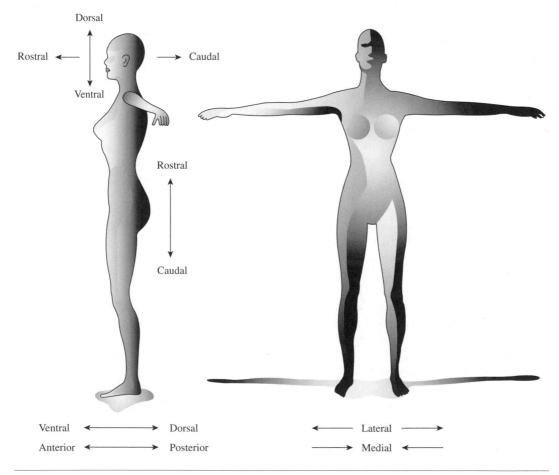

Figure 2.1   Anatomical directions. A lateral view (left) and frontal view (right) of a person, illustrating anatomical directional terms.

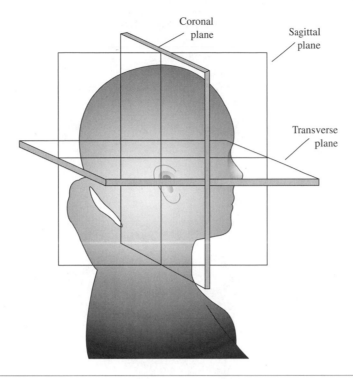

Figure 2.2   The primary views of the brain (frontal, lateral, and horizontal) are based on three planes (coronal, sagittal, and transverse) represented here.

There are many ways to look at the brain, and they reveal different perspectives. To identify the structures and describe their relative positions, we must understand the different views. Unfortunately, these views also have multiple names. It may help to visualize three planes passing through the body: the **coronal plane** (also **"frontal"**), the **sagittal plane,** and the **transverse plane** (also **horizontal**) (see Figure 2.2). The most frequent views of the brain are lateral views, based on the sagittal plane. Many images of the deeper structures of the brain are also based on the sagittal plane but more medially placed. When situated directly in the center of the brain, this is called the midsagittal view or plane. Horizontal views are based on the transverse plane and are commonly seen in brain scans (see Figure 2.9, presented later). Coronal views are based on the frontal plane.

THE STRUCTURES OF THE BRAIN

Central and Peripheral Nervous Systems

The **central nervous system (CNS)** refers to the **brain** and the **spinal cord.** The brain is made up of the **cerebrum** (the cerebral cortex and subcortical structures), the **cerebellum,** and the **brainstem** (see Figure 2.3). An average human brain weighs about 400 g (14 oz) at birth and about 1400 g (3.1 lbs) at maturity. The spinal cord is a cylinder less than 2 cm in diameter running through the vertebrae, from the bottom of the brain to the level of the first lumbar vertebra. The inner portion of the spinal cord is gray matter, or unmyelinated cell bodies and dendrites, whereas the outer portion consists of white matter, or myelinated axons. The spinal cord functions to connect the brain to the rest of the body. The **peripheral nervous system** refers to the 12 pairs of cranial nerves and 31 pairs of spinal nerves, which leave the CNS to control movement and sensation. The cranial nerves control sensory and motor function of the head and neck (see Table 2.1). The spinal nerves run from the spinal cord to the extremities of the body, controlling sensory and motor functions of the trunk, legs, and arms. The **autonomic nervous system** is a subdivision of the peripheral nervous system that **innervates** (supplies with nerves) what is called smooth

Central Nervous System (CNS) = Brain + Spinal Cord

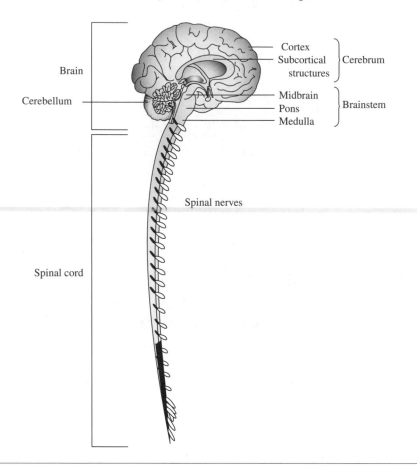

Figure 2.3   Major divisions of the nervous system.

muscle (e.g., the viscera), cardiac muscle, and the glands of the body. The autonomic nervous system functions subconsciously and regulates basic functions, including heart contractions and peristalsis of the intestines.

The Larger Structures

The brain is protected from the environment by the hard bones of the skull. Three layers of wrapping, collectively labeled the **meninges,** further protect the brain and spinal cord. The meninges consist of the dura mater (Latin: *hard mother*) lining the skull and the canal around the spinal cord, as well as the arachnoid (Greek: *spider's web*) and pia mater (Latin: *soft mother*), which hugs the brain itself and the spinal cord.

The brain also floats in an insulating bath of **cerebrospinal fluid (CSF)**, a clear liquid that circulates in the subarachnoid space surrounding the brain and spinal cord and also within the **ventricles** deep inside the brain (see below).

Below the meninges, the surface of the brain looks like a gray mass of worms. This is the **cerebral cortex** (Latin cerebrum: *brain,* cortex: *bark*), sometimes called the **neocortex.** This area is thought to have grown markedly in human evolution, and its relative size distinguishes human brains from brains of other primates. The cortex appears to be constructed of two symmetrical sides, connected by fiber tracts below the surface. These two sides are called the left and right **cerebral hemispheres.** The fiber tract connecting them is the **corpus callosum.**

Table 2.1   The Cranial Nerves

Number	Name	Functions		Method of Examination	Typical Symptoms of Dysfunction
I	Olfactory	(s)	Smell	Various odors applied to each nostril	Loss of sense of smell (anosmia)
II	Optic	(s)	Vision	Visual acuity, map field of vision	Loss of vision (anopia)
III	Oculomotor	(m)	Eye movement	Reaction to light, lateral movements of eyes, eyelid movement	Double vision (diplopia), large pupil, uneven dilation of pupils, drooping eyelid (ptosis), deviation of eye outward
IV	Trochlear	(m)	Eye movement	Upward and downward eye movements	Double vision, defect of downward gaze
V	Trigeminal	(s,m)	Masticatory movements	Light touch by cotton baton; pain by pinprick; thermal by hot and cold tubes; corneal reflex by touching cornea; jaw reflex by tapping chin, jaw movements	Decreased sensitivity or numbness of face, brief attacks of severe pain (trigeminal neuralgia); weakness and wasting of facial muscles, asymmetrical chewing
VI	Abducens	(m)	Eye movement	Lateral movements	Double vision, inward deviation of the eye
VII	Facial	(s,m)	Facial movement	Facial movements, facial expression, test for taste	Facial paralysis, loss of taste over anterior two thirds of tongue
VIII	Auditory vestibular	(s)	Hearing	Audiogram tests hearing; stimulate by rotating patient or by irrigating the ear with hot of cold water (caloric)	Deafness, sensation of noise in ear (tinnitus); disequilibrium, feeling of disorientation in space
IX	Glossopharyngeal	(s,m)	Tongue and pharynx	Test for sweet, salt, bitter, and sour tastes on tongue; pharyngeal or gag reflex by touching walls of pharynx	Partial dry mouth, loss of taste (ageusia) over posterior third of tongue, anesthesia and paralysis of upper pharynx
X	Vagus	(s,m)	Heart, blood vessels, viscera, movement of larynx and pharynx	Observe palate in phonation, palatal reflex by touching palate	Hoarseness, lower pharyngeal anesthesia and paralysis, indefinite visceral disturbance
XI	Spinal accessory	(m)	Neck muscles and viscera	Movement, strength, and bulk of neck and shoulder muscles	Wasting of neck with weakened rotation, inability to shrug
XII	Hypoglossal	(m)	Tongue muscles	Tongue movements, tremor, wasting or wrinkling of tongue	Wasting of tongue with deviation to side of lesion on protrusion

Source: Kolb and Whishaw (1996).

Note: s and m refer to sensory and motor function (or both) of the nerve.

The main features of the surface of the cerebral cortex are the ridges or convolutions and grooves or valleys. The ridges are called **gyri** (singular **gyrus**), and the valleys are called **sulci** (singular **sulcus**). The gyri and sulci are important landmarks and help to distinguish each of the four cortical lobes and to identify functional areas within the lobes.

The four lobes are named for the bones of the skull overlying them. Their demarcations are sometimes hard to see in a real brain. Figure 2.4 shows each lobe in each hemisphere along with important landmarks. The large sulcus separating the **temporal lobe** from the **frontal** and **parietal lobes** is the **lateral or Sylvian fissure.** Another important landmark is the **central sulcus**, also called the **fissure of Rolando,** separating the frontal and parietal lobes. There are two very prominent gyri running along either side of the central sulcus: the **precentral gyrus** in the frontal lobe and the **postcentral gyrus** in the parietal lobe. The precentral gyrus is also called the **motor strip** because this region controls voluntary movement of every body part on the contralateral side. The postcentral gyrus is also called the **sensory strip** because it receives sensory input from every region of the body on the contralateral side. The amount of space devoted to each body part along the motor and sensory strips is proportional to the degree of motor control and sensitivity of each region. The representation of this is referred to as a **homunculus** (see Figure 2.5).

The temporal lobe has three horizontal gyri, appropriately called the inferior, middle, and superior gyri; the frontal lobe also has prominent gyri with names reflecting their position. For example, the superior frontal gyrus runs along the superior, anterior (top front) aspect of the frontal lobes. Unfortunately, many important landmarks have names that do not reflect their position: note the supramarginal gyrus and the angular gyrus at the posterior end of the lateral sulcus. Other gyri, or parts of gyri, have multiple names: *Heschl's gyrus* and the *planum temporale* are names given to aspects of the superior temporal gyrus that lie within the Sylvian fissure.

Below the cortical surface of the brain, the two cerebral hemispheres appear more or less structurally identical. From a sagittal view within each hemisphere, you can see the inside of the hemispheres (see Figure 2.6). One important aspect of this view is the ability to see the corpus callosum, the fiber tract connecting the two hemispheres. Another aspect of this view that is not apparent in the lateral view is the ability to see the various subcortical structures. Subcortical structures are often grouped with one another, with the groupings thought to reflect functional units of one sort or another.

Along the inner surfaces of the cortical lobes, you can see what is sometimes called the **limbic lobe** or, more commonly, the **limbic system** (*Limbus;* Latin: *border* or *ring*). Originally, this name was given to identify cortical regions that border the corpus callosum. The limbic system includes many structures: the *hippocampus* (Greek: *sea horse*), *amygdala* (Latin: *almond*), mammillary bodies, fornix (Latin: *vault*), olfactory bulbs, and cingulate (Latin: *girdle*) cortex. This system is thought to be evolutionarily old. Because it was at first thought to be important for smell, the limbic system was originally labeled the *rhinencephalon* (*smell brain*). We now know that the functions of the limbic structures are varied and include, among other things, emotion, learning, memory, and spatial organization.

Another important grouping of subcortical structures is the **basal ganglia.** The basal ganglia includes the *caudate nucleus* (Latin: *nut*), *putamen* (Latin: *husk*), *globus pallidus* (Latin: *pale globe*), and the *substantia nigra* (Latin: *black substance*). To complicate things, these elements are often grouped and given other names: For example, the putamen and globus pallidus together are called the **lenticular nucleus**. The basal ganglia, along with the cerebellum, are central parts of the **extrapyramidal system,** a set of structures and connections that modulate movement. The basal ganglia have extensive connections with the thalamus and neocortex. The important role of the basal ganglia in controlling and modulating movement is corroborated by the fact that structural and/or chemical impairments of the basal ganglia, such as Parkinson's disease and Huntington's disease, result in decreased movement and involuntary movements. However, it is apparent that the basal ganglia are involved in much

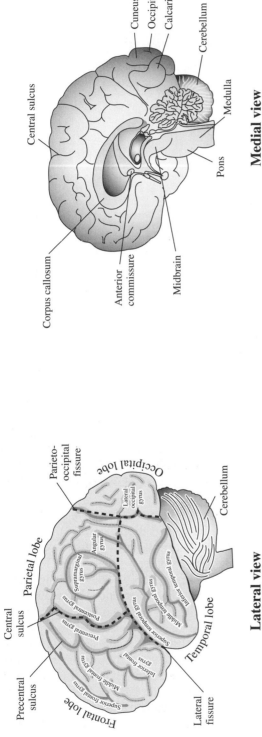

Medial view

Central sulcus · Cuneus · Occipital lobe · Calcarine fissure · Cerebellum · Medulla · Pons · Midbrain · Anterior commissure · Corpus callosum

Lateral view

Parieto-occipital fissure · Occipital lobe · Lateral occipital gyrus · Angular gyrus · Parietal lobe · Supramarginal gyrus · Postcentral gyrus · Central sulcus · Precentral gyrus · Precentral sulcus · Middle frontal gyrus · Superior frontal gyrus · Inferior frontal gyrus · Frontal lobe · Inferior temporal gyrus · Middle temporal gyrus · Superior temporal gyrus · Temporal lobe · Lateral fissure · Cerebellum

Ventral view of left and right hemispheres

Frontal lobe · Temporal lobe

Dorsal view of left and right hemispheres

Longitudinal fissure · Frontal lobe · Central sulcus · Parietal lobe · Occipital

Figure 2.4   The frontal, parietal, occipital, and temporal lobes of the human brain.

23

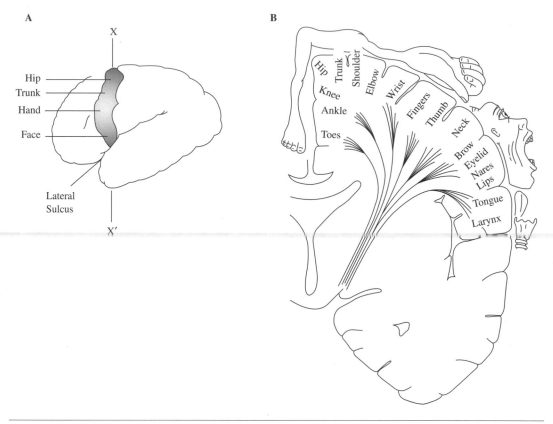

Figure 2.5   (a) The lateral surface of the left cerebral hemisphere, illustrating the location and functional organization of the motor strip along the precentral gyrus. (b) A coronal view through the motor area of the brain, showing motor homunculus and the proportional representation of the opposite side of the body.

more than controlling movement. We know this in part because patients with basal ganglia damage suffer from movement abnormalities but also suffer from dementia, depression, and impairments of cognitive function previously thought to be controlled by the neocortex, particularly the frontal lobes (e.g., Masterman & Cummings, 1997).

It is still not clear if the cognitive dysfunctions associated with basal ganglia disease are caused directly by the basal ganglia impairment or indirectly by the effect of basal ganglia dysfunction on the cortex, particularly the frontal lobes. In any case, most current theories of basal ganglia function stress much more than its historically proven and well-accepted role in motor control and emphasize the relationship between the basal ganglia, cortical regions, and higher cognitive functions, particularly those functions associated with the frontal lobes (Masterman & Cummings, 1997).

The **thalamus** (Latin/Greek: *inner chamber*) consists of several distinct nuclei that receive input from various parts of the body and brain and project to other brain regions, and each has different functions. The thalamic nuclei are involved in all interactions between higher and lower brain centers and are very important in the conscious experience of sensation, emotional capacity, and modulation of attention and learning. Another structure that is not obvious from the lateral view is the **insula,** sometimes called the insular lobe. It is the cortical tissue that lies inside the lateral fissure and can only be seen if the fissure is opened up or on a coronal view.

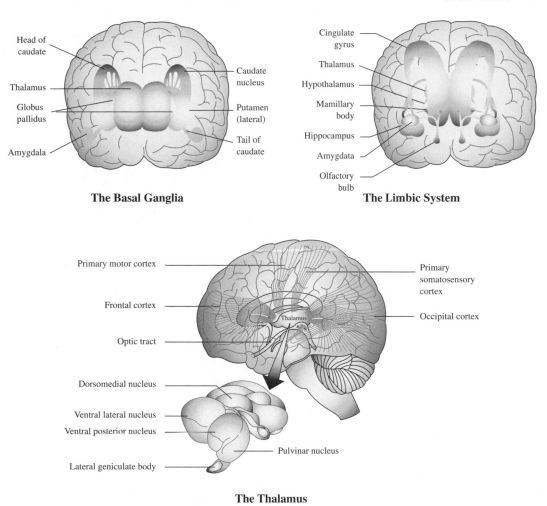

The Basal Ganglia

The Limbic System

The Thalamus

Figure 2.6 Brain structures viewed from a midsagittal plane, including important aspects of the limbic system, basal ganglia, and thalamus.

Sitting atop the spinal cord and below the structures of the basal ganglia is the brainstem. The brainstem is made up of the *medulla* (Latin: *innermost, marrow*), the *pons* (Latin: *bridge*), and the midbrain. The brainstem regulates the basic functions of heart and respiration and is also a crucial relay station between the cortex and the rest of the body. The cranial nerves arise from the brainstem. All sensory and motor information that is transmitted to and from the brain travels through the brainstem via the cranial nerves and the spinal cord.

The cerebellum (Latin: *little brain*) is the bilaterally symmetrical structure attached to the caudal (posterior) end of the brainstem. Like the cerebral hemispheres, the cerebellum has a cortex of convoluted gray matter and an internal core of white matter (see "White and Gray Matter" below). The cerebellum appears to be involved in motor coordination, balance, and posture. Because of its involvement with motor functions and connections with the basal ganglia, it is considered part of the extrapyramidal system.

The ventricular system consists of four connected cavities filled with cerebrospinal fluid. There are two lateral ventricles (one at the center of each cerebral hemisphere); the third and fourth ventricles are midline, not

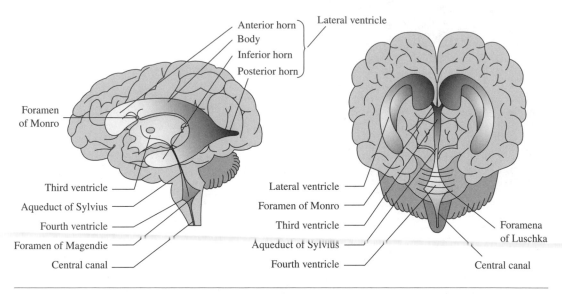

Figure 2.7   A lateral view (left) and a frontal view (right) of the ventricles.

paired, and are connected to the spinal cord (see Figure 2.7). Capillary networks in each of the ventricles generate the cerebrospinal fluid. Three openings in the fourth ventricle allow the CSF to pass from the fourth ventricle into the subarachnoid space outside the brain, where it covers the whole surface of the brain and spinal cord. CSF, absorbed from the subarachnoid space surrounding the brainstem and spinal cord, is a saline solution made up of sodium chloride and other salts and functions to nourish and cushion the brain. The ventricles are important landmarks and also are very helpful in determining the extent and location of brain damage because as brain tissue is damaged, it shrinks, and the fluid-filled ventricles expand to fill the space. Therefore, increased ventricular size indicates brain **atrophy** (shrinkage) and is generally associated with brain damage.

CONNECTING THE STRUCTURES: NERVE CELLS AND CHEMICALS

Although this book focuses on larger brain structures, it is important to understand how the brain works on a cellular level as well. There are two types of nerve cells: **neurons** and **glia.** Glia (Greek: *glue*) constitute 90% of nerve cells and are supporting cells, holding together the substance of the brain. The three types of glia are oligodendrocytes, astrocytes, and microglia. The neurons are thought to do the work of communicating and controlling sensation, movement, and cognition. Neurons exist throughout the body, and although they differ from one another in size and shape, they can be schematically represented as in Figure 2.8. The primary parts of the nerve cell are the **nucleus** (cell body), **axon,** and **dendrites.** The axons conduct impulses away from the cell body. The dendrites receive stimuli from adjacent neurons and conduct stimuli toward the cell body. The **synapse** is the contact zone between neurons where they communicate with one another. Nerve cells communicate with one another by releasing **neurotransmitters** (chemicals) at the synaptic junction. The neurotransmitters released from synaptic vesicles of one neuron cross the synapse and create an **action potential**—an electrical impulse—in an adjacent neuron. The electrical impulse travels down the axon of that neuron to a synapse, where neurotransmitters are released, stimulating receptors in the dendrites of an adjacent cell, triggering an action potential in that cell, and so on. An axon may stimulate dendrites of many other cells, and dendrites of any one

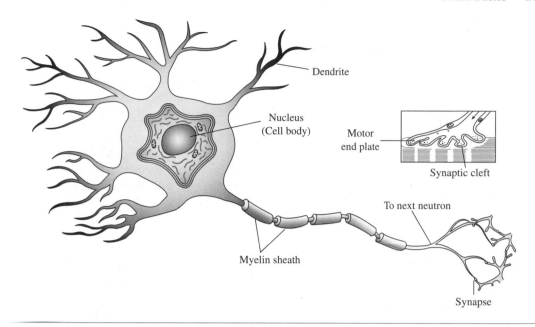

Figure 2.8   Primary parts of a neuron.

nerve cell can receive stimulation from many neurons. The communication between nerve cells can be either excitatory or inhibitory. **Excitatory effects** stimulate an adjacent neuron to fire; **inhibitory effects** prevent an adjacent neuron from firing.

Estimates of the number of nerve cells in a human being range from 10 billion to 1 trillion. Each neuron may have direct synaptic contact with several thousand other neurons, resulting in up to 60 trillion synapses. We are born with the full complement of nerve cells. During development, nerve cells grow and elaborate in response to experience. This growth and consequent synaptic development is the neuronal basis for learning. It has long been assumed that nerve cells, once damaged or dead, could not regenerate themselves. Although still believed to be generally true, it has recently been discovered that certain cell types do regenerate (Eriksson et al., 1998). In general, when we talk about neuronal activity in the brain, we are referring to large groups of very small neurons firing in concert. However, some neurons, such as the cranial nerves, are large enough to be seen with the naked eye. A group of nerve cells that arise in one area of the brain and whose axons traverse from one region of the brain to another

are referred to as a **tract.** Groups of neurons or nerve structures that work together as a unit are referred to as a **ganglion** (plural *ganglia;* Greek: *knot*).

Nerve cells in different parts of the brain vary in structure, pattern, and connectivity with other brain regions. For instance, the cerebral cortex, the outer layer of the brain, generally has six layers of nerve cells, whereas other areas of the brain have fewer layers. These layers differ in their connections with the rest of the brain: The outer four layers of the cortex receive axons from other brain regions, and the inner two layers send axons to other brain regions. A German neurologist, Korbinian Brodmann (1868–1918), completed some of the first and most important work documenting the structure of nerve cells throughout the brain, using staining techniques to develop cytoarchitectonic maps of the cortex. These maps label each neuronally distinctive area with a number, and each location is known as a **Brodmann area.** For instance, Brodmann area 44 refers to a part of an inferior frontal gyrus known to be important for language production, and this is differentiated from Brodmann areas 41 and 42, which are in the temporal lobe and important for language comprehension.

White and Gray Matter

A slang term for the brain is **gray matter.** When the skull is removed, the exposed brain does look gray. These are the nerve cell bodies. However, much of the brain below the surface is white. Part of the development of neurons is a process by which the nerve axon is covered with a fatty sheath of insulation called **myelin.** This sheath develops after birth and continues to develop until at least 15 years of age. Myelination appears to facilitate nerve firing. Because this sheath is more white than gray, areas of the brain that are predominantly made up of axons are referred to as **white matter.** This is particularly apparent below the surface of the brain, where long axons course through the lower areas. Certain disorders, such as multiple sclerosis, result if the white matter disintegrates.

Efferent and Afferent

Neurons are described as being predominantly efferent or afferent. **Efferent** means away from the center; **afferent** means toward the center. Neurons that control movement are efferent and are also called **motor neurons.** They take impulses from the central nervous system out to the so-called *end organs*—the arms, legs, mouth, and so on. The point at which a neuron contacts voluntary muscle is called the **motor end plate** or **myoneuronal junction.** Afferent neurons propagate sensation from the end organs to the brain, where the patterns of nerve firing are interpreted as sensation (e.g., pain, pleasure, heat, or cold).

The structures of the brain are well connected with one another. The connections between brain structures are particularly important for understanding certain disorders that are caused by disconnections between specific regions. There are several particularly important fiber tracts connecting the frontal and occipital lobes (**superior longitudinal fasciculus**), the superior and middle frontal gyri with the temporal lobe (**arcuate fasciculus**), and the occipital lobes with the temporal poles (**inferior longitudinal fasciculus**). Arguably, the most important and possibly largest mass of connecting fibers are the neurons that connect the two hemispheres, the **corpus callosum.** The corpus callosum is divided into *genu* (anterior portion; literally, *knee*), *body* (midportion), and *splenium* (posterior portion).

Neurotransmitters

Chemicals are very important in understanding brain function at the cellular level, as well as for understanding human behavior and emotions. Some chemicals found in the brain have been identified as neurotransmitters. These include many different classes of chemicals, including derivatives of lipid cholesterol, monoamines derived from amino acids, neuropeptides, and amino acids themselves. To be classified as a neurotransmitter, a chemical must be (a) synthesized in the neuron and stored in the presynaptic vesicles, (b) released into the synapse in sufficient amounts to affect other neurons, and (c) removed from the synapses by specific cellular mechanisms. Neurotransmitters appear throughout the brain but have particularly high concentrations in specific regions. An accessible source of information on neurotransmitters is Gilman and Newman (2003).

Brain Changes With Aging

Throughout development, some brain regions shrink due to neuronal death. This is part of a general process called **apoptosis,** which occurs throughout the life span and is sometimes called cell "pruning" or "programmed cell death" (Honig & Rosenberg, 2000). The degree of cell loss is not easy to quantify, and there are conflicting reports of how much cell loss actually accompanies early development versus healthy aging, although the consensus is that much more programmed cell death happens early in development rather than later (White & Barone, 2001). Some estimates of cell loss indicate that between 20% and 40% of brain cells may die in healthy aging (Woodruff Pak, 1997). We do know that brain cell loss is not uniform throughout the brain, affecting the frontal lobes and hippocampus more than other regions. The brainstem tends to lose fewer neurons (Digiovanna, 2000). The natural and progressive process of nerve cell death undoubtedly contributes to a decrease in brain size and weight through adulthood, from approximately 1,400 grams at 20 years of age to 1,100 to 1,200 grams at 100 years of age, a decrease estimated to be 20% for female and 22% for male brains (Svennerholm, Bostrom, & Jungbjer, 1997). This cell loss changes the appearance of the brain, with the gyri shrinking, the sulci widening, and the ventricles enlarging.

Although we assume that age-related neuron loss contributes to cognitive and functional deficits associated with aging, this has been a difficult argument to make for several reasons. First, as mentioned earlier, it is very hard to determine the degree of cell loss. Second, the cell death does not necessarily mean a decline in function. Brain cell loss in aging should be kept in perspective with respect to other periods of the life span associated with cell loss: There is more and widespread cell loss in early development than in old age. Third, remaining neurons, new synapses, and more efficient processing in older age may compensate for the decrease in neuron numbers. Finally, it has been suggested that the loss of neurons may actually improve brain function by eliminating unnecessary or poorly functioning neurons (Digiovanna, 2000; White & Barone, 2001). In contrast to apoptosis, the greatest source of cell death in aging is due to the abnormal process of cell necrosis, which frequently happens as a consequence of acute brain injuries such as stroke and head injury (see Chapter 3). However, in addition to cell loss due to the normal process of apoptosis and abnormal necrotic processes, other changes occur within the aging brain that also affect nerve cell function.

Abnormal elements appear both within and between the remaining brain cells in the course of healthy aging. **Neurofibrillary tangles,** paired double helical filaments, emerge within the bodies of the nerve cells. These result when the normal content of nerve cells (neurofibrils) become tangled. **Senile or neuritic plaques** are deposits of the protein amyloid, surrounded by degenerated cell fragments that occur between nerve cells and are thought to interfere with communication between nerve cells. Both neurofibrillary tangles and neuritic plaques are present to some degree in healthy aging but are much more common in Alzheimer's disease (Kolb & Whishaw, 1996).

There are declines and/or alterations in all the major neurotransmitter systems in healthy aging due to loss of the cells that produce the chemicals and in the numbers of receptors. Changes in the neurotransmitter production and circulation are also probably associated with normal changes in cognitive function with age (Reeves, Bench, & Howard, 2002). However, the decrease in circulating chemicals may have a minimal impact because there may also be compensatory changes, such as an increase in size of remaining synapses that may mitigate the decline in the overall amount of the circulating neurotransmitter. However, these tentative data regarding the relationship between neurotransmitters and cognitive function in healthy age pale by comparison to the large body of evidence demonstrating that a decrease or an imbalance of specific neurotransmitters is associated with specific mental and behavioral disorders, including Alzheimer's and Parkinson's diseases (see Chapters 12 and 14), two of the major neurological disorders associated with aging. Patients with Alzheimer's disease appear to have greatly decreased concentrations of acetylcholine; patients with Parkinson's disease appear to have greatly decreased concentrations of dopamine. Because depletion of these neurotransmitters is so strongly believed to be a trigger, if not the cause, of these disorders, treatments for Alzheimer's and Parkinson's diseases are often aimed at returning the brain to the proper balance of neurotransmitters.

NEUROPSYCHOLOGY: THE ASSOCIATION BETWEEN BRAIN STRUCTURE AND HUMAN BEHAVIOR

The field of neuropsychology is the branch of science devoted to mapping brain functions onto brain structures, determining what parts of the brain are responsible for what aspects of behavior. There have been two primary theories of how brain structures relate to behaviors. One is that the work of the brain is distributed across many, if not all, the structures. This view has historically been called **holism** and maintains that human mental and behavioral functions are distributed over many structures of the brain, and it is not possible to associate a specific behavior with a narrowly defined brain region. The alternative view is that certain specific brain structures are responsible for specific aspects of behavior and silent for others, a view historically called **localization of function** and more recently talked about as **modularity of function.** As we shall see, neither of these views in their extreme formulation is supported by the data.

It has not always been apparent that the brain controlled behavior. Aristotle (384–322 B.C.) conjectured that the heart controlled mental functions, and the brain merely served to cool the blood (Kolb & Whishaw, 1996). However, the relatively large size of the human brain compared to body size, the fact that nerves from the sense organs go to the brain (not the heart), and the frequent occurrence of behavior problems following brain injury have led others, including Hippocrates (460–370 B.C.), to argue that the brain was the seat of mental function. Interestingly, even once the brain was identified as the important control center of thinking and behavior, the crucial elements of the brain were not clear for many years. Galen (129–199 A.D.), surgeon to the Roman gladiators, saw firsthand the effects of head trauma and hypothesized that brain function was contained in the CSF. This notion was discredited because some nonhuman animals (that are presumably not as bright as humans) had the same amount of CSF. Descartes (1596–1650) argued that mental processes were controlled by brain tissue but picked the pineal gland as the important structure, in part because of its closeness to the ventricles and the CSF (Kolb & Whishaw, 1996).

Since these early investigations, we have learned much about the relationship between the brain and behavior, primarily from observations of abnormal behavior subsequent to brain injury. Associating brain lesions with specific behavioral deficits, called the lesion-deficit approach to neuropsychology, has guided our thinking about neuropsychology over the past 100 years. The lesion-deficit approach works in the following way: Consider a patient who cannot move his right arm and leg. We then find that the patient has a lesion in the left frontal lobe. If this finding is replicated across a number of patients, we may conclude that the left frontal lobe normally controls movement of the right side of the body. Through this type of lesion (left frontal lobe)/deficit (right-sided paralysis) correlation, we build hypotheses about how the intact brain controls behavior. Lesion-deficit mappings have led to two important neuropsychological theories over the past century: lateralization and localization of function.

Lateralization

The notion that the two hemispheres differ is relatively new. Until the 1860s, it was assumed that the two sides of the brain were identical in structure and function (Berker, Berker, & Smith, 1986). We now know that they are not. Although they look similar, they serve very different functions. The notion that the two hemispheres function differently is referred to as **hemispheric specialization** or the **lateralization of function.** The differences are not structurally apparent to the naked eye, but as we shall see in later chapters, damage to one hemisphere often has very different effects than damage to the other. One important difference between the two hemispheres is that they control movement and sensation of the opposite side of the body. That is, for example, the right hemisphere controls movement and registers sensation of the left arm and leg. The long nerves that connect the right side of the brain with the left side of the body cross at the level of the brainstem. This crossing is called **decussation** (from Latin *decem,* "10," represented by the Roman numeral X—a cross).

Lateralization of movement and sensation are relatively uncontroversial (see the visual system in Chapter 8). Lateralization of cognitive functions is harder to demonstrate and is therefore more controversial. For example, the preponderance of speech and language problems following left hemisphere lesions, a consistent finding from the 1860s through the present, has led most researchers to conclude that the left hemisphere is specialized and dominant for language. However, even this most robust of lateralized findings is not without exception and controversy. For instance, the lateralization of language functions appears to be variable in the sense that not all patients with left hemisphere lesions become language impaired. Even patients who have had their left hemisphere totally removed (a procedure called hemispherectomy, done to control intractable seizures) often develop adequate, if not entirely normal, speech and language (Code, 1997; Smith & Sugar, 1975;

Vargha Khadem, Carr, Isaacs, & Brett, 1997). This and other exceptions to the left hemisphere dominance for language demonstrate that the left hemisphere, even if it usually controls language, is not absolutely necessary for language functions. We can conclude that although language is clearly and preferentially controlled by the left hemisphere, language is not limited to the left hemisphere. This type of finding forces us to develop a more flexible notion of what it means for a function to be lateralized, a notion that involves some amount of **redundancy,** with functions being controlled by multiple areas, and **plasticity,** with brain areas being able to rededicate themselves for functions that they do not ordinarily control. We now think of lateralized functions as those functions that are frequently and preferentially processed by one hemisphere but not necessarily or only processed by that hemisphere (Kempler, Van Lancker, Marchman, & Bates, 1999).

A further complication arises when we try to explain why one function might be lateralized to one hemisphere or the other. For example, why is it that speech and language tend to be governed by the left hemisphere? Some researchers have argued that something special about language structure is associated with the left hemisphere, citing the fact that both auditory-verbal and visual-spatial languages (sign languages) are controlled by the left hemisphere (Poizner, Bellugi, & Klima, 1989). Others have argued that speech and language are controlled by the left hemisphere because the left hemisphere is specially equipped to control sequential movements (Kimura & Archibald, 1974; Mateer & Kimura, 1977).

The specialization of the right hemisphere has been even more controversial than the left hemisphere. For the first hundred years of investigation into hemispheric specialization, the right hemisphere was generally ignored. Damage to the left brain caused obvious communication deficits, but damage to the right hemisphere caused only subtle, if any, cognitive problems. Over the past few decades, it has been convincingly shown that the right hemisphere does more than just keep the left one from falling over. The functional and cognitive sequelae of right hemisphere damage may not be as striking as the inability to talk that often follows left

hemisphere damage, but they are real and measurable (Myers, 1999). It appears that, unlike the left hemisphere's proclivity to process analytic and sequential information, the right hemisphere is particularly adept at processing visual information and processing information in a simultaneous and holistic fashion (Springer & Deutsch, 1993). The different processing capabilities of the two hemispheres have caught the imagination of the public. Over the past few decades, almost every possible behavioral and psychological dichotomy has been interpreted with regard to the left versus right hemispheres, a phenomenon called *dichotomania* by Springer and Deutsch (1993). Knowledge that the two cerebral hemispheres serve different functions has also made its way into popular culture, even popular advertising. As we shall see in the subsequent chapters, damage to the left and right hemispheres does, in some instances, produce very different deficits and, in other instances, very similar problems (e.g., Springer & Deutsch, 1993).

Localization

The idea that circumscribed areas within each hemisphere control specific functions is referred to as **localization.** There is a long and heated debate about the degree to which specific functions can be localized within the brain. In the 19th century, the question of which brain structures were responsible for specific behaviors was addressed by a group of scientists called **phrenologists,** most notably Franz Josef Gall (1758–1828) and Johann Caspar Spurzheim (1776–1832). These men correlated skull shape with areas of mental superiority to derive phrenological maps. For instance, a number of people with exceptional language abilities and bulges near the eyes led to the conjecture that the frontal part of the brain housed language abilities. Although this method is inherently flawed insofar as the outer skull shape has little relationship to the brain structure, it was an early, strong, and appealing version of the theory that one can localize control of specific behaviors to specific brain regions.

Several aspects of the way in which we think about localization of neuropsychological functions have changed in the 125 years since the heyday of phrenology. For instance, we are no longer as interested in the same functions: Phrenologists localized personal qualities such as attraction to food, cautiousness, thrift, love of family, love of animals, faith, self-love, and veneration, whereas we are now more interested in motor and cognitive functions such as speech, language, and memory. We also have different assumptions about the equivalence of the two cerebral hemispheres: Phrenologists assumed that all functions were bilateral, but now we believe there are anatomical and functional differences between the two hemispheres.

However, the basic tenet of phrenology, the idea that we can localize brain functions, has continued through the present day with data from lesion-deficit mapping. As researchers identify regions that, when damaged, consistently impair a particular aspects of behavior, they are said to *localize* that behavior. For instance, it has been shown that damage to the left precentral gyrus creates right-sided paralysis. Therefore, we say that control of right limb movement is localized to the left precentral gyrus. There are, of course, functions that have proved more difficult to localize. For instance, picture naming is disrupted by damage to many regions of the left hemisphere (Goodglass, 1993). We could conclude that picture naming is lateralized to the left hemisphere but not well localized within the left hemisphere. A reasonable approach to the notion of localization is to think of some behaviors as localizable to particular brain regions and others as diffusely represented or distributed throughout a hemisphere, or even the entire brain, with some behavioral functions relying on the interaction of many brain regions.

Challenges to Lesion-Deficit Mapping

Although lesion-deficit correlations continue to be the primary way we elucidate brain-behavior relations, the method has some inherent problems. First, brains differ. A child's brain is not organized in the same way as an adult's brain. There are differences between men and women in brain organization, and there are also unexplained individual differences in the brain. Historically, there has also been significant difficulty comparing one person's evaluation and description of deficits with another's. Although physicians in 19th-century France and 20th-century America might agree on the meaning of *left arm paralysis,* they may have very different methods of assessment and criteria for problems of object recognition (see Chapter 8). Perhaps a more serious and theoretical problem with lesion-deficit correlations is that, as Hughlings Jackson (1915) pointed out many years ago, locating the lesion that destroys a function and locating that function are two different things. That is, a correlation between a lesion site and a functional deficit does not mean you have found the site in the brain where that function resides. There may be other explanations for the lesion deficit correlation. For instance, the brain damage could interfere with functioning of another adjacent or remote region that was not overtly damaged, and it could be the disruption of the input to this intermediate region or to this overall system that creates the observed deficit. Also, importantly, cognitive processes are complex and involve the coordination of many subprocesses and brain regions. For instance, picture naming minimally involves visual perception, object recognition, name retrieval, and name production. Therefore, picture naming could be disrupted by problems in any one of these contributory processes. Finally, we cannot assume that the remaining undamaged tissue is functioning in the same way as it was before the brain damage. Damage to one area prompts other areas to take over functions that they may not typically control, and they may carry out nonnative functions in different ways and with varying success. In summary, the abnormal behavior we observe is undoubtedly the result of many factors, including damage to a particular brain region, remote effects of that damage on other brain regions, the attempts of damaged regions to function, and the attempts of preserved regions to compensate and carry out functions that are usually not their responsibility.

Alternative Methods of Elucidating Brain Function

One difficulty with the lesion-deficit technique is the inherent messiness of most naturally occurring lesions: Gunshot wounds and strokes rarely disable a cleanly defined cortical region. Over the years, several other techniques have been used to perform more controlled experiments to reveal the neural bases of behavior. For instance, Flourens (1794–1857) removed various amounts of canine brains and then made careful observations of the dogs' behavioral changes to determine how the amount and location of brain excision affected behavior. The functional deficits following the brain lesions appeared related to how much cortical tissue was removed, not the location of that tissue, leading him to conclude that mental abilities (of the dog at least) were not localized. It is obviously difficult to generalize from work with dogs to human cognition and equally obvious that it is not possible to do this exact sort of research with humans. Surgical procedures in humans have allowed us to conduct similar experiments and led to important discoveries regarding human brain function. Wilder Penfield, a neurosurgeon, pioneered a technique in the 1950s by which he electrically stimulated the cortex of patients who were undergoing neurosurgery to remove tumors and control epilepsy. He reported responses to stimulation of specific brain regions, including the sensation of specific emotions, déjà vu states, vivid recall of visual and auditory experiences, production of movement, local numbness and tingling, alterations in speech, and disruptions of movement (Penfield & Roberts, 1959; Wooldridge, 1963). This work was reinvigorated and updated more recently (Ojemann, Ojemann, Lettich, & Berger, 1989). In general, data from electrical stimulation of the brain have upheld the essential left-right dichotomies: Stimulation of the left hemisphere elicits and interrupts speech production, and right hemisphere stimulation interrupts spatial processing (e.g., memory for faces and judgment of line orientation). Interestingly, the vivid memories with visual and auditory perception appear to be more often elicited by right than left hemisphere stimulation, suggesting that the right hemisphere has perceptual functions not shared by the left.

Another informative surgical technique that was designed to control epilepsy involves cutting the corpus callosum to impede the spread of seizures from one cerebral hemisphere to the other (see Springer & Deutsch, 1993, for overview). The so-called **split brain** patients were surprisingly able to carry on daily activities quite well despite their disconnected hemispheres. Assessment techniques that presented information to one or the other hemisphere (primarily via lateralized visual stimulation; see Chapter 8 on the anatomy of the visual system to understand how this is possible) elucidated the abilities of the left and right hemispheres. Data from the split-brain patients have again confirmed theories about brain lateralization derived from patients with lateralized lesions but have also added some interesting nuances. For instance, although the isolated right hemispheres of split-brain patients cannot speak, they do have some linguistic capability. Data from word and sentence comprehension indicate that the isolated right hemisphere has a recognition vocabulary of about a second grader (Zaidel, 1978). The split-brain data, however intriguing, have somewhat limited implications because of the small number of patients and the fact that most of them had longstanding epilepsy and concomitant brain damage.

A slightly more benign approach to looking at hemispheric specialization is provided by the Wada technique, in which sodium amytal, a barbituate, is injected into a carotid artery. This injection anesthetizes and disables one hemisphere for several minutes. By watching which functions are impaired after injection, observers can determine which functions are lateralized to each hemisphere. Injection of the left hemisphere reliably produces speech arrest and speech disturbance, whereas injection of the right hemisphere generally does not (Wada & Rasmussen, 1960).

Despite inherent flaws, lesion-deficit mapping has been the mainstay of neuropsychology for the past century and remains the gold standard of charting behavioral functions in the brain. Some recent advances in methodology have made the process more reliable and informative. For instance, behavioral testing has become more standardized over the past 50 years. Behavioral measurement tools have been developed, translated, and normed, allowing clinicians at research centers around the world to evaluate patients with the same techniques and compare them to standards. One historical problem—that the correlation between an abnormal behavior and brain lesion had to wait until the autopsy—has been eliminated by the development of sophisticated brain-imaging techniques that allow us to visualize in great detail brain structures at the same time as behavior is being evaluated. Newer brain-imaging techniques are rapidly becoming available that allow us to investigate brain-behavior relationships in healthy individuals while they are performing specific cognitive tasks. It is to this important area of brain imaging that we now turn.

BRAIN IMAGING

There are two broad categories of imaging techniques: those that take pictures (images) of brain structures and those that take pictures of brain function (blood flow, electrical activity, or glucose utilization).

Structural Imaging: CT Scan and MRI

X-ray **computed tomography (CT)** is an example of transmission tomography that is similar to standard radiography (see Figure 2.9). In transmission tomography, an external beam of radiation is transmitted through the tissue. The amount and distribution of X-rays transmitted through the tissue (and not absorbed or deflected) is measured by detectors in the machine. The detectors convert electromagnetic radiation into electronic pulses, and a computer uses these pulses to calculate the amount of radiation transmitted through the tissue and reconstructs an image on a point-by-point basis. The amount of radiation that passes though a given structure depends on its thickness and density. For example, bone absorbs X-rays readily, and so very little passes through it; soft tissue does not absorb X-rays as well and therefore transmits them. The contrast between the transmission versus absorption of X-rays by various tissues yields contrasts between structures and between healthy and damaged tissue. Infarcts show up as areas of decreased density, and hemorrhages show up as areas of increased density with respect to surrounding brain tissue (see also next chapter). The resolution of the CT, or the accuracy with which the image depicts increasingly smaller areas of the scan, depends on the number and geometry of detectors.

The other most common structural imaging technique uses magnetic resonance imaging (MRI). MRI is an example of emission technology, in which an image is reconstructed from internal rather than external sources. It examines energy released by a selected element, usually hydrogen atoms, in response to a large magnetic field. Atoms generally point in different directions. However, when placed in a strong magnetic field, they line up in parallel. A radio frequency current is applied to synchronize the movement of the protons (hydrogen nuclei), and after the current stops, the protons reorient to the magnetic field and emit radio signals that can be detected. Again, depending on the makeup of particular tissue, the emitted signals will differ, yielding a contrast between healthy and damaged tissue. MRI generally has better contrast in distinguishing gray from white matter and overall better resolution than CT, making it more useful for diagnosis of small lesions. MRI also has the distinct advantage that it does not involve radiation, making it safer than CT scans (see Figure 2.9).

Functional Imaging: EEG, PET, and fMRI

Structural images (CT, MRI) tell us the location and amount of brain damage. However, they cannot show brain function, that is, what part of the brain is actually working during perception, movement, or cognition. This is an important limitation for several reasons. First and foremost, we know that brain structures are intricately interconnected by blood supply, structural connections, and neurochemical interactions. We also know that brain structures affect one another in complex ways, involving both excitation and inhibition. For instance, if one brain region (A) typically stimulates another brain region (B), damage to Region A may decrease activity in Region B. Alternatively, if the damaged Region A typically inhibits Region B, damage to Region A will release the inhibition, and Region B will increase in activity. Structural imaging does not reveal how damage to one part of the brain affects other structurally intact but functionally connected parts of the brain.

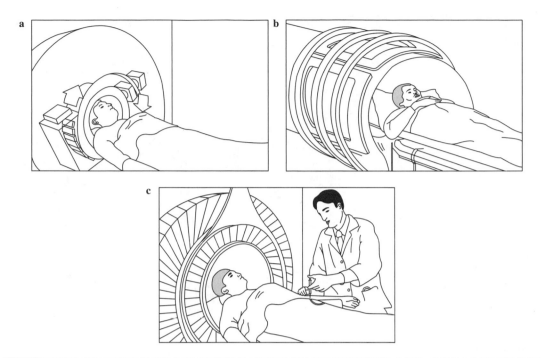

Figure 2.9 Schematic drawings of three brain-imaging techniques. (a) Computerized axial tomography (CAT or CT) is performed by moving an X-ray source around the head. The patient lies on a table with his or her head inside a large ring. The X-ray source is moved around the head, emitting radiation that is picked up by detectors on the opposite side. The amount of radiation absorbed versus passed through the head depends on tissue density. Ventricles, gray matter, spaces, and lesions all absorb different amounts of radiation. The sensors feed the information into a computer and create a series of images based on the amount of radiation that is passed through versus absorbed. The images reflect different tissue density, including structural lesions. The patient is exposed to radiation. The images obtained from this technique are exemplified in Figure 2.10 (top row) in a patient who suffered a left hemisphere stroke with resulting aphasia. (b) **Magnetic resonance imaging** (MRI or MR), like CT, allows us to create images of brain structure. MRI requires a patient to lie in a large magnet while the magnetic fields are manipulated by passing an electromagnetic wave (a radio signal) through the head. This energy alters the energy state of the proton in each hydrogen atom's nuclei. When the signal is turned off, protons that return to their prior state emit radio signals, which are picked up by sensors and fed into a computer for analysis. These signals differ from the characteristics of the energy input as well as the internal structure. Computer analysis of the resulting data is used to create images of the brain, which can show details of sulci and gyri and reveal extremely small changes in brain structure such as the loss of myelin on nerve axons. The resulting image is generally more detailed than those seen in CT scans and is acquired without exposing the patient to radiation (see Figure 2.11). (c) **Positron emission tomography** (PET) is one of the earliest and best-known methods of looking at brain function rather than structure. This technique works by introducing radioactive chemicals into the bloodstream. The chemicals are labeled with compounds that are used by the brain, such as glucose. The chemical solutions contain atoms that emit positrons. The positrons interact with electrons and produce electromagnetic radiation (in the form of photons), which is detected by sensors. Often, the radioactive isotope contains a glucose-like substance (e.g., fluorodeoxyglucose [FDG]), which is then taken up by the neurons, which typically use glucose. The computer analysis of the data detected by the sensors then reveals the patterns of glucose (i.e., glucose metabolism) in various parts of the brain. Brain regions that are structurally damaged or functioning poorly without structural damage are revealed in this technique. The technique can be used in a "resting state," which reveals the normal baseline metabolism (as in Figure 2.10, bottom row), or with stimulation, as when the patient is asked to do something particular (e.g., move a finger, read words), showing how brain metabolism changes with activities. Although often displayed in color, the color versus gray-scale coding of the images shows the same information: degree of metabolism. More recently, the technique of functional magnetic resonance imaging (fMRI) has been developed, based on the principles of MR, capitalizing on the fact that the hemoglobin that is oxygenated and hemoglobin that is not have different magnetic resonances and therefore respond differently to electromagnetic energy. fMRI shows brain function by analyzing how blood oxygen levels change with activities. It has advantages over PET insofar as it is quicker, has good spatial resolution, and is noninvasive.

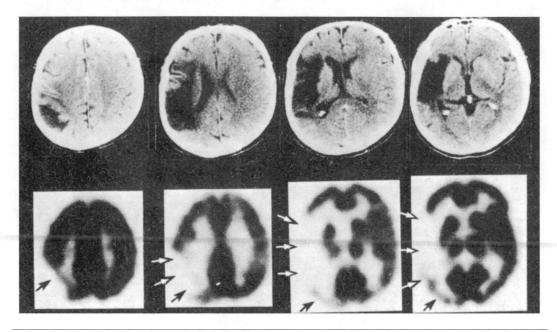

Figure 2.10 Computerized axial tomographic (CAT or CT) and positron emission tomographic (PET) scans (in a transverse plane with horizontal views) for a subject with aphasia following a stroke. The CT scan (top row) shows structural damage (dark areas) in the insula and the parietal and temporal lobes in the left hemisphere. The PET scans (lower row) show glucose hypometabolism in these and several other regions, including the temporal, parietal, and frontal lobes; the caudate; and thalamus, all on the left side. Although frontal lobe regions are not structurally damaged, they show glucose hypometabolism. The arrows indicate areas of significant hypometabolism. The right hemisphere appears normal, both structurally and metabolically. If the whole brain were healthy, the left hemisphere would look like a mirror image of the right hemisphere.

Second, structural brain imaging cannot reveal important information about recovery of behavior. Following brain damage and loss of cognitive and motor abilities, patients often recover lost function. Structural images show what tissue is damaged and highlight what brain regions are *not* participating in recovery of function. But structural images do not show what structures *are* participating in that recovery of function. It is clear that undamaged brain structures adapt and take over new functions after brain damage (Merzenich et al., 1984; Recanzone, 2000). Therefore, to understand which brain regions adapt and become involved in new function—that is, to understand recovery—we need more than structural imaging; we need to see images of brain function.

There are now several techniques for taking pictures of brain function. These are all emission techniques that depend on internal energy sources. The most widely used techniques are electroencephalograms (EEGs), **positron emission tomography (PET)** (Figure 2.10), and functional magnetic resonance imaging (fMRI).

Electroencephalography (EEG) measures electrical activity of the brain through electrodes placed on the skull. Because neuronal firing is an electrical event, EEGs can measure brain function through electrical activity. EEGs are a relatively indirect measurement of brain activity because the electrical activity is summed over millions of neurons originating in a large area of brain tissue and diffused through the skull. However, with either gross deficits and/or careful experimental methods, it is possible to use these brain waves measured on the skull to detect localized brain function and dysfunction. For instance, epileptic seizures and tumors alter the normal patterns of resting brain waves. **Evoked potentials** (EPs, sometimes called ERPs for evoked response potentials) are a more sophisticated method of using EEGs to detect neural response to specific stimuli. EPs capitalize on the finding that visual or auditory stimuli produce reliable response patterns of brain waves. These electrical responses, because they are time-locked to the stimuli, indicate where in the brain, and when in relation to the presentation, a person processes specific stimuli. Deviations from typical electrical patterns suggest brain dysfunction. Advantages of this technique are that it is noninvasive and has excellent time resolution, measuring perceptual and mental activity while it is taking place. Disadvantages include the fact that it is a very indirect measurement of brain function insofar as it has relatively limited spatial resolution, and because of the extent of irrelevant background brain activity, it is necessary to average electrical activity over many presentations to see clear response patterns.

PET and fMRI are based on the assumption that increased brain activity is associated with increased use of oxygen and glucose, and these in turn are associated with increased blood flow. PET requires the injection or inhalation of radionuclides that are metabolized throughout the body (see Figure 2.9). The radioisotopes decay by the emission of positrons. The positron combines with an electron, and that process creates two photons that are emitted 180 degrees apart. Two electronically linked detectors determine the line of origin and use that information to construct the image. The isotopes that are commonly used include (F-18)-fluorodeoxyglucose, (0–15)-water, (0–15)-carbon dioxide, (Xe-133)-xenon, and (I-123)-N-isopropyl-*p*-iodomaphetamine. The technique involves administering the radioactive isotope; engaging the patient in a particular cognitive task, which brings the labeled substance to those brain regions most involved; and then scanning the brain to see where the radioactive isotope accumulates. The amount of time it takes for the isotope to collect depends on the substance; it takes about 40 minutes for a glucose-labeled compound to be taken up by the tissue, which is a very long time to sustain any particular mental operation; labeled oxygen allows measurement of regional blood flow within several minutes and is more appropriate for controlled tasks of cognition.

Because brain activity increases the flow of oxygenated blood to the active regions, and because the magnetic properties of oxygenated blood are different from nonoxygenated blood, **functional magnetic resonance imaging (fMRI)** can quantify the degree of activity in particular brain regions. This technique is also referred to as BOLD MRI, standing for *b*lood *o*xygenation-*l*evel *d*ependent MRI. Because this technique is fast (with a temporal resolution of several seconds), affords excellent contrast, and does not involve ingestion/injection of radioactive isotopes, it is quickly becoming the preferred method for investigating brain function.

Functional brain-imaging studies have been done with healthy and impaired subjects, in a range of states from resting quietly to being actively engaged in specific cognitive tasks. The results have shown us what parts of the brain are involved in specific cognitive activities and how different brain structures affect one another by showing multiple areas of activation, highlighting neuronal circuits. Current challenges in the field of functional brain imaging include identifying the extent of individual variability in brain organization and cognitive strategies.

Brain scans used for the purpose of associating lesions with behavior typically show horizontal slices of the brain, approximately 1.5 mm apart. It is traditional to show the *left* side on the *right,* as if the person reading the scan is facing the person whose brain was scanned. However, this is inconsistent, and it is crucial, when viewing any scan, to determine which side is labeled "left" versus "right." Shades of gray and colors have different meanings in different scans. In CT scans, the darkest areas are the ventricles and lesions; the skull and brain tissues are lighter. If functional images are shown in black and white, the darker colors indicate greater activity. When functional images are displayed in color, the scale generally runs from red (high activity) to blue (no activity).

Brain-imaging techniques enable us to see with great clarity the changes in brain structure in healthy aging and disease states. Images of healthy aging brains show the overall shrinkage of the brain, with concomitant sulci widening and ventricular enlargement (see Figure 2.11). Knowing how age affects the shape of the brain enables us to differentiate the healthy brain from a brain that has been damaged by a focal lesion and/or more global deterioration.

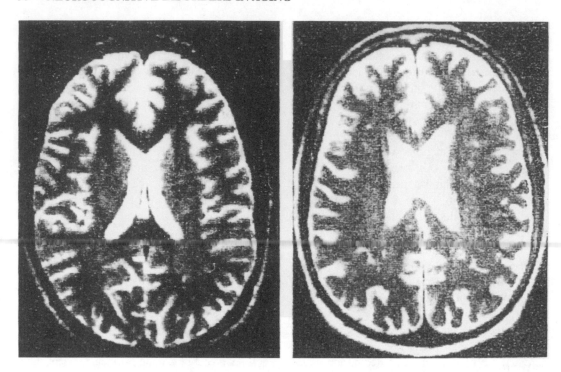

Figure 2.11   Examples of aging as seen on magnetic resonance images. The image on the left is a 23-year-old female, and the image on the right is a 77-year-old female. Both images are cross sections of the brain in a transverse (horizontal) plane. The parameters used to acquire these images emphasize changes in brain water state and content, thus highlighting the spaces surrounding blood vessels, cerebral sulci, and ventricles filled with cerebrospinal fluid. The fluid appears white, and myelinated fibers appear dark. Note the enlarged ventricles and widened sulci in the image of the older person on the right.

3

STROKE AND OTHER FOCAL NEUROLOGICAL DISORDERS

Chapter Preview

The ultimate goal of this book is to introduce students and caregivers to a wide range of cognitive impairments and other abnormal behaviors that we see in older adults. The prior chapter introduced information that will allow us to discuss the *where* question: Where are the brain structures that, when damaged, cause abnormal cognition and behavior? This chapter introduces the *how* question—how do these brain structures get damaged in the first place? This chapter focuses on the most common mechanism of brain damage in older age: stroke. Each of the subsequent chapters builds directly or indirectly on the *where* and *how* information in order to discuss the central questions of the book: *What* is going on, and *what* can we do about it?

Stroke, cerebrovascular accident (CVA), and **brain attack** are all equivalent terms to describe the sudden onset of neurological deficits due to disruption of blood flow to the brain. When blood flow to the brain is diminished, brain cells do not receive the oxygen and glucose they need to function. This disrupts their electrical functions, and if oxygen and glucose are not restored quickly, the brain cells die. Cell death due to oxygen deprivation is called **ischemia.** Behaviorally, stroke is manifested as a sudden loss of neurological function (Wilkinson, 1993). Stroke typically affects brain cells within a particular region of the brain, causing **focal neurological damage.** Stroke is by far the most common cause of focal brain injury at all ages, and the risk grows exponentially with each decade of life (Gress & Singh, 1999) (see Figure 3.1).

The relative importance of stroke as a health concern is clear. The National Stroke Association (2002) reports the following:

- Every year, approximately 750,000 Americans have a new or recurrent stroke.
- After heart disease and cancer, stroke is the third most common cause of death, killing nearly 160,000 Americans every year.
- Stroke is the largest single cause of focal neurologic dysfunction.
- Nearly 4 million people in the United States have survived a stroke and are living with the aftereffects.
- About one third of stroke survivors have mild impairments, another third are moderately impaired, and the remainder are severely impaired.

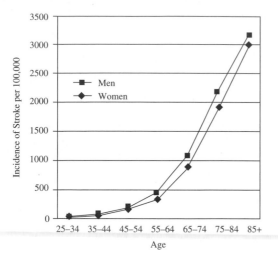

Figure 3.1 Average annual age-specific incidence rates of total stroke (first ever and recurrent) per 100,000 population in the United States in 1995 by sex.

- Stroke costs the United States $30 billion annually. Direct costs, such as hospitals, physicians, and rehabilitation, add up to $17 billion; indirect costs, such as lost productivity, total $13 billion. The average cost per patient for the first 90 days poststroke is $15,000.

The risks of stroke are disproportionately greater for older adults.

- Two thirds of all strokes occur in people older than age 65.
- For each decade after age 55, the risk of stroke doubles.
- In those older than age 70, stroke is the second most common cause of death.
- For adults older than age 65, the risk of dying from stroke is seven times that of the general population.

As we shall learn in subsequent chapters, the behavioral consequences of focal brain injury depend on what part of the brain is damaged. The following chapters describe in detail the signs, symptoms, and behavioral treatments of focal brain injury. This chapter covers the mechanisms of stroke and some of the medical treatments for stroke. Although stroke is the most common, it is not the only cause of focal brain

damage. Therefore, several other causes of focal brain damage will be briefly described at the end of the chapter.

STROKE MECHANISMS AND SUBTYPES

The vascular system feeding the brain is key to understanding the underlying mechanisms of stroke. The blood vessels supplying the brain originate in the internal carotid and vertebral/basilar arteries. The internal carotids give rise to the anterior and middle cerebral arteries, which provide blood to the front and middle portions of the cortex. The middle cerebral artery is the biggest of the cerebral arteries. The vertebral arteries join together and form the basilar artery, which gives rise to the posterior cerebral artery and irrigates the medial temporal and posterior occipital lobes. The arteries in the left and right hemispheres are joined together by the anterior and posterior communicating arteries, which together form the circle of Willis (see Figure 3.2). The circle of Willis enables the blood supply from one carotid or vertebral artery to reach the entire brain, allowing compensation of blood flow in case one of these arteries is compromised. However, during normal circumstances, with normal blood pressure and no arterial obstructions, there is little or no exchange of blood either between the two sides of the circle of Willis or between the internal carotid and posterior cerebral vessels (Walsh & Darby, 1999).

Although the brain accounts for only 2% of the adult body weight, it uses about 20% of the cardiac output when the body is resting. Normal cerebral blood flow is about 50 mL for each 100 g of brain tissue per minute (L. R. Caplan, 2000). The intensity and duration of oxygen deprivation determine the extent of ischemic brain damage. When cerebral blood flow drops below 40% of normal, the electrical functions of cells are disrupted. Dysfunctional (but not dead) brain cells (**ischemic penumbra**) can be brought back to life by resumption of blood flow (Caplan, 2000). When cerebral blood flow drops below 20% of normal for more than about 10 minutes, the cells in the affected region die (Kolb & Whishaw, 1996). Areas of dead brain cells are called **infarcts.**

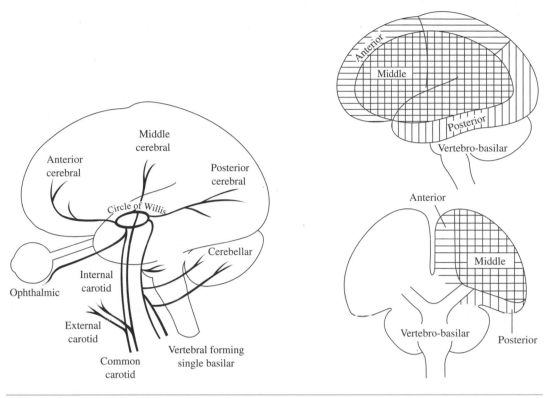

Figure 3.2   Schematic diagram showing the arteries carrying blood to the brain (left) and their distributions (right).

Obstructive Strokes

The two primary mechanisms of stroke are (a) **arterial occlusion,** in which mechanical obstruction of blood flow creates ischemic brain damage, and (b) **hemorrhage,** in which a perforation in a blood vessel causes bleeding into the brain. Obstructive strokes are divided into two types, depending on the source of the obstruction. The most common type of occlusive stroke is **thrombosis,** in which abnormal tissue narrows and occludes the lumen (the internal channel) of a blood vessel. Thrombosis generally occurs in large arteries and is usually caused by a combination of slowly developing stenosis of the artery from **atherosclerosis** (narrowing of the artery by buildup of fatty and sometimes hemorrhagic deposits, atheromas[1]), followed by rapid formation of blood clots at the stenotic site. Thrombotic strokes account for 60% of all strokes and more than 75% of obstructive strokes (Caplan, 2000).

The other type of obstructive stroke is caused by an **embolism,** a plug that moves inside a blood vessel until it becomes lodged and obstructs the flow of blood. Most emboli are fragments of lesions that develop outside of the brain, frequently formed in the heart or the carotid arteries. Emboli can be blood clots, bubbles of air, deposits of fat, tumor cells, and particulate matter from injected drugs or bacteria. Because the middle cerebral artery is the largest artery in the brain, it is the most common site of embolic strokes. Of all obstructive strokes, 20% to 30% are associated with emboli (Caplan, 2000) (see Figure 3.3).

Obstructive strokes are sometimes described with respect to the size of the vessel that is obstructed. Large vessel obstructions are relatively common in people with heart disease and cause prominent cortical symptoms. Small vessel obstructions account for about 20% of obstructive strokes, are more common in people with hypertension and/or diabetes, and frequently

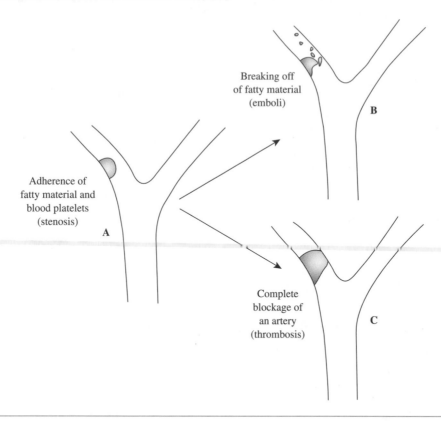

Breaking off
of fatty material
(emboli)

B

Adherence of
fatty material and
blood platelets
(stenosis)

A

Complete
blockage of
an artery
(thrombosis)

C

Figure 3.3   Mechanisms causing thromboembolic or occlusive strokes. (a) Abnormal tissue collects on the walls of a blood vessel, narrowing the lumen and reducing blood flow. (b) Material can break off of the abnormal tissue lining a blood vessel, creating an embolus. The embolus can move through the blood vessel and further obstruct blood flow. (c) Tissue lining the blood vessel can grow to the point of completely blocking the lumen of a blood vessel and stop blood flow.

affect subcortical areas. Small subcortical strokes are called **lacunar** (Latin: *hole*) **infarcts** and are associated most obviously with hemi-sensory and motor deficits (Gress & Singh, 1999) but also with depression, poor motivation, and other symptoms associated with frontal lobe dysfunction (Absher & Cummings, 1995). The extent and size of infarct from obstructive strokes will depend on several factors, including the rate of occlusion, adequacy of collateral circulation, resistance of brain structures to ischemia, and degree of secondary brain edema (swelling).

Hemorrhagic Strokes

Hemorrhagic strokes are less common than obstructive strokes, accounting for about 20% of all strokes (Caplan, 2000; Gress & Singh, 1999). Hemorrhagic strokes are caused by a weakness in the wall of a blood vessel, either present from birth or caused by hypertension. Weakness in a vessel wall often results in dilation of the artery (aneurysm), which is weak and can rupture from increased pressure. A hemorrhage causes brain damage by a number of processes, including vasospasm (constriction of blood vessels), which restricts blood flow to particular areas of the brain; brain edema; and pressure exerted on brain tissue by a **hematoma,** the accumulation of blood within the brain. There are two types of hemorrhage, differentiated by the part of the brain that becomes filled with blood. **Subarachnoid hemorrhages** release blood into the subarachnoid space around the brain, are typically associated with congenital **arteriovenous malformations** (AVMs), and affect younger people most often. AVMs are congenitally tangled arteries and veins that grow and eventually rupture and hemorrhage. They are rare (1% of all strokes). **Intracerebral** (or **intraparenchymal**) **hemorrhages** release blood directly into the brain tissue and are more frequently associated with hypertension and older age. Intracerebral hemorrhages often involve blood vessels feeding the subcortical structures and therefore are likely to affect the thalamus, basal ganglia, and brainstem. Intracerebral hemorrhages have a high mortality rate, with 26% to 29% of patients not surviving the initial hospitalization (Williams, Jiang, Matchar, & Samsa, 1999).

Other Categories of Stroke

Transient ischemic attacks (TIAs) are small strokes from which people recover within 24 hours. Although it has been traditionally assumed that there are no lasting effects from a TIA, several long-term studies have now shown that patients who have had TIAs may not fully recover, and deficits become pronounced with repeated TIAs (Delaney, Wallace, & Egelko, 1980). In addition, after a TIA, a person's risk of having a stroke is increased. The overall risk of a stroke during the 5 years after a TIA is 24% to 29%, a sevenfold increase over those who have not had a TIA. The risk of a stroke after at TIA is greatest during the first year and greater for certain groups of patients, including those with severe carotid stenosis (Streifler et al., 1992).

Silent Strokes. A fair number of strokes, called **silent strokes,** go completely unnoticed. In one study (Chodosh et al., 1988), 11% of subjects had strokes that had not produced any notable symptoms. These strokes are discovered when patients have a brain scan for other reasons—for instance, because of a later occurring stroke, or when they volunteer as a "normal control." These are typically small lacunar strokes in deep brain structures.

Nonsudden reduction of blood flow. Obstructive and hemorrhagic strokes are the most common causes of focal brain damage, but it should be noted that nonsudden reduction of blood flow can also cause ischemia. Nonsudden reduction of blood flow tends to cause diffuse rather than focal brain damage. Decreased systemic perfusion may be due to poor cardiac function or long-term thrombosis (Caplan, 2000).

STROKE INCIDENCE, RISK FACTORS, AND PREVENTION

Although it is difficult to determine the exact number of strokes that occur in a population, the estimated incidence (number of strokes per year per population) of first-time and recurrent strokes in the United States is between half a million and 750,000 (Williams et al., 1999). People are not all equally likely to sustain a stroke. Incidence rates in different populations highlight different risk factors. Risk factors for stroke are usually divided into those that are beyond the control of the individual (untreatable) versus those that can be treated. Untreatable risk factors include age, sex, race, and location of residence. Treatable risk factors typically include smoking, obesity, and certain physiological signs or diseases such as hypertension, high blood cholesterol, and diabetes. Obviously, there is great overlap between risk factors (e.g., the incidence of hypertension and diabetes both rise with age), and risk factors tend to correlate with one another (i.e., obesity, hypertension, and diabetes often co-occur). However, it is important to realize that risk factors are simply *associations* between signs or behaviors and incidence of stroke; they are not necessarily *causal*. We still do not understand why certain risk factors (e.g., location of residence; see below) are associated with a higher incidence of stroke.

Untreatable Risk Factors for Stroke

The most striking epidemiological factor about stroke is the exponential rise with age (Williams et al., 1999). Such a rise is generally attributed to the increase in atherosclerosis and heart disease with age, both of which contribute directly to the formation of thrombosis and emboli.

Men are more likely to have strokes than are women, and this is particularly notable at younger ages when there are roughly equivalent numbers of men and women in the population (Hollander et al., 2003). Because more women survive to older ages, the incidence in older people is roughly equivalent between the sexes.

Blacks are more susceptible to strokes than Whites: The incidence rate for first stroke among African Americans is almost double that of White Americans (Gillum, 1999). The explanation for the racial differences is not clear, but Blacks do have a higher incidence of other risk factors for stroke, including diabetes and hypertension.

There is an interesting and yet unexplained geographic association with stroke in the United States: Twelve contiguous states and the District of Columbia have stroke death rates that are consistently more than 10% higher than the rest of the country. These states (Virginia, North Carolina, South Carolina, Georgia, Florida, Alabama, Mississippi, Louisiana, Arkansas, Tennessee, Kentucky, and Indiana), along with Washington, D.C., are often referred to as the "stroke belt" (Howard, 1999). The higher stroke incidence and mortality may be linked to a number of factors, including a higher than average population of African Americans and older adults, dietary factors, obesity, and smoking (Howard, 1999).

Heredity is another nontreatable risk factor. Several inherited disorders and traits appear to increase the risk of stroke due to their association with heart disease, hypertension, mitral valve prolapse, arterial abnormalities, and diabetes (Caplan, 2000).

Treatable Risk Factors for Stroke: Focus on Prevention

The prevention of stroke emphasizes control over treatable risk factors, including primary prevention (prior to a stroke) and secondary prevention (after a first stroke to prevent recurrent stroke). The best-understood and treatable risk factors are hypertension, heart disease, and atherosclerosis, and these have been the primary focus of stroke prevention. Hypertension, often defined as blood pressure above 140 mm Hg systolic and 90 mm Hg diastolic, is associated with atherosclerosis and cardiac disease. Hypertension is typically controlled by a combination of medical and behavioral interventions such as diet and exercise, and many studies have now shown that treated hypertension reduces stroke incidence and mortality (Gress & Singh, 1999; Kannel, 1996).

Because blood clots, presumably of cardiac origin, have been implicated in a large percentage of strokes, medication to reduce blood clotting is now a primary part of stroke prevention. Atrial fibrillation, myocardial infarction (heart attack), and other heart abnormalities create abnormal blood flow around the heart and increase the risk of blood clots and embolic stroke. Therefore, stroke prevention often involves medications to reduce the formation of blood clots, including the prevention of blood coagulation (clotting) and platelet aggregation (adhesion and aggregation) (Caplan, 2000). Both anticoagulation (e.g., heparin) and antiaggregation (e.g., aspirin) agents appear successful in reducing myocardial infarction and stroke (Gress & Singh, 1999).

The association between hypercholesterolemia (high cholesterol levels in the blood), atherosclerosis, and carotid stenosis has led to recommendations to lower blood cholesterol. This can be achieved via a combination of diet, exercise, and medicine and, when successful, appears to reduce risk of stroke (Gress & Singh, 1999).

There has always been an emphasis on excess body weight and smoking as treatable risk factors. Obesity puts a strain on the entire circulatory system and increases the incidence of hypertension, heart disease, high cholesterol, and diabetes, which are all associated with stroke.

Smoking doubles stroke risk. Smoking damages blood vessel walls, speeds up the clogging of arteries by deposits, raises blood pressure, and makes the heart work harder. Both the amount and the duration of smoking are important factors. In one study, the total years of cigarette smoking was the most important predictor of severe occlusive carotid artery disease. Stopping smoking reduces the risk of stroke (Kawachi et al., 1993; Whisnant et al., 1990).

Diabetes is associated with an increased risk of stroke because hypertension and intracranial atheromatous diseases are more common among patients with diabetes. Diabetes, like hypertension, appears to cause thickening of the blood vessel walls, particularly in small vessels, which reduces blood flow. However, no data suggest that strict control of diabetes alters the risk of stroke (Caplan, 2000).

Needless to say, changes in diet and lifestyle, because of their correlation with various other risk factors (such as obesity and diabetes), are also often the target of stroke reduction. For instance, low-fat diets and adequate physical exercise help to reduce weight, control diabetes, and lower blood levels of cholesterol and therefore reduce stroke risk.

Alcohol use can have both a protective and a deleterious effect on the cerebrovascular system. Light to moderate consumption of alcohol, defined as two or fewer drinks per day, appears to have a protective effect against atherosclerosis and actually reduces the risk of ischemic stroke. Although there is some controversy about the type of alcohol that offers this protective effect, the most pervasive theory is that wine, because of its antioxidant flavonoids and tanins, is protective, but beer and other spirits are not. However, these data are confounded by the fact that those who drink wine tend to drink less than those who drink other alcoholic beverages, and it is clear that heavy alcohol consumption, defined as five or more drinks per day, positively correlates with stroke (Sacco et al., 1999). The role of alcohol in stroke is further complicated by the frequent coexistence of alcohol consumption with hypertension and smoking (Gorelick, Rodin, Langenberg, Hier, & Costigan, 1989; Gorelick et al., 1987).

A relative newcomer in the treatable risk category is the presence of higher than normal blood levels of the amino acid homocysteine. The good news about this risk factor is the ease of treatment: Intake of vitamin B12, B6, and folic acid appears to reduce homocysteine with no side effects (Warren, 2002).

DIAGNOSIS

Strokes are identified by a combination of history, neurological deficits, and laboratory tests. Because there are now treatments that are best given during the acute phase of stroke, it is very important for the public and physicians to be able to quickly recognize the signs of a stroke and to make an accurate diagnosis. Fast and accurate diagnoses will allow the best possible outcomes.

Sudden onset of symptoms is usually the key to diagnosing a stroke. A stroke is something that happens quickly (as in "the stroke of midnight") and unpredictably (as in a "stroke of bad luck"). Most symptoms appear in a matter of minutes, although some strokes may evolve over hours or even a few days. The most common symptoms of stroke are unilateral numbness or weakness of the face, arm, or leg; confusion; trouble speaking or understanding; visual disturbance; trouble walking; loss of balance; or severe headache.

Once a patient is identified and brought to the attention of a physician, the doctor's first priority is to determine if a stroke has indeed occurred and, if so, determine the mechanism of stroke (hemorrhage vs. obstruction), the location of brain damage, and the severity of the stroke. This information will help to implement appropriate treatment, which might include medication (beneficial in obstructive strokes), surgery (ofen indicated in hemorrhagic strokes), or neither (often preferred in mild strokes) (Odderson, 1999). Both medical and surgical interventions carry risk. Correct identification of the stroke type is imperative to prevent further harm from treatment. For instance, **thrombolysis,** a pharmacological treatment that dissolves clots, is appropriate for obstructive strokes but is thought to cause hemorrhage and edema in patients with large infarcts and severe neurological deficits, so patient selection is extremely important.

Personal history is particularly important in suggesting stroke type. A prior history of stroke would suggest a recurrent stroke in someone with new, sudden-onset neurological symptoms. History can also suggest the mechanism of a stroke: A patient who is known to smoke and have high blood cholesterol is likely to have atherosclerosis with large-artery occlusive disease (i.e., thrombosis) rather than embolic or hemorrhagic etiologies. Old age also tends to be associated with atherosclerosis so would also favor a diagnosis of thrombosis. In contrast, a personal or family history of diabetes and/or heart disease increases the chance of myocardial infarction, which increases the likelihood of cardiac-originated cerebral embolism (Caplan, 2000).

Behavioral signs and symptoms are also helpful in identifying the stroke mechanism. Sudden-onset headache, concurrent with other symptoms, suggests subarachnoid hemorrhage (SAH): Headache is almost always associated with the onset of SAH, less often associated with intracerebral hemorrhage, and rarely associated with obstructive strokes. Time of onset can also be a helpful clue. Thrombotic events are more likely to occur at rest with the deficit noted upon rising, whereas embolic strokes and hemorrhages are more likely to occur during strenuous activity when blood pressure is higher. Embolic strokes frequently occur when getting up at night to urinate, the so-called "matudinal" (morning) embolus. Decreased level of consciousness and vomiting are more frequently associated with hemorrhage than obstructive stroke (Caplan, 2000).

Symptoms are important in identifying sites of brain damage. Knowledge of how motor and behavioral functions are localized allows the clinician to hypothesize the location of damage. Unilateral left limb weakness suggests a contralateral (right) frontal lobe lesion. Neglect of left space (i.e., failure to respond to people and objects that appear on the left side) suggests a right hemisphere lesion. Trouble speaking suggests left hemisphere damage. Dizziness or weakness in all four limbs suggests a vertebrobasilar territory infarct. Purely motor deficits or pure sensory deficits suggest subcortical lesions in the area of the internal capsule or thalamus, respectively (Caplan, 2000).

Although observation of behavioral deficits is helpful, it is not objective. To allow comparisons of stroke symptoms and treatment outcomes across a wide range of patients, physicians, and countries, researchers have developed behaviorally based stroke rating scales. These scales allow clinicians to identify and quantify stroke symptoms and track improvement in a standard manner. Danish researchers have developed the Scandinavian Neurological Stroke Scale Score (SSS), which allows clinicians to rate stroke signs and symptoms on a 58-point scale. Nine areas of function are rated by assigning points for degree of function, with more points given for better function (e.g., 2 points each for orientation to time, place, and person). The nine areas of function are consciousness; eye movement; hand power; arm power; leg power (on the affected side); orientation to time, place, and person; speech/language; facial weakness; and gait.

In the United States, the National Institutes of Health (NIH) has developed a similar stroke scale (Odderson, 1999). The NIH scale takes about 10 minutes to complete, and each patient receives a score from 0 (normal) to 42 (worst possible outcome). Both the Scandinavian and American scales include evaluation of the patient's level of consciousness and ability to follow commands, see, move arms and legs, and so on. The items are designed to assess brain functions served by each of the major regions of the brain. Both scales have been used to compare the type and severity of symptoms across types of stroke, the effectiveness of treatment, and the extent of recovery and to guide treatment. For instance, patients with more severe deficits on the NIH scale (score > 20) are more likely to suffer a hemorrhage when administered medication meant to dissolve thrombi than patients with milder symptoms (Odderson, 1999).

Laboratory tests, including brain imaging, ultrasound, and lumbar punctures, provide valuable information in detecting the size, type, and location of stroke. We now have the ability to look at the brain early in the course of a stroke to determine the type of stroke and the site and size of lesion. Computed tomography (CT) and magnetic resonance imaging (MRI) of the brain can show and help to distinguish an obstructive stroke versus a hemorrhage and delineate the lesion location. The appearance of lesions on brain scans depends on the type, size, and age of the lesion, as well as the type of scan used. Small and/or early ischemic changes may not be visible at all. Various functional brain scans can also be used to identify areas of metabolic abnormality but are not now routinely provided because of availability, cost, and lack of convincing evidence that they would change the treatment.

Subarachnoid hemorrhages are often preceded by small leaks that can be easily overlooked on CT scans. However, because subarachnoid blood rapidly disseminates and is present in the cerebrospinal fluid, it can be easily detected by lumbar puncture. Ultrasound measures blood flow and velocity and therefore can be very helpful in determining the location and extent of occlusive vascular lesions in the arteries of the neck, the base of the brain, and even the intracranial arteries (transcranial Doppler ultrasound). **Cerebral angiography** uses dye injected into cerebral arteries to reveal the precise nature of vascular lesions. Because many strokes are due to emboli from the heart, diagnosis of stroke will often involve a cardiac evaluation as well.

MEDICAL AND SURGICAL TREATMENT OF STROKE

Stroke prevention is the most important treatment. However, if prevention fails and a stroke occurs, it is crucial to minimize the amount of brain damage that occurs. Until recently, medical treatment of acute stroke emphasized maintaining appropriate fluid levels, oxygen, body temperature, and blood pressure. However, treatment of occlusive stroke now includes thrombolysis, chemically dissolving the thromboembolic blockage and restoring cerebral blood flow within the first few hours of the stroke. Recombinant tissue plasminogen activator (rtPA) is the currently favored thrombolytic agent, with generally positive outcomes if administered within 3 hours of symptom onset. Standard anticoagulation and antiplatelet medications are also used during the acute phase of stroke to reduce blood clotting. Acute hemorrhages can be approached surgically, both to stop the bleeding and to remove hematomas from the brain tissue to prevent or reduce excessive pressure on brain tissue.

Various surgical approaches are used to improve blood flow to the brain after a stroke to prevent recurrence once the patient is stabilized, with the goals of maintaining function and preventing further damage. For instance, if carotid blood flow is significantly (> 70%) restricted, a **carotid endarterectomy,** which involves surgical removal of carotid lesions, is often successful in improving blood flow. This procedure eliminates a source of emboli, therefore reducing

stroke risk in nonsymptomatic patients (Caplan, 2000; Gress & Singh, 1999). Blood flow can be improved by transluminal angioplasty, which uses balloon catheters to dilate specific blood vessels. Obstructed blood vessels can also be bypassed by connecting a good blood vessel to another just beyond the obstruction.

Survival, Prognosis, and Recovery

Survival from a stroke depends on type and severity. For instance, a greater percentage of patients die from hemorrhages (26%–29%) than strokes more generally (12%) (Williams et al., 1999), although for those who survive, functional outcomes appear equal for both groups. The location and severity of stroke also play a role: Occlusion of the vertebrobasilar artery is often more severe than hemispheric strokes and carries a mortality rate of about 85% (Becker, 1999). Overall, about 80% to 90% of stroke patients survive (Jorgensen, Nakayama, Raaschou, & Olsen, 1999; Williams et al., 1999), and about 70% to 80% of those patients have persistent neurobehavioral (functional) deficits that affect their ability to perform activities of daily living (Gresham, Granger, Linn, & Kulas, 1999). In general, the deficits are most severe at onset and resolve to some extent with time and treatment. The factors underlying recovery are complex and not fully understood.

Initially after stroke, there is often a period of up to 3 months of relatively rapid **spontaneous** (or **neurologic**) **recovery.** This recovery is thought to be due largely to the return of blood flow and the reduction of brain swelling. The neural mechanisms underlying **functional recovery**—that is, the restoration of functions often long after spontaneous recovery has ceased—are less clear but appear to involve homologous areas of the undamaged hemisphere assuming functions of the damaged hemisphere (Cramer, 1999). The speed of functional recovery varies and is determined by many factors, including the patient's general health status and available treatment. The most important prognostic indicator for eventual recovery from stroke is initial severity of stroke symptoms. In a comprehensive study of 1,197 stroke patients in Copenhagen, all patients with mild strokes were discharged home compared with 75% of patients with moderate strokes, 3% of patients with severe strokes, and 14% of patients with the most severe strokes who went home (Jorgensen, Nakayama, et al., 1999). However, the number of patients discharged home is only one indicator of recovery. Independent functioning was achieved in a smaller percentage of the patients but still was clearly related to initial severity of symptoms: 68% of patients who had mild strokes became functionally independent compared with 37% of patients who had moderate strokes, 13% of patients who had severe strokes, and 4% of patients who had very severe strokes. Of stroke patients, 75% have persistent difficulty with performing basic activities of daily living (Jorgensen, Kammersgaard, et al., 1999).

OTHER FOCAL NEUROLOGICAL DISEASES

Stroke is by far the most common cause of focal neurological damage. However, any type of focal brain injury can cause similar symptoms. Tumors, head trauma, brain infections, and epilepsy occur with some regularity and are briefly described here.

Tumors

A **tumor** (or **neoplasm**) is a mass of tissue that grows independently of its surrounding structures and has no physiological use (Kolb & Whishaw, 1996). Brain tumors grow from glia and other support cells but not from neurons. The brain is the second most common site of tumors, after the uterus. Tumors are divided into those that are benign versus malignant. Benign tumors are not likely to recur after removal. Malignant tumors frequently progress, recur, and threaten life. The type of cell from which they originate also distinguishes brain tumors. About 45% of brain tumors arise from glial cells (gliomas). The second most common brain tumors are metastatic, arising from cancer outside of the brain. Meningiomas are tumors arising from the meninges and grow between the brain and the skull, frequently not invading the brain tissue itself. The incidence of brain tumors rises with age, reaching 30 to 50 per 100,000 for those older than age 45 (Walker, Robins, &

Weinfeld, 1985). Tumors cause focal brain damage by compressing brain tissue, inducing seizures, invading brain tissue, and altering hormonal patterns (Lezak, 1995). Brain tumors cause focal neurological deficits much like stroke (depending on their size and location) but differ from stroke in that the early symptoms are subtle and may fluctuate, and the symptoms progress as the tumors grow. Treatment for brain tumors can cause additional brain damage. Radiation to the brain produces both temporary and permanent changes in the brain that can affect mental function (Lezak, 1995). Surgical removal of brain tumors can also create additional functional problems due to damage caused by accessing and removing the tumor. Long-term exposure to radiation can induce abnormally high amounts of cell death and new focal lesions, a condition know as **radiation necrosis.**

Trauma

Brain trauma is a general term that includes **open head injuries,** as when a bullet penetrates the skull (10% of cases), and **closed head injuries,** as when the head comes in contact with a blunt object but the skull is not opened (90% of cases). Open head injuries often cause very specific (focal) neurological symptoms determined by the site of injury, whereas closed head injuries cause much more diffuse injury. Closed head injuries often damage the site of the brain nearest the impact, as well as the site of the brain opposite to the impact, where the brain ricochets off the skull, called a **contrecoup injury.** Additional lesions are caused throughout the brain from the shearing of nerves and widespread edema. Head trauma is most common in those ages 15 to 24 due largely to motor vehicle accidents, but it is also common in the first 5 years of life and in the elderly as a result of falls. Approximately 30% of people older than age 65 fall each year (Baker & Harvey, 1985; Downton & Andrews, 1991; Ness, Gurney, & Ice, 2003). Falls account for a great number of deaths in the elderly population, but surviving a fall in which the head is injured can mean living with the sequelae of a closed head injury (Rosin & Van Dijk, 1980). Closed head injuries often cause loss of consciousness and result in both focal neurological symptoms as well as global cognitive impairments. The "most crippling and often the most intractable disorders associated with severe head trauma are those that involve capacities for self-determination, self-direction and self-control and regulation, all of which depend on intact awareness of one's self and surrounds" (Lezak, 1995, p. 187). This type of impairment will obviously affect personality and social adjustment and how all cognitive abilities are expressed.

Infection

The brain has a natural defense system called the **blood-brain barrier** that keeps many bacteria and viruses that affect other parts of the body from entering the substance of the brain. However, some infections do get to the brain and cause damage. The brain is susceptible to viruses, bacteria, parasites, and fungi. Brain infections cause nerve cell damage by interfering with blood supply and cellular metabolism, stimulating production of pus and causing edema (Kolb & Whishaw, 1996). Infections that affect the brain cause a variety of symptoms, including fever, headache, delirium, confusion, and focal neurological signs. Diagnostic tests include cerebrospinal fluid (CSF) analysis, CT scans, and tissue cultures. Inflammation of the central nervous system is called **encephalitis.** Treatment for brain infections involves antibiotics, although many brain infections are not sufficiently treatable and must simply run their course.

Epilepsy

Epilepsy (convulsions, seizures, fits, or attacks) is uncontrolled electrical activity within the brain that disrupts normal brain function. The etiology of seizures is often unknown, although a fair number of patients suffer seizures following head trauma, as a result of a tumor, or from toxic chemical exposure, high fever, or other neurological disorders. The two major categories of seizures are generalized seizures, in which the individual briefly loses consciousness, and partial seizures, which involves less acute disruptions of consciousness. Grand mal (or tonic-clonic) seizures are the more severe type of generalized seizure, in which the person can experience convulsions for several minutes and has no memory of the event. Absence or petit mal seizures are of the generalized type and typically only induce a few seconds of convulsing. Seizures occur on a continuum from every few minutes to once in a lifetime. They are often preceded by an aura, including sensation, odors, and noises, and involve loss of consciousness and shaking movements. Subtypes of epilepsy vary depending on how much of the brain is involved and what symptoms appear. Generalized seizures, for example, seem to result from more diffuse disruption of neural activity, whereas partial seizures arise from more focal neural interruptions that induce the significantly less dramatic symptoms of the latter type of seizure. Anticonvulsant drugs (e.g., Dilantin) can control most seizures, but if they cannot be controlled medically, surgery to excise the neurological origin can be successful. Recently, implanted electrical stimulators have been used with some success for patients whose seizures cannot be controlled medically (Amar et al., 1998).

Note

1. *Atherosclerosis* is often not clearly distinguished from *arteriosclerosis,* which refers to thickening of arterial walls, making them more rigid. Some authors suggest that atherosclerosis is a subtype of arteriosclerosis (Christiansen & Grzybowski, 1999, p. 177).

4

APHASIA: DISORDERS OF LANGUAGE

Chapter Preview

In this chapter, we address five central questions:

1. What is language?

Knowledge of words and rules for combining words into sentences. This knowledge underlies our ability to talk, understand spoken language, read, and write.

2. How does language develop and change with age?

The basic elements of language are learned by the time we are about 3 years old, although we continue to learn words throughout our lives. Language knowledge is essentially stable through adulthood, despite some increasing difficulty retrieving words with age.

3. What are the behavioral characteristics and neuropathology of aphasia?

Aphasia is an acquired impairment in the ability to produce and/or understand language. Prominent symptoms include anomia (word-finding difficulty), nonfluent speech, difficulty repeating words and sentences, paraphasias (substitutions), comprehension deficits, alexia (difficulty reading), and agraphia (difficulty writing). Aphasia is typically associated with damage to the perisylvian region of the left cerebral hemisphere.

4. How are language disorders diagnosed?

Aphasia is primarily diagnosed by speech-language pathologists using tests that require patients to name objects, describe pictures, repeat words and phrases, follow simple instructions, write, and read.

5. How are language disorders treated?

Behavioral treatment for aphasia is provided by speech-language pathologists and includes practice in various aspects of speech production, reading, and writing, as well as compensation for communication deficits by using less impaired modalities (e.g., writing instead of speaking), gestures, computers, and sometimes singing. A few experimental drug treatments are also aimed at improving language through manipulation of neurochemistry.

LANGUAGE

Language is a system of communication and expression. We use language to express our emotions and our thoughts, to communicate our desires and our social identity. The flexibility and complexity of human language appears to set us apart from all other animals. Some say that language is uniquely human. Whether it is unique to our species or not, it is ubiquitously human—humans, with very few exceptions, learn their native language with great ease and use it throughout their lives. Therefore, the disruption of language is one of the most debilitating disorders discussed in this book. Language can be described as discrete but interacting domains of knowledge.

Sounds

With the exception of sign languages, the basic elements of language are sounds produced in the vocal tract. To know a language, one must know the phonology of that language—the inventory of the sounds, or **phonemes**—and how they can be combined. For instance, English speakers know that English has a *p* and a *t* but not the Swedish *Ø*, the nasalized vowels that are frequent in French, or the clicks of the Zulu. English speakers also know that sounds can occur only in certain positions within a word: English words can end with an *ng* (as in *sing*) but cannot begin with that sound, although it is physiologically possible—words in Vietnamese begin with that sound. Furthermore, certain sound sequences such as *pf* may be legal in one language, such as German, but not allowed in another, such as English. With a few notable exceptions, such as the sound *sh*, sounds by themselves do not carry meaning. They must be combined into words to do that basic work of language.

Words

In linguistic terminology, the smallest unit of meaning is the morpheme. Morphemes are roughly equivalent to words, except for the fact that some morphemes, such as the past tense marker *-ed* and the prefix *re-*, could be said to carry meaning even though they are not words,

and some words, such as *walked,* could be said to contain two morphemes, *walk + ed.* However, for the purposes of this discussion, we can consider words and morphemes to be roughly synonymous. Words are composed of sounds, and when combined with one another, they form complex words and sentences. Morphemes are divided into two broad categories based on their functions in the language. The largest group are content words, including nouns, verbs, and adjectives. Word meaning is called *lexical semantics* and is an important part of our language knowledge. Our lexical semantic knowledge includes a wide array of information:

- functional—you sit and sleep on a *couch;*
- category—*couch* belongs to the semantic category *furniture;*
- physical—a *couch* is usually upholstered, has arms and a back;
- animacy—*couch* is inanimate;
- synonymy—*couch* and *sofa* mean the same thing.

Content words are plentiful—we are estimated to have a mental word production dictionary of more than 20,000 items (Levelt, 1989). Content words change dramatically over time, with some words falling out of use (e.g., from Shakespeare's *Romeo and Juliet: beseem* 'to be suitable,' *mammet* 'a doll,' *wot* 'to know') and new words being added to the lexicon as needed (e.g., *megabyte, rollerblade*).

A smaller set of morphemes is grammatical in nature. These include articles (*the, an*), prepositions (*to, from*), conjunctions (*and, but*), and various bound morphemes such as the plural marker *-s* and past tense marker *-ed* in English. Bound morphemes are not words insofar as they cannot stand alone (e.g., *un-, re-, -ful*) but carry meaning nonetheless. Grammatical morphemes are sometimes called function words because they indicate the relationship between or function of content words in a sentence. There are relatively few grammatical morphemes in a language compared to the number of content words, and they constitute a relatively fixed set. We do not add to this group of morphemes very often, and they are slow to change historically.

Sentences

Sentences are constructed by combining words in a particular order to convey a particular meaning. Knowledge of grammar or syntax underlies our ability to use sentence structure to convey and interpret complex meanings. English syntax dictates many structural principles that sentences follow to be considered grammatical. For example, articles precede nouns as in *the coffee,* not *coffee the,* and adverbs precede adjectives as in *very hot,* not *hot very.* Grammatical structure also conveys relationships between words in sentences, and a change in sentence structure can dramatically alter meaning: *The dog chased the cat* and *The cat chased the dog* contain the same words but in a different order, and they convey different meanings.

Discourse

Language also includes larger units than the sentence. Discourse ability includes the knowledge of how to construct a story, tell a joke, and give directions. This aspect of language, as well as disruptions to it, is generally not included in discussions of aphasia but is addressed in Chapter 5.

AGE-RELATED CHANGES IN LANGUAGE

The now extensive literature on language development in children has become one of the battlefields in the fight about the extent to which human behavior is guided by nature (genes) versus nurture (environment) (Bates & Carnevale, 1993; Pinker, 1994). There is now considerable evidence for both sides of this debate. Based on evidence such as an seemingly invariant timetable of language development and a critical period for learning language, it seems that humans have an innate ability to develop language (Curtiss, 1977). However, it is not clear what about that system is innate and whether the mechanisms are specific to language or serve other cognitive domains as well (Bates, 1996, 1999). It is also clear that the environment plays a role insofar as children need to be exposed to language in a form that is usable and relevant to them in order to develop normally.

Normally developing children produce many of the sounds of their native language by they time they are age 2 and virtually all of them by age 4 (Prather, Hedrick, & Kern, 1975). There are subtle but observable changes in the way older adults produce sounds, at least in structured speech tasks, but there is no evidence that these differences interfere with communication (Parnell & Amerman, 1987).

Word knowledge develops quickly and appears stable throughout adulthood. By about their first birthday, children reliably understand and produce single words. Words are acquired slowly at first. But around the middle of the second year, there is a surge in vocabulary growth, and children acquire words quickly and easily. By the time children are age 5, they have a vocabulary of several thousand words, and by the time they graduate from high school, their vocabulary is about 40,000 words (Nagy & Herman, 1987).

There is considerable evidence that as we age, it becomes more difficult to retrieve (recall) words, including proper names. For instance, people older than age 70 have a more difficult time naming pictures than young people (Nicholas, Barth, Obler, Au, & Albert, 1997). Older people also report more word-finding difficulty in daily activities: The frequency of "tip-of-the-tongue" states rises from about 4 per month for young adults to about 6.6 per month for older adults (Burke, MacKay, Worthley, & Wade, 1991). Older adults also perform relatively poorly in timed tasks of naming such as word fluency paradigms (see Figure 4.1), with older subjects generating significantly fewer words within a specified semantic category in a limited amount of time than younger subjects (Kempler, Teng, Dick, Taussig, & Davis, 1998).

Despite some degradation in aging of our ability to retrieve and generate words, our knowledge of word meaning appears stable throughout the aging process. For example, the specific words elicited in category generation and word association tasks are the same for young and older adults (Burke & Peters, 1986). There is even some evidence that semantic knowledge, as indicated by vocabulary scores, increases with age (Salthouse, 1988). In other words, we remember word meanings and continue to learn new word meanings throughout

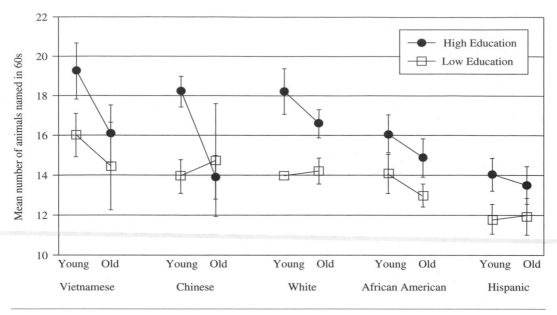

Figure 4.1   Animal naming in five ethnic groups. Mean number (and standard error) of animal names generated in 60 seconds by speakers from five ethnic groups, stratified by educational level (low = 0–8 years; high = 9+ years) and age (young = 54–75 years; old = 75–99 years).

our lives, even if we are not as efficient at retrieving them in certain contexts. Although there is no agreement on the cause of naming and word retrieval deficits in aging, there is a consensus that the problem results from processing deficits and does not reflect semantic degradation or the loss of word meanings from long-term memory (Bowles, Obler, & Poon, 1989).

Sentence structure has a similar developmental pattern. By the end of the second year, children begin to combine words in novel and flexible ways. Over the following 1 to 2 years, children master the specific sentence constructions of their language such as how to ask a question and construct a negative sentence. By the time children are age 5, they can use all the basic grammatical principles of the language. There is continued development of grammar through early school years, when the more subtle and complex sentence structures, including relative clauses, are mastered (Chomsky, 1969; Diessel & Tomasello, 2000). By late childhood, all native speakers of a language produce and comprehend a wide range of grammatical constructions automatically,

without conscious control, and are able to make uniform judgments about the grammaticality of most sentences.

Kemper (1992) has reported some subtle changes in the production of complex sentence structures in healthy aging. In a longitudinal study analyzing the syntactic structures used in diary entries over the adult life span, Kemper found that by age 70, people tended to use less complicated sentences, averaging about 1.4 clauses, whereas in their 20s, their sentences averaged about 3 clauses (Kemper, 1987). In contrast, the number of words per sentence did not change (about 9.2 at age 70 vs. 9.8 at age 20). Age does not interact with the relative complexity of particular syntactic constructions; rather, as people age, they simply produce fewer of all types of constructions. Kynette and Kemper's (1986) analysis of spontaneous speech comparing people in their 50s and 60s with those in their 70s and 80s showed similar patterns of simplification of syntax production with age.

Data on sentence comprehension in healthy aging are mixed, with some studies showing a sentence comprehension impairment for older adults and some showing no impairment (Bayles & Kaszniak, 1987; Davis & Ball, 1989). Wingfield and colleagues (Tun, Wingfield, Stine, & Mescas, 1992; Wingfield, Waters & Tun, 1997) have identified several likely contributions to auditory comprehension problems in healthy aging, including progressive hearing loss, decreases in working memory, and slower overall processing.

First, there is a well-documented and significant decrease in hearing acuity and speech perception with advancing age. Some studies estimate that up to 30% of adults between ages 65 and 74 have a hearing impairment that is likely to interfere with understanding speech. *Presbycusis,* hearing loss associated with aging, often affects higher frequency and low-energy sounds most, interfering with the perception of many phonemes, including *p, t, s, t, sh, ch,* and *th.* Speech perception in background noise is also particularly difficult for older adults (e.g., Morrell, Gordon-Salant, Pearson, Brant, & Fozard, 1996; Tun, 1998). Several studies that show auditory comprehension deficits in aging place high demands on auditory perception, such as presenting speech in noise (e.g., Obler, Nicholas, Albert, & Woodward, 1985).

Second, *working memory,* the ability to temporarily hold information in memory while processing it, declines with age (e.g., Salthouse, 1996; Wingfield, Stine, Lahar, & Aberdeen, 1988; see also Chapter 11). Auditory comprehension, by its nature, requires integrating information over time: To understand sentences and groups of sentences, people must hold some auditory information in mind while processing later bits of information. It is logical that deficits in working memory could create problems with auditory comprehension. Supporting evidence comes from many studies that demonstrate a decline in comprehension and use of methods that require substantial working memory, including long and syntactically complex sentences (e.g., Norman, Kemper, Kynette, Cheung, & Anagnopoulos, 1991); ambiguous sentences (Kemtes & Kemper, 1997); complex response requirements, such as acting out sentences with small animal and human figures (Feier & Gerstman, 1980); or sentences in which a pronoun and its referent are separated

by more than one sentence (e.g., Light & Capps, 1986). However, the relationship between working memory and language comprehension is not as simple as these data may make it appear. For instance, some patients with brain damage who have severe working memory deficits show surprisingly good comprehension of complex sentences (e.g., Wingfield et al., 1997), suggesting that there is still much to learn about the complex relationship between working memory and language (e.g., Waters & Caplan, 1996, 2001).

Finally, there is strong evidence that perceptual processing slows with aging (e.g., Salthouse, 1994, 1996). This likely causes some problems for auditory comprehension. Because speech occurs very quickly (about 180 words per minute) and the sound signal fades rapidly, successful auditory speech signals require consistently rapid processing. If it takes too much time to process even a portion of a sentence, the listener will be at a perceptual disadvantage when hearing the next stretch of auditory material. Some supportive evidence comes from the fact that older adults have significantly more difficulty than younger adults when processing rapid speech (e.g., Gordon-Salant & Fitzgibbons, 1993; Small, Rabins, et al., 1997; Wingfield, Poon, Lombardi, & Lowe, 1985; Wingfield, Tun, Koh, & Rosen, 1999).

Given the documented age-related declines in these three domains (perceptual acuity, working memory, and speed of processing), it is really quite remarkable that there is not a more dramatic or consistent impairment in auditory comprehension with aging. This is probably true for several reasons, including the following:

1. Linguistic knowledge of vocabulary and grammar is preserved in aging. Older adults retain their ability to learn and understand vocabulary, form a grammatical sentence, distinguish grammatical from ungrammatical sentences, and understand various grammatical structures (for a review, see Kempler & Zelinski, 1994).

2. There is a great amount of individual variability in healthy aging so that many older adults do not show the characteristic perceptual and memory declines that may affect language comprehension.

3. Even older adults who do have hearing loss, memory deficits, and/or slowed processing can frequently compensate for their deficits by successfully using context and "top-down processing" to "fill in the blanks" to aid auditory comprehension.

BEHAVIORAL CHARACTERISTICS AND NEUROPATHOLOGY OF APHASIA

Aphasia is an impairment of language due to brain damage, including difficulty formulating and/or comprehending words or sentences. *Aphasia* is used to describe a language deficit that is due to central nervous system damage after language has been acquired. Aphasia is most commonly seen after stroke or other focal brain injury to the perisylvian regions of the left cerebral hemisphere. In some cases, the term *aphasia* is also used to describe the language problems that occur in the context of more widespread brain and cognitive dysfunction such as Alzheimer's disease. However, aphasia in the context of dementia appears, progresses, and is treated differently than aphasia due to stroke and focal brain damage and therefore is discussed separately in Chapter 11. *Aphasia* is not used to describe difficulty with the motor component of speech output (see Chapter 13 for discussion of apraxia of speech) or psychiatric disorders such as delirium or schizophrenia (see Chapter 12). There are, of course, cases of children who have difficulty learning a language or whose language development is interrupted by brain injury; these cases are called language delay/impairment and **developmental aphasia** to distinguish them from adult-onset language problems.

APPROACHES TO THE STUDY OF APHASIA: SYMPTOMS VERSUS SYNDROMES

Historically, two general approaches to aphasia have influenced the theories, description, evaluation, and treatment of language disorders. Some authors emphasize symptoms, whereas others emphasize syndromes. As both approaches are helpful in understanding patients with aphasia, both will be presented here.

Aphasic Symptoms

The primary symptoms of aphasia are described below. Knowing these symptoms is crucial to understanding the relationship between symptoms and brain damage, the common aphasic syndromes, evaluation techniques, and treatment options.

Anomia

By far the most common symptom of aphasia is word-finding difficulty. *Anomia* is the technical term used to describe the inability to retrieve the names for concepts that were previously available to the speaker (Goodglass & Wingfield, 1997). Some authors restrict the term *anomia* to the phenomenon in which a person cannot retrieve the word, but it is not lost from memory. In this case, intact meaning can be demonstrated by recognizing the word when it is offered, demonstrating its use, or pointing to a picture of it. However, word-finding problems can also result from loss of semantic information, which would affect one's ability to recognize and understand the word as well. This type of naming difficulty is more typically associated with dementia (see Chapter 11), but the difference between a simple retrieval deficit and a loss of semantic knowledge may be one of degree rather than type. Although healthy adults experience anomia increasingly with age, these normal word-finding episodes happen on the order of four to seven times a month. In contrast, patients with aphasia often experience anomia in every sentence. Anomia is associated with lesions throughout the brain but most frequently in the perisylvian region of the left hemisphere.

Paraphasias

Paraphasias are characteristic errors made by patients with aphasia. Paraphasias are substitutions of one thing for another. These substitutions can be real words (e.g., *door* for *desk*) or nonwords (e.g., *chalana* for *desk*) (see Table 4.1). Nonwords are called **neologisms** (French < Greek: *new words*), which obey the phonological rules of the language, using only sounds and sound combinations that are possible in the patient's native language.

Table 4.1   Paraphasias

Type	Definition	Example
Literal/phonemic	Sound substitution	*boat → boot* *paper → taper*
Semantic	Substitution of a semantically related word	*plate → bowl* *asparagus → zucchini*
Phonosemantic	Substitution of a phonemically and semantically related word	*telephone → television* *broom → brush*
Verbal	Substitution of any word for another	*desk → plant* *globe → train*
Neologistic	Substitution of a nonword	*house → shalafu* *table → babeli*
Circumlocution	Substituting a description for a word, or "talking around the word"	*hourglass → it's a thing you use to measure time*

The types of paraphasic errors that patients with aphasia make may reveal the source of the problem. For instance, if a patient, when trying to name a *desk,* says "the thing that you sit at and write on," you know that his knowledge of the object is relatively preserved; if he calls a line drawing of a *mushroom* an *umbrella* or a *screwdriver* a *pen,* you might suspect a visual perceptual problem because these objects have similar shapes; and a substitution of semantically related items (e.g., *carrot* for *potato*) might lead you to suspect a semantic-level deficit.

Dysfluency

Abnormalities in the fluency of verbal production are also common in aphasia. Normally, language is fluent—that is, produced smoothly and without obvious interruption or **dysfluency.** Although there is some variability in typical fluency, language is typically produced at about 3 words per second and 180 words per minute (Levelt, 1989). Pauses occur at conceptual and grammatical junctures—that is, at the end of a thought and at the end of a sentence, although by no means at the end of every thought or every sentence. Importantly, pauses do not generally occur inside grammatical phrases (e.g., between article and noun or between an adverb and a verb). Along with normal speech rate and occasional well-placed pauses, fluent speech is also characterized by a melody or intonation

contour. Intonation contours typically bracket a whole utterance, giving it melodic coherence—intonation typically rises and falls smoothly within a sentence and falls predictably at the end of a statement (see also Chapter 6). *Fluency* refers to the form of speech—speech rate, patterns of pausing, and intonation. Speech can be considered fluent even if it contains paraphasias or even if it does not make sense at all, as in the case of many patients with a Wernicke's-type aphasia (see below). Two different types of alternations in fluency occur in aphasia: Language production can be **nonfluent**—slow and halting, with excessive pauses and a notable absence of intonation. Nonfluent speech is associated with anterior left hemisphere lesions and may be due to a combination of difficulty in retrieving words and formulating grammatical structures, difficulty with motor initiation, or difficulty with sequencing movements. Speech can also be **hyperfluent**—too fast and without appropriate breaks. Hyperfluent speech is sometimes referred to as *press of speech* and is associated with posterior left hemisphere lesions and comprehension deficits.

Agrammatism

Agrammatism is a term used to describe problems with grammatical function words and sentence construction. Agrammatic language production is characterized by the omission of grammatical morphemes such as prepositions, conjunctions, and articles. The following example of a stroke patient describing what happened to him typifies agrammatic speech: "alright . . . stroke . . . and . . . hot tub . . . two days wen- uh . . . hospital and amblance [sic]." Patients with agrammatism are nonfluent in speech production. Agrammatism can also be manifested in language comprehension. Patients who are agrammatic have difficulty understanding sentences that rely on function words and atypical sentence structure for their interpretation. This includes, for instance, passive voice sentences; for example, *The boy was kissed by the girl* requires the listener to use word order and function words to figure out that the girl is the one who did the action. Other sentences that require the use of grammatical information for comprehension include sentences with prepositions (*Put the cup on* vs. *in the box*) and sentences with relative clauses (*The boy is kissing the girl that the clown is hugging*). The presence of agrammatism in both production and comprehension suggests that it is not simply a motor problem or that patients with aphasia are not just leaving out the small words in an economy of effort—it is a problem that exists at the level of linguistic knowledge (Grodzinsky, 1991; Kean, 1995). Agrammatism is often associated with left hemisphere frontal lesions.

Comprehension Impairment

Auditory comprehension problems are widespread in aphasia and range in severity. Patients who are agrammatic may experience comprehension deficits for long and/or syntactically complex sentences. Other patients with aphasia suffer from more severe comprehension deficits that interfere with understanding simple sentences and even single words. More severe comprehension deficits are associated with posterior left hemisphere and large lesions.

Repetition Disorders

Almost all patients with aphasia have difficulty repeating what they hear. For the most part, errors made in repetition are similar to errors in spontaneous speech. If a patient's spontaneous speech is nonfluent, repetition is also nonfluent. If spontaneous speech contains many paraphasias, so does repetition. Errors include omissions and substitutions of sounds and words. Repetition deficits are associated with lesions throughout the left perisylvian region.

Perseveration

Perseveration refers to a tendency for a response to persist after it is no longer appropriate. In aphasia, perseveration is demonstrated, for instance, when a patient names a picture and then names a subsequent picture with the same label. Whether or not the initial response was correct, the repetition of that same response is no longer appropriate. Perseveration can occur in comprehension as well, as when a patient gives the same response to two different commands (e.g., pointing to his eyes when asked to point to his eyes and pointing to his eyes again when asked to point to the door). Perseveration is not limited to immediate repetition of a response: The perseverative response can be separated from the first instance by variable amounts of time and intervening stimuli and responses. Perseveration is sometimes interpreted as an indication of fatigue, as it occurs more frequently when a patient is tired or after many test items. Perseveration is a general behavioral phenomenon and not limited to aphasia.

Alexia and Agraphia

Problems with reading and writing are common in aphasia and have their own terms to describe them: Acquired reading problems are called **alexia** (**dyslexia** is usually reserved to describe developmental problems learning how to read), and acquired writing problems are called **agraphia.** In general, reading and writing problems parallel difficulties with spoken language production and comprehension. That is, if patients have word-finding difficulty in speech, they will probably also have similar problems in writing; if they are agrammatic in spoken language comprehension, they will probably also exhibit problems understanding written sentences. There are exceptions to these generalizations and other unusual reading and writing deficits that are discussed in Chapter 6.

The Major Aphasic Syndromes

The main aphasic syndromes can be distinguished by patterns of fluency, comprehension, and repetition (see Figure 4.2). All patients with aphasia have naming problems, so the presence of anomia does not help to distinguish one aphasic syndrome from another, although some syndromes are associated with particular types of paraphasias (see Table 4.2). Typical locations of brain lesions have been associated with each of the major syndromes as well. Each syndrome is briefly described as follows.

Anomic Aphasia

Anomic aphasia is characterized by relatively fluent speech output with normal speech rate, articulation, and grammatical structure but marked by anomia. Anomia affects primarily nouns, but other content word classes (verbs, adverbs, and adjectives) are affected as well. Anomic speech often contains **circumlocutions** in place of the hard-to-retrieve words. *Circumlocutions* means talking around a word or topic, as when a patient names a picture of a snail as "that's one of those slimy little animals that eats my vegetables in the garden." Anomic aphasia has also been called *nominal aphasia*

and *semantic aphasia.* At its most extreme, anomic speech output resembles the "empty speech" seen in some dementias (see Chapter 11). It is impossible to localize anomia, despite many people's efforts in this direction. Anomia can occur with damage throughout the brain (including right hemisphere and subcortical regions), although most often it occurs after left hemisphere damage. On one hand, the inability to associate damage to specific sites with anomia can be used as argument against localization of brain function. On the other hand, there are researchers who purport to have found specific lesions responsible for specific anomic deficits. For instance, a deficit in retrieving verbs may be associated with frontal lobe lesions, whereas a concrete noun-retrieval problem might be associated with left temporal lobe lesions (Damasio & Tranel, 1993).

Broca's Aphasia

Broca's aphasia is characterized by nonfluent, frequently agrammatic speech output. Speech is slow and halting and is composed primarily of content words (nouns, verbs) without the function words (articles, prepositions) (see Figure 4.3). Auditory comprehension appears grossly intact in conversation, although on testing, comprehension deficits can usually be found. Repetition, reading, and writing deficits parallel problems in spontaneous language

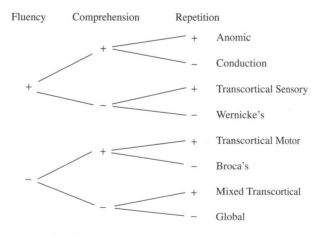

Figure 4.2   Aphasic syndromes organized by whether fluency, comprehension, and repetition are relatively intact (+) or significantly impaired (–).

Table 4.2   Definition of Aphasic Syndromes[a]

Syndrome	Type of Speech Production	Type of Language Error
A. Fluent		
Wernicke	Fluent speech, without articulatory disorders	Neologisms and/or anomias or paraphasias; poor comprehension; poor repetition
Transcortical, sensory	Fluent speech, without articulatory disorders	Verbal paraphasias and anomias; poor comprehension
Conduction	Fluent, sometimes halting, speech but without articulatory disorders	Phonemic paraphasias and neologisms; phonemic groping; poor recognition
Anomic	Fluent speech, without articulatory disorders	Anomia and occasional paraphasias
B. Nonfluent		
Broca	Slight but obvious articulatory disorders	Phonemic paraphasias with anomia; agrammatism; dysprosody
Transcortical motor	Marked tendency to speech reduction and inertia, without articulatory disorders	Uncompleted sentences and anomias; naming better than spontaneous speech
Global	Laborious articulation	Speechlessness with recurring utterances; poor comprehension; poor repetition
C. "Pure"		
Alexia without agraphia	Normal	Poor reading
Agraphia	Normal	Poor writing
Word deafness	Normal	Poor recognition; poor repetition

production and comprehension. Patients with Broca's aphasia are generally aware of their deficits. Broca's aphasia has also been called *motor aphasia* and *verbal aphasia.* There is a longstanding debate on the topic of whether the speech output problems in Broca's aphasia are essentially motoric or linguistic in nature (see discussion of Apraxia of Speech in Chapter 13). Because damage to the left frontal lobe often includes lesions in and around the motor strip, patients with Broca's aphasia frequently do have motor problems—paralysis and paresis of the right arm and leg, most prominently. Lesions associated with Broca's aphasia often involve the inferior left frontal lobe.

Wernicke's Aphasia

Wernicke's aphasia is characterized by fluent speech output with many paraphasias and marked auditory comprehension deficits (see Figure 4.3). In many ways, it is the opposite of Broca's aphasia. Sometimes, the speech of patients with Wernicke's aphasia seems very fast; these patients talk more than what seems called for in a conversational or testing context (*press of speech*), possibly because they are frequently not aware of the many errors they make. Wernicke's aphasia has also been called *sensory aphasia, temporo-acoustic aphasia* and *acoustic-mnestic aphasia,* and *syntactic aphasia,* reflecting various conceptions of what is fundamentally impaired (e.g., sensory perception, recall of acoustic information, and grammar, respectively), as well as *jargon aphasia,* highlighting the phenomenon of uninterpretable verbal output. Wernicke's aphasia is generally associated with damage to the posterior, superior aspect of the left temporal lobe, where the auditory association cortex is located (Wernicke's area).

Broca's aphasia	*Wernicke's aphasia*
OK. Goy, uh . . . huh . . . boy and a cookie yar, gar, and uh wants some, the girl, and. . . . (sigh). . . . fall down, the stool. And a . . . mother . . . and d-d-dishes. . .and (sigh). . . .full. . . . naw . . . uh. . . . (sigh) . . . sink is full of it and . . . cup, two, and dishes. I don't know.	I believe that evern in this ff-fern and turn lady and enterter her son and the mother of some lady doing acran with her lore had been her pressure to their uh tenior senior when she found off of a layer that the tang it handing over forward as she was falling off of her lockward. Along the lady of sss late of sing, that ended the mother of on her ten which is doin' ten with her foot, her chart falling in the water in front of her.

Figure 4.3   Picture descriptions of the Cookie Theft drawing by a patient with Broca's aphasia (left) and by a patient with Wernicke's aphasia (right).

Conduction Aphasia

Conduction aphasia is characterized by disproportionate difficulty with repetition. Patients with conduction aphasia have speech output that is relatively fluent and auditory comprehension that is relatively preserved, particularly in comparison to repetition abilities. However, the patients are anomic and paraphasic. Comparable deficits are also found in reading and writing. Conduction aphasia has also been called *central aphasia*. The lesion underlying conduction aphasia has long been thought to be caused by damage to the arcuate fasciculus, the white matter fibers that run between posterior areas of the left temporal lobe and the left frontal lobe, functionally connecting the posterior and anterior language zones. The standard theory to explain this phenomenon is that Wernicke's and Broca's areas remain intact, so the patient can understand and produce speech. However, the brain damage disrupts the arcuate fasciculus, the fiber tract that serves as a route by which language formulated in Wernicke's area reaches Broca's area. This is realized as disproportionate difficulty in relaying messages between the two language centers (i.e., repetition) when compared with auditory comprehension and the production of self-formulated messages.

The proposed anatomical basis for this syndrome has been difficult to confirm, although most patients with conduction aphasia do have brain damage in the perisylvian region of the left hemisphere (Kempler, Metter, et al., 1988).

Transcortical Aphasias

Transcortical aphasias, characterized by the relative preservation of repetition despite severe aphasia, are relatively rare and are included here for completeness. The symptoms of **transcortical motor aphasia** are reduced speech output, relatively good repetition, and good auditory comprehension. These patients tend to be quiet, and when they do speak, they use very few words, although their short productions can be fluent, probably depending on the extent of the lesion into the posterior frontal lobe. The neuropathology of transcortical motor aphasia is generally the left frontal lobe, superior or anterior to Broca's area. The anterior frontal lobes are important for initiation and maintenance of behavior. Therefore, damage in this region creates problems with beginning and continuing speech production. Repetition and comprehension remain relatively preserved because the temporal and parietal lobes, including Wernicke's area and the arcuate fasciculus, are not damaged. **Transcortical sensory aphasia** is similar in behavioral characteristics to Wernicke's aphasia, insofar as they produce fluent, paraphasic speech. However, these patients are distinguished from those with Wernicke's aphasia by their relatively preserved repetition ability. The brain damage underlying this disorder is to the high parietal lobe, which tends to be near the junction of the left parietal, temporal, and occipital lobes, which are classically defined as the watershed regions of the middle cerebral artery. The damage typically spares the arcuate fasciculus and the ability to repeat. Interestingly, even when it spares Wernicke's area, it effectively isolates it from much of the parietal lobe and the visual cortex, causing difficulty with auditory and reading comprehension. **Mixed transcortical aphasia,** also called isolation of the speech area, spares the ability to repeat but impairs all other communicative abilities. The brain damage, typically caused by compromised blood flow to the watershed areas of the entire left hemisphere, spares Broca's area, Wernicke's area, and the arcuate fasciculus but isolates them from the rest of the brain (Brookshire, 2003).

Global Aphasia

Global aphasia, as its name implies, is characterized by impairment affecting all modalities of language to a severe degree. Auditory comprehension is frequently limited to a few words, and speech production is sometimes nonexistent or limited to a few usually high-frequency automatic utterances (e.g., *no, goddamnit, uh-huh*). Global aphasia is associated with large lesions of the left hemisphere, including anterior and posterior regions.

SYMPTOM VERSUS SYNDROME APPROACH: WHICH IS RIGHT?

The emphasis on distinct aphasic syndromes associated with localized neuropathology can be traced back to the late 19th century. In the 1860s, Paul Broca, a surgeon and physical anthropologist, described several patients with severe language production impairments (what he called **aphemia**) but relatively preserved comprehension and lesions in the third left frontal convolution (Berker et al., 1986). There has been much debate about the nature and appropriate description of this type of language production impairment and whether it is predictably associated with damage only to Broca's area. Nonetheless, Broca's original reports are credited with providing the first strong evidence that language functions are lateralized to the left hemisphere and that at least some language processes are localized to the frontal lobe. That part of the left frontal lobe and the particular type of nonfluent aphasia that often results from damage to this region both bear his name today: Broca's area and Broca's aphasia. Several years later, Karl Wernicke (1874) described an aphasic syndrome of fluent speech production and impaired comprehension associated with damage to the left temporal lobe, a region and aphasic subtype that now bear his name (Wernicke's area and Wernicke's aphasia). Following Broca's and Wernicke's descriptions, many researchers identified specific aphasic syndromes and associated each with specific lesion sites (Damasio & Damasio, 2000; Lichtheim, 1885). Although the syndrome names have changed many times, essentially these same syndromes and underlying neuropathology are still taught and discussed today (Benson, 1993; Damasio & Damasio, 2000).

The syndrome approach is very useful insofar as it gives names to clusters of commonly co-occurring symptoms that are often associated with damage to particular brain regions. Syndrome names are very helpful in communicating a lot of information about a patient in very few words. The syndrome approach is helpful, however, only insofar as it works. That is, it is only helpful if patients fit the profiles and have the underlying neuropathology that is associated with the particular syndrome. If the symptoms of a patient are atypical or a mix of symptoms of several syndromes, or if the neuropathology is not consistent, then the syndrome names are less helpful. The syndrome approach is problematic to the degree that patients do not fit into the syndromes, or the underlying neuropathology cannot be predicted from the syndrome and vice versa.

Arguments against the syndrome approach with its localizationist associations began as soon as the syndromes were proposed in the 19th century. John Hughlings Jackson (1897), Sigmund Freud (1891a, 1891b), and Pierre Marie (1906) all offered early versions of a different, symptom-based approach to the study of aphasia. In this alternative, which is sometimes called the *holistic* approach, aphasia is not seen as a set of separate syndromes of language impairment; rather, aphasia is seen as a single disorder involving a more general intellectual deficit that is not easily localized (Eling, 1994). In this view, the similarities between patients with aphasia are emphasized, and differences between them are attributed to the relative severity of impairment and complications of other additional disturbances, such as motor speech problems, that are overlaid on the essential language disturbance. The notion of a unitary disorder is supported by a range of facts outlined below.

First, all patients with aphasia share the symptoms of anomia, comprehension impairment, and repetition deficits. Although aphasic syndromes are distinguished by their degrees of relative impairment in these symptoms, proponents of the holistic approach claim that with adequate and careful testing, these hallmark symptoms are present in all patients, even if they are not obvious.

This suggests an underlying commonality. In a strong statement about the overlap between syndromes, Marie (1906) stated,

> The only notable difference between the aphasia of Wernicke and the aphasia of Broca is that in the first patients speak more or less badly, while in the second they do not speak at all. . . . The aphasia of Broca is none other than aphasia complicated by anarthria. (qtd. in Berker et al., 1986, p. 1072)

Second, aphasia is frequently associated with other intellectual deficits. Most patients with aphasia have problems in other intellectual domains, including symbolic gesture (e.g., waving, saluting, crossing oneself) and manipulation of other symbolic systems (e.g., denominations of money, musical notation) (Duffy & Liles, 1979). This suggests that language impairment should not be seen as an isolated disability. Jackson, a strong proponent of the holistic approach, advocated looking at language disturbance in the context of thought (Jackson, 1897). He observed the fact that patients with aphasia can often produce well-formed utterances in some tasks (e.g., counting, swearing) but are unable to produce those same words in intentional or propositional tasks, demonstrating that it is the manner or purpose in which language is used that determines the level of impairment.

Third, patients with aphasia often progress from one form of aphasia to another in the course of recovery. This suggests that a single brain lesion can cause different types of aphasia and therefore undermines the notion that each syndrome is uniquely associated with a distinct brain lesion.

Fourth, there are many exceptions to lesion-syndrome mapping, and the fact that all regions of the brain are tightly interconnected has been used to argue against the view of localization that generally accompanies the syndrome approach (Basso, Lecours, Moraschini, & Vanier, 1985; Bogen & Bogen, 1976; Kreisler et al., 2000; Lecours & Joanette, 1984). The syndrome approach has been promoted, at least over the past 50 years, primarily on the basis of the examination of right-handed, adult, English-speaking men. Even in this group there are exceptions, but when we venture outside of this group, the number of exceptions increases, suggesting that a strict syndrome and localization approach holds better for some groups than others:

- *Left-handers:* The incidence of left-handedness is reported in various studies to be between 1% and 30% and probably lies somewhere between 4% and 10%. Aphasia is much more common after right hemisphere damage in left-handers (6%–50%, depending on the study) than right-handers (0.4%–3.5%). The pattern of aphasic symptoms that appears in left-handers is also different: They have less severe aphasias and a smaller incidence of comprehension deficits and a higher incidence of expressive deficits than right-handers (Joanette, 1989). These data suggest that syndrome-lesion mapping developed on the basis of right-handers cannot be easily and accurately applied to left-handers.

- *Age:* Children have strokes and other insults to the brain just as adults do. However, their pattern of deficits—in particular, aphasia—is considerably different than adults. First, perinatal strokes to either the left or the right hemisphere impair development of language, and the location of the lesion does not determine the type or extent of language delay (Kempler et al., 1999; Reilly, Bates, & Marchman, 1998). Second, the patterns—or syndromes—of aphasia deficits that we see in children are not the same as those that we see in adults. In childhood, receptive Wernicke's-type aphasia is relatively rare; most acquired aphasia in childhood is of a nonfluent variety. The explanation for this is not clear. It might have to do with the fact that children suffer fewer embolic strokes than adults and/or the fact that the brain is organized differently during development; children have much greater neural plasticity—the ability of the brain to reorganize and functionally recover—than adults, and brain damage will have different effects on an ability that is in the process of developing versus after that ability has been fully acquired (Beaulieu, 2002; Chabrier, Husson, Lasjaunias, Landrieu, & Tardieu, 2000; Dennis, 2000; Woods, 1995). These data suggest that the models of language lateralization and localization developed for right-handed adults are less successful in predicting lesions or syndromes in children (Kreisler et al., 2000).

- *Native language:* At least one syndrome, agrammatism, may be determined more by native language than by the neuropathology. The omission of grammatical morphemes in nonfluent aphasia is much more frequent in English than in languages such as German, Turkish, or Hungarian, which have very rich morphological systems for marking semantic and grammatical information on words. One explanation for this is that the grammatical morphemes are omitted in languages in which they are less important, not because of any particular neuropathology (Bates, Wulfeck, & MacWhinney, 1991).

- *Subcortical aphasias:* Although it has been assumed that language, the function that sets humans apart from other animals, is represented and controlled by the newer part of the brain, the *neocortex,* there are now many reports of aphasia stemming from damage to the evolutionarily older, subcortical regions. In particular, damage to the left side of the head of the caudate and nearby white matter in the anterior limb of the internal capsule, as well as in the left anterolateral nuclei of the thalamus, will cause aphasia (Mohr, Watters, & Duncan, 1975; Naeser et al., 1982). Cases of aphasia caused by lesions of the left thalamus have been relatively well described. These patients are typically anomic, with sparse, echolalic, and neologistic spontaneous speech; although they have relatively good auditory comprehension and reading, they have impaired writing and generally perseverative behavior (e.g., Mohr et al., 1975). The fact that subcortical lesions can cause aphasia suggests that the classic maps of cortical regions and aphasia are not adequate to describe the range of aphasia and their localizations. It is possible that the subcortical regions are themselves important in language functions (Radanovic & Scaff, 2003), that the subcortical lesions subtly damage cortical tissue (e.g., Dewitt et al., 1985, in Brookshire, 2003), and/or that the subcortical lesions decrease cortical metabolic function, which then interferes with the cortical control of language (e.g., Metter et al., 1988). In any case, clearly, an accurate mapping of aphasic symptoms or syndromes to cortical regions must somehow also take into account noncortical regions as well.

Neuroimaging data have been equivocal on the syndrome-lesion association. The advent of structural (computed tomography [CT]) brain imaging in the 1960s and 1970s provided important data for researchers looking for structure-function associations: Early reports of structural imaging data were reported as evidence that Broca and Wernicke were right about their localization theories (Kertesz, Harlock, & Coates, 1979) (see Figure 4.4). However, by the 1990s, when functional imaging (positron emission tomography [PET]) came into use, a different picture, more consonant with the holistic approach, emerged. Several studies have shown that patients with aphasia, regardless of syndrome and regardless of the location of the structural lesion, all share metabolic abnormalities in the left temporal lobe. These findings are consistent with the view that patients with aphasia share a core set of language symptoms (anomia, comprehension and repetition deficits) that are associated with temporal lobe dysfunction seen on PET. These studies suggest that the behavioral differences between patients with aphasia and the differences between the syndromes are determined by the extent of structural or functional damage in other (non-language) brain regions. For example, although patients with Broca's and Wernicke's aphasia both show functional damage to the temporal lobe, patients with Broca's aphasia also have left frontal structural damage and metabolic effects distant from that lesion in the cerebellum, which may explain their motor output problems (Metter et al., 1989; Metter et al., 1987).

The debates between those who prefer to view aphasias as distinct syndromes with identifying lesions and those who view aphasia as a single disturbance continue today. Some researchers still prefer to emphasize the uniqueness of each syndrome and associate each symptom with a particular region of the brain, whereas others view aphasic deficits in the context of other cognitive functions and emphasize the distributed nature of the neural bases for language. The primary difference between the arguments that took place in the 19th century between Broca and Marie and those taking place today is that today's arguments are bolstered by the use of standardized tests and neuroimaging data. As you have seen, the data can be used to support either perspective. Although

it is clear that the location of the lesion is an important determinant of the aphasic symptom, neither location nor size fully determines symptomatology. All researchers admit that there is quite a bit of individual variability with respect to lesion-syndrome mapping in aphasia (Caplan, 1994). The now extensive work by Kertesz (1979) and others comparing brain scans with aphasic syndromes documents what are best viewed as central tendencies for certain syndromes to be associated with certain lesions.

Remarkably, however, despite more than a hundred years of debate and greatly improved methods of investigation, the experts remain divided on the best way to characterize aphasic behavior and its underlying neuropathology. The most reasonable approach concedes that both symptom- and syndrome-dominant views have merit, but neither in their extreme formulation captures the essential facts of aphasia: Language and motor symptoms commonly cluster together and are associated with lesions in particular regions. The frequent exceptions to these associations indicate that these are at best central tendencies for localization and lateralization of specific components of cognitive functions with many exceptions (Caplan, 1994). Furthermore, it appears that the relationship of aphasic syndromes to neural areas may be due to the relatively consistent localization of lesions producing motor speech disturbances rather than the association of language functions with particular cortical regions (Caplan, 1994).

Although arguments about the best way to describe aphasia may seem academic, they are relevant to clinicians and patients because the view that a clinician adopts with respect to aphasia will determine the methods used to evaluate and treat patients with aphasia. Syndrome names are often used clinically to communicate a large amount of information efficiently. The syndrome approach is now the culturally accepted approach to aphasia, and every textbook on neurology and neurological dysfunction uses it. Therefore, the syndrome approach must be learned by every clinician. However, patients and families generally notice symptoms, and it is the symptoms that must be treated.

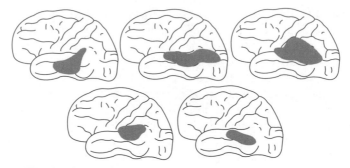

A Wernicke's aphasia

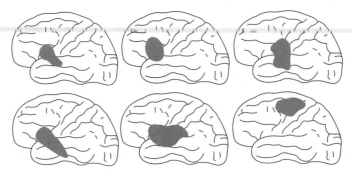

B Broca's aphasia

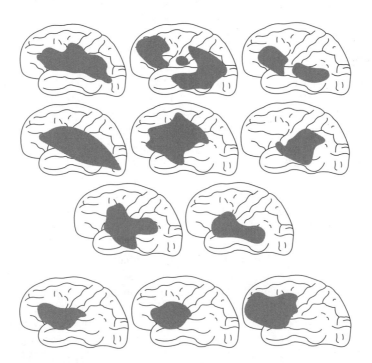

C Global aphasia

Figure 4.4   Typical lesions of individual patients that cause (a) Wernicke's aphasia, (b) Broca's aphasia, and (c) global aphasia.

DIAGNOSIS OF APHASIA

Aphasia is diagnosed by the presence of acquired language disorder due to central nervous system (brain) damage. Speech-language pathologists are the professionals who evaluate and treat the communication disorders associated with aphasia. Occasionally, neuropsychologists and neurologists will also evaluate and/or diagnose aphasia. With any language disorder, it is also crucial to determine if any part of the language problem is due to hearing loss. Particularly in the case of comprehension impairment in older patients, it is important to rule out the potential effects of **presbycusis,** hearing loss due to aging. This may be done informally, through interview and history (e.g., presbycusis is a gradually progressive disorder, whereas aphasia due to stroke tends to begin suddenly). However, because comprehension problems can also appear gradually (e.g., due to brain tumor) and hearing loss can appear suddenly (e.g., due to infection, ischemic events at the level of the cochlear blood supply, and even impacted cerumen), if there is any doubt about whether a comprehension deficit is due to aphasia versus hearing loss, it is wise to involve an audiologist, who can determine the presence and extent of hearing loss, estimate the effect on auditory comprehension, and make appropriate recommendations for aural rehabilitation and/or amplification.

The goal of a language evaluation for aphasia is to determine the domain(s) and severity of deficits. This will also identify areas of preserved ability, which is equally important because therapy will build on any strengths the patient has. The results of the evaluation will determine if therapy is feasible, what the appropriate goals will be, and, to some extent, the prognosis. Repeated evaluations are used to measure recovery and response to treatment. There are many tests of language ability (in English, at least), and the specific tests selected will depend on the philosophy of the clinician (e.g., whether it is important to come up with a syndrome diagnosis), the setting (acute hospital vs. rehabilitation setting), and patient characteristics (acuity, severity, and cooperation).

Informal assessments can be accomplished by engaging the patient in conversation to determine whether the patient is responsive enough to undergo a full evaluation and how the family can best communicate with the patient prior to rehabilitation. An informal assessment will cover basic areas of communication to determine obvious deficits and islands of preserved function. The patient's participation in an informal assessment will reveal whether the patient is grossly aphasic, as well as something about the pattern of deficits (e.g., fluent vs. nonfluent, the presence or absence of comprehension deficits), and yield a relatively good idea of the patient's ability to communicate basic needs. There are limitations of an informal assessment: Few test items can be used, and this limits the reliability of the data. Informal tests are not standardized, so the data cannot be used to compare one patient with another, compare one etiology with another, or even measure the recovery of a single patient over time. For these purposes, standardized aphasia batteries are used.

Standardized language assessment batteries offer validity, reliability, and normative data. They are administered in a standard manner, and thus the results can be compared across patients, clinicians, institutions, and even countries. There are several popular tests, the most prominent being the Boston Diagnostic Aphasia Exam (BDAE), which also has been adapted into several other languages (Goodglass, Kaplan, & Baressi, 2001); the Western Aphasia Battery (WAB) (Kertesz, 1982); and the Minnesota Test for Differential Diagnosis of Aphasia (MTDDA) (Schuell, 1965). Both the BDAE and WAB are geared toward diagnosis via aphasic syndrome. The MTDDA, developed by Hildred Schuell, is less concerned with syndrome identification than with identifying severity of impairment in numerous functional domains. All the batteries include ways to assess auditory comprehension and speech production, reading, and writing. Some simple examples can illustrate the types of questions used to assess various domains of language:

Speech Production (Spontaneous): Engage the patient in conversation. Ask general questions: *How are you feeling? Are you having any problems communicating?*

Speech Production (Elicited): Have the patient count from 1 to 20, say the days of the week, repeat some words and phrases, name objects or

pictures, complete sentences (e.g., "The grass is
_____"), respond to simple questions (e.g.,
"What do you use to tell time?"), and describe a
picture. This list exemplifies a range of tasks used
with patients of varying severity. Some may be too
simple and not reveal any problems, and others
may be too difficult for the patient to even
attempt.

Auditory Comprehension: Assess comprehension of words by placing objects or pictures of
several objects in front of patient, asking him or
her to identify each one individually when told to
point to them one at a time after hearing the verbal label (e.g., "Point to the comb"). Assess comprehension of sentences through yes/no questions
(e.g., "Are the lights on in this room?"), following
commands (e.g., "Open your mouth; make a fist;
point to your left ear; point to the window and
then to the door"), and sentence-picture matching
(e.g., read a sentence aloud and ask the patient to
select one of several pictures that matches the
meaning).

Understanding Reading: Ask the patient to
follow written commands (e.g., "Close your eyes,"
"Show me your right knee").

Writing: Ask the patient to write his or her
own name, write words and sentences to dictation,
and/or generate a written sentence.

One test battery, the Communication
Abilities of Daily Living (CADL) (Holland,
Frattali, & Fromm, 1999), is unique in attempting to reveal how patients with aphasia function
in real-life situations, such as reading a restaurant menu or bus schedule and what to say on a
visit to a doctor's office. Some batteries also
include additional nonlanguage tests of gesture,
drawing, and copying. Using a standardized test
is also essential for any research, for instance,
investigating the efficacy of one treatment
versus another.

Specialty Tests

There are several disadvantages to the language batteries: They are long and do not evaluate any particular aspect of language in much
depth. If there is reason to focus on one particular area of language ability, it is wise to select
from the broad array of specialty tests. There are
special tests to evaluate naming, grammatical

function, auditory comprehension, and reading,
among others. The Boston Naming Test
(Kaplan, Goodglass, & Weintraub, 2001) is a set
of 60 line drawings that has been used extensively to assess naming abilities in healthy and
impaired populations. It includes drawings of
objects that vary in frequency (from *bed* to *aba-
cus*), and limited norms are provided. Auditory
comprehension, an area of great interest and
widespread impairment in aphasia, is often
tested with one of the many versions of the
Token Test (de Renzi & Vignolo, 1962). This test
uses a set of 20 plastic tokens and a limited
vocabulary (six color words, two shape terms,
two size terms) to test a range of sentence constructions from simple (*Touch the red circle*) to
complex (*Touch the small yellow circle and the
large green square; after picking up the green
square, touch the white circle*). Many researchers
interested in grammar have developed ways to
assess sentence comprehension (see Figure 4.5).

TREATMENT OF APHASIA

The results of language testing will naturally
guide language therapy. The goals of language
therapy for patients with aphasia are to restore
lost function, enhance residual capacity, and/or
compensate for last function. Choice of treatment
technique will be influenced by the clinician's
view of aphasia (described above), the type and
severity of the language deficits, the goals of the
patient, and the available resources (time, therapists, family members). Several examples of
behavioral treatment approaches are described
here to provide an idea of the range of techniques
that are used. See Holland and Beeson (1995)
and Helm-Estabrooks and Albert (2004) for
succinct overviews.

Linguistic Drill Approach

Many language therapists use direct drill and
practice in specific areas of language function.
For instance, patients with agrammatic aphasia
who are thought to have a morphosyntactic
processing deficit may be drilled to produce
and comprehend specific sentence structures
(Thompson & Shapiro, 1995). Patients with
anomia are often given naming drills. Naming

Figure 4.5   Two examples from a sentence comprehension test assessing processing of grammatical constructions. A patient would be asked to point to the one drawing (in this case, of two) that best matches a spoken sentence. Left: A passive voice sentence: *The boy is kicked by the girl.* Right: A sentence containing a relative clause: *The cat that kicks the boy, kicks the dog.* Drawings by Susan Black.

drills will include a hierarchy of supportive cues presented over time, possibly such as the following:

- Repetition: Say *butter.*
- Sentence completion: *I like bread and* _____.
- Responsive naming: What do you spread on bread?
- Picture naming: What's this?
- Category generation: List three things you spread on bread.

Computerized treatment programs are particularly well suited to presenting and monitoring performance and progress in linguistically based drill approaches.

Cognitive-Contextual Approach

Although most clinicians use drills to facilitate recovery of specific functions, there is some evidence that a more indirect, holistic, and contextualized approach might be as beneficial. Some patients with aphasia actually produce more and better language, incidentally, when engaged in nonconfrontational tasks than when completing tasks designed to elicit particular words or structures (Holland, 1989). This is reflected in approaches that emphasize functional or pragmatic communication in group therapy and real-world settings. One specific pragmatic approach, called promoting aphasic communicative effectiveness (PACE), emphasizes interpersonal communication using all available communication strategies, verbal and nonverbal; success is judged by overall communicative effectiveness in the exchange of information (Davis & Wilcox, 1985; Holland & Beeson, 1995). Almost any context can become a therapeutic opportunity—for instance, patients communicating with the therapists about what picture is presented on a card or what they would like to order at a restaurant.

If a clinician believes that language is intimately related to nonlinguistic cognitive abilities (attention, memory, and visual processing) or that deficits in these areas have been identified in a particular patient, a cognitive approach might be used. A cognitive approach to language therapy will include strategies to improve attention and memory and necessary underpinnings of verbal/auditory communication. These strategies often function to reduce any disruptive behaviors that may interfere with communication, such as spatial neglect (see Chapter 8), inattention (Chapter 9), and perseveration.

Use of Automatic
Speech and Residual Abilities

Many patients with aphasia have two predictable islands of preserved ability: automatic speech and singing. Automatic speech includes production of overlearned, familiar utterances and sequences—most notably, counting the days of the week and months of the year—and social interaction formulas ("Hi, how are you?"). These sequences and utterances are generally produced with better fluency and fewer errors than spontaneous speech, even if the spontaneous speech contains the same words. Singing, particularly of familiar songs, such as "Happy Birthday," "Silent Night," and the "Star Spangled Banner," is also generally better than spontaneous speech. The reason that familiar sequences and songs are preserved is not known for sure, but it is likely that they are at least in part supported by intact right hemisphere mechanisms (Van Lancker, 1987, 1991). Several therapeutic techniques take these preserved modes and build on them, making them more flexible. Automatic sequences and familiar phrases can be made useful by introducing other words into fluently produced frames (e.g., I like him > I like her > I like them > I like you). Melodic intonation therapy is a particular approach for patients with aphasia that involves communication with intoned speech, using the preserved melodic ability to sing what they want to say (Albert, Sparks, & Helm, 1973).

Augmentative and
Alternative Communication

Some patients with aphasia will remain so severely aphasic that the best hope of restoring communication is nonverbal. This may include a gestural system that the family and the patient are trained to use (American Sign Language is generally too complex for this purpose). Another alternative communication modality is the use of pictures or icons selected for the individual patient to facilitate daily communication. Pictures can be placed in a notebook, organized by topic, and used efficiently to request objects and activities. One approach uses a computer-based icon system whereby the patient can string together icons, using a computer mouse and keyboard, into nonverbal sequences for communication (Lynch, 1993; Nicholas, 2004).

Effectiveness of Behavioral
Language Therapy

Does language therapy work? Because aphasia is so common after stroke, it is one of the more frequently treated disorders covered in this book. Therefore, it makes sense to ask, and some data address whether treatment for aphasia works. It is very difficult to conduct efficacy studies on language therapy because of great variability: Each patient is different, and each treatment is different. Furthermore, properly constructed studies would involve a control group, which would require denying treatment to a group of patients with aphasia, an idea that is anathema to most rehabilitation professionals. Nonetheless, several studies of aphasia treatment have been completed and, in general, indicate that aphasia treatment helps. Some of the more interesting results of these studies indicate that patients benefit from therapy regardless of whether it is provided during the first 4 months or 12 months after onset (Poeck, Huber, & Willmes, 1989). Another set of studies demonstrated that treatment is most effective when provided by a trained speech therapist, but it can also be effective when provided by trained volunteers, and both of these options provide more benefit for the patient than no treatment at all (Marshall et al., 1989). The effects of lesion site/size and age, although presumed important, have turned out to have only a questionable effect on treatment. More severe aphasia and other health problems are negative prognostic indicators.

New Directions in Aphasia Treatment

Although the mainstay of aphasia treatment continues to be behavioral therapy guided by speech-language pathologists, there is now also experimental evidence that pharmacological treatment may be able to augment the effects of traditional therapy (Mimura, Albert, & McNamara, 1995). Several single-case and small-group studies have looked at the effectiveness of using various drugs. For instance, on the assumption that damage to the left temporal lobe produces a relative deficit in cholinergic activity, a study investigated the effect of administering a cholinergic agent during therapy. The results showed a significantly greater improvement in those patients who received the drug therapy than those who did not (Tanaka, Miyazaki, & Albert, 1997). Another study suggested that the use of piracetam, in addition to traditional speech therapy, augments the effects of speech therapy alone (Huber, Willmes, Poeck, Van Vleymen, & Deberdt, 1997).

5

Alexia and Agraphia: Disorders of Written Language

Chapter Preview

In this chapter, we explore the following six questions:

1. What is written language?

A system of mapping between graphemes (letters and characters) and sounds.

2. How do reading and writing develop and change with age?

In literate societies, children learn to read and write between the ages of 6 and 8. However, individuals vary greatly in their reading and writing proficiency, and older cohorts are less literate than younger cohorts. Because of this variability, reading and writing is an area of great concern and potential misdiagnosis for older patients. Once acquired, reading ability declines in healthy aging, but most of the problems can be attributed to decreased speed or impairments in selective attention and working memory. Age-related changes in writing are associated with motor control deficits rather than linguistic impairments.

3. What are the behavioral characteristics of reading and writing deficits?

Alexia, impairment in reading, is demonstrated by difficulty reading words aloud and understanding written text. *Agraphia,* difficulty in writing, is demonstrated by difficulty forming letters and arranging them on a sheet as well as assembling written words into sentences.

4. What is the neuropathology of alexia and agraphia?

Alexia and agraphia are most commonly associated with damage to the perisylvian region of the left cerebral hemisphere.

5. How are alexia and agraphia diagnosed?

Reading tests require patients to read words aloud and answer questions about written text. Tests of writing require patients to write spontaneously, copy written material, and/or write to dictation. Error patterns determine the type and severity of the disorder.

(Continued)

(Continued)

6. How are alexia and agraphia treated?

Reading and writing disorders are treated primarily with behavioral therapy provided by speech-language pathologists. Therapy includes drills to improve residual abilities and compensate through, for example, writing with the nondominant hand.

WRITTEN LANGUAGE

Written language evolved more recently than spoken language and is considerably less common than spoken language around the world. Although spoken language emerged about 100,000 years ago, written language can be traced back only about 5,000 years. There are somewhere between 3,000 and 10,000 spoken languages (Crystal, 1994), but most of them do not have a written tradition. Written language is derived from spoken language insofar as it is used in conjunction with spoken language and to reflect spoken language. The importance of this overlay status is that reading and writing rely on knowledge of spoken language but require additional functions such as vision and therefore use somewhat different brain regions than spoken language.

Writing may have emerged from the use of early symbols to represent ideas, or *ideograms,* seen in early cave drawings. Ideograms lacked the flexibility of spoken language and were either replaced by or evolved into other writing systems.

There are three major types of writing systems in use today. Chinese characters are an example of a **logographic** system in which each symbol stands for a word. English and most other languages also use logographs in a limited way, for instance $, %, #, &, and the so-called international signs.

A syllabary is a system in which each written symbol represents the pronunciation of a syllable, generally a consonant and a vowel. Japanese is the only major language that uses a syllabary. Japanese uses about 100 different symbols to represent syllables, called **kana.** Kana are derived from Chinese characters but have now come to represent syllables rather than whole words and are used in combination with Chinese characters, called **kanji.**

The alphabetic system uses graphemes to represent each sound. Alphabetic systems vary tremendously in how regular the relationship between the graphemes and sounds are: Spanish has a relatively close relationship, where each letter is generally pronounced similarly each time; English uses an alphabetic system notorious for exceptions, including so-called "silent letters" (lis*t*en, de*b*t), letters with multiple sounds (*th*ought vs. *Th*omas), and sounds that are written in a variety of ways (*aye,* b*uy,* d*ie,* Th*ai*). Alphabetic systems have developed in several regions of the world using different symbols: Many Slavic languages use the Cyrillic alphabet, derived from the Greek alphabet, and many Arabic languages use the Semitic alphabet.

Theories of reading have been developed primarily to explain the processes underlying learning, use, and disorders of using alphabetic scripts. Models of reading generally presume that there are two ways to read any alphabetic text (see Figure 5.1a).

1. We can sound out each letter, using **grapheme-to-phoneme conversion rules.** These rules could also be called *letter-to-sound correspondences* because they essentially tell a reader what letter goes with each sound. We rely on these rules overtly when we sound out new words and nonsense words to give them a reasonable pronunciation (e.g., *shamanaki*). This is the phonics method often discussed in elementary school pedagogy (Rieben & Perfetti, 1991) and stands in contrast to whole-word reading.

2. Whole-word or lexical reading, called **whole-language** reading in the education literature, does not rely on grapheme-to-phoneme

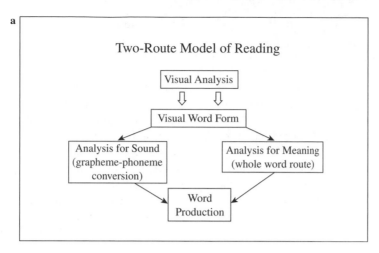

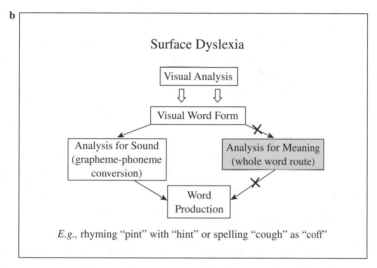

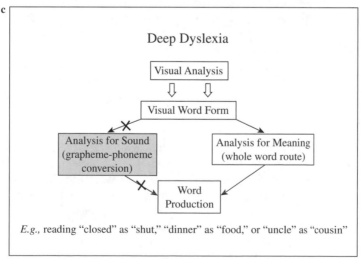

Figure 5.1 (a) The two-route model of reading. (b) Illustration of the impairment in surface dyslexia. (c) Illustration of the impairment in deep dyslexia.

rules. Rather, the whole word is analyzed as a single unit and mapped directly onto the pronunciation and meaning. We rely on this method frequently when we pronounce irregular words (e.g., *yacht, reign*) and abbreviations (e.g., *kg, tsp*) and when we read very frequently encountered words (e.g., *the, STOP*).

It is clear that we normally use both of these reading routes and that we use both of them simultaneously. Some models of reading state explicitly that there are two cognitive and neuroanatomic routes, but other researchers favor an integrated approach in which both types of reading can result from a single system containing orthographic, phonemic, and semantic units that are interconnected (Coltheart, Curtis, Atkins, & Haller, 1993). Although the appropriate characterization of the normal reading process is not fully resolved, the description of the two reading routes is a useful heuristic to understanding the effects of brain damage on reading and writing.

AGE-RELATED CHANGES IN READING AND WRITING

Everyone learns to speak and understand his or her native language with virtually no instruction and at a very early age. This is not true of reading and writing. Reading and writing are mastered later than spoken language and less universally. Even in cultures where reading and writing are common, mastery is often limited to various segments of the population. For instance, the literacy rate in the United States is generally higher than in developing nations (half of all nonliterates are in India and China), but literacy is far from universal even in the United States: 10% to 20% of the U.S. population is functionally illiterate (Crystal, 1994), many reading at or below a fifth-grade level. Literacy is highest for the younger population. Older generations in the United States still have a relatively low literacy level.

Spoken language is learned spontaneously long before children go to school. In contrast, learning to read and write is explicitly taught, both at home and at school, if it is taught at all. Learning to read and write is a process that takes

several years. Children in the United States usually learn the grapheme-phoneme rules between 6 and 7 years old. By the time they are about age 8, they can read simple stories and have a reading vocabulary of about 3,000 words. The ability to read and read quickly continues to increase through young adulthood.

Assuming one learns to read by adulthood, we can ask how healthy aging affects our ability to produce and comprehend written language. A national adult literacy survey begun in 1992 demonstrated that adults older than age 60, when compared to younger adults, have a limited ability to read news stories, poems, job applications, bus schedules, checkbooks, ordering forms, and loan advertisements (Brown, Prisuta, Jacobs, & Campbell, 2000). This is probably due to a combination of factors that limit the early development of reading skills in older cohorts, including limited access to educational opportunities, lower ultimate level of educational attainment, and lack of practice or disuse in later years (Freer, 1994). Many psychological studies of language abilities in aging have used written language in experiments, providing another source of data on how aging affects our ability to read. One almost universal finding from this literature is that older adults read more slowly than younger adults (Hartley, Stojack, Mushaney, & Kiku Annon, 1994). However, it is important to note that the slower pace of reading is not necessarily associated with impaired comprehension (Harris, Rogers, & Qualls, 1998). Many studies have attributed reading impairments in older adults to age-related impairments in nonlinguistic functions. Rousseau, Lamson, and Rogers (1998) found a decrease in visual acuity and contrast sensitivity. Duchek, Balota, and Thessing (1998) reported that sensitivity to distractions resulted in disrupted attention while reading. Kemtes and Kemper (1997) found poor performance in recall tasks and in tasks with ambiguous texts in which several meanings must be kept in mind, indicating that a difficulty with working memory affected reading results. Despite these measurable deficits in sensory and cognitive abilities that are involved in reading, overall, if older subjects are given sufficient time to read, can adequately see the material, and are left without distractions or heavy demands on working memory, they appear to understand the material as well as younger subjects (Harris et al., 1998).

There are relatively little data on the effects of age on writing. In content of writing, older adults use shorter and simpler sentences in writing as well as speech. These differences are generally attributed to declines in working memory rather than the mechanics of writing (Kemper, 1990). However, writing does have a manual motor component that makes it susceptible to age-related changes in motor coordination. Detailed analyses of handwriting movements in younger versus older adults showed more stroke-to-stroke variation for older than younger adults. Another difference between older and younger adults' handwriting is the fact that external cues (e.g., lines vs. no lines, pens with ink vs. no ink, wearing goggles vs. not) appear to effect older adults and younger adults differently. Older adults but not younger adults are slower, have more cycles of acceleration and deceleration, and are overall less efficient when there are visual cues (lines) than when there are no visual cues, apparently using the visual information to modify their writing movements (Slavin, Phillips, & Bradshaw, 1996). This is explained by greater "field dependence" in older adults; that is, they are more affected by external stimuli than younger adults. Although there are some subtle similarities between the handwriting of healthy older adults and older adults with neurological conditions (e.g., Parkinson's disease), in most cases, there are dramatic differences. For example, adults with Parkinson's disease tend to produce very small handwriting (*micrographia*), whereas healthy older people do not (see Chapter 13 for more information on Parkinson's disease).

BEHAVIORAL CHARACTERISTICS AND NEUROPATHOLOGY OF READING AND WRITING DEFICITS

Alexia refers to acquired problems in reading. This term is generally reserved to talk about reading deficits that occur after normal development of reading skills (Friedman, Ween, & Albert, 1993; Kirshner, 1995a, 1995b). This is distinguished from typical use of the term *dyslexia,* which refers to problems learning to read in childhood. *Agraphia* refers to acquired problems in writing. As with disorders of spoken language, there are many patterns or syndromes of reading and writing problems. The cognitive context of alexia and agraphia and specific types of errors help to distinguish one syndrome from another. The major subtypes are described as follows.

Aphasic Alexia and Agraphia

As mentioned in Chapter 4, aphasia is typically accompanied by disruption of reading and writing. Although the disturbance may not be to the same extent across spoken and written language, the symptoms are frequently comparable. For instance, patients who are agrammatic omit grammatical function words in speech production and writing and have difficulty understanding grammatical function words in auditory comprehension and reading. Patients with anomia are anomic in writing as well as speech. When patients with Wernicke's aphasia produce neologisms in spontaneous speech, they are as neologistic in reading aloud and writing. We can assume that in these cases, damage to the underlying language system is affecting both spoken and written language. The neuropathology of **aphasic alexia** and **aphasic agraphia** is the perisylvian left hemisphere language zones discussed in Chapter 4.

Surface and Deep Alexia/Agraphia[1]

A relatively rare subgroup of patients with aphasic alexia produce interesting errors that inform us about how the reading and spelling systems work and how they can be fractionated by brain damage. In particular, these disorders provide evidence for the two routes of reading discussed above (see Figure 5.1a). Surface and deep alexia and agraphia are characterized and diagnosed by their peculiar error patterns, which are only notable in closely controlled tasks.

Surface alexia and **surface agraphia** are characterized by difficulty with the whole-word route in reading and writing, respectively (Figure 5.1b and c). Surface alexia is also sometimes referred to as *reading-by-sound*. The patients make reading and writing errors predominantly with irregularly spelled words that cannot be sounded out (e.g., *sword, yacht, cough*). They may pronounce *pint* to rhyme with *hint* and spell *cough* as *coff*. These exception words do not follow the most frequent spelling-sound correspondence rules and are generally hard to learn to read and write. Because they do not fit the most productive spelling-sound rules, they cannot be easily sounded out and are generally recognized as whole words. Note, however, that some words are more irregular than others are. For instance, some irregular words belong to a subpattern (e.g., *bought, caught, thought*), whereas others appear to be examples of rarer or truly exceptional spelling rules (e.g., *gist, aisle, phlegm, syncope, yacht*). Patients with surface alexia and agraphia can read and write regularly spelled words and even figure out how to pronounce and write nonwords (e.g., *blik*) by use of intact spelling-sound rules.

Deep alexia and **deep agraphia** are characterized by the inability to use the spelling-sound (grapheme-phoneme) correspondence rules and some impairment in the whole-word route as well (Figure 5.1c). Deep alexia is also called *reading-by-sight vocabulary*. The most dramatic errors that these patients make are semantic substitutions, called **paralexias** in reading and **paragraphias** in writing. For instance, errors made by patients with deep alexia include reading *close* as *shut, uncle* as *cousin,* and *dinner* as *food.* Notice that the words they produce are not phonologically related to the target but are semantically related to it. These errors suggest that the patients are not sounding out the words at all but nonetheless can derive some meaning from them. Patients with deep agraphia make spelling errors of the following type in dictation: *time → clock; sky → sun; yacht → boat; laugh → smile* (McCarthy & Warrington, 1990). It is relatively easy to make the argument that these patients are not able to use the sound-spelling rules efficiently and instead are relying on a whole-word or semantic route. However, it is also clear that the semantic route is not working too well, or else the target words would have been produced correctly. Patients with these disorders also make errors that suggest they have an easier time with words of high semantic content and more difficulty when semantic content is minimal:

- They make errors in reading and writing nonwords (e.g., *wug, blik*), presumably because there is no semantic association possible with them.
- They have difficulty reading and writing grammatical function words (e.g., *and, the, for, be*), possibly because there is little semantic information available (compare the semantic content of *be* vs. *bee*).
- They make morphologically related errors, reading *wise* as *wisdom* and *birth* as *born,* likely because the affixes in these cases are low in semantic content.

Although these disorders are very interesting because of the way they disrupt reading and writing, they are not particularly common and appear to be caused by relatively heterogeneous lesions in the left hemisphere— the same regions that cause aphasia. The lesions that cause surface alexia often involve left temporoparietal cortex, frequently the superior temporal gyrus. The lesions underlying surface agraphia appear to involve areas in and around the left angular gyrus, including adjacent subcortical white matter. Deep alexia appears to be associated with relatively large lesions of the left temporoparietal region, generally including the supramarginal gyrus (McCarthy & Warrington, 1990).

Alexia With Agraphia (Parietal Agraphia, Parietal Alexia)

Alexia with agraphia is behaviorally similar to aphasic alexia and agraphia but occurs in the absence of significant aphasia. Symptoms include deficits in all aspects of reading and writing, including spelling and comprehending orally spelled words. Alexia with agraphia occurs after damage to the left angular gyrus, at the posterior region of the perisylvian language areas. The angular gyrus sits at the junction of the visual and auditory cortex and has significant input from the somatosensory cortex. Because damage to the angular gyrus produces reading and writing deficits without other major cognitive or behavioral problems, this suggests that it is uniquely important for reading and writing (Benson, 1979; Goodglass, 1993).

Pure Alexia and Pure Agraphia

There are two disorders of relatively pure disruption of reading or writing, appropriately called pure alexia and pure agraphia. **Pure alexia,** also called *alexia without agraphia, pure word blindness, letter-by-letter reading,* and *angular alexia,* is a reading disorder that is not accompanied by either aphasia or agraphia; hence, it is pure. The striking behavioral characteristic of this disorder is that patients can write but cannot read what they have themselves just written. These patients often discover that they can cue themselves by spelling words out loud. By using this letter-by-letter strategy, they hear the letters and then identify the word and its meaning. This, of course, takes quite a bit longer than regular reading and is more prone to error, particularly with longer words (Coltheart, 1998).

This syndrome is sufficiently bizarre in its behavioral consequences that many have tried to explain it. Most researchers describe pure alexia as a disconnection syndrome, in which visual processing in both occipital lobes and language processing in the left perisylvian language zone are intact, but there is a disconnection between the visual input from the occipital lobes and the left and right hemisphere language regions. That is, the angular gyrus is intact but isolated from crucial visual input. Pure alexia often occurs after occlusion of the left posterior cerebral artery, which damages the left occipital lobe and the posterior regions (i.e., the splenium) of the corpus callosum (Kirshner, 1995a, 1995b). Both lesions are necessary to isolate the angular gyrus from visual input. These patients can still see because right hemisphere occipital structures are intact, although a right visual field deficit is typical. They can write because the left angular gyrus is intact. However, they cannot read because the left hemisphere damage prevents visual information from being transmitted from the left occipital lobe to the left hemisphere language zones; the splenial damage prevents visual input from the right hemisphere from getting to the left hemisphere language zones. Thus, the left hemisphere language zones are disconnected from visual input (see Figure 5.2). However, the disconnection must not be complete because these patients can still recognize and name letters to perform oral letter-by-letter reading. Once the letters are named out loud, the intact auditory input to the left hemisphere language areas allows the words to be identified by the intact language zones.

Pure agraphia is a rare disorder of writing without aphasia or alexia. Patients with pure agraphia make well-formed letters but spelling mistakes. These symptoms are thought to be due to damage to the second frontal convolution on the left, Exner's area. However, these symptoms have also been reported after damage to the left parietal lobe and subcortical structures, including the left caudate and internal capsule. There are

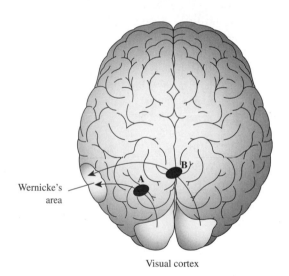

Wernicke's area

Visual cortex

Figure 5.2 The lesions that cause pure alexia disrupt (A) the left visual cortex or its connections to Wernicke's area and (B) the transfer of visual information from the right visual cortex to the left hemisphere through the corpus callosum. This has the effect of isolating Wernicke's area from both the left and right visual cortices, which impair a patient's ability to read. However, connections between Wernicke's area and the frontal motor planning and control regions remain intact, preserving the patient's ability to write.

probably several different disorders that have been described under this name.

Neglect Alexia and Agraphia

One of the ways that reading and writing differ from spoken language is that visuospatial abilities are central to reading and writing and largely irrelevant to spoken language. It is not surprising, then, that visuospatial deficits affect reading and writing more than they affect spoken language. Visuospatial deficits are discussed in Chapter 7 in more detail, but it is worth noting here the particular effects that visuospatial impairments, particularly unilateral neglect, have on reading and writing. **Neglect alexia** is characterized by difficulty reading on the left, usually due to right hemisphere damage. Some patients neglect the entire left side of the page, whereas others misread or omit the left sides of words, even if the words are on right side of the page. Errors include the deletion of letters on the left (e.g., reading *cage* as *age*) or substituting letters on the left (reading *yellow* as *pillow*) (Friedman et al., 1993). More rarely, we see neglect of the right side of words due to left hemisphere damage.

Neglect alexia and agraphia are typically associated with right parietal lesions and frequently accompanied by other manifestations of neglect, such as being unable to copy simple figures on the affected side. Occasionally, neglect may affect reading more than other visual functions.

Unilateral neglect of space affects writing in predictable manners. Patients with **neglect agraphia** will write only on the right side of the page, completely ignoring the left side of page (see Figure 5.3). These patients will also often have trouble writing on a horizontal line and will introduce extra strokes and extra spaces. Neglect agraphia is commonly associated with right parietal damage.

Apraxic Agraphia

Apraxia is a motor disorder of learned movements (see Chapter 13). Apraxia can affect skilled movements of any type, including speech, hand and arm gestures, and writing. Errors include substitutions of inappropriate movements. Patients with **apraxic agraphia** have difficulty forming letters accurately. Some patients will substitute one letter for another, and other patients will write unrecognizable letters. Sometimes, patients cannot even copy letters accurately. These patients are also frequently apraxic for other hand movements such as gestures. Lesions causing this type of writing disturbance are often in the dominant

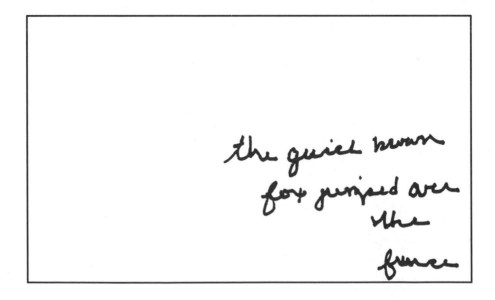

Figure 5.3   The sentence *The quick brown fox jumped over the fence,* written to dictation by a patient with right hemisphere damage and left neglect.

left parietal lobe. Lesions of the second left frontal convolution, Exner's area, are also thought to give rise to impairments confined to the formation of letters.

DIAGNOSIS OF ALEXIA AND AGRAPHIA

The primary goals of testing reading and writing are (a) to identify patterns of errors and (b) determine if the reading and writing problems are based in visual, motor, or linguistic processes. Speech-language pathologists typically guide diagnosis and treatment of reading and writing disorders. This section reviews tests of reading and writing per se, but because reading and writing involve vision and movement, full evaluations will also include independent testing of these domains. Tests of visual function, particularly neglect, are discussed in Chapter 8; tests of motor control or praxis are discussed in Chapter 13.

Reading and writing disorders can only be diagnosed with knowledge of how well the patient was able to read and write before the onset of brain injury. Therefore, prior to assessment of reading and writing, it is necessary to at least estimate a patient's premorbid reading and writing ability. This can be done by asking the patient and/or family members how well, how much, and what types of materials the patient read and wrote prior to the illness. Level of education, work, and hobby history are also helpful in determining premorbid reading and writing skills.

Tests of Reading

Tests of reading comprehension can be found within intelligence tests (Terman & Merrill, 1973), academic achievement batteries (MacGinitie, 1978), and aphasia batteries (Goodglass, Kaplan, and Baressi, 2001; Kertesz, 1982; LaPointe & Horner, 1998). Basic assessment of reading comprehension will include reading of letters, words, sentences, and paragraphs. Examples of each level are provided as follows.

Letter reading can be tested in a match-to-sample procedure in which letters are matched to each other from an array of letters that vary in case and font. This will determine if a patient

can recognize letters in a variety of forms (e.g., *G* and *g; F* and *f*).

Word reading can be tested by asking the patient to select the picture that matches a written word. Other tests will have the patient select from several words the one that labels a single picture (see Figure 5.4). This method can incorporate different types of distracters, including words that look alike (*sub-bun-bus*), words that sound alike (*sky-pie-buy*), and words that have related meanings (*pipe-smoke-cigar*). Differential performance with different types of distracters reveals visual, phonological, or semantic problems. Some word-level tests include several categories of words, most commonly nouns, verbs, and colors, because some patients appear to suffer from deficits that affect relatively specific grammatical or semantic categories (see discussion in category-specific semantic agnosias in Chapter 8).

Sentence reading can be tested by having a patient follow written commands (e.g., *Shut your eyes, Point to the door*). Sentence comprehension is also frequently tested in a multiple-choice format, in which the patient selects the most appropriate continuation from a set of written choices (e.g., *A mother has a _____ TREE - COOK - CHILD - TRUCK*) (Kertesz, 1979) or matches a sentence with a picture. Sentence

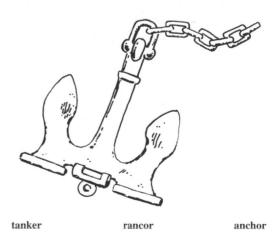

tanker   rancor   anchor

Figure 5.4   An example of a single-word reading test item. The patient selects or reads the word that matches the picture. In this case, the distracter words are phonologically related to (they sound like) the target word (*anchor*).

comprehension can also be assessed by having the patient select from a set of sentences the one that means the same thing as a target sentence (i.e., a paraphrase) (Lezak, 1995). Test items should vary in length and complexity because patients may be able to understand simple but not complex sentences.

Paragraph reading can be assessed by paragraph completion as in the following examples from the Reading Comprehension Battery for Aphasia (first example) (LaPointe & Horner, 1998) and the Nelson Reading Skills test (second example) (Hanna, Schell, & Schreiner, 1977):

Example 1: The connection between sanitation and disease became clear when Pasteur showed that food would not decay if germs were killed by heat and then sealed out. Sterilization by heat is a result of:

> SANITATION
> GOOD FOOD
> PASTEUR'S DISCOVERY
> GERMS.

Example 2: Kansas, "The Wheat State," grows more wheat than any other state. It grows hard red winter wheat that is used to make flour for bread. Over 100 years ago, a group of Christians called Mennonites moved from Russia to Kansas because they didn't believe in being soldiers. In Kansas they were free to practice their religion. Most of them were farmers. They brought a hard winter wheat called Turkey Red with them. Turkey Red was so successful that other farmers soon ABANDONED soft wheat and began growing this new hard wheat.

Turkey Red is not grown now but its improved descendants still make Kansas the nation's breadbasket.

1. ABANDONED means
   A. adopted
   B. bought
   C. gave up
   D. harvested

2. Flour from hard red winter wheat is used to make
   A. bread
   B. crackers
   C. noodles
   D. pancakes

3. Kansas is called the nation's breadbasket because it
   A. grows so much wheat
   B. makes so many baskets
   C. makes so much flour
   D. produces so much bread

4. Kansas farmers stopped growing soft wheat because
   A. soldiers didn't like it
   B. the Mennonites made them
   C. Turkey Red was much better
   D. it was against their religion

5. Where did the Kansas Mennonites come from?
   A. Mennon
   B. Russia
   C. Turkey
   D. It doesn't say

6. Mennonites moved to the United States so they wouldn't have to be
   A. Christians
   B. religious
   C. soldiers
   D. farmers

7. Where does the name Turkey Red come from?
   A. The Kansans
   B. The Mennonites
   C. The Russians
   D. It doesn't say

Items and tests vary with regard to "passage dependency." Readers can often select the correct answer by reading just the final (even incomplete) sentence, without reading the paragraph at all for paragraphs with low "passage dependency" (Nicholas, MacLennan, & Brookshire, 1986). The Nelson Reading Skills Tests (Hanna et al., 1977) appears to be a more accurate gauge of paragraph reading than items from the Reading Comprehension Battery for Aphasia or the paragraph comprehension items on other popular aphasia batteries (Nicholas & Brookshire, 1986). Several tests assess functional reading by having the patient read practical material such as a bus schedule, an invitation to a birthday party, a doctor's appointment card, a checkbook register, calendar, or weather forecast (Holland et al., 1999).

Tests of Writing

Writing examinations must be able to detect impairments in vision, movement, and language that cause writing problems. Spontaneous writing samples in response to general directions such as "write a sentence about anything you want" or "write a paragraph about a familiar topic" can often elicit adequate data to be analyzed. Common writing errors include visually based problems such as neglect of space on one side or odd spacing between letters, poor letter formation, spelling errors, odd word choice, and grammatical deficits. However, spontaneous writing is not useful for all patients: Some patients may not generate any spontaneous writing at all, other patients will write something so simple that there are few opportunities for errors, and still others make so many errors that it is hard to tell where the problems lie. Therefore, structured writing tasks help to elicit more useful information in these cases.

The patient writing her or his own name will usually elicit optimal performance because this is the most practiced writing task. Writing a description of a picture limits the topic and the range of words that are appropriate and also helps the patient focus. Writing to dictation and copying offer the most control and are useful to determine exactly where a breakdown may occur. Dictation will include letters, numbers, words, phrases, and sentences. Dictation is particularly helpful in identifying deficits in specific word types (nouns vs. verbs, regular vs. irregular spelling). Copying does not involve auditory perception or language generation, so it is a good technique to identify visuospatial and motor problems.

For patients who are blind or paralyzed, some aspects of the writing system can still be assessed. For instance, oral spelling, in which the examiner spells a word aloud (*D-O-G*) and the patient identifies it (by saying *dog*) or the examiner says a word (*dog*) and asks the patient to spell it aloud (*D-O-G*), tests a patient's spelling ability without any writing at all.

If reading and/or writing disorders are thought to affect a particular route of the writing system or a particular class of words, special word lists need to be prepared for dictation. These frequently include words with regular versus irregular spelling (e.g., *desk* vs. *ache*) (Blair & Spreen, 1989; Langmore & Canter, 1983), content versus function words (e.g., *be* vs. *bee*), nouns versus verbs (e.g., *trout* vs. *bleed*), concrete versus abstract words (e.g., *table* vs. *justice*), long versus short words (e.g., *dog* vs. *rhinoceros*), and common versus rare words (e.g., *girl* vs. *ibex*).

TREATMENT OF ALEXIA AND AGRAPHIA

Treatment of reading and writing disorders is a relatively neglected field. This might be due to the fact that rehabilitation of spoken language functions is considered more important for communication. Treatment of reading and/or writing is extremely important in several scenarios, including for patients with mild impairments who require reading and writing for a return to functional status and work, and for patients with severe impairments, for whom written language is one of the more preserved or "open" modalities that can be facilitated and used to compensate for impaired auditory/spoken communication. Obviously, the key to successful rehabilitation in this area is understanding the premorbid skill level, the underlying deficit, and the patient's goals. A few examples of successful therapeutic programs are presented as follows.

Deep Alexia and Surface Alexia

The great interest and research in the dual-route model of reading over the past few decades has yielded some practical and theoretically motivated approaches to rehabilitation. Recall that the dual-route model is essentially a description of two strategies that we use simultaneously in reading: sound-spelling correspondences and whole-word reading. Therefore, if one of the routes is impaired, it is possible to improve function of the impaired route or, alternatively, compensate via the relatively intact route. Both of these approaches have been used with success.

For example, a patient with deep alexia who was particularly impaired in the use of the sound-spelling rules was explicitly retrained to use the sound-spelling route. By pairing each letter with a common word that begins with that letter (*a* is for *apple*), the patient was eventually able to produce a sound corresponding to each letter and subsequently improve word reading (de Partz, Seron, & Van der Linden, 1992). This is similar to phonics used in teaching children to read.

Patients with surface alexia, deficits in whole-word reading, have been taught to associate individual written words with a particular pronunciation. They do this by grouping words with similar spelling-sound patterns, as in *ow* in *mow* and *grow* versus *ow* in *cow* and *clown,* essentially relearning the irregular patterns in terms of their "neighborhoods" (Friedman & Robinson, 1991).

Moss, Gonzalez Rothi, and Fennell (1991) designed another type of treatment program for a patient with surface alexia. All the tasks required the patient to use aspects of the impaired lexical route. Three separate therapy tasks were used: (a) assigning a semantic category to written words, (b) reading irregularly spelled words (e.g., *jealousy, epistle, mystique,* and *ocean*), and (c) selecting the appropriate homophone in sentences such as *The rose is a beautiful flour/ flower.* After 10 treatment sessions, the patient was able to read more quickly without any sacrifice in accuracy, suggesting that these exercises facilitated reading.

For patients who have pure alexia or reading impairments not complicated by language or visual deficits, there are several successful therapeutic techniques. Many of these patients discover letter-by-letter reading on their own (i.e., spelling words out loud to access their meaning). Another method that has been used spontaneously by patients and explicitly taught in therapy is the use of kinesthetic feedback. For instance, patients can be trained to trace letters on their hands, which often stimulates recognition of the letter and pronunciation, or to trace the letter in the air with eye or head movement. The kinesthetic feedback helps the patient to recognize the letter, and by putting the letters together, the patient can read, however painstakingly (Lott & Friedman, 1999; Seki, Yajima, & Sugishita, 1995).

1	Neglect alexia and agraphia are also amenable to therapy.	1
2	Increasing awareness and developing a habit to look to the left has a positive effect	2
3	for those patients who neglect to read or write on the left side of the page. A simple	3
4	but successful treatment strategy is to have the patient copy a paragraph. This	4
5	involves both reading and writing. At first, many cues are used to help the patient	5
6	keep track of where he is, and to facilitate scanning from the ends of lines on the	6
7	right side of the page to the beginning of the next line on the left side. Initially, the	7
8	paragraph may have line numbers on both the left and right margins and an	8
9	anchoring horizontal line along the left margin, as in this paragraph. The anchor line	9
10	and the numbers along the left margin give the patient something to search for	10
11	when looking for the beginning of the line. The lines on the right margin match	11
12	numbers on the left margin and reduce the possibility of skipping lines while	12
13	scanning to the left. When the patient is successful with this strategy, the right	13
14	margin numbers can be dropped; eventually, all the numbers are dropped and	14
15	only the anchor line remains; and finally, no cues are needed. (Sohlberg & Mateer, 1989)	15

Agraphia due to motor deficits requires a different approach. Patients with left hemisphere damage are often weak or paralyzed on their right side. Because most people are right-handed, this creates an obvious obstacle for writing. These patients need to be taught to write with their nondominant hand, a slow but often successful treatment. There have also been some attempts to facilitate writing with the paralyzed right hand via a limb prosthesis. This device, a sort of skateboard attached to the right arm, allows movement to be directed from proximal (e.g., shoulder) muscle control (Brown, Leader, & Blum, 1983). In addition, strengthening and coordination exercises for the paralyzed arm help.

NOTE

1. This collection of reading disorders is often called *dyslexia,* despite the general tendency for acquired reading disorders to be called *alexia.*

6

PRAGMATIC COMMUNICATION DEFICITS

Disorders of Prosody, Discourse, and Nonliteral Language

Chapter Preview

1. What is pragmatics?

The term *pragmatics* refers to the conventions for using language in context. Three major areas of pragmatics are prosody, discourse structure, and nonliteral language.

2. How does aging affect pragmatics?

Certain aspects of pragmatics are essentially stable through older adulthood, including use of prosody and nonliteral language. Aspects of discourse structure appear to change with age, including an increase in off-topic and tangential remarks in conversation. In this area, there is considerable variability across individuals and cultures, as well as substantial overlap with certain pragmatic deficits, causing some potential diagnostic confusion.

3. What are the behavioral characteristics of pragmatic deficits?

Pragmatic deficits are manifested by inappropriate verbal and nonverbal communication, including monotone speech, tangential comments, and concrete interpretations of nonliteral language.

4. What is the neuropathology of pragmatic deficits?

Pragmatic deficits appear to be associated with right hemisphere damage.

5. How are pragmatic deficits diagnosed?

Pragmatic deficits are diagnosed through analysis of spontaneously produced conversation and narratives, as well as by specific tests of production and comprehension of prosody, discourse structure, and idioms.

6. How are pragmatic deficits treated?

Pragmatic deficits are treated by speech-language pathologists with a combination of practice and compensation.

PRAGMATICS

Knowledge of word meaning and sentence structure is a basic element of language and is central to communication. Disorders in the use of words and sentence structure are called aphasia and result from left hemisphere lesions (see Chapter 4). However, communication also encompasses a range of other rules and conventions that govern how people actually talk. The principles or rules governing appropriateness of language use make up the domain of **pragmatics** (i.e., the practical and functional aspects of language use in social interaction). Pragmatics includes a number of diverse domains, including the following:

- traditionally nonlinguistic, paralinguistic, or extralinguistic parameters such as body language and facial expression (e.g., when giving a lecture, you generally face the audience; when giving sad news or expressing sympathy, you generally do not smile);

- prosody—the melody of speech—which conveys linguistic, attitudinal, and emotional information;

- rules of constructing and interpreting discourse, including when to talk, how much information to give, and how to arrange the sentences to form a coherent narrative, lecture, or joke; and

- how to convey and interpret nonliteral meanings (e.g., when to interpret *John kicked the bucket* as *John died* vs. *John used his foot to move the pail*, or how to convey someone is a real loser by saying the opposite: *He's a real winner*).

The rules of pragmatics are very different from the linguistic rules governing word and sentence structure discussed in Chapter 4. For the most part, rules of word and sentence structure are regular—they are consistent from situation to situation: It is always ungrammatical to say *keys the found I* to communicate *I found the keys*. Rules of pragmatics, because they govern appropriateness, a concept that is itself vague and difficult to define, vary from context to context and are often subtle and not simple to characterize. Consequently, violations of pragmatic rules are

generally harder to describe and quantify than frank aphasia. For instance, the rules governing when to take a turn in a discourse are not absolute: It might be perfectly appropriate to occasionally interrupt a friend in an animated conversation, but it is less appropriate to interrupt a prospective employer in a job interview and even less appropriate to interrupt a speaker during a formal lecture. Because of this acceptable range of appropriateness, we tolerate much more individual and cultural variability in the realm of pragmatics than in other aspects of language.

The notion of pragmatics includes many disparate aspects of communication. In the field of communication disorders, pragmatics and pragmatic deficits constitute a group of sometimes unrelated functions, made coherent and associated with one another in part by patterns of neurobehavioral disorders. First, pragmatics are often spared in aphasia, highlighting the fact that they should be considered separately from core linguistic impairments that define aphasia. Second, pragmatic functions are often disrupted by right hemisphere damage, suggesting that they have a common neurological substrate.

Aphasic disturbances have been well described for more than 120 years (Broca, 1865; Freud, 1891a). Deficits in pragmatic aspects of communication after brain damage have been much less frequently and less thoroughly characterized. We are now beginning to categorize and label particular types of pragmatic deficits in much the same way we distinguish between aphasic symptoms, and this in turn will open the door to diagnosing and treating pragmatic deficits in a coherent manner. This chapter first describes some of the general communication phenomena that are not included in the discussion of aphasia (Chapter 4) but are associated with pragmatic deficits. It then addresses in detail three relatively distinct disorders of pragmatic communication that have received significant scrutiny: prosody, discourse structure, and nonliteral language.

Pragmatic Deficits

A patient with pragmatic communication deficits may communicate adequately, especially in brief interactions about familiar topics. The signs of a problem may only be apparent in longer discourses such as conversations and stories. His voice may be monotone, which is liable to be interpreted as depression, apathy, or disinterest. His facial expression and body language may also not match the context. He may talk too much or too little and wander from topic to topic. His behavior may seem rude. He may omit the small talk and typical introductions (e.g., *Hi, how are you?*) and closings (e.g., *Well that's about it for now*) that usually bracket a verbal interaction.

Pragmatic communication deficits may be easily but erroneously explained as problems of mood or personality, being dismissed by health care providers, family, and friends as depression or other psychological adjustment problems. It should also be noted that many of the pragmatic deficits discussed here are similar, if not identical, to some of the symptoms of schizophrenia, including *flat affect* (monotonous speech and little change in facial expression), *inappropriate affect* (tone of voice or body language not matching the context), *poverty of speech* or *alogia* (talking too little), and problems with discourse structure (Andreasen & Olsen, 1982). Although the deficits in psychiatric disorders and focal brain damage may be similar, this discussion will be limited to pragmatic deficits typical after focal brain damage. To make things even more confusing, a patient with pragmatic deficits may not recognize that anything is wrong or may deny a problem when asked directly. Denial of deficits—**anosognosia**— often makes pragmatic deficits difficult to evaluate and treat. Imagine being confronted with a person who acts apathetic and rude, has trouble constructing a coherent story, but thinks everything is fine. That is typical of patients with pragmatic deficits.

PROSODY

Prosody is the linguistic term used to describe variation in pitch, loudness (volume), and timing of speech. Taken together, variation in these aspects of the speech creates the characteristic melody that accompanies sentences. Each aspect of prosody corresponds to a distinct acoustic parameter. Pitch corresponds to frequency of sound waves, measured in cycles per second (Hz); a higher frequency sound is perceived as a higher pitch. Loudness corresponds to sound intensity, or amplitude of sound waves, measured in decibels. Speech timing corresponds to the duration of speech sounds and pauses in speech, measured in seconds. These three parameters are discussed under the single term *prosody* because they vary together, and it is often difficult to distinguish the individual contributions of each. For example, an emphasized word is, louder, longer, and higher in pitch than the same word in a neutral context.

Prosody does not fit neatly into either the core-linguistic or pragmatic domains of communication but rather cuts across linguistic, emotional, and pragmatic aspects of communication.

Linguistic prosody refers to instances when prosodic variation conveys core linguistic information, including (a) distinguishing word meaning by stress alone (e.g., *conVICT* vs. *CONvict*), (b) determining the internal structure of utterances (e.g., distinguishing a compound word [*greenhouse*] from an phrase consisting of an adjective and a noun [*green house*]), and (c) identifying whether an utterance is a statement, question, or command: Questions tend to rise in pitch at the end; commands are level in pitch and contain longer pauses; and statements have a characteristic fall in pitch on the last word (e.g., *You are going?* vs. *You are going*).

Affective prosody refers to prosodic variation that conveys the emotional state or mood of the speaker: Happiness is signaled with variable and high pitch; sadness with low volume, little pitch variation, and longer duration; anger with high volume; and surprise with high volume, high pitch, and fast speech rate. In contrast to linguistic prosody, in which forms are categorically distinguished from each other (the word is either *conVICT* or *CONvict*, not something in between), **emotional prosody** is a continuous and graded variable; degrees of sadness, happiness, and other emotions can be expressed.

Less frequently discussed is the notion of **pragmatic prosody**—the use of prosodic variation to communicate information that lies in between the linguistic realm of word and sentence meaning and the emotional realm of mood often involving both. One element of pragmatic prosody is emphatic stress—the use of pitch, volume, and word length to convey the speaker's attitude toward an element of the discourse (*you know, I really **HATE** peas*). Pragmatic prosody, through a combination of pitch contours and pausing, is also used to distinguish between literal and nonliteral meanings in sarcasm or irony: *I'm so impressed* versus *I'm sooo-o-o-o impressed.* Nonliteral meanings of idioms are also signaled prosodically: The literal meaning of *She's skating on thin ice* is marked by slower speech rate, more pauses, and more local pitch contours than the idiom (Van Lancker, Canter, & Terbeek, 1981). Speech timing, particularly pauses, is also used systematically to signal the pragmatically important notion of turn-taking in conversation (Schegloff, 1998).

Age-Related Changes in Prosody

Prosody is used very early in life. Infants intone babbling, making otherwise unintelligible utterances sound like sentences in their native language (Halle, de Boysson Bardies, & Vihman, 1991). Children from a very early age respond to prosodic cues in speech directed to them (Dehaene Lambertz & Houston, 1998; Papousek, Bornstein, Nuzzo, Papousek, & Symmes, 2000).

The very few studies of prosody in aging indicate minimal or no changes in older adults' ability to produce and comprehend prosodic variation. Kjelgaard, Titone, & Wingfield (1999) evaluated younger and older adults' ability to use prosodic contours to distinguish between the two interpretations of who was rushing in sentence fragments such as *Whenever Jean rushed her workers. . . .* Both younger and older adults were sensitive to prosodic variations and were able to make sensible continuations to the sentence fragments (e.g., *Whenever Jean rushed her workers, they made mistakes* vs. *Whenever Jean rushed, her workers made mistakes*). These data suggest that at least this aspect of linguistic prosody is well preserved in healthy aging.

Some older adults appear to talk more slowly than younger adults. In general, the longer and more frequent pauses in the speech of older adults are interpreted to be a result of word-finding difficulty that increases with age (Ska & Joanette, 1996). It is also possible that slower speech is due to a generalized psychomotor slowing rather than to word-finding.

There is one area in which prosody does cause difficulty for older adults, but it is not because of a problem in the older adults' use of prosody. Older adults frequently inspire the use of **elderspeak.** Elderspeak is a speech register used when talking *to* older adults, characterized by a number of prosodic features, including high pitch, slow speech rate, increased loudness, and exaggerated intonation, as well as simplified grammar, elementary semantic content, and limited eye contact (Caporael, 1981; Kemper, 1994; Ryan, Maclean, & Orange, 1994). Similar speech accommodations have been identified in speech to young children, called *motherese,* and speech directed to nonnative speakers (Snow & Ferguson, 1977). Although these largely prosodic speech accommodations appear to have some beneficial effect on older adults' comprehension in specific experimental contexts (Kemper, Othick, Warren, & Gubarchuk, 1996), they are also responsible for older adults' dissatisfaction with many interactions. The speech accommodations are elicited largely on the basis of social stereotypes about disabilities in older adults, such as hearing loss, that may or may not be true and therefore may be unnecessary, demeaning, and disrespectful (Garcia & Orange, 1996; Ryan, 1996). The negative impact of using overaccommodated speech to older adults is identified as part of the *communication predicament of aging,* in which speech modifications based on a "presumption of incompetence and dependence . . . limit the older person's chance for a meaningful conversation . . . [and] convey a sense of declining . . . capability, loss of control and helplessness." These feelings, in turn, "contribute to the negative feedback loop within which the elder's self-esteem and opportunities for satisfying communication decline" (Orange, Ryna, Meredith, & MacLean, 1995, p. 23).

Behavioral Characteristics and Neuropathology of Prosodic Deficits

Prosodic deficits are categorized in several ways. A primary distinction is made between deficits in prosody used to convey linguistic versus emotional information. Like other language deficits, prosodic impairments can occur in production and/or comprehension. The terms used to describe prosodic deficits are **aprosodia** and **dysprosody.** These terms are used interchangeably.

Deficits in linguistic and pragmatic prosody appear in conversation most commonly as flat pitch contours (Colsher, Cooper, & Graff Radford, 1987). This gives an overall monotone quality to speech and interferes with the patients' ability to signal linguistic and pragmatic differences. In several studies, patients with right hemisphere damage were impaired in their ability to produce emphatic stress, in which one word in a sentence is stressed for emphasis, and exhibited prosodic differences among declarative, interrogative, and imperative sentences (Behrens, 1988; Shapiro & Danly, 1985; Weintraub, Mesulam, & Kramer, 1981). In language comprehension as well, patients with brain damage are often impaired in the use of prosody to distinguish words from other words (*PROduce* vs. *proDUCE*), words versus noun phrases (*whitehouse* vs. *white house*), and imperative versus interrogative sentences (Emmorey, 1987; Pell & Baum, 1997a, 1997b).

Emotional dysprosody results in difficulty conveying and interpreting emotional states. Stroke patients will sometimes complain that they have a difficult time making their tone of voice match their mood (Ross & Mesulam, 1979). These subjective reports have been experimentally confirmed: When patients with brain damage, especially those with right hemisphere damage, are asked to produce semantically neutral sentences (e.g., *Johnny is walking his dog*) with a specific emotion, judges have a difficult time determining the emotion they intended (Tucker, Watson, & Heilman, 1977). The difficulty with emotional prosody extends to perception, as patients with brain damage also have difficulty determining the mood of other speakers when they are forced to rely on prosodic cues. Van Lancker and Sidtis (1992) also used semantically neutral sentences (e.g., *Lizzie is petting her cat*) recorded by a professional actress to convey four different emotions: happy, angry, sad, and surprised. The researchers played the sentences for patients with unilateral brain damage and asked them to select one of the four line drawings of a happy, angry, sad, or surprised face, accompanied by the corresponding written label for emotion. Patients with both left and right brain damage were significantly impaired compared to patients who did not have brain damage.

There is ongoing controversy with regard to the psychological/cognitive explanation for dysprosody. One possible explanation is that emotional prosodic deficits are the result of a patient's actual mood experience (i.e., if patients are not able to experience emotions, they will have a difficult time expressing and interpreting them via speech). In support of this theory, a group of nondepressed stroke patients and a group of depressed nonstroke patients were judged to sound similar (House, Rowe, & Standen, 1987). However, this cannot be the general explanation because stroke patients frequently sense a dissociation between their intact emotional state and their impaired expression of emotion: Some patients can experience emotion but cannot express it through prosody; others express emotion (e.g., through crying) when they do not feel it. An underlying lack of emotion is also unlikely because many dysprosodic stroke patients have no difficulty conveying and interpreting emotion through words (e.g., *I'm happy*). Finally, an explanation based on impoverished emotional experience does not explain deficits in linguistic or other uses of prosody. A more plausible and general theory to explain dysprosody is that stroke patients are capable of experiencing emotion but are impaired in their ability to produce and comprehend the prosodic cues in appropriate circumstances.

Dysprosody results from lesions to a wide range of brain regions, including both left and right hemispheres. Van Lancker (1980) and others (Pell & Baum, 1997a, 1997b) have raised the possibility that linguistic and emotional dysprosodia are different disorders with distinct neuropathologies, most often associating linguistic dysprosody with left hemisphere damage and emotional dysprosody with right hemisphere damage. The association of left hemisphere damage with linguistic dysprosody is supported by consistent findings of many linguistic deficits after left hemisphere damage.

The association of emotional dysprosody with right hemisphere damage is appealing because there is a longstanding theory that the right hemisphere plays a greater role than the left in modulating the expression of emotion generally (Mills, 1912), and recent evidence shows that patients with right hemisphere damage have difficulty with the expression of emotional prosody (Borod, 1993; Wertz, Henschel, Auther, Ashford, & Kirshner, 1998). However, the picture is more complex than that, as both hemispheres appear to contribute to emotional prosodic abilities. Pell and Baum (1997a, 1997b) found that patients with either left or right hemisphere damage had difficulty identifying emotional prosody, but patients with left and right hemisphere damage did not differ from each other. Van Lancker and Sidtis (1992) found that patients with either left or right hemisphere damage erred in identifying emotional prosody, but they did so for different reasons: patients with damage to the right hemisphere were unable to use pitch cues, whereas patients with damage to the left hemisphere could not use timing cues, suggesting that aspects of emotional prosody may be differentially disrupted.

The focus on the roles of left versus right hemisphere damage in dysprosody is somewhat misleading because subcortical structures such as the basal ganglia are also important. In one study of dysprosody, patients with basal ganglia disease were as impaired as patients with damage to the left and right hemispheres in both prosodic production and comprehension (Cancelliere & Kertesz, 1990). However, the precise contribution of the basal ganglia to dysprosody is still mysterious: It is not clear whether the basal ganglia modulates prosody directly or whether it influences prosody through connections to the limbic system and frontal lobes. The frontal lobes are likely important because of their involvement in fine motor control, necessary for modulation of pitch, loudness, and timing of speech. Both the frontal lobes and limbic system are also involved in modulation of emotions. The picture that is emerging after almost 20 years of scientific investigation into the neuropathology of dysprosody is that "prosodic processes are made up of multiple skills and functions distributed across cerebral systems" (Van Lancker & Sidtis, 1992, p. 963).

Diagnosis of Dysprosody

A clinician can observe in conversation whether the patient's prosody appears to lack variation. The simplest evaluation is to use a rating scale to guide and quantify the subjective impression of prosody. One simple scale from the Boston Diagnostic Aphasia Exam (Goodglass, Kaplan, & Barresi, 2001) uses subjective impression during conversation to rate volume (normal/low/loud), voice (normal/whisper/hoarse), speech rate (normal/slow/rapid), and intonation, which is rated on a subjective 7-point scale ranging from *no sentence intonation* (1) to *normal sentence intonation* (7), with the midpoint (4) being *sentence intonation limited to short phrases*. More formal tests of prosodic production have the advantage of a range of controlled items to evaluate. Most of the ideas for assessing prosody that follow (Table 6.1) are adapted from Cancelliere and Kertesz (1990) and Myers (1999). For tests assessing prosody in sentences as opposed to words, it is useful to have a prepared set of emotionally neutral simple sentences (e.g., *The book is on the table, The movie starts at 7:00, You are going to the store*) to be used in each of the sentence tests. In any assessment of prosody, it is important to be aware that facial expression also conveys much of the same pragmatic, linguistic, and emotional information that is conveyed by prosody, so it is important to limit the amount of facial expression seen by the patient during comprehension assessment (e.g., the examiner should turn away or cover his or her face when speaking the test sentences). Table 6.1 provides sample assessment procedures for production and comprehension for linguistic, pragmatic, and emotional prosody.

Treatment of Dysprosody

Linguistic dysprosody is generally less of a functional problem than emotional dysprosody and therefore receives less therapeutic attention. Fewer communication problems arise due to linguistic dysprosody because there are

Table 6.1   Sample Tasks Used for the Evaluation of Dysprosody

	Production	*Comprehension*
Linguistic	Ask the patient to read sentences with interrogative and declarative intonation. Use sentences that can be a statement or question, such as *Jennifer loves to go skydiving.* Do not use sentences that are unambiguously questions, such as *Where is the car?* and *Is it too late?* Note if and how the patient uses pitch versus loudness versus facial expression to signal declarative and interrogative meanings.	The clinician reads simple sentences, such as *The movie starts at 7,* with either declarative or interrogative intonation. The patient indicates whether each utterance is a question or a statement.
Emotional	Ask the patient to read or repeat a list of emotionally neutral sentences with specific emotions expressed via intonation, such as *happy, sad, angry,* and *surprised.* Have the patient read each sentence with each emotion. Rate whether the emotions are conveyed and how well they are distinguished from one another. Note if and how the patient uses pitch versus loudness versus facial expression to signal emotions.	The clinician reads sentences to convey specific emotions via intonation (typically *happy, sad, angry,* and *surprised*), and the patient indicates which emotion was used, either verbally or by pointing to the words and/or line drawings of faces depicting the emotions. Be sure the clinician covers or hides his or her face during the production of emotional sentences so that facial expression is not an available cue for the patient.
Pragmatic	Ask the patient to read printed sentences, stressing one of the words. Rate if the patient can emphasize individual words and whether this is done via loudness, pitch, and/or lengthening. Typically, an emphasized word is louder, longer, and higher in pitch.	Give the patient a list of simple written sentences. The clinician reads each sentence, emphasizing one of the content words. The patient identifies the emphasized word in each sentence. Rate accuracy.

generally other available cues; for example, a question can be cued by verb-first word order (*Are you going?*) or a question word (*what, who, where, how*), eleminating the need to rely on interaction. That said, each patient, caregiver, and clinician will need to determine if linguistic and/or emotional dysprosody is a priority for treatment for any given individual.

The first step in treatment is to explain any prosodic deficit to patient, family, and caregivers. This increases awareness of the problem and minimizes misunderstandings between the patient and family or other interlocutors. Restoration

of prosody production can be accomplished through practice drills starting with simple repetition of prosodic contours. That is, the clinician produces nonsense syllables, words, phrases, or sentences with a specific prosodic contour, and the patient repeats them. If the patient can repeat the prosodic contours, therapy progresses to various elicitation techniques in which the patient uses more subtle cues to produce appropriate prosody. Compensation for dysprosody involves practice using nonprosodic ways to convey the same information such as words (e.g., explicitly stating emotions), sentence structures

Table 6.2   Sample Tasks Used for the Treatment of Dysprosody

	Production	*Comprehension*
Linguistic	Because statements and questions generally have distinct structures, this is probably not a high priority for anyone in terms of rehabilitation. But for some patients, these exercises might have the benefit of drawing attention to the issues and improving overall prosodic range. Have the patient produce sentences with declarative, interrogative, and imperative intonation. If this is difficult, emphasize that these differences can also be conveyed linguistically via question words and subject-verb inversion (e.g., *Are they coming over for dinner?* rather than *They are coming over for dinner?*).	The clinician produces words and sentences that are ambiguous in writing but can be disambiguated in speech via prosody in speech (e.g., *conVICT* vs. *CONvict*) and sentences with declarative versus interrogative prosody (*You won't eat your breakfast* vs. *You won't eat your breakfast?*). The patient identifies the intended target by defining words or labeling question versus statement.
Emotional	Practice producing emotional prosody. The patient produces emotional prosody consistent with various contexts. For example, ask the patient to say what someone would say and how that person would say it after his or her dog died. Provide a story with a final line that is clearly emotional, and have the patient produce the line with appropriate prosody.	If the patient is having difficulty interpreting emotional prosodic information, encourage family members to use explicit verbal labels in discourse directed to the patient. Ask the patient to label emotions associated with various words, situations, and contexts, such as: 1. *An earthquake destroyed our home;* 2. *I just won the lottery;* and *My lost dog was returned to me.* 3. Practice labeling emotions in various discourses, such as *I am sad today* or *The boy is happy because....*
Pragmatic	Emphatic stress lends itself to some specific facilitatory techniques. Ask counterfactual questions, such as "Is it the 5th of March?" on another date. The target response would be, "No, it's the **6th** of March." (or the correct date) Patients can be cued to make emphasized words louder, longer, and higher in pitch.	The clinician reads a sentence aloud emphasizing a word. The patient identifies the emphasized word.

(e.g., using question words rather than intonation to ask a question), and facial expressions. Treatment for comprehension deficits related to prosody typically works on identification and recognition of prosodic cues, progressing from exaggerated stimuli and simple contexts (e.g., distinguishing between two theatrically produced emotional contours) to more natural stimuli and complex contexts (e.g., identifying and recognizing a variety of prosodically conveyed meanings in conversational speech) (see Table 6.2).

DISCOURSE STRUCTURE

Discourse refers to units of language that contain more than a single sentence. There are many different genres of discourse, including narratives, jokes, and instructions. When more than one person is involved in creating discourse, we call it a conversation. The structure of discourse is guided by principles outlined by Grice (1975), who described several maxims of good communication. These principles relate to quantity (be succinct, provide as much information as necessary but not more than is necessary) and relevance (stay on topic, be informative). When discourses adhere to these principles, they **cohere**—the sentences follow from one another, main themes are developed, and the gist of the discourse is easy to follow.

Discourse rules vary from context to context. There is no one-to-one mapping between Grice's (1975) maxims and actual discourse structure because each **discourse structure** varies in content, purpose, and participants. For instance, the admonition to give the right amount of information is sensible enough, and we generally have a notion of approximately how much information to give. However, this notion is difficult to quantify because it changes from context to context: Asking a friend how the weather is outside should elicit a short one- or two-word response such as *nice, hot,* or *very windy.* However, a response by a meteorologist to a TV anchor asking a how the weather is outside should yield a lengthier response involving precise temperatures, wind velocity and direction, barometric pressure, cloud levels, and surf or snow conditions, not to mention the predictions for change over time. Both types of responses are appropriate but only within their context.

In addition to the amount of information, the structure of that information is also crucial. Conversations and narratives must maintain internal **thematic coherence.** This means that the individual sentences must be relevant and interpretable with respect to what came before and what follows, and they must also relate to overarching topics of the discourse. Discourse coherence helps a listener to extract the main theme (sometimes called the **macrostructure**) from the narrative. During discourse, a speaker relies on the listener to make inferences about how the sentences relate to one another because not all information is spelled out explicitly. The speaker and the listener will use both explicit linguistic information and nonlinguistic context to construct the discourse macrostructure. One of the primary ways to maintain discourse

coherence is by use of clear references, so that listeners always know who or what is being talked about. This is done in part by judicious use of names (*John*), nouns (the *boy*), and pronouns (*he*). Pronouns are particularly useful, pointing backwards to specific participants and tying sentences together. However, poor use of pronouns can also disrupt the coherence of a discourse because without proper and clear antecedents, pronouns are ambiguous and make a discourse very hard to follow (i.e., *he* can refer to a number of people). The two sentences below (from Light & Capps, 1986) illustrate how pronouns bridge sentences to build coherence and how listeners use linguistic and other contextual cues to infer the meaning of discourse coherence.

1. Henry spoke at a meeting while John drove to the beach.

2. He lectured on the administration.

Any listener would need to decide whether *he* in the second sentence refers to Henry or John. Given that Henry is speaking at the meeting, and *lecturing* is related to *speaking* at meetings, most listeners effortlessly infer that *he* refers to Henry, not John (Light & Capps, 1986). This exemplifies how (a) the use of particular words (*spoke at a meeting* and *lectured*) helps maintain thematic coherence, (b) speakers use reference to facilitate discourse structure (in this case, the use of *he* to refer back to Henry adds to the coherence), and (c) listeners use any context available to make inferences to extract or build a coherent discourse meaning.

Another example of a discourse structure that helps speakers and listeners construct and interpret discourse is knowledge of **scripts.** Scripts are typical sequences of events involved in certain activities. For instance, we all know that eating at a restaurant involves specific actions in a particular order: being seated, ordering food, getting food, eating, paying, and leaving. Speakers and hearers then use this script information to structure and interpret discourse. For instance, knowing the restaurant sequence, it is trivial for a listener to make sense of the sentences: *Liz and Aina went out to eat last night. They paid with a credit card.* However, if you didn't know that paying was part of the restaurant script, the two sentences would not make sense together. Compare a similar discourse in which the script does not support the inferences: *Liz and Aina went out to stargaze last night. They paid with a credit card.*

It is important to remember that each discourse genre has its own set of pragmatic rules. For instance, conversations involve rules about turn taking. Narratives do not usually involve turn taking but generally involve a sequence of elements proceeding from the initial setting, through complicating events and finally to the resolution. Instructions, also called *procedural narratives,* contain a different internal discourse structure, typically containing very carefully sequenced steps.

Age-Related Changes in Discourse

By and large, healthy older adults produce coherent, relevant, and appropriate discourse. They take turns appropriately in conversation and construct narratives by appropriately introducing topics, building on them, and referring back to them (Boden & Bielby, 1983; Garcia & Orange, 1996; Ska & Joanette, 1996). However, there are subtle differences in older adults' ability to construct and interpret discourses.

Older adults are more talkative and produce more tangential speech than younger people (Arbuckle & Gold, 1993; James, Burke, Austin, & Hulme, 1998). When describing personal events (e.g., a vacation, their education), older adults use more words and wander from the topic more often. This phenomenon, called **off-topic verbosity** or off-topic speech, appears to be limited to personal narratives and does not occur in less personal narratives such as picture description (James et al., 1998). One excerpt from James et al. (1998) illustrates an older adult's off-topic speech (in italics) when asked to talk about her education:

I started in grammar school in Porterville, Ohio and, uh we lived about a block about 8 blocks and I use to go home for lunch. *One of the things I remember so vividly was a fire across the street and they pulled a lady out on a stretcher and I was very, very upset. And upset for a long, long time.* I remember my second-grade teacher. Her name was Lucy Keller and she had buck teeth and when I looked up she scared the daylights out of me.

As an adult, as I knew her better, why she probably was one of the most wonderful people I'd ever met but uh as a child. . . . I've thought of that with my own children. If they run into something I kind of check what uh what's cooking because it could be something simple like a very tall person with uh buck teeth (p. 367).

Another area of difficulty in discourse with aging is pronominal reference. Older adults are more likely than younger adults to use pronouns (*he, she, they*) ambiguously (Pratt, Boyes, Robins, & Manchester, 1989; Ulatowska, Hayashi, Cannito, & Fleming, 1986). **Referential ambiguity** was studied by Pratt et al. (1989), who found that people in their 20s and 40s produced about five unspecified referents in narratives, whereas people in their 70s produced an average of eight unspecified referents.

Older adults also have more difficulty understanding and remembering discourse when reference is maintained with pronouns. In the pair of sentences (1) and (2) (previous page), Light and Capps (1986) showed that older adults use pragmatic knowledge to accurately assign reference to pronouns, correctly interpreting *he* in the second sentence to refer to Henry in the first sentence. However, when another sentence intervened between the two sentences, placing demands on memory, older people showed reference assignment deficits, that is, assigning *he* to *John* in the example above.

There have been three primary explanations for these subtle changes in the discourse of older adults (Kwong See & Ryan, 1996). Many aspects of cognitive aging, including off-topic verbosity, have been explained by an inhibition deficit (Hasher & Zacks, 1988). That is, older adults mention tangential information because they have difficulty inhibiting (i.e., ignoring) irrelevant information. However, because off-topic verbosity occurs only in personal narratives, it is not likely due to a general deficit in suppressing irrelevant information. Another, more benign explanation for what seems like off-topic and verbose speech is that older adults have developed different goals for their talk about themselves than younger adults; older adults want to communicate a meaningful description of life events rather than a concise description of facts (James et al., 1998).

Other discourse changes in aging have been explained by declines in **working memory** (see Chapters 10 and 11 for more discussion of working memory). The increase in ambiguous pronouns can be linked to memory deficits if the older speaker has forgotten to establish reference, thought that he or she already did, or has forgotten the names of characters (Pratt et al., 1989). In comprehension as well, a working memory deficit could explain poor comprehension of longer discourses or texts in which pronouns and their antecedents are separated by other material (Light & Capps, 1986).

One of the difficulties explaining discourse deficits in aging stems from the fact that discourse does not uniformly or dramatically deteriorate in healthy aging. In fact, some areas of discourse may improve with age. The ability to build a coherent, interesting story—a macrostructure—is one example of how age can enhance performance. Several studies have analyzed the overall structure of narratives told by younger and older people about important incidents in their lives—such as their first love. In two studies, narratives were produced orally (Kemper, Rash, Kynette, & Norman, 1990; Pratt & Robins, 1991), and in the third, written extracts from diaries kept over a lifetime were used (Kemper, 1990). The older adults' stories were rated as appropriate in terms of overall structure: introductions of characters, complex and coherent episodes, and endings that accurately summarized the outcomes of the actions. Surprisingly, however, stories produced by older adults are better remembered and rated as more interesting, more informative, and having a better story quality than narratives produced by younger people (James et al., 1998; Mergler, Faust, & Goldstein, 1984). This may be related to the values and goals that older adults have for communication as well as their rich life and storytelling experiences (James et al., 1998).

In summary, studies of discourse show some pragmatic changes in aging, including increased talkativeness, more digressions, and overuse of ambiguous pronouns. Equally notable, however, is that these changes are accompanied by overall improvement in other discourse skills such that the narratives of older adults are rated as more interesting, more informative, and of better story quality than narratives produced by younger speakers. Therefore, we are left with a paradox: Despite measurable impairments in some discourse abilities as people age, the narratives of older adults are often rated more favorably than those produced by younger adults. One explanation for this paradox is that older people have extensive experience with language and may be able to mitigate or eliminate the impact of discourse problems via superior story structures or other mechanisms.

This is not the case for people with discourse deficits due to brain damage, who often cannot compensate for frank pragmatic impairments and produce confusing and inappropriate discourse.

Behavioral Characteristics and Neuropathology of Discourse Deficits

Some of the effects of brain damage on discourse appear to be exaggerations of the effects of healthy aging on discourse, and others appear unique.

Discourse production after brain damage is often marked by digressions and **tangentiality,** making speech seem off-topic and verbose at times. These patients use many more words and include more irrelevant information than people who do not have brain damage when conversing and producing narratives. One patient's description of what is happening in a Norman Rockwell painting depicting a young man leaving home for university demonstrates the introduction of irrelevant details that disrupt the ability to extract a coherent story from the words.

> Well, collie or Lassie—looks like they're going to take him back to college. That's State U, or U State, State U. And they've had car trouble somewhere. Old Dad's still puffin' on cigarettes. This is before cigarettes went out of fashion. They better watch out about that porch they're sitting on there. Isn't it a mess? It's all rotted away. Termites must be at it. Look at those bumper shoes that kid—he's a collegiate. Look at the socks. Striped socks and he's got those snub-nosed kickers on. Must be gonna be the kicker for the team. He's got a yellow handkerchief in his shirt—coat jacket—and he thinks he's very dapper. You'll find this hard to believe, but that is an Atlas tire, and I sold those stinkers for 20 years. Now how do I know? I know because of the figuration on the side of the tire. That's an Atlas Junior, sold by Atlas TBA

Company to Exxon, and American Oil, and Chevron on a wire wheel and that tire is probably 475 by 17. I mounted many of those. That's a Model A Ford truck. (Myers, 1999, pp. 116–117)

The overall verbosity and tangentiality of speech is reminiscent of the off-task verbosity previously described in healthy aging but differs in several respects. First, whereas healthy older adults get to the point eventually, patients with brain damage often get so distracted by irrelevant details that they never communicate a main point. Second, healthy older adults are verbose only when discussing personal topics; if patients with brain damage are off-topic and verbose, they are so in all contexts.

Brain damage sometimes produces the opposite effect on discourse as well: too little speech. Too little speech, called paucity of output or poverty of speech, is illustrated by a stroke patient with right hemisphere damage describing a typically elaborate Norman Rockwell painting: "Looks like the mother's got a turkey. That's it" (Myers, 1999, p. 116). This limited amount of information, although accurate, is less than expected and less than what subjects without brain damage produce. In some cases, too little speech appears rude or is interpreted as an emotional problem.

Discourse comprehension is also affected by brain damage. Patients with right hemisphere damage often have trouble distinguishing relevant from irrelevant information in a text. Rehak (1992) asked patients with right hemisphere damage to judge the coherence of discourse containing tangential material. Patients often judged tangential conversations as normal and thought the tangential inserts were on the same topic.

Patients with brain damage are also impaired in extracting the main themes of narratives. Hough (1990) had patients listen to a story and then answer comprehension questions and select a main theme. Patients with right hemisphere damage were able to see a main theme if the text provided help—by presenting a clear topic near the beginning. However, if the topic was presented near the end of the paragraph, the patients were not able to come up with the main theme, suggesting that they could not provide their own thematic organization as they were processing the story.

The same cognitive explanations offered for discourse-level processing deficits in healthy aging can explain discourse processing after brain damage. Inhibition deficits are invoked to explain why patients include irrelevant information in discourse production and why they have difficulty distinguishing relevant from irrelevant information in discourse comprehension. An impairment in attention and working memory systems may explain tangential speech and poor discourse comprehension by appealing to a disturbance in concentration that disrupts organizing and recalling verbal information.

Most authorities associate discourse-level impairments with right hemisphere damage (Joanette, Goulet, Ska, & Nespoulous, 1986; Myers, 1999). However, several caveats must be mentioned along with that generalization. First, many of the studies that have explored discourse-level deficits have compared patients with right hemisphere damage with patients without brain damage but did not include control patients with damage to the left hemisphere. Therefore, although we know that right hemisphere damage *does* interfere with discourse, we cannot be sure that left hemisphere damage *does not.* The reason for excluding patients with left hemisphere damage from these comparisons is straightforward: They are frequently aphasic and therefore cannot perform tasks involving story retelling and other discourse productions. Interestingly, when patients with left hemisphere damage can be included in studies of discourse, deficits are noted. Second, most authorities agree that discourse-level deficits are due to other, more basic, cognitive impairments either in attention or activation/suppression of information. Although these basic functions may be associated with the right hemisphere, they are functions that are distributed widely across the brain and involve many different regions working together for smooth functioning. This is perhaps why discourse disorders are associated with damage to widespread regions of the right hemisphere as well as lesions elsewhere in the brain.

Diagnosing Discourse Disorders

Discourse Production

Engaging patients in a conversation or story-telling about their life, education, family, or a vacation is an excellent informal way to assess discourse ability. The clinician can judge if the patient is appropriate in the amount of talking, turn taking, reference, and topic maintenance. Picture description is helpful because, unlike conversation, the topic can be tightly controlled. The limited theme of a picture enables the clinician to judge the patient's ability to integrate specific details and contexts and draw inferences. There are no widely available norms for what details and inferences are normally elicited by specific pictures, but Myers (1999) provides a list of literal and interpretive concepts that are likely to be mentioned in describing a commonly used line drawing (the Cookie Theft picture from the Boston Diagnostic Aphasia Exam; see Figure 4.3 in Chapter 4) as well as some Norman Rockwell illustrations. For the Rockwell illustrations, Myers (1999) presents the percentage of patients without brain damage along with patients with right hemisphere damage who mentioned several specific concepts, illustrating substantial variability in both healthy individuals and patients. Therefore, there are no clear criteria to identify abnormal performance. A disadvantage to using pictures is the fact that many patients with right hemisphere damage have visual inattention and/or neglect (see Chapter 8), which may interfere with their ability to attend to and/or see the stimuli.

Discourse Comprehension

Story comprehension protocols assess the patients' ability to understand explicit and implied information in paragraph-length verbal material. Typically, story comprehension is assessed by presenting to the patients a written or spoken story, asking them a series of questions about the story, and asking them to summarize and discuss the story. Answers to questions indicate whether the patients understand, can recall, and draw inferences from the narrative. The Reading Comprehension Battery for Aphasia (LaPointe & Horner, 1998) assesses discourse comprehension through reading and includes questions addressing both factual and inferential information, as in the following example, which provides a paragraph for the patient to read followed by two multiple-choice questions asking about factual information presented in the paragraph and two questions asking about information that was not stated but could be inferred from the text:

Paragraph:
   Snoring sounds are made by vibration of the soft palate at the back of the mouth. More men snore than women, because more men sleep on their backs, a position that is more likely to produce snoring. Though there is nothing physically wrong with loud snorers, many have black and blue ribs.

Factual questions:
   Snoring sounds are made by the: *teeth/soft palate/gums*
   Most snoring is done by: *women/men/neither*

Inferential questions:
   One way to stop snoring is to: *play soft music/be very quiet/wake the person up*
   The one most likely to snore would be a: *man sleeping on his back/woman sleeping on her side/man sleeping on his bed*

Treatment of Discourse Deficits

Treatment for discourse structure deficits involves using pictures and stories to elicit narratives. The patient's task is to interpret succinctly and accurately the pictures or verbal information to arrive at a theme, avoid tangential remarks, and maintain thematic cohesion. The clinician provides models and cues to inhibit tangential output.

One useful technique to elicit main themes is to have a patient read short news summaries and stories or even look at complex pictures and arrive at a single sentence title. This requires extracting important information and ignoring less important information.

Story continuations also provide a format to practice appropriate discourse structure. The patient reads a short story and produces a short ending. The endings can be selected in a multiple-choice format initially and be self-generated at a more advanced level. This activity requires extracting and tracking key discourse facts and inferences to provide a coherent ending.

Justine was racing through the hospital to the emergency room. Her son, Rob, had had an accident and she didn't know what his condition was. When she got there, she was met by her husband, and she immediately asked him_____

Multiple choice responses	Rating
How is Rob?	Appropriate, related, plausible
How are you?	Related, plausible
How was your day?	Related, inappropriate
Where's the cafeteria?	Unrelated, inappropriate, implausible

(Myers, 1999, p. 230)

There is a range of exercises designed to heighten awareness of discourse structure by having the patient monitor and correct discourse problems. This can be done by having the patient review written materials that contain obvious discourse errors, including tangential material and ambiguous references. The patient's aim is to identify the problem, describe what is wrong, and then correct it. Not all patients will be able to perform all aspects of this task right away.

NONLITERAL LANGUAGE

When we use the usual word meanings to interpret a sentence, we derive a literal meaning. But utterances often have nonliteral interpretations as well—meanings that are conventional or idiomatic and cannot be derived from analysis of the usual meanings of the words. This is true for (a) **idioms,** such as "She's got him eating out of her hand"; (b) **ironic** or **sarcastic** statements, such as saying "That's great" with sarcastic intonation to convey that something is horrible; and (c) **indirect requests,** such as saying "This food needs some salt" as way of requesting someone to pass the salt shaker. In these cases, a correct interpretation must disregard or go considerably beyond the literal meanings of words to arrive at the nonliteral or figurative meaning.

We do not understand how we correctly arrive at nonliteral interpretations. Some experts think that a listener derives both the literal and nonliteral meanings, compares them to the context for appropriateness, and then selects the most appropriate meaning. So in the case of hearing *John kicked the bucket,* we would compute both the literal meaning, *John hit a pail with his foot,* and the nonliteral meaning, *John died,* and decide which one is most likely given

the context. This probably happens when we encounter an unfamiliar nonliteral expression such as *She had the face of a queen* or *She had a laugh made of spikes.* However, it is also likely that in at least some instances, particularly with very familiar phrases, we derive the nonliteral interpretation initially without first accessing the literal meaning (Gibbs, 2002; Recanati, 1995). For instance, because of our familiarity with the idiom "kick the bucket," coupled with the fact that we rarely talk about people actually kicking buckets, we may not even attempt a literal interpretation or analysis of the phrase but process the whole phrase more or less like a single word, meaning *die.* In addition to context and frequency of expression, we also use prosody to help us choose a literal or nonliteral interpretation. Van Lancker et al. (1981) showed that speakers make more pauses and use local pitch contours to convey the literal meaning of ambiguous sentences, such as *He was skating on thin ice.*

Age-Related Changes in Nonliteral Language

There is now a growing literature on the neuropsychology of **nonliteral language,** with particular emphasis on the development and neuropsychology of idioms and proverbs (Cacciari & Tabossi, 1993). We know, for instance, that the production and comprehension of idioms develop much later than abilities to produce and understand literal language (Kempler et al., 1999; Nippold, Uhden, & Schwarz, 1997). In production, children can speak in full grammatical sentences and even complete sentence frames logically by the time they are 3 and 4 years old, but they cannot accurately complete familiar idioms and proverbs often until they are 9 or 10 years old. Even a cursory perusal of 7- and 8-year-olds' proverb completion demonstrates a dissociation between good literal language and reasoning abilities versus poor knowledge of idioms and proverbs (e.g., Don't cry over _____ "a cliff—you might fall in"; If the shoe fits _____ "then, I'll keep them"; A bird in the hand _____ "might fly away").[1] In comprehension, children understand literal sentences well by the time they are 3 years old but perform randomly on idiomatic expressions of the same length and grammatical complexity until about 10 years old (Kempler et al., 1999). Children do not reach adult proficiency with idiom comprehension until about age 15. The very late development of nonliteral language might be due to (a) limited exposure to particular expressions in the early years and (b) limited conceptual maturity necessary to understand the complex meanings of these expressions. Furthermore, if literal and nonliteral language are subserved by different cerebral hemispheres (see below), the different rates of development of the hemispheres may also play a role (e.g., Corballis & Morgan, 1978).

Only a few studies have looked at the production and comprehension of nonliteral language in later adulthood. Kempler, Van Lancker, and Read (1988) found no decrement in idiom comprehension in older adults. Nippold et al. (1997) found a slight decrement in proverb explanation for adults in their 70s compared with younger adults, but these differences could be attributed to lower educational level of the older population rather than age.

Although I know of no formal studies, it is clear that idioms enter and leave the language relatively quickly; therefore, there are bound to be substantial cohort effects that will determine what idioms are known to what generations. For example, I suspect that idiomatic phrases such as "the sun is over the yardarm," "I like the cut of your jib," and "he bought the farm" are more familiar and meaningful to older generations, whereas "it's raining cats and dogs," "she's driving me up the wall," and "I'm seeing stars," will be relatively more interpretable to younger generations. This suggests that any testing of frozen, idiomatic, or proverbial phrases across the generations must be careful to establish cohort familiarity before interpreting errors as deficits.

Behavioral Characteristics, and Neuropathology of Nonliteral Language Deficits

Literal interpretation of nonliteral utterances is frequently used for humor, as when someone answers yes to the conventional indirect request, *Do you know what time it is?* However, it is not so funny when patients with brain damage take things literally, which they often do.

Many authors have shown that patients with brain damage have a difficult time interpreting idioms and proverbs in a verbal explanation or multiple-choice format (Kempler et al., 1999; Tompkins, Boada, & McGarry, 1992; Winner, Rosenstiel, & Gardner, 1977) (see Figure 6.1).

Many things can go wrong on the way to a nonliteral interpretation. Because nonliteral interpretations are often cued by nonlinguistic context, inattention or insensitivity to these contextual cues could lead to a literal interpretation (Molloy, Brownell, & Gardner, 1990). As mentioned earlier, nonliteral meanings are also often cued by prosodic contours (Van Lancker et al., 1981), and any impairment perceiving prosodic cues might interfere with deriving nonliteral interpretations.

If listeners typically derive both the literal and nonliteral meanings, compare them to the context for appropriateness, and then select the right one, that process could break down at a number of points. If patients are either not able to activate multiple meanings initially or are not able to suppress the inappropriate meaning, they will have difficulty arriving at the correct interpretations. Tompkins et al. (1992) measured how long subjects took to identify words that appeared in an idiom and in an neutral context (e.g., how long it took for them to recognize the word *rat* in the phrase *I smell a rat* vs. *I see a rat*). Patients with unilateral left or right hemisphere damage and healthy older adults were all faster to identify the word in the idiomatic phrase than in the neutral context, and there was no difference between the groups. This contrasted with an idiom explanation task in which both groups of patients with brain damage performed more poorly than the healthy subjects. This indicates that patients with brain damage process idiomatic phrases, at least through the initial stages of recognition, in the same way as healthy subjects as they hear them. This also suggests that the problem is not at the initial stages of comprehension but that the problem occurs later in the process, possibly at the point of deriving a full meaning or in the conscious selection of alternative meanings, as must be done in picture-pointing or verbal interpretation tasks.

Figure 6.1 Sample picture arrays for comprehension test of idiomatic and literal sentence comprehension. A patient would be asked to point to the one of the four drawings that best matches a spoken sentence. In this test, the comprehension of idiomatic phrases is compared to the comprehension of literal phrases of similar length and structure. Sample items from the Familiar and Novel Language Comprehension Test (Kempler & Van Lancker Sidtis, 1996). Top: The idiomatic phrase, "He's got his head in the clouds." Bottom: The literal sentence, "He takes his pets in the car." Drawings by Susan Black.

An impaired **theory of mind** may also account for literal interpretations (Happé, Brownell, & Winner, 1999). Theory of mind is the notion that we all, as we talk, take into account the listener's perspective. That is, we have a "theory" about this person's beliefs, knowledge, motivations, and intentions. These beliefs allow us to make certain decisions and inferences. For instance, if we watch a basketball game together in which your favorite basketball player played a lousy game, and then I say *he played a really great game,* I could expect you to interpret that sentence sarcastically because I know that you know he did *not* play a great game. Communication problems might emerge if my theory of your mind is inaccurate. For instance, if I thought you saw the game, but you did *not,* and therefore have no idea how well or poorly the star played, you might reasonably interpret *he played a really great game* literally. Therefore, my theory of what you know and do not know is crucial in both my decision to use nonliteral language and your success interpreting it. Obviously, if a patient is no longer able to imagine what someone knows or intends, this can cause problems interpreting nonliteral utterances.

The bulk of evidence suggests that nonliteral language interpretation is most problematic for patients with right hemisphere damage (Kempler, et al., 1999; Van Lancker & Kempler, 1987). However, there is growing evidence that both hemispheres contribute to nonliteral language interpretations. For instance, interpreting indirect requests and providing definitions of idioms are equally impaired in patients with right and left hemisphere damage, although probably for different reasons (Molloy et al., 1990; Tompkins et al., 1992). It may be that patients with left hemisphere damage perform poorly due to aphasia, whereas patients with right hemisphere damage perform poorly because of deficits in attention, prosody, and theory of mind.

Diagnosis of Nonliteral Language Deficits

The simplest and most straightforward way to assess nonliteral language is to ask patients to give verbal interpretations of common idioms and/or proverbs (Gorham, 1956). Three difficulties with verbal interpretation of idioms and proverbs are as follows:

- Patients will often give partially correct answers, making it difficult be sure whether they do or do not understand the nonliteral meaning.
- Speech production impairments will interfere with performance.
- Aphasia will interfere with performance, making it hard to tell how much of the problem is due to aphasia versus a nonliteral language impairment.

The first difficulty, ambiguity of patient response, is generally resolved by scoring systems that include several levels of abstractness (see Table 6.3).

The second problem, the interference of speech intelligibility, can be resolved by eliciting answers in a multiple-choice format, using either written explanations or pictures as choices. Verbal multiple-choice formats present the idiom or proverb in writing along with several paraphrases, from which the patient chooses the correct one (Gorham, 1956; Nippold & Haq, 1996). A verbal or written multiple-choice format might give the following possibilities for the proverb "Rome wasn't built in a day": great projects take time (correct); it took many years to construct the Italian capital (concrete); one cannot love and be wise (incorrect); Rome wasn't built to meet today's standards (incorrect) (D. Delis, no date).

In sentence-picture matching, idioms are presented verbally, and the patients are shown two, three, or four pictures and asked to choose the one that depicts the meaning of the idiom (Kempler et al., 1999).

The third problem, distinguishing between aphasic and nonliteral language impairments, can be solved by assessing both literal and nonliteral language in the same format (see Figure 6.1).

Nonliteral language performance is affected by native language status and educational level. Facility with nonliteral language, particularly idioms and proverbs, requires a lifetime of exposure to native speakers and written material and can be seen as part of an individual's crystallized verbal intelligence. Therefore, caution should be used when evaluating nonliteral language of a nonnative speaker or someone with

Table 6.3   Examples of a Guide to Scoring Proverb Interpretations

Proverb	Abstract (2 points)	Semi-abstract (1 point)	Concrete (0 points)
Where there's a will there's a way	• If you have the desire, you can accomplish anything. • If one has determination, he will succeed. • If a person really wants to do a thing, he can.	• If you want to, you can. • If you keep trying, you will succeed. • There's always a solution to your problem. • Determination	• There is always a right way to do a thing. • There is always a way for everything. • A person should be willing to do things.
Let sleeping dogs lie	• Don't stir up old troubles. • Let well enough alone. • Let the past be in the past. • Let people alone when they are not bothering you.	• Don't make troubles. • When one is all right, leave him alone. • Leave bad situations alone. • Leave things as they are.	• Because he might bite. • Let those who don't wish to learn alone. • Be kind to dumb animals.

Source: Adapted from Gorham (1956), a proverbs test for clinical and experimental use, available from Psychological Test Specialists.

limited (e.g., less than ninth grade) education and, as mentioned before, when selecting idioms that are appropriate for the generation/cohort.

Treatment of Nonliteral Language Deficits

Nonliteral language is typically not the central focus of cognitive rehabilitation programs because nonliteral language deficits may not disrupt communication sufficiently to warrant rehabilitation. However, there are exercises, including discussion and drills, to enhance a patient's facility with nonliteral language. Explicit discussion of inference and what nonliteral meanings are, as well as identification of the cues for nonliteral meanings, are good starting points. Idioms and proverbs can be explicitly taught, although each expression is

relatively rare, so improved performance relies on generalization. If patients learn and generalize a limited number of expressions, they may learn and interpret unpracticed nonliteral expressions without guidance. Another approach is to directly treat underlying deficits in theory of mind through discussion of what speakers and listeners in specific contexts know and do not know and how that would affect interpretation of particular utterances. For instance, contexts could be established (as in the basketball player example above) and ambiguous sentences presented; contexts can then be altered to bias a literal or nonliteral meaning.

NOTE

1. Examples courtesy of Elizabeth Tone.

7

VISUOSPATIAL DEFICITS

Chapter Preview

1. What is normal visuospatial function?

Normal visuospatial function underlies our ability to move around in and think about space. It is accomplished through a combination of visual sensation, perception, recognition, exploration, and vision-guided movement.

2. How do peripheral visuospatial functions develop and change with age?

By 6 months of age, a child has visual acuity comparable to an adult. Visual deficits occur in a large number of otherwise healthy individuals due to changes in the eye, including presbyopia, cataracts, glaucoma, and macular degeneration. These deficits create a range of functional impairments, from difficulty reading without glasses to functional blindness. In contrast to the changes that commonly take place in the eye, aspects of visuospatial abilities controlled by the brain change little in otherwise healthy older adults.

3. What are the behavioral characteristics of central visuospatial impairments?

Visuospatial impairments due to brain damage cause a wide variety of deficits, including (a) partial or complete blindness, (b) failure to notice some visual stimuli despite intact vision, (c) difficulty managing one's own body, (d) impairments in managing 'space' immediately around the body, and (e) topographic disorientation. Functional deficits range from occasionally getting lost to requiring full visual assistance.

4. What is the neuropathology of visuospatial impairments?

Because the visual system traverses so much of the brain, damage to many different brain regions causes visuospatial deficits. Right hemisphere damage is likely to cause neglect of left space. Left hemisphere damage is likely to cause oversight of details in viewing complex scenes. The occipital and parietal lobes are particularly important.

5. How are visuospatial disorders diagnosed?

Tests of visuospatial function include assessment of visual acuity, visual attention, and the ability to read, copy, and make sense of complex visual images. Functional assessment of daily

(Continued)

(Continued)

activities involves visuospatial skills such as dressing and finding one's way around a familiar environment.

6. How are visuospatial disorders treated?

Restorative therapy includes sensory stimulation, practice in visual scanning and functional tasks such as map reading. Compensatory strategies might include using written notes to remind patients to do important tasks, and rearranging the environment to facilitate movement.

VISUOSPATIAL FUNCTION

Visual function involves both peripheral and central components.

Vision begins when light enters the eye and is bent (refracted) by the **cornea** and the **lens** to focus images on the photoreceptor cells of the **retina.** The **macula**, the middle of the retina, contains at its center a specialized region particularly dense in photoreceptor cells, used for high visual acuity, called the **fovea.** The retina contains two types of receptor cells—rods and cones—that function to turn light energy into action potentials. Rods are sensitive to dim light and are used mainly for night vision. Cones mediate color vision and are better suited to function in bright light. Within the retina, the rods and cones stimulate bipolar cells, which in turn stimulate ganglion cells. The axons of the ganglion cells exit the retina and form the optic nerve, which takes the information to the brain.

The optic nerves from each eye partially cross at the **optic chiasm** (Greek: *cross-piece*). This partial crossing results in information from both eyes entering both cerebral hemispheres. Nerve fibers from the portion of the retinas closest to the nose represent the **temporal half-fields** and cross; the fibers from the lateral potions of the retinas represent the **nasal half-fields** and do not cross. This results in information from the **left visual field** of each eye being transmitted to the right hemisphere and information from the **right visual field** of each eye being transmitted to the left hemisphere (Figure 7.2).

The fibers in front of the optic chiasm are called **optic nerves;** fibers behind it are referred to as the **optic tracts.** The optic tracts continue to the left and right lateral geniculate nuclei of the thalamus, where they stimulate other nerve cells in a topographic pattern representing the information from the visual fields. Neurons from the thalamus give rise to fibers that form the **geniculocalcarine tract,** also called *optic radiations,* which takes information to the primary visual areas of the occipital lobes (Brodmann area 17). The primary visual cortex is sometimes called the **striate cortex** because of a characteristic horizontal stripe of white matter within the gray matter, particularly notable in the areas around the calcarine fissure on the medial side of the occipital lobe. At all levels from the retina to the visual cortex, visual images are inverted and reversed. In the visual cortex, this means that the upper part of the visual field is represented below the calcarine fissure and the lower part of the visual field above the calcarine fissure.

In addition to the primary sensory cortex, visual information is also transmitted to what are called the secondary or visual association areas, located in regions adjacent to the primary visual cortex: the peristriate cortex and the inferior temporal and middle temporal gyri (Mesulam, 2000b).

Generally, the further along in the visual system a neuron lies, the more complex the visual stimulus must be to excite it (Kolb & Whishaw, 1996). Although neurons in the primary visual cortex respond to the presence of light, neurons in the visual association areas respond to complex stimuli such as light of a particular orientation, motion in a specific direction, or stimuli of a particular shape. The visual association areas are further divided into two separate systems: a **ventral visual system,** located in the occipital-temporal regions, and a **dorsal visual system** in the dorsal occipital-parietal region (see Figure 7.1). The ventral system appears specialized to process and recognize objects, faces, and words, called the "what" system. Deficits in this system often lead to visual agnosia—difficulty recognizing familiar objects and people—which is discussed in detail in Chapter 8. The dorsal system appears to process spatial information, including the ability to reach toward visual targets and visual search, often called the "where" system (Mesulam, 2000b). Heteromodal association areas throughout the brain provide connections between visual areas and nonvisual cortical regions, integrating vision with other cognitive and motor functions. These association areas are called *heteromodal* because they integrate different types of information, including vision, motion, and language (Greek: *hetero* = other; Latin: *modus* = manner).

It is appropriate to make a distinction here between *sensation* and *perception.* Sensation typically refers to a basic description of how the sense receptors are stimulated, the physiological responses to stimulation, and neural pathways that are involved. Our perception that accompanies sensory stimulation is affected by many factors, including our prior experience of these stimuli and sensations, as well as the context in which they are perceived. Perception is a product of the neocortex, where basic neural information is integrated with other information.

Age-Related Changes in Peripheral Visuospatial Function

At birth, vision is the least developed of the senses, but by age 4 months, infants respond to their mother's facial expression and recognize their mother's photograph. By 6 months, their visual acuity approaches 20/20 (Berger, 1988). Changes in vision that most commonly accompany healthy aging are associated with changes in the eye, not the brain (Christiansen & Grzybowski, 1999). Unfortunately, these peripheral changes are common and can significantly interfere with visuospatial function. Four changes are particularly frequent.

Presbyopia (Greek: *old vision*) is the reduced ability of the older eye to accommodate or adjust focus to see objects clearly at any distance. This is normally accomplished by contraction of small ciliary muscles that change the shape of the lens, which focuses the image on the retina. With age, the cornea becomes flatter and loses refractive power, and this requires more lens adjustment. Simultaneously, the lens loses elasticity, compounding the problem and making it difficult to adjust focus for different distances. By age 45 or 50, most people have noticed a decrease in accommodation and have difficulty focusing at near distances. Corrective lenses are commonly used to compensate for this nearly universal problem.

Cataract refers to any decrease in the transparency of the lens. Cataracts restrict the amount of light that can pass through the lens. Cataracts begin by the time people are age 30 and progress over time at various rates to cause dim vision and eventually blindness. Surgical cataract extraction, done on an outpatient basis, is the most commonly performed operation in the United States. After cataract excision, an artificial lens is put in place, which restores excellent vision in the vast majority of cases.

Glaucoma is the buildup of pressure within the eye. If the drainage ducts for the aqueous humor are blocked, pressure builds up within the eye, eventually pushing the lens into the posterior chamber. This pressure can cause damage to the retina, affecting the periphery of the retina first. If left untreated, it can result in tunnel vision. Treatment is usually successful with either surgery or medication to allow normal drainage.

Macular degeneration is the most common cause of blindness in the elderly and also the least treatable. There are more than 200,000 new cases in the United States each year, and it occurs most frequently in the seventh decade of life. Macular degeneration is age related, but otherwise the cause is unknown. Degeneration of the macula results in impaired central vision and interferes dramatically with reading and writing, although patients can perform many other daily activities without difficulty. Only a small number of cases are treatable with laser photocoagulation (Rechtman, Ciulla, Criswell, Pollack, & Harris, 2002).

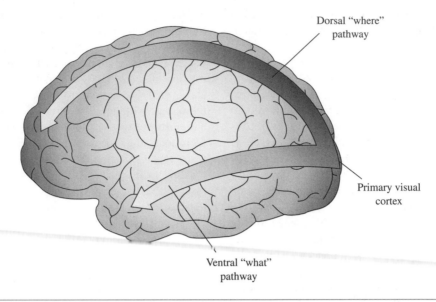

Dorsal "where" pathway

Primary visual cortex

Ventral "what" pathway

Figure 7.1   Two visual pathways. "Where" information travels from the primary visual cortex in the occipital lobe dorsally through the parietal lobes. "What" information travels from the primary visual cortex in the occipital lobe ventrally through the temporal lobes. Both streams converge in the frontal cortex.

BEHAVIORAL CHARACTERISTICS AND NEUROPATHOLOGY OF VISUOSPATIAL IMPAIRMENTS

Visual impairment is one of the most frequent disorders following focal brain injury. In fact, *sudden trouble seeing in one or both eyes* is one of the five National Stroke Foundation's warning signs of stroke. Because the visual system involves so much of the brain, damage to many different regions can create visual impairment. On the positive side, because vision is represented in so many regions of the brain, focal brain damage generally affects only part of the visual system and therefore frequently causes partial, rather than total, vision loss.

Impairments in the use of vision and space are referred to as **visuospatial, visuoperceptual,** or **visuoconstructive** deficits and are sometimes called impairments in **spatial cognition** or **spatial behavior** (Benton & Tranel, 1993; Bradshaw & Mattingley, 1995; Kolb & Whishaw, 1996). This chapter covers five types of visuospatial deficits: (a) blindness and visual field defects, (b) visual neglect, (c) constructional deficits, (d) disorders of body schema, and (e) topographical disorientation. Although

these five deficits are theoretically distinct, they often co-occur, affect one another, and all disrupt a patient's ability to move about in and use space.

Blindness and Visual Field Defects

For the purposes of discussing visual loss, it is useful to talk about **visual half-fields.** Each eye has two half-fields: the *temporal half-field,* the area of vision toward the side, and the *nasal half-field,* the area of vision toward the center, or nose. The pattern of visual field defect, colloquially called a *visual field cut,* depends entirely on where along the visual pathway the damage occurs. Damage to the retina or optic nerve of one eye causes **monocular blindness** (i.e., loss of vision in both half-fields of that eye). Because of the anatomy of the visual system, damage at or behind the optic chiasm frequently produces **hemianopia** (Greek: *half-blindness*), loss of sight in one visual half-field. Damage at the optic chiasm, severing the crossing fibers, produces **bitemporal hemianopia,** loss of vision in both temporal half-fields. A lesion to one side of the optic chiasm causes ipsilateral **nasal hemianopia,** loss of vision in the nasal half-field on the same side as the lesion. Damage at any point along the optic tract or in the lateral geniculate body of the thalamus typically causes contralateral **homonymous hemianopia,** loss of vision in the half-fields of both eyes on the side opposite the lesion. Therefore, damage to the *right* optic tract creates blindness in the temporal (i.e., *left*) half-field of the left eye and the nasal (i.e., *left*) half-field of the right eye, impairing vision in the left half-fields of both eyes. Because damage to many areas can cause homonymous hemianopia, it is the most common type of visual field defect. If a lesion destroys only part of one optic tract, only a portion of the half-field will be affected, creating a **quadranticanopia,** affecting either the top or bottom of the contralateral half-field (see Figure 7.2).

Damage beyond the optic tracts, in the cortical lobes themselves, causes different types of visual problems, depending on whether the lesion is in the primary or association cortex. Small lesions in the primary visual areas of the occipital lobe can produce small blind spots or **scotomas,** often sparing macular (central) vision. More severe cortical damage can cause total blindness, appropriately called **cortical blindness.**

Sometimes, cortical blindness is accompanied by a mismatch between the actual visual defect and awareness of the visual impairment. **Anton's syndrome** is cortical blindness accompanied by a denial of blindness. **Blindsight** refers to the phenomenon of a cortically blind patient being able to perform some visual tasks, such as pointing to flashes of light in his or her blind visual field. These conditions are often transient. The neuroanatomical basis of the sense of being able to see in Anton's syndrome and the preserved ability to perform limited visual tasks in blindsight are unclear but are probably due to intact retinal function and some visual pathways connecting the eye with the parietal cortices, giving the patient at least some of the cortical signals typical of looking and seeing despite severely impaired vision (Damasio, Tranel, & Rizzo, 2000).

The functional consequences of visual field defects are obvious: Some things are not seen. If the visual field defect is only a scotoma, the natural and constant small scanning eye movements (called *nystagmus*) may actually fill in the defect, and it is hardly noticed. However, a homonymous hemianopia, affecting half-fields of both eyes, will interfere with seeing objects placed on the blind side, particularly in the contralateral temporal half-field. The degree to which the impairment is functionally debilitating depends, to a large extent, on how aware a person is of the deficit. Those patients who are aware of the deficit can compensate for it by consciously scanning the visual environment. Interestingly, awareness of the deficit varies with the hemisphere that is damaged: Patients with right hemisphere damage and left visual field defects tend to be less aware of the deficit than patients with left hemisphere damage and right visual field defects. This raises questions about the ability of patients to direct their attention to portions of space and the notion of visuospatial neglect.

Visual Neglect/Visual Inattention

Neglect is a general term used to describe failure to respond to information presented on the side opposite of the brain lesion (Myers, 1999). Although the observed behaviors can be similar to a visual field defect, neglect is a distinct clinical phenomenon. Visual field defects are impairments in visual sensation, whereas neglect is a deficit in attending to information on one side. To put it another way, visual field defects are impairments in seeing, and visual neglect is an impairment in looking and exploring (Mesulam, 2000a). In practice, it can be very difficult to distinguish a visual field defect from visual neglect. This is because some of the prominent symptoms are the same and the two impairments often co-occur. The common and prominent behavioral characteristics of both visual field defects and visual neglect are failure to react to or notice words, objects, and people on the side of space contralateral to the lesion. Therefore, patients with either a left homonymous hemianopia or left-sided neglect will only read words on the right side of the page and/or ignore objects placed on their left.

However, several other symptoms help to distinguish a visual field defect from unilateral neglect. First, patients with neglect often deny or minimize their problems. Denial of deficit—called **anosognosia**—can manifest itself in subtle ways. A patient may dismiss a problem

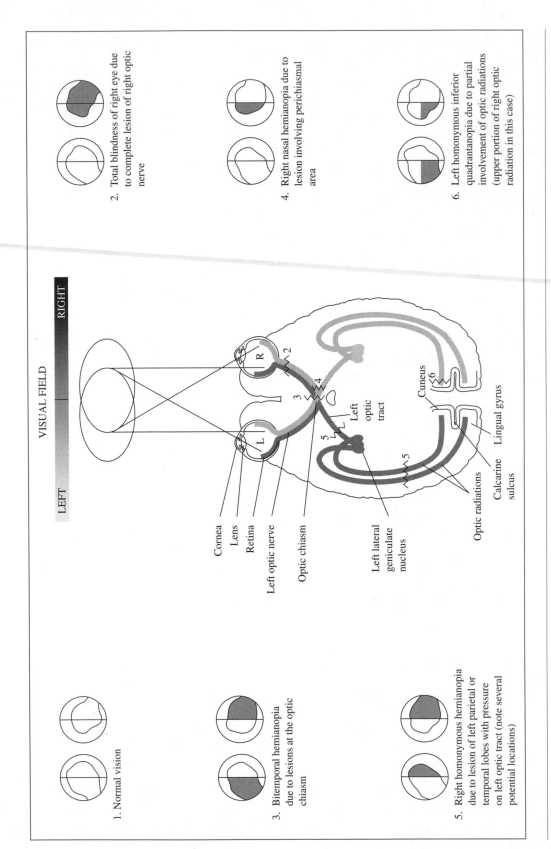

Figure 7.2 Visual defects caused by damage at various locations within the visual system.

reading the leftmost portions of sentences by saying, "I never did like to read, I guess I need new glasses" (Myers, 1999) or "I have my glasses, but they aren't working very well." However, occasionally, the deficit is so obvious to all around that the denial is shocking, as when patients deny that there is anything wrong with their own hemiplegic leg or arm or even deny that their own hemiplegic limb is their own (Sacks, 1990; see also the section on unilateral body neglect later in this chapter).

Second, and related to denial of deficit, patients with neglect tend not to compensate for their deficits. Patients with a visual field defect without neglect are aware of the problem and may develop compensatory strategies and use other cues to make up for the visual impairment. For instance, a patient with a left visual field defect may volitionally scan the left side to compensate for the visual field defect. Likewise, even though they may not be able to easily see their left shoe to tie the lace, they know that they have two shoes and will therefore remind themselves to look over to the left to attend to the left shoe. However, patients with neglect, because they are often not aware of the problem, generally do not spontaneously compensate for the impairment. Even prompting them to look over to the affected side is of little help if their neglect is severe. For patients with visual neglect, the affected side of space simply does not exist.

A third difference is that unilateral neglect is often not restricted to visual impairment but also extends to other senses and movement. Patients with unilateral neglect, even without hemiplegia, may fail to move one side of their body, letting their neglected arm fall by their side; they may also drag a foot while walking, not use the neglected hand to eat, and not use neglected limbs for balance. They may also ignore auditory information coming from the neglected side.

Because neglect is not due to sensory impairment, explanations are cognitive in nature. The most convincing explanations of unilateral neglect come from theories that explain the phenomenon by either impaired mental representation of space or impaired attention. Theories of impaired mental representation presume that the left side of space is mentally represented in the right cerebral hemisphere and that right space is represented in the left hemisphere. When one hemisphere is damaged, the representation of contralateral space is impoverished to the point that patients do not know that side of space exists. Several experiments support this theory. Perhaps the most ingenious and often reported study of mental representation in patients with neglect comes from Italy. Bisiach and colleagues (Bisiach, Capitani, Luzzatti, & Perani, 1981; Bisiach & Luzzatti, 1978) asked several patients with neglect to recall details of a city plaza in Milan. Crucially, the task does not involve any actual vision—performance is based only on mental representations. The patients described the plaza twice, once from the vantage point of facing the cathedral and once from the vantage point of their backs to the cathedral. From both perspectives, they reported more details on the right side. Because some details were described when facing one direction but not the other, the omission of details is not due to memory impairment. Rather, the authors propose that the defect is an impoverished mental representation of space on one side. Hornak (1992) asked patients with neglect to search a dark room to find out if a light was present and obtained a similar result. Control subjects searched the entire space, but patients with left neglect searched only the right side of the room. This indicates that even in the absence of visual input, exploration of the left side of space is diminished.

An alternative theory posits that neglect is due to impaired attention. That is, patients have full mental representations, but they are not attending to parts of them. This is supported by the fact that cueing a patient to look toward the neglected side improves performance in both mental image and external visual tasks (Riddoch & Humphreys, 1987a, 1987b, 1987c).

Although both of these models of neglect have found some empirical support, there is growing evidence that neglect cannot be accounted for by a unitary deficit of representation or attention. Rather, neglect emerges from multiple impairments in representation and attention as well as from deficits in arousal and possibly other cognitive domains (Mesulam, 2000a).

Unilateral neglect occurs after damage to either the right or the left hemisphere, although it is more frequent, more severe, and longer lasting with right hemisphere lesions. The incidence of neglect ranges from 31% to 66% after right hemisphere damage and 2% to 15% after left hemisphere damage (Myers, 1999). Neglect is most commonly associated with damage to the inferior and posterior portions of the right parietal lobe (Vallar, 1993). However, neglect has also been reported after frontal lobe, thalamic, and basal ganglia lesions. Larger lesions involving the parietal lobe and frontal or subcortical areas are generally associated with more severe and longer lasting neglect.

One of the mysteries of neglect is why it is more prominent after right than left hemisphere lesions. One theory of neglect posits that (a) each cerebral hemisphere directs attention to contralateral space, and (b) the right hemisphere has additional attentional capacity that enables it to attend to both left and right space (see Figure 7.3). In this model, damage to the left hemisphere impairs ability to attend to right space, but the right hemisphere, because of its superior attentional capacity, can somewhat compensate for this. This explains the less frequent and severe nature of neglect after left hemisphere lesions. Right hemisphere damage diminishes the ability to attend to left space, and because the left hemisphere is "attentionally challenged," it cannot compensate by directing attention to the ipsilateral (left) side, resulting in severe left-sided neglect.

Data from both healthy adults and patients with brain damage support this theory. Heilman and Van Den Abell (1980) used electroencephalograms (EEGs) to measure each hemisphere's involvement in attention. In the experiment, healthy subjects saw a red light in either the left or right visual field just prior to seeing a green light in center vision. They were asked to press a switch as soon as they saw the green light. Paying close attention to the red *warning* signal speeds reaction time because it prepares the brain for the green light. The authors found that the left parietal lobe reacted most to right-sided warning signals, but the right parietal lobe responded equally to left- and right-sided warning lights. These data suggest that the right parietal lobe dominates attentional processes. In their words,

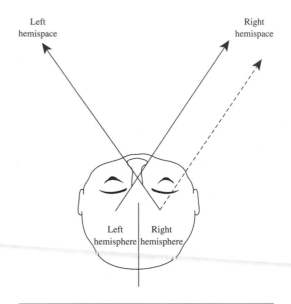

Figure 7.3   The left and right hemispheres direct attention toward the contralateral hemispace (solid lines). The right hemisphere has some capacity to attend to ipsilateral (right) hemispace as well (dotted line). When the left hemisphere is damaged, the right hemisphere can compensate by attending to the right hemispace, resulting in relatively rare and/or minimal neglect. However, when the right hemisphere is damaged, because the left hemisphere lacks a similar capacity to compensate, left-sided neglect is relatively common and severe.

The right parietal lobe attends to stimuli presented to both the right and the left sides, and if there was a lesion of the left parietal lobe, the right parietal lobe could continue attending to ipsilateral (right-sided) stimuli. However, because the left parietal lobe cannot attend to ipsilateral stimuli as well as the right parietal lobe can, lesions of the right parietal lobe are more likely to induce a more profound contralateral sensory inattention than lesions of the left parietal lobe. (Heilman & Van Den Abell, 1980, p. 328)

Evidence for greater involvement of the right hemisphere in attentional abilities also comes from experiments with patients with brain damage. Bub, Audet, and Lecours (1990) asked patients with no brain damage, left hemisphere damage, and right hemisphere damage to press a button as soon as they heard a tone, which appeared at variable intervals. The experimenters wanted to know if damage to either hemisphere slowed down response times or altered the ability of the patients to pay attention to the tones. They found that brain damage slowed down reaction times but did so equally for both the groups of patients with left and right hemisphere damage. Hemispheric differences appeared in the pattern of responses over the course of the experiment. The patients with no brain damage and left hemisphere damage both got faster as the experiment progressed. However, the patients with right hemisphere damage actually slowed down and became more variable over the course of the experiment. The authors concluded that right hemisphere damage impaired the ability to sustain attention.

Although neglect may indeed be due to, at least in part, impaired attention, we would then need a clear definition of attention, a difficult and thorny topic (see Chapters 10 and 11). One thing is clear about the nature of attention: It is not a single ability. The ability to attend to stimuli requires sufficient arousal and awareness, as well as the ability to direct or focus attention, ignore irrelevant information, and sustain focus over time. It is likely that each of these aspects of attention can be selectively impaired by damage to specific brain regions and has distinct effects on performance. At this point, the data are insufficient to make strong claims about localization with respect to attentional subcomponents (see also Chapter 9).

Other Visuospatial Disorders

Visual field defects and visual neglect are the most obvious, the most common, and among the most debilitating visuospatial deficits, but there are others. This section summarizes three categories of common and functionally disruptive problems of visual processing, divided roughly into three domains of space: the body, the "grasping space" immediately surrounding the body, and the rest of the world.

The Body

To move successfully through our environment, we develop a relatively detailed and accurate **body schema** or **body image,** a spatial representation of our body parts. This includes semantic information such as body part names, left-right discrimination, relationships between body parts such as the fact that the knee and ankle are both joints, and functional information about body parts—you hear with the ear and see with the eye. Our body schema also includes specific spatial representations, including body part location (the hip is above the knee), proximity information (the foot and ankle are contiguous), boundary information (the finger ends at the third knuckle), and part/whole information (the nose is part of the face). The most common spatial disruptions of body schema after brain damage are (a) unilateral body neglect, (b) left-right disorientation, (c) body part agnosia, and (d) dressing apraxia. Most disorders of body schema are associated with a breakdown in other cognitive abilities, mainly language and spatial attention.

Unilateral body neglect, also called *personal neglect* and *hemi-asomatognosia,* is the inability to use information from one side of the body. This disorder often accompanies visual neglect, but patients with visual neglect may or may not neglect half of their body and do so to different degrees (Heilman, Watson, & Valenstein, 1993). Patients with body neglect may forget to shave one side of their face, put lipstick on one side of their lips, or dress one side of their body. Severe body neglect can manifest as anosognosia, in which patients do not recognize a left-sided paralysis ("it is tired," "it always was a lazy arm") or even that their own paralyzed limbs belong to them:

> When I was put in bed, this arm was sticking out. I told the nurses and doctors. They think it's my arm, but it's not. That's been sticking out like this ever since I was put in here. . . . It was here when they put me in bed. I always had an idea I was laying on top of a corpse because this hand was lying out there motionless. (Zoltan & Siev, 1996, p. 82)

One story recounted by Sacks (1990) illustrates the potential depth of denial. A patient was found lying on the floor staring at one of his legs. By the patient's account, when he awoke, he found "someone's leg" in the bed—a severed human leg! He explained it to himself by figuring that the hospital staff were drunk and, as a joke, had placed a cadaver leg in his bed. However, he was not humored by the joke and threw the leg out of the bed. But when he threw it out of the bed, he somehow came after it, and now, sitting on the floor, he was discovering that the leg was attached to him: "Have you ever seen such a creepy thing? I thought a cadaver leg was just dead. But this is uncanny! And somehow— it's ghastly—it seems stuck to me." He tried to rip the leg off his body, dissuaded from mutilating it by the doctor. However, the denial was so dense that the physician's calm reasoning with him about the physically obvious fact that this was his left leg had little impact. When the doctor asked, "If this is not your left leg, then where is your own left leg?" the patient replied, "I don't know. I have no idea. It's disappeared. It's gone." Unilateral body neglect most commonly affects the left side following right hemisphere lesions.

Left-right discrimination, as applied to sides of the body, is a verbal-spatial concept that is normally not learned until about 7 years of age and not fully mastered by many otherwise healthy adults. However, if it was mastered, it is often impaired after brain damage. Impairment identifying left and right on one's own body is limited primarily to patients with aphasia, whereas patients who do not have aphasia and even those with right hemisphere damage may have difficulty with identifying left versus right on another person (Benton & Sivan, 1993). Problems with left-right discrimination are most frequently associated with left parietal lobe damage and aphasia, although the impairment in understanding left-right distinctions may be disproportionately severe compared to other aphasic symptoms. It is one of the identifying symptoms of Gerstmann syndrome, a combination of impairments in left-right discrimination, agraphia, acalculia, and finger agnosia (see below) associated with lesions of the angular gyrus.

Body part agnosia, also called **autotopagnosia,** is the inability to recognize body parts. This is demonstrated by not being able to name body parts or to point to body parts when they are named. It can occur without aphasia. For example, a patient with a left parietal lesion made errors when pointing to body parts on himself, a doll, and a photograph of a man. He indicated, for example, the wrist for elbow and at other times made excuses, saying, "I can't

reach that" or "That seems to have disappeared." Interestingly, he could name body parts when the examiner pointed to them, indicating the problem was not due to aphasia. He could also point to parts of a truck, a sink, and an elephant, indicating that the problem was limited to the human body (Ogden, 1985). The inability to identify fingers is a more specific and more common problem than the inability to identify body parts generally. Gerstmann first used the term *finger agnosia* to describe the inability to identify the fingers on one's own hand or another person's hand (Benton & Sivan, 1993). The problem is elicited by finger naming, pointing to a finger named by an examiner, or identifying the finger touched by an examiner either in or out of view. Finger agnosia is associated with poor dexterity (Zoltan & Siev, 1996). Gerstmann identified finger agnosia with the other symptoms of Gerstmann syndrome, linking it to the left angular gyrus.

Dressing apraxia is the inability to dress oneself. The patient with dressing apraxia may put clothes on backwards, upside down, or inside out; may put multiple layers of clothing on; or may be unable to find the correct sleeve of a shirt. Although apraxias are generally considered movement disorders, dressing apraxia appears due to disordered body schema or spatial dysfunction (Denny-Brown, 1958; Fitzgerald, McKelvey, & Szeligo, 2002). Depending on the error, dressing apraxia may be explained by problems sequencing actions, as when a patient puts shoes on before pants; deficits in self-monitoring or executive skills (see Chapter 9), as when a patient puts on several pairs of pants; or difficulty visualizing the relationship of clothing to the body, as when a patient cannot find the appropriate sleeve in a shirt. Sometimes, dressing apraxia can be attributed to unilateral body neglect, as when the patient does not dress the left side of the body or puts both legs in one pant leg. Zoltan and Siev (1996) quote Pehoski's description of a patient with a typical dressing apraxia and hemiplegia who was trying to put on a shirt (Pehoski, 1970):

- The subject was unable to find the correct sleeve. He looked at the shirt in a puzzled manner and finally put his involved arm into a sleeve, but it was the wrong sleeve.

- He then had some difficulty getting the sleeve up the involved extremity, but he finally managed to slide it past the elbow and onto the involved shoulder.

- He then reached around the back as a normal response to find the other sleeve. Since the correct sleeve had not been used at the beginning, the second arm hole was not in back as it should have been, but remained in front. He then came back to the material in front of him and found the second arm hole and put his uninvolved extremity in. The shirt was then on as if it were to be buttoned down the back. He looked puzzled for a moment and then put the material that was in front over his head to the back. Now he had the bulk of the material behind his neck with the two shirt tails hanging over his shoulder in front. Feeling at the back of his neck, he asked, "Where is the collar?" After several seconds of fumbling for the collar and trying to pull the shirt down, he said, "I've fouled up somewhere along the line. The collar is nowhere." (p. 167)

Grasping Space

Visuoperceptual deficits, *constructional* impairments, and Balint's syndrome are examples of visuospatial deficits that dramatically affect behavior in grasping space, the space right around the body.

Spatial perception underlies our ability to interpret and manipulate what we see. Judgment of line orientation is perhaps the purist test of spatial perception and is used to test what are called visuoperceptual deficits. The task deals with very simple stimuli and requires simple responses with minimal movement. Various versions of this simple task exist, but all require patients to determine whether lines are the same or different in slope and orientation. In some tasks, patients are shown two lines and are asked if they are the same or different. In other tasks, they are must "match to sample," selecting from a multiple-choice array the best match to a particular stimulus line. Performance declines slightly with age but significantly with brain damage: Impaired performance is documented in 46% of patients with right hemisphere damage and 10% of patients with left hemisphere damage (see Benton, Sivan, Hamsher, Varney, & Spreen, 1994, for full description and data).

Constructional deficits, or **constructional apraxia,** refer specifically to deficits in copying line drawings, drawing figures, or building constructions out of blocks or sticks. These tasks involve visual perception, spatial organization, and movement. Because constructional deficits are elicited through movement, they often fall under the term *apraxia* (see also Chapter 13). But because the problem is primarily in reproducing spatial arrangement of elements, it is included here as a visuospatial deficit. The errors made in constructional tasks depend on the task and the location of brain damage. Patients with right hemisphere damage often neglect the left side of the construction, possibly due to hemianopia, visual neglect, or both. Their drawings are likely to include details but miss the overall structure or gestalt of the image, lack perspective, and not have any overall plan for using the space on the page. In contrast, patients with left hemisphere damage will often produce copies or drawings that capture the overall idea but err on the internal details. Their drawings are often very simple with features omitted (Lezak, 1995; Zoltan & Siev, 1996). Some of these differences are illustrated in Figure 7.4. Constructional apraxia is a common disorder, affecting approximately half of all subjects with a unilateral lesion (Benton, 1967), and is frequently associated with parietal lesions. It is equally common following parietal lesions on both sides of the brain (Benton & Tranel, 1993).

Balint's syndrome is a rare visuospatial impairment generally arising from bilateral damage to the lateral parietal and occipital lobes (Cummings & Mega, 2003). Originally described in 1909, it is characterized by three major deficits: a fixed angle of gaze that the patient cannot easily shift; perseveration of eye gaze on a single, prominent stimulus; and optic ataxia. *Optic ataxia* was the term used by Balint to describe a person's difficulty in movements that require continual visual guidance such as grasping an object or pouring liquid into a glass (Kolb & Whishaw, 1996). Although a person with Balint's syndrome might be able to shift eye gaze with verbal prompting, the patient will usually be unable to attend to more than one object, even in visually stimulating picture scenes. This causes difficulty in reading, as the person may

Left hemisphere lesion

Right hemisphere lesion

Figure 7.4   Drawings of a house by a patient with left hemisphere damage (left) and right hemisphere damage (right). Notice the drawing by the patient with left hemisphere damage lacks internal detail, whereas the drawing by the patient with right hemisphere damage lacks overall structure.

become fixated on a single word or letter in a sentence and will be unable to move to subsequent words. Balint's syndrome also appears to cause deficits in depth perception and attribute discrimination and is likely due to the occipital lobe lesions.

The Rest of the World

Topographical disorientation describes difficulty finding one's way around familiar places and learning new routes despite minimal or no basic visual impairments.

We generally navigate space by identifying landmarks or features of places. For example, we know that the Washington Monument is a tall pointed structure with no windows or that the New York library has statues of lions in front. We also use topographic relationships between landmarks; for example, the Washington Monument stands across from the Lincoln Memorial, or the library is behind the lion statues. Together, these elements form a mental map of the world, and they can break down separately (Patterson & Zangwill, 1944). **Topographical agnosia** is disorientation due to failure to recognize landmarks. For example, a person previously familiar with the Washington Monument will see it and fail to recognize it. **Topographical amnesia** is disorientation due to an inability to recall relationships between landmarks. In this case, for example, a person previously

familiar with the buildings surrounding the Mall in Washington, D.C., might recognize the Washington Monument but no longer remember that the Lincoln Memorial stands across from it. Symptoms of topographical disorientation include getting lost in familiar territory, difficulty describing familiar settings such as one's own home, giving directions, describing routes, and locating places on a map. A case description from Meyer and reported by de Renzi (1982) captures the behavioral manifestations:

> Whenever he left his room in the hospital, he had trouble in finding the way back, because at any chosen point of the route he did not know whether to go right, left, downstairs or upstairs (on one occasion, he walked from the main floor down to the basement, instead of going up to the first floor, where his bed was located). When he eventually arrived in front of his own room, he did not recognize it unless he chanced to see some distinguishing feature, such as the black beard of his roommate, or a particular object on the bedside table. . . .
>
> Required to provide verbal information concerning routes or places well known before the disease, he performed fairly well, as long as he could rely on purely verbal knowledge. Thus he was able to give the names of the intermediate stations on the railway line he used daily or the location of the main building of the city. Yet, he met with considerable difficulty when the way

had to be retraced from spatial memory; for instance, when required to tell how he would walk between two sites chosen at random in the city, he could only say the initial street and then he became confused.

He grossly mislocated cities and states on a map of his country as well as of Europe, a task with which he was familiar since he had been a post office clerk. (p. 213)

Topographical disorientation can occur independently of visual field defects and visual neglect, but, of course, visual problems would exacerbate topographical impairment. Deficits in describing familiar routes appear to be relatively rare, affecting only 1% of those with left hemisphere damage, 6% with right hemisphere damage, and 8% with bilateral damage (Benton, Levin, & Van Allen, 1974; Benton & Sivan, 1993). In nonverbal assessments of geographic orientation, such as finding cities and states on a map, the incidence of topographic disorientation is about 22% and is similar in patients with left (20%) and right (25%) hemisphere damage. Topographical disorientation is associated with posterior cortical and occasionally hippocampal damage.

DIAGNOSIS OF VISUOSPATIAL DISORDERS

Visual Field Defects and Visual Neglect

Visual field defects can be assessed in detail by **perimetry.** The subject fixates on a black dot in the middle of a large white field. A small light is moved around the field, and the subject indicates when it can be seen. Performance is mapped on a drawing of the visual fields and indicates the areas of blindness (Kolb & Whishaw, 1996). In a simpler clinical procedure, a clinician, generally a neurologist, will ask a patient to look straight ahead and indicate when he or she can see the clinician's fingers, which move into and around the visual field. Paper-and-pencil tasks are also used to determine the presence and severity of visual field defects and neglect.

The simplest test of visual field defects and visual neglect is line bisection. Patients are asked to put a mark in the middle of an 8- to 10-inch horizontal line, placed at their midline. Healthy subjects get within about ¼ inch of the center on a 10-inch line (Hausmann, Waldie, & Corballis, 2003). Patients with left neglect place their mark to the right of the center, and patients with right neglect do the opposite. Visual field defects and visual neglect can also be screened by line cancellation tasks. Patients cancel or mark each line on a sheet of paper placed at their midline, containing many short, randomly placed lines at different angles. Assuming there are equal numbers of lines to cancel in each hemifield, the number of lines missed in the left versus right hemifield indicates the location and extent of visual defects or neglect. Note, however, that because the patients are not asked to fixate on a center point, they can visually scan the page and compensate for a visual field defect. These tasks are very helpful for assessing neglect, vigilance, visual attention, and visual strategies by observing any patterns in patients' approach to the task. Copying and drawing figures are excellent ways to assess visual field impairment and neglect as well as constructional apraxia. Patients copy or draw a relatively complex picture such as the Rey-Osterrieth figure (see Figure 7.5) or a scene with several objects in it. The number of elements missing or distorted from each side of the product indicates the location and severity of impairment. Drawing common objects such as a flower or a clock, because they are naturally symmetrical, yields helpful information about the use of left and right space.

Performance on these tasks does not distinguish a visual field defect from visual neglect. If a patient is suffering from one and not the other, it should be apparent in other ways. For instance, although patients with a visual field defect and no neglect will often spontaneously compensate for the deficit, patients with a neglect syndrome are more likely to exhibit anosognosia, not correct themselves, and show neglect in other modalities, including motor inactivity on the affected side in the absence of paresis or paralysis (Mesulam, 2000a).

Body Schema Tests

Body schema tests use naming, pointing, and yes/no questions. In body part naming, the examiner points to body parts on herself or

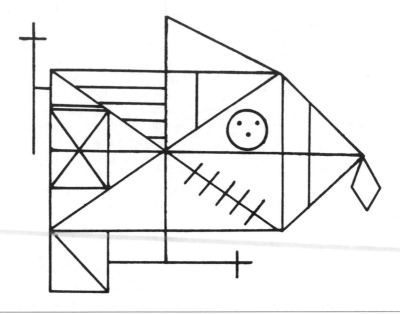

Figure 7.5   The Rey-Osterrieth figure.

himself or on the patient, and the patient names them. To test comprehension, the examiner asks the patient to point to body parts as they are named (e.g., *show me your knees*). Body part visualization and space concepts can be assessed via specific questions (e.g., *Is your mouth above your eyes?*). Finger agnosia is elicited primarily by finger naming (the examiner points to a finger and asks the patient to name it) and by finger identification (e.g., *show me your pinky*). Left-right discrimination is usually tested by having the patient show the examiner various body parts on both himself or herself and the examiner (e.g., *show me your left hand; show me my right eye*). Unilateral body neglect and dressing apraxia are problems that become apparent without explicit testing in the course of a normal day's activities.

Visuoconstruction

Visuoconstruction is assessed by copying, drawing, and building block structures. One of the most popular tools for assessing construction is the Complex Figure Test, also called the Rey-Osterrieth figure (Osterrieth, 1944; Rey & Osterrieth, 1993). This figure (see Figure 7.5) has been well normed (to 70+ years), has several usable scoring systems, is simple to administer,

and is sufficiently complex to elicit a variety of visuospatial deficits (Lezak, 1995). The figure is placed in front of the patient along with a blank sheet of paper. The clinician records how long it takes the patient to copy or reconstruct from memory the figure and tracks the precise order and direction of lines made. Scoring is tabulated by looking for each of 18 elements, giving 2 points for each element that is present and placed properly and 1 point for each element that is either there but not placed properly or distorted and placed properly (Lezak, 1995). The 18 scored elements are as follows:

1. Cross upper left corner, outside of rectangle

2. Large rectangle

3. Diagonal cross

4. Horizontal midline of 2

5. Vertical midline

6. Small rectangle, within 2 to the left

7. Small segment above 6

8. Four parallel lines within 2, upper left

9. Triangle above 2 upper right

10. Small vertical line within 2, below 9

11. Circle with three dots within 2

12. Five parallel lines within 2 crossing 3, lower right

13. Sides of triangle attached to 2 on right

14. Diamond attached to 13

15. Vertical line within triangle 13 parallel to right vertical of 2

16. Horizontal line within 13, continuing 4 to right

17. Cross attached to 5 below 2

18. Square attached to 2, lower left

Performance is relatively constant across age groups. Patients with frontal lobe damage tend to lose track of what has been copied and repeat elements and/or transform a design element into a familiar representation, as when the circle with three dots becomes a *happy face*. Patients with left hemisphere damage tend to break up the design into small units and simplify elements, possibly due to poor motor control with the nonpreferred hand. Patients with right hemisphere damage are more likely to omit elements altogether, possibly due to visual neglect.

Freehand drawing of the human figure, a house, a bicycle, and other familiar objects is also used to elicit constructional deficits. Because freehand drawings lack a model, they make scoring a bit harder because the examiner may not know precisely what was intended. Clock drawing is particularly useful because it involves a very familiar object and allows assessment of several aspects of visuospatial functions. There are considerable normative data from a wide age range (20–90) and from patients with neurological and cognitive impairments on clock drawing. Age does have a significant effect on the task, with the most common errors occurring in those older than age 70 and including incorrect proportion (length) of clock hands and incorrect placement of the minute hand. Patients with right hemisphere damage may omit the outer configuration (circle) and hands, place numbers in a disorganized way or even outside the clock face, and clump numbers together on the right side, whereas the left side of the clock may not be round at all and the left-sided numbers missing or misplaced (Freedman et al., 1994). Patients with left hemisphere damage tend to draw clock faces with fewer details, sometimes omitting many numbers and/or one or both hands, particularly on the right side, or perseverate on numbers (Freedman et al., 1994; McFie & Zangwill, 1960). Patients with frontal lobe damage resulting in executive dysfunction (see Chapter 9) have difficulty planning appropriate spacing and can be easily misled by asking them to set the time to times in which the time of day does not match the relevant numbers on the clock. For instance, a frequent error of this type is elicited by asking the patient to set the time at "10 after 11," which requires recoding "10 after" as the number "2" and then drawing a hand pointing at the "2" with no hand pointing at the "10." Patients with frontal lobe damage have difficulty with this process (Freedman et al., 1994).

Construction abilities are also commonly assessed by the Block Design subtest of the Wechsler Adult Intelligence Scale (Wechsler, 1997a). The patient is given a set of blocks, each having two sides that are red, two sides that are white, and two sides that are half red and half white on a diagonal. The patient is shown a model design constructed out of similar blocks or in picture form and asked to construct the same design with a set of blocks. The test is scored by accuracy and the time it takes to complete each design. Performance is significantly affected by age, with older subjects performing the task much more slowly than younger subjects. Block design performance is commonly and most severely impaired after right parietal lobe lesions. In a block design task, in which the patient must reconstruct a pattern made up of multiple square blocks, patients with right hemisphere damage may begin on the right side and work toward the left, omit a section on the left, rotate some of the blocks, and even lose the overall square pattern of the reconstruction (Lezak, 1995). In contrast, patients with left parietal damage will work from left to right as do healthy subjects but often perform slowly and simplify the design. Patients with frontal lobe damage tend to make mistakes due to impulsivity, not seeing or correcting errors (Lezak, 1995).

Topographical Orientation

Topographical orientation can be tested by having a patient locate prominent cities on an outline map of the country. Lezak (1995) asks patients to write a number to identify particular points (e.g., *Write 1 where the Atlantic Ocean is; 2 for Florida; 3 for Portland*). The places should be familiar to the patient and should include an equal number of places on the right and left sides of the map. When patients have difficulty finding their way around very familiar areas, it may also be worthwhile to have them draw a floor plan of the problem space and compare it with an accurate floor plan.

TREATMENT OF VISUOSPATIAL DISORDERS

Occupational therapists treat visual-spatial disorders, with the goal of improving the patient's ability to accomplish daily activities. Speech-language pathologists treat left neglect as it pertains to reading and writing. In what follows, I describe some common techniques that can be used to facilitate recovery of visual function to compensate for visual impairments.

Visual Field Defects

Visual field defects without neglect can often be overcome relatively easily. In fact, patients often automatically compensate without even realizing that there is a problem. A student recently told me that he just discovered, in a routine eye examination, that he sees nothing in either left half-field—he has left homonymous hemianopia. He has evidently had this problem since birth, and it went undiagnosed because it had not affected his behavior in any obvious way. In retrospect, it may help explain his poor performance in sports, in which keen awareness to balls in peripheral vision is key. Upon neurological examination, a right parietal lesion of unknown etiology explained the defect. Likewise, patients who acquire visual field defects as adults can often compensate well with minimal disruption to function. The process of compensation for a visual field defect by an adult was clearly described by a neuropsychologist (Kolb & Whishaw, 1996). The patient (B.K.) awoke one morning and discovered that he was hemianopic in the left visual field, apparently due to a migraine-induced stroke. For the first 2 or 3 days, the visual field appeared dark, as if he were looking through a piece of smoked glass. On the 4th day, the darkness was replaced with visual noise called a scintillating scotoma. On testing, no points of light were perceived in the blind field. Immediately after the stroke, B.K. was able to read with great difficulty, missing parts of the word on the left side. About 2 weeks after the stroke, he would enter a room and not see people on the left side that he was looking for. In at least one case, the person was there but on the left side of the room talking on a telephone. B.K. assumed that his colleague was not there and therefore left without waiting. The colleague on the phone assumed B.K. had seen him on the phone and gone outside to wait for him. This created a misunderstanding and was annoying and confusing to both parties. Normal reading returned within about 6 weeks as B.K. learned to direct his gaze to the left and upward. Over the period of 4 to 6 months, the area of blindness decreased and acuity improved, but vision remained poor in the left upper quadrant. The blindness was partial insofar as he could identify color and movement but not identify objects placed in the affected field. He slowly returned to playing squash and tennis, again compensating for the field defect. Face recognition was slow. He has learned to compensate by *overscanning* a scene when looking for someone or something (Kolb & Whishaw, 1996).

Visual Neglect/Visual Inattention

Visual neglect is a different matter. It is possible to compensate for unilateral left visual neglect by cues to *look to the left*. Although this verbal cue helps at the moment it is given, it is seldom internalized because for many patients with unilateral neglect, the neglected side of space simply does not exist, and despite reminders, they continue to behave *as if nothing of any importance could be expected to occur there* (Mesulam, 1985). Therefore, the benefit of the verbal cue is tied to the presence of the verbal cue, and because the goal of therapy is functional independence, a transitory cue such as a verbal reminder is not an optimal rehabilitation strategy. As always with focal deficits, it is instructive to see what coping mechanisms patients develop themselves. One patient described by Sacks (1990) suffered a massive stroke affecting the posterior right hemisphere and experienced a severe left neglect. She made up only half of her face and ate only half of the food on her plate. After being continually reminded that the rest of her food was on the left side of her plate, she developed the strategy of turning her wheelchair in a circle to bring into view the remainder of her food, finding this particularly successful "if her portions seem too small . . . or . . . if she cannot find her coffee or dessert." She sometimes had to make two or three rotations because each time she bisected her remaining food, seeing only half. Although

it might seem easier to rotate the plate or simply look to the left, "her looking, her attention, her spontaneous movement and impulses, are all now exclusively and instinctively to the right" (p. 78). This example illustrates that although the more straightforward therapeutic strategies such as cueing someone to look to the left may fail miserably, other, possibly more cumbersome and unintuitive strategies, such as turning a full circle in the opposite direction, can restore a lost part of the world.

1	Visual reminders are helpful in reading. Marks are used to draw the patient's	1
2	attention to the left side of the page. These range from a simple line drawn	2
3	down the left margin as an anchor to more complex guiding cues such as a	3
4	sheet of paper with lines numbered in both the left and right margins to help	4
5	guide the patient to stay on the same line and scan to both margins, matching	5
6	up the numbers at the end of each line (on the right) with the subsequent	6
7	number on the left of the next line (see example and discussion in Chapter 5	7
8	on diagnosis and treatment of reading problems). Restructuring the	8
9	environment is also useful. Objects such as telephones can be placed in the right	9
10	hemispace relative to where the patient likes to sit, to improve the patient's	10
11	success at finding them. It can also be useful to intentionally place objects	11
12	and people in the neglected hemispace to encourage the patient to get in the	12
13	habit of scanning to the left. Repetitive exercises that emphasize leftward	13
14	scanning are used in treatment, including reading words and sentences	14
15	that don't make sense when only the right side is seen, picture recognition	15
16	with items that cannot be recognized by viewing only the right half, scene	16
17	description with elements on both left and right sides, line cancellation, and	17
18	writing. Computer treatment programs present randomly placed targets on	18
19	a screen and provide practice scanning arrays. Because visual neglect is	19
20	likely associated with attentional impairments, treatment may also attempt	20
21	to address underlying inattention (see Chapters 10 and 11).	21

Because anosognosia often accompanies left neglect, therapeutic approaches must initially determine the degree of deficit. Because most therapeutic approaches require the patient's cooperation and participation in working toward a goal, increasing awareness of deficits is often a first step in the rehabilitation of neglect. Explicit discussion and demonstration, even

videotaping the patient to illustrate deficits, can improve awareness of deficits. Several experimental techniques, such as fitting patients with special vision-distorting prism glasses or stimulating the ear canal with cold or warm water (caloric stimulation), appear to improve performance on standard tasks of neglect, but carryover and usefulness in activities of daily living have yet to be shown (Rossi, Kheyfets, & Reding, 1990; Rubens, 1985). Pharmacological treatment, including dopamine agonist therapy, has been found to reduce neglect, although only minimal and equivocal research is available to evaluate the usefulness of pharmacotherapy (Grujic et al., 1998).

Treatment for Body Schema Disorders

Treatment for body schema disorders may be unnecessary, depending on how much they disrupt function. For instance, finger agnosia is frequently identified in a neurological examination but may not be sufficiently disruptive to warrant direct treatment. On the other hand, we should not assume that any deficit, no matter how arcane it seems, is benign without full exploration. For instance, finger agnosia, although it seems unrelated to most daily activities, is often associated with sensory deficits on the fingers that affect dexterity and therefore can affect everything from buttoning shirts to cooking (Zoltan & Siev, 1996). If finger agnosia needs treatment, sensory stimulation of fingers may be appropriate as well as environmental adaptations, such as Velcro shirt closures. Left-right discrimination can be disruptive, particularly in cases where the words *left* and *right* are used in directions. Compensation might involve recommending caregivers to avoid using the terms *left* and *right* and, if necessary, marking left and right objects like shoes with visual cues (e.g., placing red tape on the bottom of the right shoe). Unilateral body neglect, which can affect dressing and self-care, may be treated by sensory stimulation (e.g., rubbing the neglected arm or leg) and by external cues, such as a note on the mirror to remember to shave both sides of the face or a checklist after shaving and dressing to help monitor the neglected side of the body.

Constructional Deficits

Constructional deficits, often documented in nonfunctional tasks such as block design and figure copying, are often exacerbated by visual field defects and neglect and associated with functional impairments in dressing and meal preparation. If visual field defects and neglect are contributing factors, the strategies outlined above would be used to reduce visual field defects and neglect. In addition, practice in nonfunctional tasks, such as building three-dimensional models of blocks, and more functional tasks, such as learning numbered sequences in a table setting, have also been used to treat constructional deficits.

Topographical Disorientation

Treatment for topographical disorientation is naturally tailored to each patient. Once a deficit is clearly identified (e.g., the patient cannot find his or her way to the dining room), a specific set of landmarks such as pictures, icons, or written signs can be designed to facilitate getting about.

8

AGNOSIA: DISORDERS OF RECOGNITION

Chapter Preview

1. What is recognition?

The ability to identify objects and people. Recognition involves perception and recall of previous experiences.

2. How do recognition abilities develop and change with age?

Age-related decreases in vision, hearing, and touch can impair the ability to recognize stimuli. These changes can have functional consequences of decreasing the speed and accuracy of recognizing voices on the telephone, familiar faces on the street, and so forth.

3. What are the behavioral characteristics of agnosia?

Agnosia is the pathological inability to recognize objects or people that cannot be attributed to basic sensory deficits, anomia, or amnesia. Agnosia can affect recognition through any modality. Patients with agnosia have difficulty naming or otherwise demonstrating that they recognize stimuli ranging from a pencil to their own child.

4. What is the neuropathology of agnosia?

Damage to the occipital-parietal regions of either hemisphere can cause agnosia.

5. How is agnosia diagnosed?

Most tests for agnosia ask patients to name objects that are presented in clear view, partially obscured, or shown in an atypical perspective. Special tests of face recognition ask patients to recognize either famous faces or match samples of unfamiliar faces.

(Continued)

(Continued)

6. How is agnosia treated?

Therapy includes drills in sorting and selecting objects from groups, as well as compensation through preserved modalities. For example, a person who no longer recognizes a rose when he sees it will recognize it immediately when he smells it.

What Is Recognition?

You are walking down the street and you see an old friend. You recognize her face instantly and confidently. Your mother calls on the telephone and says "Hi, dear" and you know, even before she has finished the "Hi," exactly who it is. You know this because you recognize the sound of her voice. You reach your hand in your pocket or purse and blindly search for your house key and, with your fingers, recognize and grasp it. These are instances of effortless recognition of familiar objects and people. You also rapidly and accurately recognize hundreds of common but unfamiliar objects every day: You recognize an unfamiliar object as a chair even if you have never seen one just like it; you identify a picture of a dog as a dog even if you have never seen that breed before. You can perform this act of recognition even in difficult circumstances, too, such as recognizing a chair in the unlikely position of being placed not on four feet but tipped over on its back, a word even when it is scrawled in unfamiliar penmanship, or a friend through a screen door.

There are two broadly defined models of the process of recognition: serial and parallel. Serial models assume that there are three stages to recognition: sensation, perception, and cognition (Bauer, 1993; Lissauer, 1890).

- Basic sensory abilities include, for instance, visual awareness of light and dark, visual acuity, perception of movement, auditory threshold, and sensitivity to heat and cold.
- *Perception* can be defined as the active processing of sensation. This includes, for example, discrimination of the number of lines on a page or of different pitches in a melody. Perception also includes identification of similarities, differences, and patterns in the stimuli, allowing us to recognize, for example, that three lines form a triangle or that three sounds constitute a melody.
- The final stage of recognition in this model involves conceptual-semantic processes and relies on the notion of stored mental representations. Mental representations define concepts—for example, cats and dogs are domestic animals with four legs, a tail, and fur.

In this type of model, recognition involves first analyzing sensory stimuli to perceive forms and then matching these perceptions to stored representations. In a sense, we are recalling or remembering the stored representation. When perceptions match a prior experience closely enough, we recognize (*re + cognize;* Latin: *to know again*) the object of the perception. Recognition in this model is therefore matching a particular perception with prior experiences and thereby attaching meaning to it.

Because most sensory stimuli come to our awareness with some meaning already attached, it is sometimes difficult to distinguish the various stages of recognition. For instance, when we see a bright light, we instantly know if it is the sun or a bare light bulb, blurring the boundaries of sensation, perception, and recognition

An alternative to the serial model views recognition as a unitary phenomenon that cannot be easily dissected into component parts. These models of recognition, based on the early work of Gestalt psychology, emphasize the perception of whole units without analysis of parts and make less of distinction between the components of the recognition process. A contemporary version of this model is found in the parallel distributed or integrated models of recognition that do not presume that stored representations exist at all. In these models, previous experience is simply a pattern of neural activity, and when that pattern of neural activity recurs, we recognize the object or person (Damasio, 1989).

AGE-RELATED CHANGES IN RECOGNITION

Because we do not really understand well the psychological mechanisms underlying recognition, it is difficult to describe age-related changes in it. However, we can assume that recognition requires sensory, perceptual, and semantic abilities, whether they take place serially or simultaneously. We can then ask how these component abilities change in healthy aging.

Sensory perception is notoriously affected by aging: Deterioration of hearing and vision is a well-known and relatively well-understood part of the aging process (see Chapters 4 and 7). Deficits in these areas, if severe enough, will undoubtedly affect our ability to recognize visual and auditory stimuli.

At the semantic level, there is little evidence that meaning categories deteriorate in aging (see Chapter 4). However, concepts certainly do develop and change over time. For an object to be recognized, it, or something like it, must have been experienced and categorized before. Therefore, a person's previous experiences are relevant to recognition of objects: An older person might not readily recognize pictures of computer terminals or Rollerblades, having had much less experience with them, not because of a recognition deficit per se.

The many and subtle decreases in sensory perception with age take their toll on recognition, but mostly in terms of speed and efficiency (e.g., Cerella, 1990). Luckily, the decreased efficiency in recognition that accompanies sensory declines in aging can often be compensated for by either devices (hearing aids and glasses) or by reliance on context to fill in the missing perceptual cues.

Young or old, many of us have failed to recognize a friend's face in an unusual context, a familiar flavor in a meal, a well-known song on the radio, or a friend's voice on the telephone. Our recognition can be partial (e.g., we know it is a woman from work, but we do not know her name), and at other times, we successfully recognize someone or something, but we are slow to arrive at the point of recognition. These experiences give us a glimpse into the phenomenon of **agnosia** (Greek: *without knowledge*)—failure to recognize an object or a person. These experiences also illustrate a couple of important aspects of the recognition process. First, recognition is not all-or-nothing; we can have partial and/or slow recognition. Second, recognition is affected by many factors. Seeing work buddies at work helps us to recognize them because of the right context, but hearing a familiar melody in a noisy environment will impede our recognition because the context is distracting. This illustrates the complexity of the recognition process and that it can break down to various degrees for a number of reasons. The term *agnosia* is reserved for pathological cases of recognition failure—frequent, consistent, and persistent failures. Pathological instances of agnosia can often be distinguished from the occasional failure to recognize a colleague, for instance, in the same way that a normal tip-of-the-tongue phenomenon can be distinguished from aphasia: by frequency and severity.

BEHAVIORAL CHARACTERISTICS AND NEUROPATHOLOGY OF AGNOSIA

Agnosia is the failure to recognize objects and people that cannot be attributed to elementary sensory deficits such as blindness or deafness, amnesia, anomia, or unfamiliarity with an object. The person with agnosia perceives adequately, but that perception is *a percept stripped of its meaning* (Teuber, 1968). Agnosia is often modality specific, so that if a patient cannot recognize an object presented visually, he or she can often identify it when allowed to touch or hear it. Agnosia is most commonly described for the visual modality but can appear in both auditory and tactile modalities as well.

Munk (1881) described agnosic behavior in dogs that had undergone bilateral occipital lobe lesions. The dogs avoided obstacles placed in their paths but did not react appropriately to the objects. For instance, they tried to eat stones, defecated in their beds, and ignored other dogs. He called this condition *Seeleblindheit* (mindblindness). Soon after, similar disorders were described in humans. Lissauer (1890) provided the first detailed report of agnosia in man. Lissauer's terminology persists today, despite more than a century of contentious discussions of his views and definitions. He distinguished two stages of recognition, proposing that each stage could be disrupted independently. The first stage was called **apperception,** the conscious perception of a sensory impression—piecing together of separate visual attributes into a whole. He called a problem with this stage *apperceptive mindblindness.* The second stage of recognition was **association,** or linking the perception to a previous experience, thereby giving it meaning. Difficulty with this stage was called *associative mindblindness* (Bauer, 1993). Freud (1891a, 1891b) introduced the term *agnosia,* replacing the term *mindblindness* to emphasize the fact that these disorders were not sensory in nature (i.e., not blindness) but were impairments in recognizing previously known objects.

Despite the fact that agnosia is a relatively rare disorder in focal brain damage, it is striking when it appears by itself, and it is relatively more common as a symptom in cortical dementias such as Alzheimer's disease. When it appears in cortical dementias, due to the context of widespread brain damage and multiple cognitive impairments, it is often difficult to determine what is causing it, either anatomically or cognitively. Therefore, much of our information comes from the many detailed case studies that have been reported since Lissauer's (1890) publication. Unfortunately, each case appears slightly different, and therefore there is still little agreement about the characteristics or neural bases of agnosia. For instance, there are those who maintain that agnosic disorders, particularly visual agnosias, result from a combination and interaction of primary sensory abnormalities, various degrees of inattention, and dementia (Bender & Feldman, 1972), suggesting that there is nothing unitary or unique about agnosia and that we may be able to explain it by looking at the perceptual and cognitive abilities that accompany it. However, many experts still believe that agnosia, as an independent and interesting disorder, exists and

is worth studying, diagnosing, and treating (e.g., Saumier, Arguin, Lefebvre, & Lassonde, 2002).

For the purposes of this discussion, I will describe agnosic behavior in three different modalities—visual, auditory, and tactile—and, when possible, attempt to locate the primary problem generally within the perceptual (apperceptive) or semantic (associative) realms.

VISUAL AGNOSIAS

Patients with **visual agnosia** cannot identify visually presented material. The problem is not one of visual acuity, anomia, or memory lapse. Sometimes, patients mislabel an object they are shown. At other times, they say they do not know what it is. On occasion, they will make excuses for their deficit—for instance, saying that the lighting is poor, that they have not had much experience with the objects, or that the drawings are of poor quality.

Following Lissauer's (1890) original distinction between apperceptive and associative agnosia, several different patterns of agnosia will be described with respect to the degree of impairment in perceptual versus semantic processes.

Perceptually Based Visual Agnosia

One group of patients with agnosia has adequate visual acuity but demonstrates specific perceptual deficits. These patients correspond to Lissauer's (1890) category of apperceptive agnosia. Some patients, for instance, cannot distinguish the difference between shapes: A square and a rectangle of different dimensions appear the same to them, as do two lines of different lengths. Functionally, these patients describe their visual world as "very indistinct and distorted," saying that things look "just like blobs" (McCarthy & Warrington, 1990). One patient with a shape discrimination impairment, when shown a drawing of a carrot, was not able to name the object but was able to describe the details the drawing: "I have not even the glimmerings of an idea. The bottom point seems solid and the other bits are feathery. It does not seem to be logical unless it is some kind of a brush" (Humphreys & Riddoch, 1987, cited in McCarthy & Warrington, 1990, p. 28). This patient was evidently not able to take information about details and mentally organize them into a unified and recognizable shape, a gestalt. It is worth noting that these patients, in their descriptions of their problems, are neither anomic nor amnesic, and they appear to be able to see the details of the objects, even if they cannot make fine shape distinctions.

Another perceptual symptom of patients with agnosia is difficulty attending to more than one object in the visual environment. One patient saw the tip of a cigarette held between his lips but failed to see a match flame offered to him and held several inches away (Bauer, 1993). When describing a picture of a flag, another patient said, "I see a lot of lines, now I see some stars." When describing a dollar bill, the patient said "a picture of George Washington" (Tyler, 1968). These descriptions indicate a deficit in integrating details, even when individual parts are recognized. This is slightly different than the case with the carrot described above because that person could not even accurately identify its subparts. Patients with agnosia with this sort of problem are also easily disrupted by slight movement of the object they are attempting to recognize.

Another symptom of perceptually based visual agnosia is somewhat subtler and is seen only on special testing. Many patients with agnosia have relatively good recognition in daily life but have recognition difficulty in unusual situations. Therefore, presenting atypical views of stimuli disrupts their recognition. This includes stimuli with extraneous lines such as letters with decorative serifs; degraded stimuli, as in drawings with some omitted lines, shadows, or uneven lighting; or objects seen from unusual views, such as a chair shown from above (Figure 8.2) or pictures of object parts in atypical configurations (e.g., Hooper, 1983).

Patients who demonstrate perceptual deficits, such as the loss of shape discrimination and/or difficulty attending to more than one part of a visual scene, tend to have bilateral, posterior parietal-occipital cerebral lesions. In some cases, the agnosia may be confined to one visual half-field, contralateral to the lesion. Those rare patients who have the isolated symptom of difficulty identifying objects in unusual views have had unilateral right parietal lesions.

Semantically Based Visual Agnosia

Associative visual agnosia is thought to be a problem with higher order semantic deficits, or impairment in linking an intact perception with its meaning. This type of agnosia is thought to be a problem of semantic association and not one of perception.

Patients with associative agnosias have recognition deficits but no identifiable perceptual deficits. A patient with **associative agnosia** can generally describe, copy, and even draw an unrecognized object, demonstrating intact perception. Interestingly, even after successfully drawing an object, a patient with associative agnosia is still not able to identify it. One patient, after copying a picture of a train, described it as "a wagon or a car of some kind" (Rubens & Benson, 1971). On further testing, a clear semantic deficit often emerges. For instance, although patients with this type of agnosia can draw and match pictures of various glasses, they may have trouble recognizing that a wine glass and a juice glass belong in the same semantic category (i.e., drinking vessels) (Bauer, 1993). They also have difficulty identifying other semantic information about stimuli that they do not recognize, for example, whether a lion is dangerous or a zebra is striped (McCarthy & Warrington, 1990).

Semantically based agnosias are also sometimes limited to a specific semantic category. For instance, several patients could recognize objects from certain semantic categories (animals, foods, plants) but not others (tools, clothing, musical instruments). Other patients could recognize only inanimate objects, whereas still others demonstrated even more specific deficits in recognizing, for example, foodstuffs, minerals, vegetables, and things found indoors (Dixon, 2000; Farah, 1992; Farah, Hammond, Mehta, & Ratcliff, 1989; Farah, McMullen, & Meyer, 1991; Warrington & McCarthy, 1994). Researchers argue about the appropriate explanation for these highly selective category-specific deficits. Some authors suggest that these findings are spurious artifacts of testing and should be attributed the relative complexity of the pictures or familiarity of the objects used in each study (Damasio, Tranel, & Damasio, 1993). Other researchers explain these patterns of deficits through detailed analysis of the categories. For instance, animate objects such as animals are known by their sensory properties (e.g., four legs, fur, tail). In contrast, inanimate objects are known by their function (e.g., a hammer is used to pound nails). Therefore, sensory and functional knowledge may be associated with different brain regions and their recognition selectively disrupted (Martin, Ungerleider, & Haxby, 2000; see also discussion of category specific anomias in Chapter 4).

It is often not easy to distinguish apperceptive from associative agnosias. For instance, with regard to specific semantic category agnosias, certain categories such as animals and living things may be confusable because they are visually more similar to one another than artifact categories such as tools (Farah et al., 1991; Warrington & McCarthy, 1987). That is, some semantic categories are more perceptually rich and challenging than others. Because one would need more refined perceptual abilities to distinguish animals from one another than to distinguish articles of clothing from one another, a perceptual deficit would be more likely to impair the semantic category of animals than other semantic categories. Patient performance would depend greatly on the degree of perceptual impairment, the amount of detail in the pictures, and the confusability of the pictures used.

It is also clear that testing is insufficient in many cases to determine the contribution of perceptual versus semantic deficits. Because one of the key diagnostic criteria for associative agnosia is documenting intact perception, thorough perceptual testing is very important, although most patients have not have undergone rigorous perceptual testing. It might be that with adequate testing, all patients with agnosia would have subtle perceptual problems.

The neuropathology may help to distinguish the two types of agnosia: **Apperceptive agnosia** is most often associated with right or bilateral posterior lesions and associative agnosia with perisylvian and posterior left hemisphere damage (Warrington, 1985), although there are exceptions (Levine, 1978). Some authors go even further in localizing these deficits, reporting anterior-posterior differences, depending on

the type of category impaired. In a careful study of patients with well-defined brain lesions, Tranel, Damasio, and Damasio (1997a, 1997b) documented impaired category-specific knowledge in a number of patients with brain damage and found clear anatomical differences in those patients who were impaired naming and recognizing animals and those who could not name or recognize tools. All of the 28 patients with impaired knowledge of animals had lesions in the medial occipital lobe. Interestingly, half were in the left hemisphere and half were in the right hemisphere. The 8 patients with impaired naming and recognition of tools had lesions involving the posterior left middle temporal gyrus.

As the cases of visual agnosia are reviewed in more detail, the distinctions between subtypes of visual agnosias become less clear. The generalization that comes from more than a century of work on this topic is that there is a range of agnosic deficits, and they occur along a continuum from perceptual to semantic. The lesions underlying the disorder correspondingly vary. Predominantly right posterior lesions appear to cause perceptual deficits, posterior left hemisphere lesions seem to cause semantic problems, and bilateral lesions likely cause both.

Color Agnosia

Colors are unlike other visual stimuli. Although people and objects can be identified by voice recognition, tactile exploration, or other senses, colors can only be identified by direct vision. Several acquired color disturbances deserve mention, although some are not technically **color agnosia.**

Central achromatopsia is a loss of color vision due to brain damage. Patients describe their visual world as "black and white, all gray, washed out, or dirty" (Bauer, 1993). Occasionally, achromatopsia can create other visual effects: One patient felt that all objects were covered with a gold paint (Critchley, 1965). These patients will perform poorly on color-matching tasks but retain knowledge of colors and can answer questions about colors (e.g., reporting that a banana is yellow). The brain damage in question can be either unilateral or bilateral and is usually in the inferior ventromedial region of the occipital lobe, involving the lingual gyrus.

Other patients perform well on tests of color perception but have difficulty with color associations in verbal tasks only. Some have only color anomia but can still answer questions about inherent qualities (*What color is grass?*). Other patients have difficulty with both color naming and answering questions about the colors of objects. In essence, this is an aphasia limited to colors, sometimes called *color agnosia* and sometimes called *color aphasia*. It is distinguished from typical aphasia because it is limited to colors. The lesions associated with these color anomias/agnosias tend to be in the distribution of the posterior cerebral artery and functionally disconnect both the left and right visual cortices from the posterior left hemisphere language areas.

PROSOPAGNOSIA

An isolated deficit in the ability to recognize previously familiar faces is called **prosopagnosia**. Patients with prosopagnosia can discriminate and match faces, demonstrating adequate perception. Memory deficits and language impairment do not cause the face recognition problem. The deficit can involve famous faces, the faces of friends and family, and even the patient's own face in the mirror. Despite the lack of facial recognition, some patients can identify characteristics of faces, including age, facial expression, and gender. Difficulties range from laborious but eventually successful recognition to frank misidentifications. Some patients have difficulty learning and then recognizing *un*familiar faces in a memory test, but this is generally thought to be a separate disorder from prosopagnosia and presumed to be associated with separate neuropathology.

There has been a lively debate about the proper way to describe this deficit. There is some indication that the problem is not limited to human faces and may in fact be a more general problem recognizing subtle visual distinctions. The fact that it is not always limited to human faces comes from some patients with prosopagnosia for recognizing individual cows (in the case of farmers) and birds (in the case of

birdwatchers) (e.g., Bornstein, Sroka, & Munitz, 1969). These data fit nicely with the findings that expert recognition, as in the case of expert birdwatchers or trained musicians, is accompanied by distinct cognitive (Bub, 2002) and brain processes (e.g., Tanaka & Curran, 2001). Experts differ from nonexperts, at least in part, because they have learned to identify, what seem to the novice, to be similar items within a category. With this in mind, given that we are all, in a sense, experts at face recognition and able to distinguish very subtle and complex perceptual differences between them, the problem of agnosia might be a general impairment affecting the ability to distinguish visually similar objects—in this case, faces. In this theory, faces are more affected than other objects in agnosia because they are so similar to one another.

Prosopagnosia is often associated with other visuospatial disorders, including achromatopsia, and sometimes with other right hemisphere dysfunctions, including dressing and constructional apraxia (see Chapter 7). The lesions that cause prosopagnosia are found in the cortex and white matter in the inferior and mesial visual association cortices. There is some debate about whether unilateral right or bilateral lesions in these areas are necessary to cause prosopagnosia, but most cases in which the defect lasts beyond the acute stage have bilateral lesions (Damasio et al., 2000). Patients with unilateral left or right lesions appear to have incomplete prosopagnosia. Those with right hemisphere damage recognize some faces but do so slowly. Patients with left hemisphere lesions recognize the general category to which the face belongs (e.g., politician, actor) but do not recognize the individual (Damasio et al., 2000).

AUDITORY AGNOSIAS

Failure to recognize auditory stimuli despite intact hearing is called **auditory agnosia.** Auditory agnosia is distinct from **cortical deafness,** in which patients have sustained cortical damage to the primary auditory cortex, located in the lateral fissure along the superior surface of the temporal lobe (a.k.a. Heschl's gyrus, Brodmann areas 41–42). Patients with cortical deafness are not aware of sounds and have abnormally elevated auditory thresholds. Patients with auditory agnosia may have difficulty recognizing specific subsets of auditory information: speech, nonspeech sounds, music, and voices, either in combination or separately. Each is briefly described.

Pure word deafness, an auditory agnosia limited to speech sounds, is the most common and most debilitating of the auditory agnosias. Patients with pure word deafness experience speech as "an undifferentiated continuous humming noise without any rhythm," and normal speakers sound to them "like foreigners speaking in the distance" (Klein & Harper, 1956). This syndrome is distinguished from aphasia insofar as the patient's reading, writing, and speech are relatively normal. Of course, symptoms of pure word deafness can also occur within the context of aphasia, particularly Wernicke's aphasia. In that case, however, it would be presumed to be part of the comprehension deficit and not an agnosia per se. Patients with pure word deafness can rely on lip-reading, nonlinguistic context, prosody, and limited verbal comprehension to help understand some of what people say to them. The lesions causing pure word deafness are typically bilateral, symmetric, cortical-subcortical lesions involving the anterior part of the superior temporal gyrus, sparing Heschl's gyrus on the left. Some patients have unilateral left subcortical lesions within the temporal lobe (Bauer, 1993).

Auditory sound agnosia is an auditory agnosia limited to nonverbal sounds. It is either rare or so rarely disabling as to not be reported by patients but may be identified by clinicians. Patients with auditory sound agnosia have difficulty identifying common nonspeech sounds such as a train whistle or a birdsong. In several documented cases, the patients have intact hearing and unaffected language. Lesions underlying auditory sound agnosia have been identified in the right temporal-parietal region (Spreen, Benton, & Fincham, 1965), the left hemisphere (Saygin, Dick, & Bates, 2001), and bilaterally (Bauer, 1993).

Amusia, a problem recognizing music, is difficult to diagnose because of the variable level of musical aptitude and training in the general population. Because of the great variability

in musical skills and because music appreciation involves many different subskills, such as production versus appreciation and melody versus rhythm, the patterns and characteristics of amusia vary tremendously. For instance, people with no known musical skill or training are likely to suffer amusic symptoms involving tonal memory following right hemisphere damage but impairment of processing rhythm after left hemisphere damage, suggesting that different aspects of musical ability are controlled by each hemisphere (Kaplan & Gardner, 1989; Zatorre, 1984). Gardner and colleagues (Gardner, Silverman, Denes, Semenza, & Rosenstiel, 1977) asked patients with left or right hemisphere damage to select a picture that went with 20 seconds of a melody played on the piano. Patients with left hemisphere damage were relatively impaired with items that required knowledge of the lyrics (e.g., matching a picture of a rowboat with the song "Row Row Row Your Boat"). Patients with right hemisphere damage were relatively impaired with items that matched a situation to a melody without lyrics (e.g., matching a picture of a wedding to Mendelssohn's *Wedding March*). Thus, when language is involved in the musical task, patients with right hemisphere damage outperform patients with left hemisphere damage; when language is not involved, patients with left hemisphere damage outperform patients with right hemisphere damage.

There are now several cases of professional musicians who, after a left hemisphere stroke and with significant aphasia, returned to composing and teaching, suggesting a right hemisphere dominance or compensatory ability for music (Kaplan & Gardner, 1989). Musicians sometimes regain their ability to perceive and appraise music but not to compose or perform, suggesting dissociations between comprehension and production analogous to those seen in aphasia. In these cases, there are predictable differences in lesion location, with production problems associated with anterior lesions and comprehension problems associated with posterior lesions.

Interestingly, singing along with old songs appears to be relatively spared in patients with Alzheimer's dementia and widespread cortical damage (Brotons, Koger, & Pickett-Cooper, 1997). This suggests that very familiar melodies and lyrics, much like automatic sequences of counting and the days of the week, are relatively immune to brain damage due to their overlearned nature. This, of course, is motivation for music therapy as a way to engage various, even severely impaired, patient populations (Chavin, 2002).

Phonagnosia is an impairment in recognizing familiar voices. It is not as obvious or as debilitating as pure word deafness but nonetheless can disrupt social interaction in some patients, particularly on the telephone. To determine if and how the ability to recognize people by the sound of their voice is affected by brain damage, Van Lancker and colleagues (Van Lancker, Kreiman, & Cummings, 1989) asked healthy adults and patients with either left or right hemisphere damage to (a) discriminate between unfamiliar voices and (b) identify famous voices (e.g., John F. Kennedy). The authors found that both patients with left and right hemisphere damage performed poorly on the unfamiliar voice discrimination task, and performance appeared related to temporal lobe damage. On the famous voice recognition task, patients with right parietal damage performed significantly worse than patients with either no brain damage or left hemisphere damage.

TACTILE AGNOSIA

We generally rely on visual guidance to identify objects. However, in the absence of vision, in a dark room, or in the depths of a pocket, we use our sense of touch to distinguish objects. **Tactile agnosia,** called **astereognosis,** is diagnosed if a patient has difficulty using touch, particularly with the hands, to identify shapes or objects that cannot be attributed to basic sensory deficits, anomia, or amnesia. This disorder is of notable interest because of its parallel with the other agnosias. However, as you can imagine, the functional consequences are relatively minor compared with a deficit in visual recognition, unless, of course, one is also visually impaired.

As with the other agnosias, there is a continuum of deficits from the frankly sensory and perceptual, parallel to apperceptive visual agnosia, to those associated with higher level dysfunction, parallel to associative agnosia. Cortical damage to the postcentral gyrus will produce decreased tactile sensation in the contralateral hand. Usually, only the hands are tested because it is primarily the hands that we use to explore and identify objects by touch. The most relevant cases are those patients who have grossly intact sensation to pain, pressure, temperature, or vibration but have difficulty identifying objects placed in their hand. Some patients with only mild sensory deficits have disproportionate difficulty identifying shapes by touch (Bauer, 1993). The lesion in these cases appears to be in the right superior parietal lobe and affects perceptual identification in both hands. This suggests that there is a right hemisphere–based spatial function that is used in sensorimotor exploration and recognition.

Occasionally, patients are identified who have symptoms of tactile agnosia without sensory deficits. This parallels associative visual agnosia because these patients have intact sensation but still cannot recognize objects placed in their hands. In these cases, cortical lesions have been identified in the parietotemporal regions of either hemisphere but more commonly in the right hemisphere (Bauer, 1993).

As with other agnosias, there are those who believe that symptoms of tactile agnosia can be explained by elementary sensory disturbance or anomia. Defenders of the notion of astereognosis are at a particular disadvantage because there are so few cases reported. Again, the lack of reported cases may not reflect incidence as much as the fact that we do not rely on touch for object identification or recognition, so symptoms are not reported by patients.

DIAGNOSIS OF AGNOSIA

Although there are no definitive tests of agnosia per se, there are many ways to identify recognition deficits in visual, auditory, and tactile modalities. For each modality, examples of appropriate materials for testing sensation and recognition are discussed. To diagnose agnosia, one must rule out or at least identify the degree of sensory, memory, and language impairments. Therefore, in addition to specific recognition tests, basic sensory, memory, and language evaluations are a necessary part of testing. Needless to say, it is critical whe testing recognition that sensory corrections such as hearing aids and eyeglasses be used if necessary.

The most common way to identify an object is to name it, so in much of the testing described here, the patient is required to give verbal responses. Therefore, it is essential to know if a poor response is due to recognition failure or to a language problem. One way to distinguish between a problem of recognition and a problem of naming is to observe language ability outside of the recognition tasks. Patients who are purely agnosic have difficulty naming or describing an object that they are asked to identify, but they demonstrate relatively normal language production otherwise. Patients with aphasia, however, generally exhibit language production problems across all speech tasks.

Because anomia is such a common effect of brain damage, many patients with agnosia may be both agnosic and anomic, making it difficult to sort out how much of an object identification problem is due to recognition versus naming deficits. Therefore, assessment of recognition should also include nonverbal tests of recognition. Recognition can be conveyed nonverbally by gesture (e.g., pretending to drink from a cup to indicate *cup*), by sorting (e.g., placing a picture of a cup with pictures of other drinking vessels), or by word-picture matching. Below are some guidelines and examples of ways to test agnosia in various modalities. Like other test lists in this book, this list is not exhaustive; it is only illustrative.

TESTING FOR VISUAL AGNOSIA

Assuming the patient can see, visual agnosia is identified by a patient's lack of recognition of common objects, colors, words, or faces in drawings, photos, or real life. Visual recognition is determined by a combination of verbal and nonverbal tests.

Picture naming is usually the first test to be given. The patient is asked to name pictures of objects. Errors commonly include frank misidentifications (e.g., calling a *horse* a *car*) as well as comments about why the patient cannot identify the object, such as, "I never knew what that was." If a patient fails to name particular objects, further scrutiny is given to those items

to establish if they belong to a single semantic category and the degree of recognition in non-verbal formats. The third edition of the Boston Diagnostic Aphasia Exam (Goodglass et al., 2001) includes many items from several semantic categories, including animals and tools.

Naming errors are followed up with nonverbal tasks. The Test of Visual Form Discrimination (Benton et al., 1994) requires matching of complex geometric stimuli—on each trial, the patient selects one of four drawings that matches a particular stimulus. Copying, drawing, and/or picture matching can indicate status of visual perception. Ability to copy, draw, or match identical pictures indicates intact visual processing and suggests the problem is not perceptual but rather semantic or associative. The models for copying should have clear outlines and internal detail to elicit problems with either aspect. Patients who have problems copying or drawing but who have intact picture matching may have motor or constructional deficits.

There are many special tests to assess the high-level visual perceptual abilities that are often impaired in patients with visual agnosia. These visual perceptual tests generally require the patient to integrate pieces of visual information presented in atypical images. These are sometimes called tests of visual organization and include assessing gestalt perception (see Figure 8.1), identifying overlapping figures, and recognizing objects in unusual angles (see Figure 8.2) or with extraneous lines or shadows. The Hooper Visual Orientation Test requires object recognition from line drawings that consist of object parts rotated in atypical configurations (Hooper, 1983). The Benton test of facial recognition assesses complex visual perception (Benton & Van Allen, 1968) (see Figure 8.3). In this test, the patient sees a single black-and-white photograph of a face and must select the same face from a set of six other photographs. The correct matches might be an identical front view, the same face from a side view, or a view with different lighting. Patients with right parietal lesions do particularly poorly on this test, but patients with aphasia who have comprehension deficits also perform poorly. Age affects performance on this test, with 10% of healthy people older than age 70 years performing poorly (Lezak, 1995).

Figure 8.1   An example of a Gestalt closure visual perception test item, in which part of the visual image is missing and the patient must make sense of fragmentary visual information.

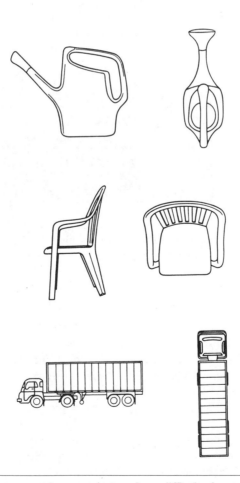

Figure 8.2   Patients with apperceptive agnosia may have difficulty in recognizing an object when it is shown from a usual angle (right).

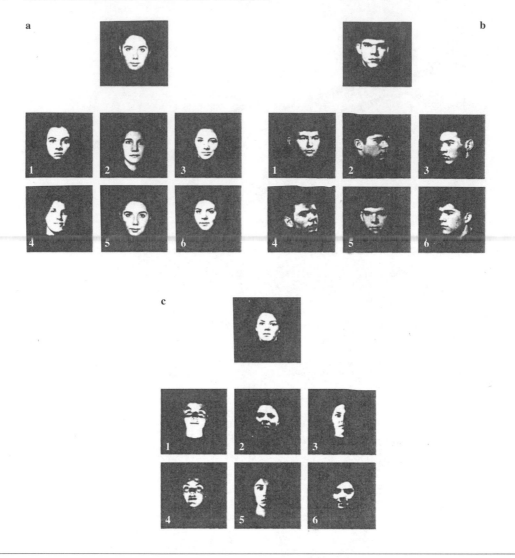

Figure 8.3 Test of Facial Recognition. These photographs illustrate three parts of the test: (a) matching identical front views, (b) matching front view with three-quarter view, and (c) matching front view under different lighting conditions.

Testing for semantic associative problems in visual agnosia includes sorting items into semantic categories and pairing similar but not identical objects from the same category. If a category-specific recognition deficit is suspected, a large number of items from many categories should be tested.

Prosopagnosia requires other specialized testing. A test of famous or personally familiar faces can be constructed from photographs (Van Lancker & Klein, 1990). Obviously, the clinician must be sure that the patient would have recognized these images prior to brain damage. The patient can be asked to name individuals shown in the pictures, select the appropriate name(s) from a written list, or see several photographs at once and select the one that matches a name presented verbally, in writing, or both.

Color recognition deficits are identified by first ruling out color blindness. This is done by a number of tests, including the Ishihara (1979) test or others that present cards printed with different-colored dots that form recognizable figures against a ground of contrasting dots.

A patient who cannot distinguish colors will not be able to see the figure. Other useful tests, such as the Farnsworth-Munsell 100-Hue and Dichotomous Test for Color Vision (Farnsworth, 1957), involve arranging colored paper chips according to hue or sorting like colors together. Once it is determined that the patient is not color-blind, several strategies can identify the extent of difficulty with color terms, including the following:

- Naming: Show the patient a color and ask, "What color is this?"
- Pointing on command: Show the patient an array of colors and ask him or her to point to one: "Show me the green one."
- Verbal association: "What color is a banana?"
- Multiple-choice association: Show an array of colors and have the patient select the appropriate color for an object or line drawing: "Show me the color of blood."
- Erroneous color detection: Show the patient correctly and wrongly colored pictures (e.g., a red apple, a purple banana, and a green grape) and let him or her select the one that is the wrong color.
- Sentence completion: *Grass is* _____.
- Question answering: "What color is snow?"
- Category fluency: "Name as many colors as you can in 60 seconds." "Name as many red things as you can in 60 seconds."

TESTS FOR AUDITORY AGNOSIA

To ensure that audition is adequate, patients suspected of having auditory agnosia should undergo standard audiometry to determine the *speech reception threshold,* the softest sound at which one can detect speech, and *pure tone testing,* the softest sound at which one can detect tones of different pitches. Standardized auditory recognition tests exist in the areas of speech and music but not for some of the other realms of auditory stimuli, such as environmental sounds and famous voices. Pure word deafness is assessed by standard auditory comprehension tests (see the aphasia testing section in Chapter 4). Musical ability can be tested with the Seashore Test of Musical Talent, which contains many subparts, including rhythm discrimination in which

patients are asked to discriminate between like and unlike pairs of musical beats (Seashore, Lewis, & Saetveit, 1960). Informal assessment of musical ability can be accomplished by asking the patient to identify familiar songs such as "Happy Birthday," "Star Spangled Banner," "La Cucaracha," "Silent Night," and "Battle Hymn of the Republic," which are sung or hummed by the examiner. If patients are not able to do this, musical discrimination can be tested by asking patients to distinguish sequences of pitches played on a pitch pipe, rhythms tapped out on a hard surface, or melodies, identifying if pairs of stimuli contain two of the same or two different sequences. Voice recognition can be tested by asking patients to identify the speaker of recorded voice samples (Van Lancker et al., 1989). If the patient cannot name familiar melodies or the people who go with the voices, multiple-choice formats can be used with either written names or pictures for voice recognition.

TESTS FOR TACTILE AGNOSIA

Both hands should be tested independently for basic perception, including touch, temperature, vibration, two-point discrimination, texture, shape, and size. For object recognition, the simplest procedure is to have patients close their eyes and identify common objects placed in their hand. If a patient fails this task, the deficit can be further explored by having the patient draw unrecognized objects or select matching objects in either the same tactile modality or in another modality, such as from a verbal list or a visual array. Accuracy as well as hesitation and degree of exploratory behavior are important indicators of difficulty.

TREATMENT OF AGNOSIA

Agnosias, particularly visual agnosias in our visually guided world, can be extremely disabling. However, these patients somehow get through life for the most part without walking into doors or eating rocks. How do they do it? Several case studies provide hints about the cues that patients with agnosia use to make sense of their world and what treatment approaches work for them. One famous patient with visual agnosia, known as "Schn.," suffered bilateral posterior brain injury in World War I and was studied by the famous neurologist Kurt Goldstein and other scientists (Gardner, 1974). Schn. functioned relatively normally in day-to-day life but could not recognize objects or words when they were presented briefly, as degraded stimuli, or with distracting lines around them. Watching him successfully read and recognize objects at his own speed revealed an interesting adaptation: He traced the contour of words and objects with his body—by moving his hands or eyes/head. This often gave him enough information, via a motoric route, to identify many words and objects. He was sidetracked by any extraneous lines or unusual perspectives in a drawing and helped by clear and suggestive defining features such as the hands of a clock. He was able to verbalize his compensatory technique by reporting that he looked for cues that provided a unique definition of objects, saying, for instance, that men and vehicles are distinguished because "men are all alike—narrow and long, while vehicles are wide; one notices that at once" (Gardner, 1974, p. 145).

Other patients with visual agnosia are reported to use other senses to identify objects, including audition, touch, and even smell, illustrating how the specificity of these disorders allows for compensation with other modalities. One patient with agnosia, who had been a doctor, described a stethoscope as "a long cord with a round thing at the end" and asked if it could be a watch. But he accurately identified it as a stethoscope when he was allowed to touch it (McCarthy & Warrington, 1990). Another patient with agnosia described a rose as "about six inches in length . . . a convoluted red form with a linear green attachment," demonstrating intact perception and language skills despite lack of recognition. However, when he smelled the flower, he immediately recognized it, exclaiming, "Beautiful! An early rose. What a heavenly smell!" (Sacks, 1990, p. 14). Patients with prosopagnosia are able to identify people by the sound of their voices, using auditory recognition when face recognition fails. Very frequently, patients with visual agnosia use prominent and identifiable parts to recognize whole objects and people (e.g., a picture of Einstein is recognized by his unique hair).

Specific therapeutic techniques have been developed primarily by occupational therapists to improve visual and tactile discriminatio and identification. For visual discrimination, the clinician can present pictures of people, objects, and colors and help the patient pick out cues in each picture that can be connected to particular people or objects. Practice matching identical objects and photos can help improve visual discrimination. Once the patient can identify several objects, they can be placed in an array, and he or she can be asked to select particular objects from that array. Increasing the number of objects placed together and the visual confusion of the array challenges the patient to improve. Tactile exploration can also be used to aid visual discrimination of objects.

Tactile agnosia has been treated with stimulation of the touch receptors by rubbing the forearm, hand, and fingers with a rough cloth to stimulate pressure receptors. The stimulation should be done only at a comfortable level and should feel good to the patient. The patient is then asked to grasp objects. Tactile object recognition can be practiced by having the patient look while touching various textures and objects and then discriminating and identifying the same textures and objects without looking.

Auditory agnosia is often treated by speech-language pathologists. Environmental sound and word discrimination is practiced, although it is not usually very successful. Compensation through other modalities, particularly writing and reading, appears more successful.

Obviously, agnosias come in a variety of modalities with degrees of apperceptive and associative deficits along with other cognitive, sensory, and motor deficits. Treatment is matched to the deficit and often is determined by preserved skills. For the most part, agnosias tend to be relatively specific, so compensatory strategies can be found in preserved abilities.

9

PROBLEM-SOLVING DEFICITS

Chapter Preview

1. What is normal problem solving?

Problem solving involves assessing the present state, defining a desired state, and finding ways to transform the former to the latter (Willis, 1996). Problem solving requires many cognitive skills, but most prominent are attention, reasoning, and planning.

2. How do problem-solving abilities change with age?

Older adults tend to gather less information and use fewer pieces of information than younger adults, but they reach decisions and solutions faster and earlier in the problem-solving process.

3. What are the behavioral characteristics of problem-solving impairments?

Patients with problem-solving deficits cannot generate possible solutions to simulated or real problems. They have difficulty figuring out how to find out what time a train leaves, how to get a library card, or how to go to the market. They are often impulsive and distractible, which prevents them from selecting an optimal solution and carrying it out. Problem-solving impairments are also manifested as problems in social interaction and are therefore often attributed to changes in personality.

4. What is the neuropathology of problem-solving impairments?

Problem-solving deficits are associated with diffuse brain damage and damage to either the left or right cerebral hemispheres, particularly the frontal lobes.

5. How are problem-solving disorders diagnosed?

Problem-solving deficits are often apparent in real life, for example, when a patient does not follow through with basic plans. Evaluations include assessment of underlying deficits in attention, reasoning, and planning as well as tests of problem solving in naturalistic contexts.

6. How are problem-solving disorders treated?

Behavioral treatments use drills to restore attention and memory, as well as logical reasoning tasks that involve planning and sequencing to accomplish a particular goal. Compensatory approaches

(Continued)

(Continued)

include altering the environment to make it less distracting and using devices from simple labels to complex planning books.

PROBLEM SOLVING

We solve all sorts of problems. Some problems are routine, familiar, and solved subconsciously on a daily basis, such as obtaining meals and getting from one place to the other. Other problems require conscious planning and extended periods of time, as when we plan a vacation, a job change, or retirement. When we fail to solve problems, the consequences range from missing an appointment to being fired from a job. More than any other ability discussed in this book, problem solving requires the integration of many different cognitive skills.

There have been many attempts to describe the underlying psychology of problem solving, but no single coherent theory is generally accepted. The Gestalt psychologist Goldstein described problem solving as a single ability to *abstract* (Goldstein, 1944). For him, abstraction included the ability to grasp the whole of a situation, analyze its component parts, and plan ahead. He attributed problem-solving impairments to a disturbance of abstraction.

Another approach is typified by the great Russian neuropsychologist Alexander Luria, who described problem solving as a sequence of discrete steps: (a) strategy selection, (b) application of operations, and (c) evaluation of outcomes (Luria, 1966). He based this analysis on observation of many patients who had difficulty solving problems and who also demonstrated impairments in these more elementary cognitive functions.

Reflecting the complexity of solving problems, recent accounts often include up to five distinct components, starting with (a) the crucial element of focused attention, which is needed to (b) identify appropriate goals, (c) formulate strategies, (d) use inference and flexibility to compare and select the most appropriate course of action, and (e) evaluate performance

(Channon & Crawford, 1999; McCarthy & Warrington, 1990). Discussions about the psychology of problem solving can be hard to follow because the various concepts overlap, and each description emphasizes different aspects of the process. This is in part because any general description of problem solving must accommodate a large range of problems that vary in their modality, familiarity, and complexity. Proble solving undoubtedly involves all of the elements listed above and some that were not mentioned as well. For the purposes of this chapter, I focus on three somewhat distinct areas of cognition:

- Attention and working memory
- Reasoning, including concept formation and abstraction
- Planning, covering the ability to develop strategies and evaluate outcomes

At first glance, these cognitive domains may not seem like a coherent group. In fact, they are seldom discussed together. However, they share some crucial characteristics that make them a natural class insofar as they (a) are global areas of cognition that are relatively free of specific content, and can be applied to problems in any content area, whether it is verbal/language or spatial or motoric; (b) are used in the service of complex thought and decision making; (c) rely heavily on the frontal lobes; and (d) can be used to predict problem solving in real life. Each is defined in more detail below.

Attention

The term *attention* refers to several different capacities related to how people become receptive to certain stimuli, as well as the ability to coordinate multiple tasks simultaneously. William James said it clearly:

Everyone knows what attention is. It is the taking possession by the mind, in clear and vivid form, of one out of what seem several simultaneously possible objects or trains of thought. Focalization, concentration, and consciousness are of its essence. It implies withdrawal from some things in order to deal effectively with others. (qtd. in Hartley, 1992, pp. 4–5)

Attentional processes may be automatic (i.e., subconscious) or controlled (i.e., voluntary) (Shiffrin & Schneider, 1977). Contemporary discussions of attention usually break it down into several distinct functions (e.g., Lezak, 1995; Strub & Black, 1988):

- **Selective or immediate attention** allows us to notice one aspect of the environment more than others. This is important initially, as well as during the process of problem solving, because when we notice that a problem exists, it allows us to ignore irrelevant bits of information in the environment and inhibit self-generated irrelevant thoughts and poor solutions to concentrate on a better solution. This is sometimes called simple or immediate attention, operationally defined as the capacity to process information within primary or immediate memory (see Chapter 10), taking place over a period of less than 30 seconds.
- **Sustained attention** allows us to attend to the problem and solution over time. This is important because problem solving typically requires planning and follow-through, which take place over time. Sustained attention can be operationally defined as concentration to process information for more than 60 seconds.
- **Divided attention** allows us to respond to more than one task at a time or to multiple elements within a task simultaneously.
- **Alternating attention** is the flexibility to shift attention back and forth between relevant elements in the environment or task.

All these elements of attention are important in solving a routine problem such as how to program an electronic appliance: You will need to focus attention on the appliance, familiarize yourself with the location of buttons and displays, concentrate on the task, not be distracted by irrelevant conversations, and divide and alternate attention between the written instructions and the machine itself. Although it might seem simple when all goes well, impaired attention can negatively affect performance on all of the elements of solving this and other similar problems, even if all other specific cognitive functions such as language and visual spatial ability are intact (Lezak, 1995; Sohlberg & Mateer, 1989).

The concept of **working memory** is closely linked to attention and augments the notion of attention by hypothesizing a general mechanism for short-term holding and computational processes that include both the immediate aspects of simple attention, as well as more complex manipulation that is needed to hold and process information simultaneously. These functions are associated with a wide range of cognitive tasks (Baddeley, 2000; Daneman & Carpenter, 1983). Simply, it refers to our ability to store and manipulate information during the first 30 seconds after registration. Working memory has several components. Two are responsible for verbatim storage of information over the period of several seconds: the **phonological loop,** which allows for storage of speech material for about 2 seconds, and the **visuospatial sketchpad,** the visual analog of the phonological loop. The **central executive** is the "most important but least well understood component of working memory" (Baddeley, 2000, p. 300). The concept of working memory is invoked to describe how we accomplish simple tasks such as holding a phone number in mind while searching for the telephone: We use the phonological loop to repeat the phone number to ourselves and use the central executive to allocate a portion of our mental resources to repeating the number, and other portions to recalling where we put the telephone, looking around the house for it, and then dialing. Deficits in attention are sometimes referred to as impairments of the central executive component of working memory.

Reasoning and Concept Formation

Some authors emphasize the role of **reasoning** in problem solving (Sohlberg & Mateer, 1989). Reasoning is the ability to draw inferences or conclusions from known or assumed facts. It is often divided into two types.

Deductive reasoning: thinking from the general to the specific, such as listing exemplars of a category.

Inductive reasoning: thinking from the particular to the general such as generating a category name from exemplars.

Concept formation is another way to talk about reasoning. Concept formation is the process of identifying features and relationships between features to derive abstract categories. For example, given *a saw* and *a screwdriver,* inductive logic leads to the concept *tools.* This process is also called **abstraction** because in the process of generating a concept, you find abstract common features—in this case, something like *used for fixing things* to derive the new concept *tools.* Concept formation is intimately involved with problem solving—seeing the solution to a problem often depends on the ability to see abstract connections between elements of the problem and between the current state and the desired state.

Planning and Executive Functions

Planning is the ability to develop a strategy to achieve a particular goal. Arriving at a good plan involves the following:

- assessing the current situation,
- formulating a goal,
- considering various sequences to attain that goal by anticipating the consequences of particular action(s),
- initiating a plan, and
- modifying a plan based on feedback and comparing the outcome with the initial goals.

An example will illustrate. Consider planning a trip to visit a relative in another state. The plan may involve (a) finding a good date based on work and other schedules; (b) deciding the mode of transportation, taking into consideration cost, speed, and convenience; (c) preparing for the trip by packing and buying a gift; and (d) taking the trip. Of course, this is a simplification, but it illustrates that the plan has sequenced steps, and each step involves several parts that are also sequenced. Reversing the order of those steps

would not work. Each segment of the plan was arrived at by anticipating the results and evaluating the anticipated outcome. This example also illustrates the importance of continuous monitoring and revision of a plan based on feedback: The specifics may have to be changed due to unforeseen weather conditions, changes in health, and so on.

We go through similar planning for even mundane activities, such as planning how to eat dinner and get to a movie on time. In many cases, planning is assisted by reliance on familiar sequences called *schemas* or *scripts* (see Chapter 6). These are prepackaged plans for particular procedures. For instance, we could insert *going out to eat* as part of the plan for how to accommodate dinner and a movie in one evening. In that case, our plan for eating is relatively easy because we have a familiar, almost frozen sequence already stored in memory for how we go out to eat: call for reservations, arrive, be seated by the hostess, look at menus, order, eat, pay, and leave. There are many such schemas that assist planning on a daily basis, such as how to make a sandwich and how to drive to work. The more familiar and specific the schema, the less on-the-fly planning is needed.

Planning cuts across cognitive domains and occurs in verbal, spatial, and motoric modalities. Verbal planning might include, for instance, determining whether to summarize a story at the beginning or the end. Spatial planning would be involved in designing a garden, taking a hike, or drawing a human figure. Motor planning is involved in figuring out how to develop a new skill, such as ice-skating, using a new hand tool, tying a tie, or brushing hair in front of a mirror.

Evaluation is an integral part of formulating a plan. For instance, in the dinner-and-movie scenario above, we might compare how long it would take to make dinner versus ordering pizza versus going to a restaurant in considering how to plan the evening so that we get to the movie on time. Once a plan has been initiated, we continuously evaluate progress toward the goal: For instance, if we decide to go out to eat and there is a line at the restaurant, which will delay dinner and make us late for the movie, we may choose to go to another restaurant or eat after the movie. Finally, we evaluate the outcome of our plans after completion. This is important for future plans: If we miss the beginning of the movie, we are unlikely to repeat that strategy; but if the plan was a success, we will store that plan and possibly use it again.

Current discussions of cognition and problem solving often subsume the elements of attention, working memory, and planning within the notion of **executive functions** (Sohlberg & Mateer, 1989; Stuss, 1992; Stuss & Benson, 1987; Woodruff Pak, 1997). Executive functions do not represent discrete processes but operate as umbrella functions that come into play in all realms of cognitive processing. They are called *executive* because they control other cognitive functions. Executive functions include anticipation, goal selection, planning, initiation, self-monitoring to sustain activity, and use of feedback to inhibit inappropriate action and shift attention when necessary. These abilities, when they function well, allow us to direct and organize our independent, goal-directed, persistent, and flexible behavior (Lezak, 1995; Zoltan & Siev, 1996). "Questions about executive functions ask how or whether a person goes about doing something (e.g., Will you do it and, if so, how?)," which differ from questions about cognitive function, which ask, "How much do you know? and "What can you do?" (Lezak, 1995, p. 42). Disruption of executive functions, like deficits in attention and working memory, can affect many aspects of behavior. Deficits in executive function can cause irritability, excitability, impulsivity, carelessness, rigidity, difficulty shifting attention, poor personal grooming, lack of initiation of activity, decreased or absent motivation (anergia), poor planning, and inability to carry out goal-directed behaviors. These deficits can persist even in the context of relatively good performance on cognitive tests.

AGE-RELATED CHANGES

Three bodies of literature are relevant to problem solving and aging: (a) a vast literature on intelligence in aging (Schaie, 1994; Woodruff Pak, 1997); (b) a literature using psychometric tasks of attention, working memory, and executive functions in aging (e.g., Cerella, 1990;

Salthouse, 1996; Verhaeghen & Vandenbroucke, 1998); and (c) a body of literature on everyday problem solving in aging (Willis, 1996).

Intelligence Testing and Aging

Intelligence is difficult to define, but most reasonable definitions sound something like problem solving: the ability to carry on abstract thinking (Terman, 1921) or the capacity of an individual to act purposefully, to think rationally, and to deal effectively with the environment (Wechsler, 1944). Not surprisingly, therefore, reasoning and problem-solving abilities have historically been part and parcel of intelligence testing. For example, the Wechsler Adult Intelligence Scale (WAIS III) (Wechsler, 1997b) includes the Similarities and Picture Arrangement subtests. The Similarities subtest asks people to state how two concepts—for example, *an eye* and *an ear*—are alike, testing their ability to generate the abstract concept *sense organs,* which requires, in our jargon, reasoning and concept formation. The Picture Arrangement subtest presents a sequence of cartoon pictures that, when put in order, tells a sensible story. This subtest requires the ability to use reasoning to derive a logical sequence of events. It should be noted that although many tests are directly related to problem solving, some are not. For instance, tests of vocabulary (e.g., *What does "repair" mean?*) and information (e.g., *What is the shape of a ball?*) assess basic factual knowledge that might be used in problem solving but are not crucial elements of the problem-solving process itself.

The literature on aging and performance on intelligence tests suggests that some relevant elements of intelligence decline with age, whereas others do not. There have been many attempts to characterize which aspects of intelligence decline with age and which do not. The most widely recognized model is that of *fluid* versus *crystallized* intelligence developed by Cattell (1971) and Horn (1982). Crystallized intelligence depends on the accumulation of experience over a lifetime, including many verbal subtests such as information and vocabulary, and tends to remain stable or increase with age (La Rue, 1992), at least until advanced old age (Bosworth, Schaie, & Willis, 1999). Fluid intelligence is the ability to quickly perceive relationships, patterns, and solutions given novel stimuli. Fluid intelligence is often associated with performance subtests in part because they are often timed. These tend to decline with age. The relative stability of crystallized abilities and the vulnerability of fluid abilities have been substantiated by many studies (Botwinick, 1977; Horn & Cattell, 1967; La Rue, 1992; Schaie, 1994; Woodruff-Pak, 1997). However, it is important to realize that many tests require a combination of both crystallized and fluid abilities, and generalizations about aging are based on averages of many subtest scores, which may obscure age-related declines on specific tasks. To take an obvious example, although verbal and crystallized abilities are thought to be relatively stable in aging, this is true for the verbal subtests of information and vocabulary, but not similarities, which is also verbal but declines. This is likely because the similarities task requires one to perceive patterns and extract abstract relationships in a relatively short time. Likewise, the decline on fluid abilities holds true for the timed visuospatial task of block design but not picture arrangement, possibly because the patterns presented in the block design task are novel, whereas many of the sequences in the picture arrangement task, are familiar from past experience (e.g., a worker building a house). From this body of data, we can cautiously conclude that age-related declines in some intellectual abilities such as concept formation, as tested by similarities, will affect problem solving. However, equally important skills for problem solving, such as logical sequencing as tested by picture arrangement, are relatively stable through older adulthood (e.g., Sands, Terry, & Meredith, 1989; Schaie, 1996).

There are also data from specific tests of reasoning. Raven's Progressive Matrices is a commonly used test of nonverbal reasoning for which there is ample aging data (Raven, 1960). It is a set of multiple-choice analogy problems using visual designs (see p. 152). It is particularly interesting because it was developed to be a culturally fair test of general ability that does not rely on language, experience, or education. Performance on this test consistently shows a negative correlation with age (see Salthouse, 1992, for a review and chapter on reasoning).

Attention and Working Memory

A vast literature on attention and working memory in aging (e.g., Hartley, 1992; McDowd & Shaw, 2000; Zacks, Hasher, & Li, 2000) shows that different aspects of the attentional system change differentially with age.

Selective or immediate attention is typically assessed by span tasks that require subjects to hold increasingly long bits of information in mind for a brief period to time. This can be in auditory or visual domains. For instance, auditory tests may require repeating increasingly long series of auditorily presented digits. Visual tests may require pointing to increasingly long series of visual sequences. Attention is determined by the accuracy of immediate recall. These are often the same tasks used to assess "primary" or "immediate" memory (see Chapter 10). The literature on older adults' performance of this type of task is quite consistent: Age has either a very small or no effect on span tasks in either visual or auditory modalities (e.g., Filley & Cullum, 1994; Hartley, 1992; Myerson et al., 2003).

The research on focused and sustained attention in aging often uses tests of vigilance such as monitoring a stream of auditory or visual information to identify particular targets. For instance, a subject might listen to a list of digits for occurrences of a particular pattern such as three odd, nonrepeated digits in sequence. Typically, the accuracy of identifying the targets decreases over the task period for both younger and older adults. Although some earlier studies suggested no greater effect with older adults (Parasuraman, Nestor, & Greenwood, 1989), more recent studies have shown age effects suggesting an age-related decrement in the ability to continuously process information and maintain concentration over time (e.g., Filley & Cullum, 1994).

Divided attention, the ability to attend to more than one thing at a time, has been studied by having adults perform two tasks that, when performed individually, are not that difficult but, when performed simultaneously, require divided attention. These "dual-task studies" come from many domains such as detecting auditory signals, performing motor tasks, and making semantic decisions (for review, see also Anderson, Craik, & Naveh-Benjamin, 1998; Hartley, 1992). One example will illustrate. Fernandes and Moscovitch (2003) presented younger and older adults with a list of 16 words to remember for later recall. During one trial, they recalled the words while doing nothing else (i.e., no distraction). During a divided-attention task, they recalled the words (the "primary" task) while simultaneously doing one of two distraction tasks: (a) a semantic decision task, in which they saw nouns appear on a computer screen and said whether they were animate or manmade, or (b) an odd-digit task, in which they saw digits on a computer screen and pressed a key when they saw an odd number. The results of this and many other similar tasks are that (a) both younger and older adults perform more poorly when the two tasks are similar (in this case, recalling words and making semantic decisions about words creates more interference than recalling words and judging digits); (b) older adults are slower, make more errors on the distraction tasks, and recall fewer words on a primary task than younger adults overall (this last point, interestingly, is not true if the older adults have two learning opportunities instead of one); and, most important (c) performance of both younger and older adults are equally affected by the divided-attention task. The increased errors and decreased speed on the distraction tasks suggest that older adults may have less efficient attentional systems overall, but the similar effects for both groups on the primary memory task suggests that older adults are not more vulnerable to interference on a primary task when their attention is divided than younger adults. The conclusion drawn by Hartley (1992) still appears apt:

> Processes involved in doing two things concurrently are probably qualitatively quite similar in younger and older adults. The differences are caused by the fact that each of the component processes [in this case, memory and performance of the distraction task] is affected by aging. (Hartley, 1992, p. 32; but see Kemper, Herman, & Lian, 2003, for an exception)

The effects of age on working memory are complex because working memory contains several different subparts. In general, the effects of age on working memory echo the findings from attentional tasks: The age effects depend on the complexity of the task. Working memory spans are typically assessed by tasks that vary along a continuum with respect to the degree to which they require storage only versus storage plus processing. Digit or word span measures are used to test storage in isolation. However, "storage plus processing" tasks require two separate and simultaneous tasks. Generally, they require subjects to perform relatively simple processing task on a series of stimuli while remembering (i.e., storing) some item from each stimulus. The processing part might be a series of simple math calculations ($5 + 3 = ?$; $8 + 4 = ?$; $4 + 1 = ?$) (Babcock & Salthouse, 1990) or sentence acceptability judgments ("It was the gangsters that broke into the warehouse," "It was the warehouse that broke into the gangsters") (Waters & Caplan, 2001). During these tasks, the subjects perform the simple calculation or acceptability judgment on an increasingly long series of items while holding part of the stimulus in memory (e.g., the last number from each math problem or the last word in each sentence) and reporting those in sequence at the end of a series. Typically, older adults are less impaired on the simple storage aspects of working memory (either digit span or the simple calculations in the examples above) but relatively more impaired when they have to engage both storage and processing simultaneously, leading to the plausible conclusion that aging reduces the ability to coordinate simultaneous demands on storage and processing but not to storage per se (e.g., Salthouse, 1990, 1991; Salthouse & Babcock, 1991; Salthouse, Babcock, & Shaw, 1991).

The differences between younger and older adults in many of these tasks are often explained by theories of general changes in cognition that affect performance on attention, working memory, and other tasks. Two of the most prominent relevant theories are (a) decreased inhibition (e.g., Hasher & Zacks, 1988) and (b) cognitive slowing (Cerella, 1985; Salthouse, 1996). The theory of decreased inhibition works like this: To function and attend to problems or tasks, we constantly inhibit many aspects of information, both internal (e.g., random intrusive thoughts) and external (e.g., visual distractions, noise, etc.), so that we can focus on the relevant information for any particular task. Hasher and Zacks (1988) proposed that older adults lose the ability to inhibit information, which allows irrelevant information to remain active in memory and interfere with the relevant information to perform a particular task. This impairment leaves older adults with a more cluttered working memory, which in turn leads to relatively poor performance compared with younger adults on many tasks. This allows, for instance, intrusions of personal information into recall tasks and increased topic shifts during conversation (Hasher & Zacks, 1988).

The theory of cognitive slowing is probably the most influential theory of cognitive aging. It maintains that we undergo a relatively general and ubiquitous (although not necessarily uniform) slowing of processing speed as we age, and this decrease in processing speed affects performance on not only sensory and motor tasks but perceptual-cognitive tasks as well (Salthouse, 1996). In the vast majority of tests of memory and reasoning, older adults perform more slowly, with a consistently high correlation of about .45 between age and measures of cognitive speed (e.g., Salthouse, 1985). This is true for both cross-sectional studies as well as longitudinal analyses (e.g., Schaie, 1989) and is true for a wide range of tests, including relatively simple tasks such as digit copying (e.g., Salthouse, 1996) and cognitively more complex tasks such as recall and recognition of word lists (e.g., Verhaeghen & Vandenbroucke, 1998). One of the crucial aspects of this theory is that it accurately predicts the fact that we not only show an increase in the typical "speed-accuracy trade-off" as we age (i.e., we become less accurate if we do something in a short period of time) but also become less accurate overall, even if there is no time limit (Verhaeghen & Vandenbroucke, 1998). This is due to what Salthouse (1996) calls the "simultaneity mechanism":

> Products of early processing may be lost by the time that later processing is completed [and] . . . relevant information may no longer be available when it is needed. . . . Information

decreases in availability (i.e., quantity or quality) over time as a function of either decay or displacement. (Salthouse, 1996, p. 407)

This interplay between processing speed on one task and the (in)ability to perform subsequent tasks helps to explain why older adults are both slower and less accurate even when time is not an issue. This aspect of cognitive aging, although discussed most often in terms of processing speed, is also another way of talking about limited resources or processing capacity often associated with the concepts of attention and working memory.

Real-Life Problem Solving

Finally, there is a literature looking at real-life problem solving and the relationship between real-life problem solving and various laboratory tests. It is very difficult to extrapolate from the laboratory tests of mental functions reviewed above to real-life problem solving because, simply put, laboratory tests are not very similar to real life. Attempts to correlate performance on intelligence tests and real-life tasks, such as interpreting medicine bottle labels and understanding the newspaper, have yielded variable results, making it difficult to draw conclusions about if and how laboratory testing predicts real-life performance (e.g., Schaie, 1996).

The difficulty in finding correlations between laboratory testing and real-life problem solving stems from many differences between the two. One important difference is the physical context: Tests are given in testing rooms, but everyday problems are solved in rich, supportive contexts that often help define and guide the problem-solving process. Second, the time course of laboratory problems and real-life problems is dramatically different: Laboratory reasoning problems often take less than a minute to solve, whereas most everyday problems are solved over hours, days, or even years. For these reasons, it is difficult to draw conclusions about everyday problem solving from laboratory test data. Luckily, we do not have to.

There is now a significant literature investigating how younger and older adults solve everyday problems, including practical activities of daily living such as making meals, taking medications, reading maps, and obtaining appropriate healthcare (Diehl, Willis, & Schaie, 1995; Marsiske & Willis, 1998; Willis, 1996).

Diehl et al. (1995) created a protocol to observe older adults solve problems in their own homes. The protocol involved simulations of how to bake a cake using a cooking chart, a microwave oven, and a timer; take medicines by using information on medicine bottle labels; and check itemized calls on a phone bill. Surprisingly, less than half of the 62 subjects ages 66 to 87 were able to perform the tasks correctly. Analysis of demographic data and performance on other tasks indicated that poor real-life problem solving was associated with poor performance on measures of both fluid and crystallized intelligence.

Other research has shown that at least in some domains, older adults can solve problems just as well as younger adults but do so differently. For instance, Meyer, Russo, and Talbot (1995) asked women of various ages to make decisions based on a written scenario about cancer treatment. They found that all age groups reached the same decisions but did so in different manners and at different points in the process. The older women sought less information than younger women, based their decisions on less information, and made their decisions earlier in the process.

Explanations for differences between young and older adult problem-solving strategies often invoke the notion of prior experience. Because older adults have more experience with various domains of knowledge, they are experts at solving some problems. This expertise enables them to use previously developed scripts and personal beliefs to facilitate decision making with less information gathering. This results in fast and personalized problem solving. In contrast, younger adults have less experience and tend to solve problems by gathering objective data to inform their decisions. Another way to conceptualize these differences is captured by the contrast of *bottom-up* and *top-down* processing. Bottom-up processing is characterized by the methodical collection and consolidation of information, beginning with basic information, and building on that in a piecemeal fashion to arrive at a solution. This is typical of

younger adults' problem-solving style. Top-down processing is characterized by beginning with abstract, often intuitive, solutions and applying them. In reality, of course, people use both approaches. However, the relative reliance on one more than the other may change as we age, with older adults using a less explicit and more intuitive approach (Labouvie-Vief & Hakim Larson, 1989).

BEHAVIORAL CHARACTERISTICS AND NEUROPATHOLOGY OF PROBLEM-SOLVING IMPAIRMENTS

Many patients with problem-solving impairments have no frank cognitive deficits: They are not aphasic, have no visuospatial deficits, and appear to have intact memory. But in real life, they have difficulty figuring out how to find out what time a train leaves, how to get a library card, or how to go to the market. Patients make various types of errors: Some cannot initiate plans; some are impulsive, using the first solution that occurs to them without considering other possibly better solutions; some have difficulty monitoring their own performance or ignore feedback that their plan is not working; some fail to consider relevant information when choosing a solution to a problem; and many are distractible. Their responses may be perseverative, reverting to prior solutions rather than generating a novel solution. Problem-solving impairments can often be attributed to deficits in attention, reasoning, or planning. Patients with problem-solving deficits also often have poor insight (i.e., limited appreciation of their condition) and poor judgment (i.e., limited ability to plan and take care of routine tasks from making appointments to tending to their finances).

Several case descriptions illustrate how deficits in executive functions and problem solving manifest themselves. Phineas Gage was a foreman of a railroad construction gang who survived an explosion that blasted an iron tamping bar through the front of his head in 1848. (Macmillan, 1996). Prior to the accident, he was of average intelligence, "energetic and persistent in executing all his plans of operation." Remarkably, he recovered well both physically and in terms of many mental functions. He was able to talk, and his memory of past events was good. However, several abnormalities were documented in detailed accounts by Harlow (1848, 1868):

> He is fitful, irreverent, indulging at times in the grossest profanity . . . impatient of restraint or advice when it conflicts with his desires, at times pertinaciously obstinate, yet capricious and vacillating, devising many plans of operation, which are no sooner arranged than they are abandoned in turn for others appearing more feasible. (Harlow, 1868, qtd. in Macmillan, 1996, p. 247)

This description captures typical changes in personality, social behavior, and the inability to plan that often accompany frontal lobe damage. The impulsive nature of many patients with problem-solving abilities is also highlighted. Although Gage never returned to work as a foreman, he was apparently able to work at simpler jobs such as caring for horses (Macmillan, 1996).

A more recent case was described by Damasio and colleagues (Damasio & Anderson, 1993; Eslinger & Damasio, 1985). This is the story of a gentleman with an unremarkable early adulthood. He graduated from a business college, married, had two children, became a church elder, and rose to a supervisory rank in his company. He then became "unreliable, could not seem to complete his usual work and experienced marital difficulties." The doctors discovered that he had a tumor compressing both of his frontal lobes, which was removed. However, problems persisted. What makes this case so interesting is the contrast between preserved overall intelligence, as gauged by standard intelligence testing and normal performance on basic neuropsychological tests, compared to his behavior, which was marked by poor judgment. He was fired from several jobs because he could not "keep reliable standards" and because of "tardiness" and "lack of productivity." He entered into bad business ventures against sound advice, his marriage broke up, and he remarried within a month after his divorce, again against advice. The second marriage also ended in divorce. Interestingly, his deficits were

seen by psychiatrists as reflecting emotional and psychological adjustment problems and attributed to personality style. This case demonstrates a strong link between what we often perceive as personality characteristics and deficits in executive/problem-solving functions. What is most striking in this case is the patient's inability to plan appropriately and hold gainful employment despite normal intelligence and good motor, sensory, and communication skills.

The frequent association of problem-solving deficits and personality changes is no coincidence—they share cognitive components and are subserved by overlapping brain regions. Problem solving and personality are similar in that they are distinct from specific cognitive domains (such as language), and yet they can influence all realms of cognitive processing. Problem-solving deficits and personality problems can have a negative influence on behavior in any domain because they direct and organize behavior generally. The combination of personality changes and deficits in problem solving conspires to create problems in interpersonal interactions (Dimitrov, 1996).

Further evidence that deficits in problem solving and changes in personality are closely related comes from the fact that they are frequently impaired together, by damage to the frontal lobes, on either the left or right side (Luria, 1969; McCarthy & Warrington, 1990). Although there are many different behavioral consequences of frontal lobe damage, one consistent finding is that patients with damage to either the left or right frontal lobe are compromised in their ability to guide behavior appropriately and to plan for the future (Damasio & Anderson, 1993).

The frontal lobes are distinct from the other cortical lobes in that they developed rather recently in evolution and remain more mysterious in their function than other brain regions. They have been described as a riddle (Teuber, 1964); the youngest, the most complex, and the least studied portion of the cerebral hemispheres (Luria, 1969); and the most mystifying of the major subdivisions of the cerebral cortex (Nauta, 1971). The human frontal lobes are also quite large compared to the other lobes, occupying more than one third of the human cerebral cortex

(Damasio & Anderson, 1993). They are characterized by having distinct anatomical regions and a high level of connectivity with other cortical and subcortical regions (Goldman-Rakic, 1987; Tekin & Cummings, 2002). Because of this high level of connectivity, particularly with subcortical regions, the deficits most associated with frontal lobe lesions can also occur after damage to connected subcortical regions. Therefore, frontal syndromes are sometimes described as "frontal-subcortical" syndromes.

The areas of the frontal lobes are distinguished by different cytoarchitectonic subdivisions (Stuss & Benson, 1987), as well as connectivity to other brain regions and their primary functions (Damasio & Anderson, 1993) (see Figure 9.1). It is helpful to eliminate from this discussion the regions of the frontal lobes concerned primarily with movement and motor control: the precentral gyrus and the supplementary motor cortex, which are those regions of the frontal lobe closest to the parietal lobe. It is the **prefrontal cortex** that is most relevant to the behavioral syndromes that interfere with problem solving. This includes the **orbitofrontal cortex,** the regions just above the eye sockets; the **dorsolateral frontal cortex,** the regions at the most anterior reaches of the frontal lobes, also called the frontal convexity; and **medial-frontal cortex,** the regions of the anterior cingulate cortex, wrapping around the anterior portion (genu) of the corpus callosum.

There have been many attempts to further associate specific behavioral abnormalities with portions of the frontal lobes.

Luria (1969) associated damage to the medial-frontal areas with deficits in concentration and attention and the more lateral aspects of the frontal lobes with failures in the procedural aspects of problem solving. Milner (1971) emphasized the importance of the dorsolateral sections of the frontal lobe in causing impairments in certain problem-solving tasks, but others have suggested that the more severe behavioral disturbances arise from damage to the medial surface (Drewe, 1975). For instance, Damasio and Anderson (1993) describe a study that compared the behavioral deficits in patients with medial versus other frontal damage. The group with medial frontal damage consistently demonstrated poor ability to organize and carry out normal activities, leading to poor decision making, the breakup of personal relationships, and financial disaster. Damage elsewhere in the frontal lobes showed less behavioral disruption.

Cummings & Mega (2003) summarize the current literature on the frontal lobes and impairments that Result from frontal lobe damage.

The orbitofrontal cortex mediates self-monitoring, and lesions can produce disinhibition of behavior, impulsiveness, tactlessness, loss of interpersonal sensitivity, poor social judgment, limited insight, irritability, mood lability, hypomania, depression, poor hygiene, and neglect of personal care.

The dorsolateral frontal cortex receives input from a wide range of cortical areas, including sensory association regions. The dorsolateral-subcortical circuit is parallel but separate from the orbitofrontal-subcortical circuit and also involves the caudate nucleus, globus pallidus, substantia nigra, and dorsomedial thalamus. This region is responsible for focused attention, and lesions are associated with memory retrieval problems, difficulty altering set-in responses to changing contingencies, impaired strategy generation for solving complex problems, poor abstraction, reduced mental control, and depression.

The medial-frontal cortex is associated with motivation, and lesions can lead to reduced interest, poor motivation, impaired initiation, overall reduced activity, impaired task maintenance, and decreased emotional concern (Cummings & Mega, 2003).

A review of 28 studies looking at the incidence of problem-solving deficits after left versus right frontal damage found deficits associated with right frontal damage in 6 studies, left frontal damage in 14 studies, and either left- or right-sided damage in 8 studies. The authors concluded that "a considerable proportion of tasks appear to be affected by damage to either the right or left frontal regions," and they suggested that this lack of asymmetry within the frontal lobes with regard to problem solving reflects the fact that problem-solving tasks are complex and involve multiple processing systems (McCarthy & Warrington, 1990, p. 356).

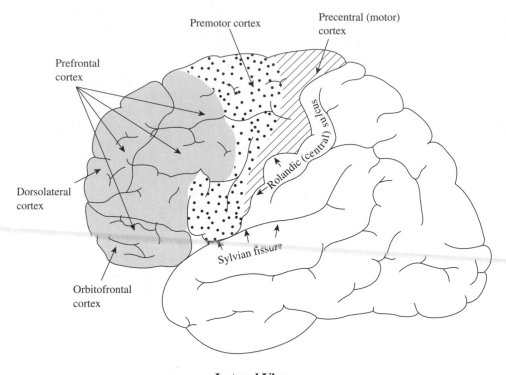

Lateral View

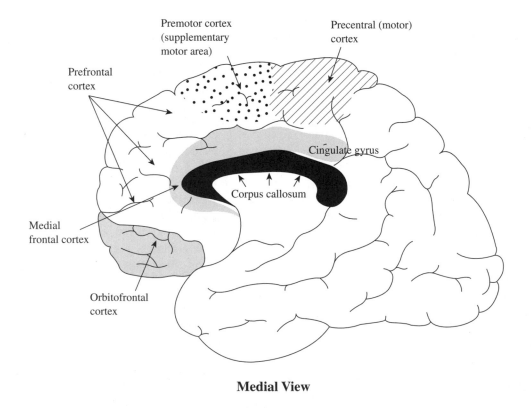

Medial View

Figure 9.1   Important aspects of the frontal lobes.

DIAGNOSIS OF PROBLEM-SOLVING DISORDERS

Poor performance in everyday problem solving is probably the best way to diagnose problem-solving impairments because it is in real contexts that the subtle effects of problem-solving deficits appear: The patient misses appointments, gets married and quickly divorced, or makes obviously poor business decisions. Although real-life problem-solving deficits are informative, they are difficult to measure and quantify and are, therefore, for diagnostic purposes, typically supplemented with formal tests of problem solving. Because problem solving is so complex, any evaluation of problem-solving deficits must not only assess success at problem solving but also the processes used to solve problems, at what point in the process difficulties are encountered, and the patient's insight into his or her own impairment. There are several broad categories of tests to assess problem solving: (a) tests of attention, and working memory (b) reasoning, (c) planning and (d) measures of problem solving that simulate everyday contexts.

Attention and Working Memory

Because attention is so fundamental to problem solving and because so many patients have underlying deficits in this domain, clinicians want to determine the degree of attentional impairment. As Lezak (1995) points out, "There are no tests of attention . . . one can only assess a certain aspect of human behavior with special interest for its attentional component," and inattention "appears as distractibility or impaired ability for focused behavior" (p. 352). Simply put: Attention can be gauged by performance on any activity or test, regardless of content.

Vigilance and span tests assess the immediate registration and temporary storage of information. They are often included in the discussion of immediate and/or working memory. These require the patient to repeat increasingly long sequences of material. Span tests form a continuum from those that test attention using repetition of digits to those that test working memory using simultaneous storage and processing tasks.

Assessment of working memory often uses modified span tests. The patient is given increasingly long sets of elements and has to hold them in mind while processing them in some way and then report them back. In general, performance on working memory tasks declines with age and is notably impaired in patients with Alzheimer's disease (e.g., MacDonald, Almor, Henderson, Kempler, & Andersen, 2001; Salthouse, 1991; Waters & Caplan, 2001). Words are the most flexible medium, and therefore there are many verbal span tests, but span tests are also available to test processing of visuospatial information.

Tests of vigilance assess focused attention. They typically present a sequence of auditory or written stimuli and ask the patient to indicate by tapping or raising her hand when a particular target appears. An auditory test of vigilance might present a series of 60 or more digits, asking the patient to tap when upon hearing a particular number. A visual version presents a page of numbers, and the patient is asked to cross out all instances of a particular number. The number of missed targets and, in the written version, the time taken to complete the task indicate the degree of attentional impairment. These tests show a decline in performance with age, demonstrated both in terms of increased time to complete and increased number of errors (Lezak, 1995).

Digit span is the most common forward span task. The examiner says numbers at about one digit per second, and the patient repeats them verbatim. The shortest list is two digits, and the longest list is seven or eight digits, depending on the test. It assesses only the simple and momentary storage of information. It does not involve remembering information for more than a few seconds or processing the information at any more than the most superficial level. Digit span is sensitive to left hemisphere damage and head trauma. Median recall for digits is about seven for adults ages 65 to 69 but depends on the list given and the age of the subject (Lezak, 1995). Variants of verbal span tasks use letters and words.

Visual span tests require the patient to repeat a pointing sequence. The examiner points to a series of printed squares or blocks, and the patient repeats the pointing sequence (Wechsler, 1997b). Because of the novelty of this sort of task, it requires more effort than digit span for both the examiner and the patient. Median forward visual span for 65-year-olds is about seven. Performance on the visual span tests is impaired by visual field defects and sequencing problems.

In backward digit span, the examiner presents digits as in forward span tasks, but the patient repeats the increasingly long series in the reverse order. Backward visual span likewise requires the patient to watch the examiner's pointing sequence and then repeat that sequence in the reverse order. Both backward digit and visual span are more challenging than forward span tasks because they require remembering the forward sequence and processing that sequence (i.e., reversing it). Median backward span for 65-year-olds is about six.

Other working memory tasks are more complicated because they introduce distractor tasks to prevent rehearsal of material in short-term memory. The many variations of the Peterson technique (Peterson & Peterson, 1959) present patients with a visual or auditory stimulus, often a consonant trigram (e.g., "QLX"). Immediately following the stimulus presentation, the patient begins counting backwards from a given number (e.g., "386") until told to stop and report the stimulus. The delay between stimulus presentation and recall is varied to determine the effect of different delays on memory, with longer delays associated with poorer recall (Lezak, 1995). Although older healthy subjects perform slightly less well than younger healthy subjects, age appears to have a minimal effect (Stuss, Stethem, & Poirier, 1987).

In sentence span tasks, the patient reads or the examiner presents sets of sentences, and at the end of each set, the subject recalls the last word in each sentence (Baddeley & Wilson, 1985; Daneman & Carpenter, 1980). As the sentences are presented, the patient also reports if each sentence makes sense. So, for instance, a patient might read or hear the sentence "The policeman ate the apple" and "The girl sang the water" (Lezak, 1995). The patient reads or listens to each sentence and responds yes or no after each, depending on whether they make sense. Then, at the end of the set, the patient reports back the last words of the sentences—in this case, "apple,

water." Sentence lists increase to sets of five or six sentences. Performance on sentence and digit span tests is highly correlated (Daneman & Carpenter, 1980; MacDonald et al., 2001).

A few examples of span tasks of this sort are given below. Sample stimuli are on the left of the arrow, and the correct response is to the right of the arrow.

Digit ordering: 3–7–2–6–8 ⇒ 2–3–6–7–8 (Kempler, Almor, Tyler, Andersen, & MacDonald, 1998; MacDonald et al., 2001)

Month ordering: October–June–December ⇒June–October–December (Kempler, Almor, et al., 1998)

Sequencing letters and numbers: L–3–R–9–D–5 ⇒ 3–5–9–B–L–R (Wechsler, 1997b)

Divided and alternating attention, like working memory, involve focusing on two aspects of the environment. Divided attention can be tested by having a patient perform two tasks at once, such as crossing out all odd numbers and numbers above seven on a list of digits. Alternating attention can be tested by having a patient alternate addition and subtraction on a series of number pairs. A classic test of alternating attention is the Trail-Making Test, in which patients connect labeled points on a piece of paper. In Part A, patients connect consecutively numbered circles. In Part B, patients alternate between circles labeled with numbers and letters, with the correct trail leading from 1 to A to 2 to B to 3 to C and so forth (Lewis, Kelland, & Kupke, 1990; Reitan, 1958).

Reasoning

Many tests assess what is variably called concept formation, abstraction, and reasoning. Both verbal and nonverbal tests are used. Common verbal test formats, along with a sample item, are given as follows:

- Two-word similarities: In what way are a *piano* and a *drum* alike? (Wechsler, 1997b)
- Three-word similarities: What do *book, teacher,* and *newspaper* have in common? (Terman & Merrill, 1973)
- Differences: What are the differences between a *bird* and a *dog?* (Terman & Merrill, 1973)

- Odd man out: Which word does **not** fit with the others: *spade, saw, ax, log?* (Luria, 1966)
- Verbal absurdities: What is odd about seeing icebergs that had been melted in the Gulf Stream? (Terman & Merrill, 1973)
- Open-ended questions: If you were lost in the forest, how would you go about finding your way out? (Wechsler, 1997b)
- Proverb interpretation: What does it mean to say *Don't count your chickens before they hatch?* (Gorham, 1956)

Test items, even within one format, vary in difficulty. The degree of difficulty or abstraction affects performance. Compare the difficulty of defining the similarity between *yellow* and *green* versus *poem* and *statue* versus *hibernation* and *migration*. As discussed in Chapter 6, proverbs also vary in difficulty, depending on their familiarity.

Patients' responses to open-ended questions are often neither right nor wrong. This necessitates the option of scoring semi-abstract responses and giving partial credit. The following possible responses to the *hibernation* and *migration* similarity item illustrate the degrees of abstraction (Wechsler, 1997b):

- Errors/concrete: Bears hibernate, birds migrate;
- Semi-abstract: Both happen in winter;
- Fully abstract responses: These are ways animals adapt to their environment and methods animals use to adapt to seasonal or climactic changes.

Visual reasoning tests are useful for testing problem-solving ability in patients with aphasia. The visual tasks also allow assessment of the patient's ability to shift between categories, or **set shifting.** The Wisconsin Card Sorting Test (Berg, 1948; Grant & Berg, 1993) is a popular test of visual reasoning and set shifting. The test consists of a pack of cards. Each card shows one, two, three, or four repeated shapes (triangle, star, cross, or circle) in one of four colors (red, green, yellow, or blue). For instance, one card shows a green triangle, another a blue triangle, another three green circles, another three yellow stars, and so on. Four stimulus cards are placed in front of the patient, each containing a

different number of symbols, different symbols, and different colors (e.g., one red triangle, two green stars, three yellow crosses, four blue circles) (see Figure 9.2). The patient must sort the deck of cards on the basis of rules derived from number, color, or form. For example, all 2s go together, all reds go together, or all stars go together. In the standard administration, the patient simply starts placing cards under the stimulus cards and has to discover the rule the examiner has in mind, based on the examiner's feedback. Once the patient places 10 correct in a row, the examiner changes the rule. The number of trials it takes for the patient to figure out the new rule indicates how well he or she can shift from one category to another. There are several alternative ways to administer the test. For example, some clinicians accept the patient's first sort as correct and then overtly tell the patient to find another rule after 6 consistent responses within any one category (Nelson, 1976). Performance is scored by the number of categories achieved and the number of perseverative errors. Perseverative errors indicate problems in using feedback and limited conceptual flexibility. Performance on the Wisconsin Card Sorting Test is sensitive to age and the presence of brain damage (e.g., MacPherson, Phillips, & Della Sala, 2002). Older adults make more errors than younger adults, which appear to be due to a difficulty in "updating working memory"—that is, integrating the feedback given by the tester into their next decision (Hartman, Bolton, & Fehnel, 2001). Older adults perform at the same level as young adults if they are given additional visual cues, such as an arrow that accompanies the examiner's feedback, pointing at the "correct" sort (Hartman et al., 2001). Older healthy subjects and patients with frontal lobe damage, when compared to younger control subjects, achieve fewer categories (Drewe, 1974) and make more perseverative errors (Grafman, Jonas, & Salazar, 1990). Poor performance on this test has been associated with damage to the dorsolateral prefrontal regions (MacPherson et al., 2002) but is not restricted to this area; impaired performance is also evident after posterior lesions (Teuber, Battersby, & Bender, 1951), diffuse head trauma (Stuss & Benson, 1987), and in Parkinson's disease (Taylor, Saint-Cyr, & Lang, 1986).

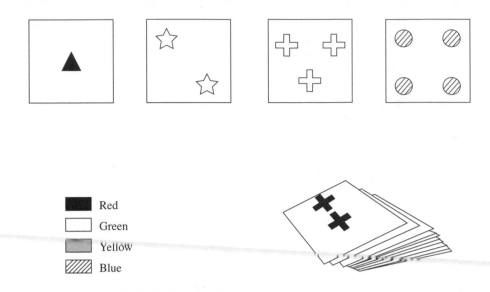

Red
Green
Yellow
Blue

Figure 9.2   The Wisconsin Card Sorting Test.

Progressive Matrices is a test of nonverbal reasoning first developed by Raven (Raven, 1960) and now adapted by others (Wechsler, 1997b). Each item presents a figure with a missing part. The patient has to select from an array of solutions the one that best completes the picture or the pattern. Some items are simple pattern matching or part/whole completion, and some require analogical reasoning. Performance on the perceptually based items is most affected by right hemisphere damage; the conceptually based items are more affected by left hemisphere damage (Villardita, 1985). As with most other tasks, impulsive and distractible performance is indicative of frontal lobe damage.

A visual analog to verbal absurdities requires the patient to identify what is wrong with pictures that are missing a logically important element (e.g., Picture Completion subtest of the Wechsler Scales [WAIS-III]; Wechsler, 1997b). One example is man looking in a mirror, but his reflected image does not have his beard. The patient can identify the problem verbally or by pointing (see Figure 9.3).

Planning

Several tests of general problem-solving ability focus on the patient's ability to plan and develop a strategy. Tower tasks present a series of rings on sticks in a particular configuration. The task is to rearrange them to reach a particular target configuration, constrained by color and/or size. The task requires planning because the goal is to attain the desired pattern with the minimum number of moves in the fewest steps possible. This requires anticipating what moves are required and the most efficient order in which to make them. The versions of the tower test vary the level of difficulty. The Tower of London (Shallice, 1982) uses three balls of different colors; the Tower of Hanoi (Glosser & Goodglass, 1990) uses three rings of different sizes and stipulates that any time two or more rings are on a particular stick, the smaller must be on top of the larger; and the Tower of Toronto (Saint-Cyr & Taylor, 1992) uses four rings of different colors but the same size.

Maze tracing also explicitly involves looking ahead and is therefore used to test planning ability. The Porteus Maze Test (Porteus, 1959, 1965) presents a drawn maze; the patient's task is to trace the maze from beginning to end without entering any blind alleys. There are many different mazes that vary in complexity. The number of mazes completed successfully and the time required to completion are both sensitive to brain damage.

Figure 9.3   An example of a nonverbal reasoning test. The patient is asked to identify what is logically wrong with the picture (from the Modified Picture Completion Test, developed by and described in Dick, Teng, Kempler, Davis, and Taussig (2002). Drawing by Susan Black. Used by permission of the authors.

Tests of Everyday Problem Solving

Problem solving is influenced by context more than many other cognitive domains. With this in mind, there are now several batteries that evaluate problem-solving ability in naturalistic contexts.

The Test of Everyday Attention (Robertson, Ward, & Ridgeway, 1996) assesses selective attention, sustained attention, and attentional switching in plausible contexts. During the test, subjects pretend they are in real-life situations and are confronted with a problem to solve. Problems include searching for symbols on a map, working an elevator, searching for telephone numbers in a directory, and playing the lottery. In the map subtest, for example, the patient is given a colored map and 2 minutes to find as many restaurant logos as possible. In the lottery subtest, the patient pretends to be listening for winning numbers, which are known to end in 55. To do this, the subject listens to a string of numbers and writes down the two letters preceding all numbers that end in 55.

The Behavioral Assessment of the Dysexecutive Syndrome (Wilson, Alderman, Burgess, Emslie, & Evans, 1996) also assesses skills involved in problem solving. Again, problems are embedded in somewhat familiar contexts, and patients must pretend they are encountering real-life challenges. For instance, the temporal judgment subtest asks the patient to estimate how long a routine dental appointment will last. To assess strategy formation, patients demonstrate how they would search for a set of lost keys in a field. A test of planning asks patients to identify a route to visit 6 of 12 locations on a zoo map. Wilson et al. (1996) also developed the Dysexecutive Questionnaire, which asks individuals to rate how often certain behaviors occur. For instance, one item assessing impulsivity states, "I sometimes act without thinking, doing the first thing that comes to mind."

Royall and colleagues (e.g., Royall, Mahurin, & Gray, 1992) developed the Executive Interview, a 25-question assessment protocol for executive functions that takes about 10 to 15 minutes to administer. This test includes items, designed to evaluate the types of executive problems commonly seen in patients with frontal lobe damage, including motor and cognitive perseveration, verbal intrusions, loss of spontaneity, and disinhibition. The test correlates well with more complex and time-consuming tests of executive function, such as the Wisconsin Card Sorting Test, and distinguishes well between those patients with and without disruptive behaviors (Royall et al., 1992).

Research protocols have been reported that might be too cumbersome and time-consuming for routine clinical evaluations but provide excellent ideas for other ways to assess everyday problem solving. Cornelius and Caspi (1987) developed the Everyday Problem Solving Inventory (EPSI) to assess problem solving in healthy older adults. It involves presenting problem situations in writing, along with four solutions.

Situations involve consumer issues, home problems, or difficulties with social interaction. The solutions represent different approaches to problem solving, including (a) problem-focused attention, (b) cognitive problem analysis, (c) passive dependent behavior, and (d) avoidant thinking and denial. The patient rates each response for appropriateness. This test obviously relies on visual and language skills and should be adapted to impaired populations with caution. That said, it has been used with good success with patients with frontal lobe damage, about half of whom demonstrate different responses than normal controls (Dimitrov, 1996).

Sample Problem:

You would like to get some friends to come visit you more often.

Possible Solutions:
- Try to figure out why they do not seem to make an effort to visit you.
- Invite them to your home.
- Do not be overly concerned about it and turn your attention to other things.
- Accept the situation and do nothing.

Channon and Crawford (1999) attempted to increase the ecological validity of problem-solving assessment even further by showing real-life problems on videotape. The Predicaments Test presents reenacted, awkward situations and then asks patients to (a) generate solutions to the problem, (b) choose an optimal solution, and (c) judge whether alternate solutions are good. This type of task takes a lot of time to produce, administer, and score, but it mimics real-life problem solving by providing verbal and visual contexts in an untimed open-ended response format. Research with this protocol suggests that frontal lobe damage impairs everyday problem solving more than posterior brain damage and that there are few differences in problem-solving deficits after left versus right hemisphere damage (Channon & Crawford, 1999).

TREATMENT OF PROBLEM-SOLVING DISORDERS

Occupational therapists, speech-language pathologists, and/or clinical neuropsychologists generally provide behavioral treatments for problem-solving deficits. Therapeutic approaches to problem solving include exercises to improve underlying cognitive deficits and real-world function. The following are examples of therapeutic activities designed to address specific aspects of problem solving from a component abilities perspective and from a functional perspective.

Component Abilities: Attention Working Memory, Reasoning, and Planning

Activities designed to improve **attention** and working memory are similar to the tasks used in assessment. It is important to create therapeutic tasks that are challenging but not impossible for the patients' current level of abilities.

Activities designed to improve selective attention often incorporate distracting and irrelevant information into a simple attention task. For instance, during a number monitoring task the numbers would be presented in the context of other irrelevant auditory information, such as a radio program in the background or an overheard conversation.

Sustained attention tasks might require the patient to tap every time he or she hears a certain number in a sequence of random numbers. In a more advanced version, the patient taps every time he or she hears a number that is preceded by the number one lower than it (e.g., 4–7–6–7*–8*–2–5–6*) (Sohlberg & Mateer, 1989).

Improving divided attention requires activities that have the patient focus on two tasks simultaneously. An example of this sort would be having the patient sort playing cards by suit but also turn over cards that have another characteristic, such as even numbers.

Alternating attention is facilitated with tasks that include two operations that alternate during a single task. An alternating attention task might have the patient switch between crossing out even and odd numbers on a verbal cue.

The example tasks given here use numbers, but the content is incidental to the type of attention that is required. A therapist adapts any of domains and level of task difficulty to challenge the patient (Sohlberg & Mateer, 1989).

Therapeutic tasks to improve **reasoning** ability often involve generating information about patterns and categories. The activities listed under diagnostic procedures for reasoning can all be adapted and expanded as treatment activities. The following are a few other common therapeutic activities to improve abstraction and reasoning:

- Generate superordinate categories: What category does *chisel* belong to? ⇒ *tool*
- Generate exemplars of general categories: List three examples of *flowers* ⇒ *rose, tulip, daisy*
- Generate opposites: What is the opposite of healthy? ⇒ *sick*
- Twenty questions: The examiner thinks of an object, and the patient asks yes/no questions to discover the object.
- Analogies: *Car* is to *engine* as *kite* is to ⇒ *wind*
- Identify the pattern in a letter or number series: 2–4–6–8–10; 1–1–2–3–5–8–13

Therapeutic activities to facilitate **planning** include sequencing tasks that provide opportunities to anticipate and evaluate outcomes. Visual sequencing tasks involve arranging pictures in a logical order to depict elements of a complex activity. Planning can also be improved by verbal exercises in which the patient describes how to perform inherently sequential activities, such as preparing meals or planting a garden.

FUNCTIONAL APPROACHES

Functional approaches to problem solving use everyday contexts to develop problem-solving skills and insight. Zoltan and Siev (1996) suggest a range of activities, all using the Yellow Pages: The clinician gives the patient hypothetical problems, and the patient's task is to find appropriate resources using the phone book. Describing each step and its logical connection to other steps, predicting outcomes of each step, and labeling each step are all part of the exercise. Of course, there is nothing like the real thing: Therapeutically designed and supervised tasks such as buying something at a store, preparing a meal, understanding drug doses, reading a train schedule, or planning a vacation involve all of the fundamental elements of attention, reasoning, and planning and provide the practice necessary to recover problem-solving skills.

Naturally, some patients will not be able to regain the skills necessary to solve problems independently but can make use of (a) environmental adaptations, (b) adaptive devices, and (c) appointing a guardian and/or power of attorney. Environmental adaptations often help primarily by reducing distractions. Eliminating extraneous noise and visual clutter will help patients maintain focus on the target object or activity. This can be accomplished by physically changing the patient's environment during therapy for the purpose of learning to focus. It can also be accomplished by adapting the patient's home environment so that it is less distracting—for example, turning off TVs and radios during other activities, limiting the number of people talking at once, emphasizing face-to-face interaction rather than talking over noise or between rooms, and organizing cabinets, closets, and drawers so that objects are easy to locate. Complex written directions can be simplified by visually highlighting the key parts to help patients discriminate important from irrelevant elements (Zoltan & Siev, 1996).

Adaptive devices include mnemonic aids such as computerized planners, wall calendars, labeled pillboxes, and lists. Simple written reminders can help: A list of things to do before leaving the house will help avoid obvious problems such as leaving the stove on.

10

AMNESIA: DISTURBANCES OF MEMORY

Chapter Preview

1. What is memory?

Memory is a general term that encompasses several distinct processes, including learning, storage, and retrieval of information.

2. How does memory change with age?

Although more than three quarters of older adults report difficulty with their memory, fewer than 40% actually show memory impairments. Retrieval of recently learned information is the most common aspect of memory to show decline with aging.

3. What are the behavioral characteristics of amnesia?

Amnesia describes pathological memory problems. Patients with amnesia have difficulty learning new information and retrieving information of all types.

4. What is the neuropathology of amnesia?

Amnesia is most reliably associated with damage to the medial-temporal lobes, particularly the hippocampi.

5. How are memory disorders diagnosed?

Memory disorders are diagnosed by assessing the ability to learn and retrieve verbal and nonverbal information after various time delays.

6. How are memory disorders treated?

Memory disorders can be ameliorated by exercises to improve learning and recall through use of cues and practice, as well as the use of compensatory techniques ranging from handwritten notes to automated systems that store information.

INTRODUCTION

As children, we play memory games such as Concentration and Simon. As young adults, we develop conscious strategies to remember things, and we make lists and even read books on how to enhance memory. As we approach middle age and later adulthood, we become anxious about the increasingly frequent episodes when we cannot find the right word, recall someone's name, or find our car keys. We become anxious because memory lapses can disrupt daily function, cause embarrassment, and may herald dementia. Memory loss is one of the most frequent, feared, and disruptive disorders of aging.

WHAT IS MEMORY?

Memory allows us to mentally record an experience and retrieve it later. Memory involves many different psychological processes, most prominently the following:

Learning: The initial perception and acquisition of new information.

Retention: After information is learned, it is stored—or retained—for a period of time. The process of storing information is gradual, lasting months or even years, and is sometimes referred to as consolidation of memory (Bauer, 1993; Squire, Cohen, & Nadel, 1984).

Retrieval: Once information is stored in memory, we access it by a process called retrieval. We retrieve information through active recall, as when we search for and remember a name or a word. We also retrieve information from memory in less active ways, as when we merely recognize a face that we see, essentially matching current and past experiences. The act of knowing something, such as a word, or having a sense of familiarity with something, despite the lack of conscious recollection of an encounter with it, is a type of passive memory retrieval.

Forgetting: Memory is also defined by instances when it fails. We say that we forget something when we have trouble recalling or recognizing information that we previously knew.

We distinguish aspects of memory by the type of material remembered, how the material is remembered, and the time period during which it is remembered. These distinctions allow us to characterize the type of memory problems we encounter in healthy aging and memory disorders.

Procedural memory and **declarative memory** describe types of material remembered. Procedural memory concerns the acquisition and retrieval of motor and cognitive skills that underlie specific procedures, for example, learning to walk, ride a bicycle, type, or drive an automobile. These skills are often learned without conscious awareness and, once learned, are typically recalled and used without awareness, a phenomenon called **implicit memory.** Procedural memories are typically retained in healthy aging and in cases of memory disorders.

Declarative memory pertains to the ability to learn and remember information about events and the world (Lezak, 1995). This is the type of memory that most people refer to when they report memory problems. Declarative memory is also sometimes called **explicit memory** because it often results from a more conscious and intentional effort to learn. This is familiar from schoolwork in which we study and rehearse specific material to enhance later retrieval for test performance. Declarative memory is subdivided into episodic and semantic memory. **Episodic memory** refers to memory for specific events and personal experiences—a wedding you attended or the last time you had an ice cream cone. **Semantic memory** refers to learning and recalling specific facts and general knowledge, including the meaning of words and facts such as what year the United States gained independence from England. Semantic memories are theoretically independent from the episodes in which they were acquired. For instance, retrieving the meaning of a word or historical fact does not require you to remember the original occasion in which you learned that word or fact.

Memories are is also classified by the modality of the material that is remembered. Nonverbal memory refers to learning and retrieval of visual information, melodies, tactile sensations, and smells. Verbal memory concerns learning and retrieval of words and other information encoded by language. Declarative memories often have verbal and nonverbal components, as when you remember a conversation, recalling the information content (verbal) and the face of the person talking to you (visual). Procedural memories can be also either verbal, such as learning to pronounce a complex word, or nonverbal, as in learning a new route to school.

A common classification of memory and memory disorders relates to the length of time that material is remembered (see Table 10.1). The most fundamental time-based distinction in memory is short-term versus long-term memory. Sometimes the terms *primary* and *secondary memory* are also used to refer to short-term and long-term memory. These terms are rather vague. *Short-term memory* can relate to information retained over seconds, minutes, hours, or even days (Lezak, 1995). *Long-term memory* relates to periods that overlap with short-term memory, essentially anything longer than 60 seconds, but extends to years. The difficulty defining even this basic dichotomy illustrates the fact that there are few clear distinctions between time frames—memories for recent events blend into memories for events that happened just before them, and so on, into earliest childhood memories. The following is a clinically useful four-way memory classification based on time.

Sensory Stage (Less Than 2 Seconds)

The first important component of memory is perception and recognition of the to-be-remembered object, information, or experience. The **sensory stage** is the essential first step for learning any information. If you cannot perceive or recognize the information to be remembered, the process of memory will be derailed from the beginning. The sensory organs (eyes, ears) and the sensory cortices are essential for this aspect of the memory process. This very short-term information storage capacity, estimated to range from a third of a second to possibly as long as 2 seconds, is sometimes referred to as **iconic memory** in the visual system and **echoic memory** in the auditory system (e.g., Dick, 1974; Harrell, Parente, Bellingrath, & Lisicia, 1992).

Immediate and Working Memory (0–30 Seconds)

People register new information and can repeat it or re-create it without rehearsal or manipulation during the first several seconds after they experience it. Verbal memory span is the amount of information we can retain verbatim, usually between seven and nine words. This important and early stage of memory is sometimes subsumed under the terms *attention, short term, primary,* or *immediate memory.* During this early stage of memory, we often manipulate information. In the simplest case, we rehearse in order to retain. Frequently, we do something else with it—for example, label an image, categorize words on a word list, or mentally compare new information with other memories. These manipulations affect our memory, sometimes improving it, as with rehearsal and labeling. We use the concept of working memory to distinguish verbatim and iconic memory from what happens when information is stored and manipulated simultaneously (see Chapter 9). Working memory has three components. The phonological loop allows for short-term storage of speech material. The visuospatial sketchpad is the visual analog of the phonological loop. The central executive modulates and directs attention and other mental resources, affecting how much and how well information can be stored (Baddeley, 2000). The central executive helps explain the effects of information manipulation and distraction on short-term memory.

The association areas of the neocortex, as well as the prefrontal regions, are important for immediate and working memory. The time frame for this stage is from 0 to about 30 seconds (Lezak, 1995). This stage of memory allows us to recall a new name just after hearing it (La Rue, 1992) and rehearse a phone number to better remember it while searching for the telephone or while dialing the number.

Recent Memory (30 Seconds to Several Days)

The next stage in the memory process is the point at which information is consolidated and learned so that it lasts more than a few seconds.

Table 10.1   A Schematic to Differentiate Several Possible Components of Memory

Memory Stage	Phase	Time Course	Name	Required Anatomy	Test	Disease
Sensory	Perception of information	Immediate	Perception recognition	Basic sensory (neo) cortex		
Primary Short-term	Processing registration	Few seconds	Short-term, working, or immediate memory; phonological loop; visuospatial sketchpad; central executive	Sensory, motor, and association cortex (e.g., language areas for digits); prefrontal cortex; central executive areas	Digit span tests	Aphasia
Secondary Long-term	Storage/learning consolidation	Minutes, hours, days	Recent memory	Limbic system; hippocampi and amygdala; mamillary bodies; dorsal medial nuclei of thalamus; cortex for storage and retrieval mechanism	Orientation questions; new learning word lists	Korsakoff syndrome; Alzheimer's disease; case of H.M.
	Retrieval	Years	Remote memory; old memory	Left and right association cortex	Autobiographical questions	Alzheimer's disease

160

The time frame for this stage ranges from 30 seconds to a few days, sometimes longer (Lezak, 1995). A period of several minutes would obviously be considered short term. However, because the process of memory consolidation can be gradual, lasting months or even years, this phase is sometimes included under long-term memory (Lezak, 1995; Squire et al., 1984). This stage of memory allows you to recall a new name after meeting several other people in the course of an evening or over the period of a week (La Rue, 1992).

Researchers speculate that a particular change at the level of the synapse, called **long-term synaptic potentiation,** accompanies and explains this aspect of memory (Bear, Conners, & Paradiso, 2001; Hebb, 1949). Long-term potentiation refers to the fact that the temporary synaptic changes that accompany all events can become permanent by altering the structure of the synapse. These changes strengthen synaptic transmission over time and lead to neurons firing more readily than they did originally, in concert, creating a new cellular circuit. It is these new circuits that we suspect underlie consolidation of memories. Memory, then, at this level, is a particular assembly or circuit of neurons firing at the same rate or in the same pattern as when we first experienced an event. As the circuit is reignited, we reexperience the event. At the level of larger brain structures, it appears that the medial-temporal lobes (hippocampi, amygdala) and the diencephalon (dorsomedial nuclei of the thalamus and mamillary bodies of the hypothalamus) are crucial for this stage of learning and memory.

Remote Memory
(A Few Days to Many Years)

This aspect of memory describes the oldest memories, including historical facts and childhood recollections. It is impossible to draw a clear distinction between recent and remote memory because there are no clear breaks in memory, at least in the healthy individual.

The brain structures that appear involved in storage and retrieval of the oldest memories are the left and right association cortices. The time frame for this stage can be as short as a few days but is usually measured in years. This stage of memory allows us to recall, for example, names of distant relatives we have not seen or mentioned in years (La Rue, 1992).

AGE-RELATED CHANGES IN MEMORY

Incidence

Older adults often report that their memory has deteriorated (for a review, see Bolla, Lindgren, Bonaccorsy, & Bleeker, 1991; Ryan, 1992; Smith, 1996). In daily life, older adults report difficulty remembering names, where they put their keys and coat, telephone numbers, words, faces, directions, and the thread of a conversation (Bolla et al., 1991; Burke et al., 1991; Zelinski, Gilewski, & Thompson, 1980). Although as many as 84% of healthy 60-year-olds report memory difficulty, this number is less impressive when you consider that 73% of healthy 40-year-olds also complain of memory difficulty (Bolla et al., 1991). In a group of 199 healthy subjects between 39 and 89 years old, only 19% had *no* memory complaints, suggesting that memory complaints are quite common in general (Bolla et al., 1991). Nonetheless, the older participants reported more frequent incidences of forgetting and more frequent use of mnemonic devices, such as appointment books and grocery lists, than younger subjects. Interestingly, although older adults complain about memory loss, their subjective experience is not highly correlated with actual memory loss (Bolla et al., 1991). Factors other than age are important determiners of the severity of subjective memory complaints; higher depression scores and lower vocabulary levels correlate with memory complaints.

Characteristics

By most reports, age-related memory impairments are greater for episodic than semantic or procedural memory, recall than recognition, and recent than immediate or remote memory (Smith, 1996). From this characterization, it is clear that some aspects of memory deteriorate more than others. This captures the fact that older people are not generally amnesic but have specific, even isolated, problems with certain aspects of memory.

Older adults have relatively preserved immediate memory, allowing them to echo lists of numbers as accurately as younger adults. Procedural learning and memory underlying everyday tasks, such driving a car or riding a bicycle, are minimally impaired by aging. Insofar as they are affected, problems are generally attributed to motor slowing rather than memory per se. This is replicated in laboratory tasks in which older adults show the same learning and memory patterns as younger adults when acquiring procedural motor tasks such as tracing patterns in a mirror (Woodruff-Pak, 1997).

However, older adults have marked difficulty retrieving recently learned information. In laboratory tests, which primarily use word list learning, age differences demonstrate that older adults have more difficulty than younger adults recalling a list of words after a short delay or following interference from another task (e.g., Schonfield & Robertson, 1966; Woodruff-Pak, 1997).

Remote memories appear relatively stable with age. Bahrick, Bahrick, and Wittlinger (1975) tested adults' recall and recognition of high school classmates' names and faces. The participants ranged from 17 to 74 years old or, more important, from 3 months past high school graduation to more than 50 years past high school graduation. Hence, some subjects were asked to recognize people they may not have seen or thought about in more than 50 years. Subjects recognized about 90% of the faces up until 35 years after graduation. There was a slight decline in the oldest group, but even they, some 50 years after graduation, recognized 70% to 80% of their classmates. These data suggest that older memories are relatively stable for very long periods of time.

Explanations

Learning Versus Retrieval

This decline in memory could be due to problems in the process of learning or in the process of retrieval. If the difficulty is in the retrieval process, performance would be helped by cues or a multiple-choice format. Better performance with cues would indicate that they did learn the material initially but just had trouble retrieving it when asked. This appears to be the case: Aging affects recall much more than it affects recognition. That is, older adults have a harder time than younger adults recalling items from a list of learned words but can identify the forgotten items if they are given a multiple-choice or other recognition test. This is demonstrated by teaching word lists to adults and asking them to (a) recall the words and then (b) recognize them by picking the words out of a larger set. Recognition memory ("supported retrieval") is better than recall ("unsupported retrieval") for all age groups, but this difference is even greater for the old than for the young (Craik & McDowd, 1987). This suggests that aging impairs the retrieval process, particularly recall, but does not dramatically affect the learning process. As they age, older adults can learn word lists, and other information, as competently as when they were younger; but they cannot as easily retrieve the newly learned information.

Reduced Resources

A more general explanation for memory changes in healthy aging attributes the decline to reduced mental resources—in speed, energy, and attention. This theory acknowledges that each memory task requires different amounts of (a) environmental support, (b) deliberate processing, (c) integration of the to-be-remembered information with context, (d) suppression of irrelevant information, (e) working memory, and (f) speed. The more that each of these underlying resources is required, the greater the age-related decline that is observed (Smith, 1996).

Reduced mental resources can be used to explain why older adults perform as well as younger adults on recognition memory tests but more poorly than young adults on recall tasks. Although this is described as impaired "recall memory" and preserved "recognition memory," that characterization is not actually accurate because performance is not fully preserved in recognition tasks or totally impaired in recall tasks. Performance on both recall and recognition tasks varies with task demands. Reduced resources explain this phenomenon by acknowledging that older adults perform better on tasks that offer maximum environmental support. Recognition tasks, by nature, provide environmental support in that all of the possible responses are provided in the environment and the learner does not have to recall anything. In contrast, in recall tasks, the learner must initiate and generate previously heard or seen items without environmental support, relying exclusively on internal mental processes. Therefore, the performance differences in recall versus recognition memory can be recast like this: Older adults perform well when they can use the environment to aid performance but not when they have to perform memory tasks without help from the environment.

The reduced resources model fits well with the fact that memory impairment is a graded phenomenon and that performance differs depending on the task demands, education of the subject, fatigue, and many other factors. It also allows a way to conceptualize the interaction of multiple resources. For instance, older adults are slower at processing material than younger adults (Salthouse, 1996). This will affect some material more than others: Information that must be deliberately processed (e.g., word-learning paradigms) will be disproportionately affected. Automatic or implicit processing is less likely to be affected because it does not involve as many resources as explicit memory recall tasks.

Depth of Processing

One influential theory that attempts to explain which aspects of memory are preserved versus impaired in aging is referred to as *depth of processing*. The theory is that older adults engage in less extensive, less "deep," and less efficient initial processing than younger adults when they are presented with new material. The depth-of-processing explanation works like this: If material is processed less completely or in a shallow manner at first, the memory will be degraded from the outset, less permanent, and more difficult to retrieve (Craik, 1977; La Rue, 1992). Shallow processing does not affect sensory and immediate memory because little processing is needed to perceive and echo stimuli. Shallow processing would also not interfere with remote memories because they were initially processed and learned prior to the onset of any memory difficulties. Only information that is learned during old age, when depth of processing is diminished, is hard to retrieve.

Laboratory data support this theory. For example, when faced with a memory task, younger adults report spontaneously using verbal or visual association strategies, whereas older adults do not describe using these mnemonics (Hulicka & Grossman, 1967). Several experiments show that introducing and training older adults to use deeper processing improves their memory performance. For instance, when older adults sort a list of words by their initial letter or sort objects by some other criteria during learning, their memory performance is increased compared to when they try to remember the list without sorting. These overt strategies improve older adults' memory more than younger adults, possibly because younger people spontaneously use mnemonic strategies when they learn information (Mitchell & Perlmutter, 1986; Sharps & Gollin, 1988).

Labels and Objective Criteria

Benign senescent forgetfulness, **age-associated memory impairment (AAMI),** age-consistent memory impairment, late-life forgetfulness, aging-associated cognitive decline, and mild cognitive impairment all describe age-related memory problems (see Sherwin, 2000, for review). These labels are minimally helpful because they are broadly defined and characterize a large number of people with heterogeneous problems. The fact that there is so little agreement on the terms and characteristics of age-related memory impairments highlights the points that (a) older adults do have memory problems, and (b) the problems are hard to characterize with much clarity. The prevalence of memory problems in older adults is difficult to determine, in part because there are no clear criteria and in part because subjective reports of memory problems do not always correspond to objective memory impairments. Subjective reports of memory problems are frequent, ranging from 76% to 84% (Bolla et al., 1991; Koivisto et al., 1995), but as mentioned earlier, they are more closely related to personality traits and depression than actual memory function (Barker, Jones, & Jennison, 1995; Koivisto et al., 1995; Schmand, Geerlings, Jonker, & Lindeboom, 1998). The subjective and somewhat unreliable nature of memory complaints has inspired researchers to develop more objective criteria to identify age-associated memory impairment. One set of inclusionary diagnostic criteria was developed by a National Institute of Mental Health task force in 1986:

a. Men and women at least age 50 years.

b. Complaints of memory loss reflected in such everyday problems as difficulty remembering names of individuals following introduction, misplacing objects, difficulty remembering multiple items to be purchased or multiple tasks to be performed, difficulty remembering telephone numbers or ZIP codes, and difficulty recalling information quickly or following distraction. Onset of memory loss must be described as gradual, without sudden worsening in recent months.

c. Memory test performance that is at least one standard deviation below the mean established for young adults on a standardized test of secondary memory (recent memory) with adequate normative data.

d. Evidence of adequate intellectual function, as determined by a scaled score of at least 9 (raw score of at least 32), on the Vocabulary subtest of the Wechsler Adult Intelligence Scale (Wechsler, 1997a).

e. Absence of dementia, as determined by a score of 24 or higher, on the Mini-Mental State Examination.

Exclusionary criteria include the following:

a. Evidence of delirium, confusion, or other disturbances of consciousness.

b. Any neurologic disorder that could produce cognitive deterioration, as determined by history, clinical neurologic examination, and, if indicated, neuroradiologic examinations. Such disorders include Alzheimer's disease, Parkinson's disease, stroke, intracranial hemorrhage, local brain lesions (including tumors), and normal-pressure hydrocephalus.

c. History of any infective or inflammatory brain disease, including those of viral, fungal, or syphilitic etiologies.

d. Evidence of significant cerebral vascular pathology, as determined by a Hachinski Ischemia Scale score of 4 or more or by neuroradiologic examination.

e. History of repeated minor head injury (e.g., in boxing) or a single injury resulting in a period of unconsciousness for 1 hour or more.

f. Psychiatric diagnosis of depression, mania, or any major psychiatric disorder.

g. Current diagnosis or history of alcoholism or drug dependence.

h. Evidence of depression, as determined by a Hamilton Depression Rating Scale (Hamilton, 1960) score of 13 or more.

i. Any medical disorder that could produce cognitive deterioration, including renal, respiratory, cardiac, and hepatic disease; diabetes mellitus, unless well controlled by diet or oral hypoglycemics; endocrine, metabolic, or hematologic disturbances; and malignancy not in remission for more than 2 years. Determination should be based on complete medical history, clinical examination (including electrocardiogram), and appropriate laboratory tests.

j. Use of any psychotropic drug or any other drug that may significantly affect cognitive function during the month prior to psychometric testing.

These criteria take into account both subjective complaints and objective measurement of memory. Estimates of prevalence using these criteria vary from 13.5% to 38.4% of the older population (Barker et al., 1995; Koivisto et al., 1995; Schroder et al., 1998). The prevalence reports are variable because the choice of objective tests and cutoff points varies from study to study. Nonetheless, well over half and possibly up to 85% of the older population do not experience measurable decreases in their memory function, despite frequent subjective memory complaints.

For most older adults, the key question is whether occasional forgetfulness is a harbinger of worse things to come. That is, does an occasional memory lapse portend the onset of amnesia or dementia? Prediction is always a tricky endeavor, and no less so in this field. Of course, it would be very valuable to find the early warning signs of any progressive disorder, particularly a disorder that could be effectively treated in the early stages. Unfortunately, there is little agreement about whether AAMI is a phenomenon of healthy aging versus a risk factor for a pathological condition such as Alzheimer's (Sherwin, 2000). In attempts to determine if age-associated forgetfulness is a warning sign of future dementia, several longitudinal studies have followed large cohorts of elderly people. The results suggest that memory complaints and AAMI provide a "small but significant amount of diagnostic information." That is, the presence of AAMI increases the chance of later diagnosis of dementia, from 1 to 25 times, but it is only one risk factor among many, including age, education, and family history (see also Chapter 11).

Can genetic, neuroimaging, and neurochemical data help to distinguish those cases of AAMI that will develop into dementia? The apolipoprotein allele (apoE) has been one target of investigation because it is implicated in at least some cases of memory loss due Alzheimer's. Bartres-Faz et al. (2001) reported an association between AAMI and the apolipoprotein epsilon 4 allele (apoE4), suggesting that it might be a way to determine which cases of AAMI are likely to go on to develop Alzheimer's. Although this association is far from universal (Palumbo et al., 1997), the presence and number of copies of the apoE4 allele do appear to indicate which people with AAMI are most at risk for developing Alzheimer's (e.g., Howieson et al., 2003; Small et al., 1999).

The search for predictive markers in brain morphology has focused on the medial-temporal and frontal lobes, areas implicated in memory disorders and dementia. Definitive markers common to AAMI and dementia are elusive (Hanninen et al., 1997; Laasko et al., 1996).

Some data show hippocampal hypoperfusion (decreased volume) in both AAMI and Alzheimer's, suggesting a common pathology in the two groups, and that brain imaging might help to diagnose early Alzheimer's disease (Parnetti et al., 1996). Other interpretations of brain imaging suggest that "memory impairment [is] a better predictor of dementia than atrophy of the medial temporal lobe" (Visser et al., 1999, p. 477).

Neurochemical parameters also have the potential for identifying memory disorders and predicting which older adults will go on to develop more serious memory problems. The cholinergic system, because of the known cholinergic abnormalities in Alzheimer's disease, is a likely culprit. However, so far, the results are equivocal (Sherwin, 2000).

The fact that there are "diagnostic" criteria for AAMI suggests a pathology and implies the need for treatment. Mnemonic strategies and drugs are frequently touted as interventions for memory failures in healthy aging. Both are discussed below in the section on treatment.

BEHAVIORAL CHARACTERISTICS AND NEUROPATHOLOGY OF AMNESIA

Amnesia is a memory problem due to brain dysfunction and not attributable to other serious perceptual or cognitive disturbances. The differences between memory problems associated with aging versus amnesia are (a) amnesia is more severe, and (b) amnesia typically results from an identifiable brain dysfunction.

Like AAMI, amnesia typically leaves immediate, working, procedural, implicit, and semantic memory intact. The obvious difficulties are found in learning/episodic memory, that is, consolidating information from immediate into recent and then remote memory. Unlike AAMI, amnesia often involves difficulty retrieving remote memories. Amnesias are characterized as either anterograde or retrograde.

Anterograde amnesia describes a problem learning information and remembering events that occur after the onset of amnesia. Patients with anterograde amnesia often cannot remember even very basic new information such as the location of their own room or what they had for a meal earlier in the day. These patients may be able to carry on a coherent conversation as long as it does not depend on current events or information that took place after the onset of the amnesia.

Retrograde amnesia is difficulty recalling events that were experienced and known prior to the onset of memory problems. All patients with amnesia typically have difficulty recalling some things that happened before the onset of the memory problem, although the temporal gradient and the memories affected vary from patient to patient. Some patients will remember everything up to a few years before the onset; others may remember events up to within a few days of the onset. Some may remember personally relevant information but not current events. Typically, older memories are better recalled than newer memories. The primary deficit in amnesia is usually a significant anterograde amnesia with a variable retrograde component.

Information about the location of brain damage that causes amnesia has come from two bodies of research, one searching for the location of long-term memories in nonhumans and the other focusing on the loss of memory in a single human patient, H.M.

Karl Lashley, a pioneer in memory research, wanted to find where learned habits are stored in the brain. By working with rats that had learned particular tasks and then by systematically removing portions of their brains, he hoped to find the brain region that disrupted those memories, that is, the brain tissue where those memories were stored. In the long run, he was not successful, eventually concluding that

> it is not possible to demonstrate the isolated localization of a memory trace anywhere in the nervous system. Limited regions may be essential for learning or retention of a particular activity, but . . . the engram is represented throughout the region. (Lashley, 1950, quoted in Kolb and Whishaw, 2003 p. 449)

The modern tradition of using nonhumans to study the neurology of memory might have begun in earnest with Lashley (1950), and his study still provides one of the best models for the study of learning and memory. For instance, macaque monkeys can learn to distinguish particular shapes and associate one with food. A lesion in the inferior temporal lobe preserves basic visual ability but impairs the monkey's ability to perform the discrimination task, suggesting that this focal cortical region is crucial for the storage of the type of discrimination ability that underlies object recognition and that, in turn, is crucial for the memory association (e.g., De Weerd, Peralta, Desimone, & Ungerleider, 1999). Lashley may have been right that memories involve many cortical regions. But in the monkey at least, it appears that very local cortical regions are crucial for specific memory associations. This is true for monkeys and appears true as well for humans.

One person with amnesia has contributed more to the study of memory in humans than any other. He is known as H.M. In 1953, a neurosurgeon named William Scoville removed both the left and right medial-temporal lobes, including the hippocampi, of this 27-year-old man to control seizures that had worsened since the time he was about age 10. Although several other patients have undergone similar procedures, H.M. is the most extensively studied single patient in neuropsychology over the past half century, if not ever (Hilts, 1996). H.M. is interesting because (a) the location and extent of his brain lesion is known, and (b) his memory deficit is severe, relatively well circumscribed, and extremely well documented. This is a very potent combination and has in large part shaped our views on the neuropsychology of memory. The area of the brain that was removed was the medial half (8 cm) of each temporal lobe, including the prepyriform gyrus, uncus, amygdala, and anterior two thirds of the hippocampus and parahippocampal gyrus, bilaterally. The temporal neocortex was not removed (Parkin, 1996; Scoville & Milner, 1957).

H.M.'s memory is characterized by severe anterograde amnesia. He has not been able to learn or recall almost any information since the surgery. In formal testing, he does not remember photographs or geometric designs when asked to recognize them 2 minutes later. However, on tasks such as motor learning, in which he traces a design while looking at the pencil and design in a mirror, he shows normal improvement after multiple attempts, indicating that he implicitly learned how to do the task. He performs normally on many tasks of perceptual and unconscious learning, showing the normal improvement over time, even though he does not consciously remember performing the task before. This dissociation between aspects of the memory system gives anatomical support to the theoretical distinctions between procedural and skill learning, on one hand, and semantic and episodic aspects of memory, on the other.

H.M.'s case highlights the fact that short-term memory, the foundation of new learning, relies crucially on the medial-temporal lobes, particularly the hippocampi. H.M. illustrates that without the hippocampi, one can learn fragments such as he did in motor and skill learning. This case demonstrated clearly the fractionation of memory abilities, showing that short-term memory and learning arc functionally independent from general intelligence, semantic memory, and long-term memory, which all appear more or less intact in his case. On the basis of many studies of H.M., scientists have developed theories about what exactly the hippocampi do during learning. One reasonable theory is that the hippocampi function to bind together all the aspects of sensation and movements into a single image. This includes many aspects of an event, including what you have seen, heard, and felt; what movements were taking place; the time and location of the event; and so forth—all of the elements needed to create a total representation of the event. Although H.M.'s case is truly fascinating and has taught us a lot about the functional and anatomical architecture of human memory, this type of case is quite rare. Therefore, H.M.'s bilateral medial-temporal lobe excision does not show us what types of memory problems we are most likely to see in the clinic. For that, we turn to other types of amnesia.

Head injury is probably the most common cause of amnesia in younger adults. However, in older adults, stroke and dementia are the most common causes. Memory problems are often an early and prominent symptom of dementia, but because they occur in the context of other cognitive deficits in dementia, they are discussed in the next chapter. Causes of relatively isolated memory problems are covered here.

STROKE

As discussed in Chapter 3, strokes disproportionately affect the elderly and can strike any part of the brain. The type of memory problem caused by a stroke depends on the location of the stroke. Damage to the neocortical lobes produces memory problems specific to each cortical region, generally affecting retrieval of previously learned information, as opposed to new learning (Parkin, 1996; Yanagihara, 1991). The effects of neocortical stroke have in part been discussed in earlier chapters under other names: prosopagnosia is a memory deficit for familiar faces due to parietal and occipital lesions (see Chapter 8), topographical agnosia is a memory impairment for environmental routes and landmarks associated with left and right hemisphere parietal lesions (see Chapter 8), and anomia is a deficit in retrieving object names subsequent to left hemisphere perisylvian lesions (Chapter 4). These examples illustrate that the effects of cortical stroke on memory function are localized and lateralized, determined by the type of material being retrieved. Lateralization of memory deficits is particularly marked after medial-temporal lobe damage, with right-sided lesions creating difficulty learning and retrieving nonverbal material and left-sided damage creating difficulty with memory for verbal material (Kolb & Whishaw, 2003; Yanagihara, 1991).

Frontal lobe damage creates its own distinctive brand of memory deficit. Recall that frontal lobe damage interferes with attention, concentration, and planning. Insofar as these abilities are needed for learning and memory, patients with frontal lobe damage will show memory impairment. These problems interfere with working memory, probably secondary to inattention. Frontal amnesia is characterized as not being able to remember to remember, that is, a problem with prospective memory. Patients with frontal amnesia perform poorly on free recall of word lists and stories but show normal learning curves with recognition trials on word lists and improved recall with indirect questions in the case of stories. That is, they have learned the information, but they are not able to select the appropriate information from memory to answer questions (e.g., Janowsky, Shimamura,

Kritchevsky, & Squire, 1989). Frontal lobe damage interferes with the ability to use context to organize what is learned. For instance, patients do not appear to use organizational strategies to group words from a list into logical categories to assist their memory. This is probably related to their deficit in recalling contextual information for what they do remember— thereby eliminating a generally helpful strategy in learning and recall. This is sometimes referred to as *impaired source memory,* that is, inability to remember accurate and sufficient information about the original source—the thing to be remembered. Frontal lobe damage interferes with the ability to accurately recall the relative timing of events. This leads to errors in making judgments about how recently something happened. Patients with frontal lobe damage are easily distractible. Therefore, their learning is often derailed by interference from external distractions or internal associations during the learning process. These problems create a serious challenge to independent functioning. Patients with frontal amnesia can have difficulty remembering their work schedule, chores, appointments, and habits of daily living such as bathing. Damage to the anterior communicating artery and the basal forebrain region typically create an amnesia accompanied by disinhibition or apathy. The anatomical source of this problem is not clear. It might be via ischemia to parts of the hypothalamus, the head of the caudate nucleus, and the fornix and/or via disruption of the cholinergic input to the cortex and hippocampus by virtue of damage to the basal forebrain, which provides much of that chemical input (Cummings & Mega, 2003).

Yanagihara and Petersen (1991) reviewed memory disorders and cerebrovascular disease using data from autopsy, computed tomography (CT), and magnetic resonance imaging (MRI) and found that damage to three subcortical areas—the medial-temporal lobe, medial thalamus, and basal forebrain—all consistently cause amnesia. In general, the amnesia associated with these limbic structures is "predominantly anterograde with a variable degree of retrograde amnesia, implying that the structures in the limbic circuit are more pertinent for new memory formation or learning than for retrieval of consolidated information" (p. 216).

"The majority of amnestic episodes occur with cerebral ischemic events in the posterior part of the cerebral hemisphere and the thalamus supplied by the basilar circulation" (Yanagihara & Petersen, 1991, p. 198). The posterior cerebral artery gives rise to several smaller arteries that supply the hippocampus and inferior surface of the temporal lobes, areas known to be important for memory from the study of H.M. Infarction of the left posterior cerebral artery and its distributions may cause prominent memory impairment that is accompanied by visual field defects and alexia without agraphia. The posterior cerebral artery also supplies the dorsomedial and the ventrolateral nuclei of the thalamus. In many cases, damage to the medial thalamic regions produces amnesia, deficits in executive functions, and changes in personality, particularly apathy. Damage to the left thalamus produces aphasia with anterograde verbal memory deficits; damage to the right side produces visuospatial and anterograde visual memory impairments.

TRANSIENT GLOBAL AMNESIA

Transient global amnesia (TGA) is a syndrome of a sudden and brief period of anterograde and retrograde amnesia. In most cases, the patients have no other significant neurological deficits. The amnesia generally lasts between 2 and 12 hours. During the episode, the person cannot form new memories of any type, verbal or nonverbal—hence the term *global.* The patient can pay attention and hold information in mind only for about 30 seconds. The retrograde amnesia can go back as far as 20 or 30 years but is variable and incomplete. The patients' environment often seems unfamiliar to them, and therefore they ask questions about their surroundings. Because of the anterograde amnesia, they forget that they have already asked and received answers to the questions, and therefore they repeat the questions. They often remember enough to be able to carry out previously learned complex activities such as driving a car.

Patients with transient global amnesia are typically aware that something is frighteningly wrong but seldom say that they have a memory problem. Mild memory deficits can linger after the episode, but ultimately, most resolve in the subsequent days or weeks. After anterograde amnesia resolves, retrograde amnesia improves, except for permanent amnesia for the episode itself and a short time, about 30 minutes, before onset.

The TGA episodes are often preceded by exertion such as sexual intercourse, swimming or other strenuous physical activity, bathing or showering in very hot or cold water, intense pain, or emotional stress. The episodes recur in about 24% of cases (Miller, Petersen, Metter, Millikan, & Yanagihara, 1987). The cause is unknown but can be the result of temporary reduction of blood supply to the brain, which is known as brief cerebral ischemia. Occasional association with migraine and prior or subsequent cerebrovascular accidents suggest that these two diseases may cause TGA, but the association is true for only about 25% of the cases (Miller et al., 1987). Concussion, hypoglycemia, and epilepsy are also possible causes. Generally, the patients are in good health for their age, and TGA does not appear to increase the subsequent risk of transient ischemic attack (TIA) or stroke. The underlying neuroanatomy is also unclear, but the thalamus, because of its known role in memory processes, is a likely site of dysfunction.

Transient global amnesia is most common in middle-age and elderly populations. In one series of patients, the mean age was 63 years old, with a slight predominance of men (Miller et al., 1987).

KORSAKOFF SYNDROME

Korsakoff syndrome is a memory disorder caused by long-term chronic alcoholism. Although the signs and symptoms of alcohol intoxication do not vary across the life span, sustained periods of alcohol abuse put a drinker at risk for lasting memory problems in the form of Korsakoff syndrome. Because Korsakoff syndrome is due to the long-term cumulative effects of alcoholism, older adults succumb more frequently than younger adults. Older adults use alcohol more than other mind-altering substances, and perhaps as many as 10% of adults abuse alcohol to some extent. About 5% of

chronic alcoholics eventually develop Korsakoff syndrome (Heindel, Salmon, & Butters, 1991). Chronic alcoholism causes the disorder by interfering with the body's ability to store and use thiamine (vitamin B_1). The syndrome can be progressive unless the patient is given vitamin B_1, which stops, but does not reverse, the progression. Korsakoff syndrome is probably underreported and underdiagnosed, making prevalence difficult to determine. Based on autopsy, prevalence is between 0.4% and 2.8% (Harper, Fornes, Duyckaerts, Lecomte, & Hauw, 1995).

Korsakoff syndrome is sometimes referred to as Wernicke-Korsakoff syndrome, recognizing Carl Wernicke's early description of the acute symptoms and S. S. Korsakoff's description of the chronic amnesia that follows. Both men wrote in the 1880s and described parts of the syndrome but were not aware that their two syndromes occurred sequentially in the same patients (Heindel et al., 1991).

The following excerpt from Korsakoff's original description is as illuminating and descriptive as any since:

> After the first days of agitation a considerable confusion appears: the patient begins to mix words, he cannot speak coherently, and confuses facts. Day after day the confusion increases. The patient begins to tell implausible stories about himself, tells of his unusual voyages, confuses old recollections with recent events, is unaware of where he is and who are the people around him. Sometimes in addition, there occur illusions of sight and hearing which confuse the patient still further. At times in this state of confusion the patient is perfectly calm, while at other times he is restless. The restlessness occurs most commonly toward evening: the patient begins to be agitated, becomes demanding, makes preparations to go away somewhere, and grows angry at not being given the effects which he requests. Sometimes the agitation reaches an extreme degree and may amount to an almost complete loss of consciousness.
>
> Together with the confusion, nearly always a profound disorder of memory is observed, although at times the disorder of memory occurs in pure form. In such instances the disorder of memory manifests itself in an extraordinarily peculiar amnesia, in which the memory of recent events,

those which just happened, is chiefly disturbed, whereas the remote past is remembered fairly well. Mostly the amnesia of this particular type develops after prodromal agitation with confusion. This excitement may last several days and then the patient again becomes calm and his consciousness clears; he appears to be in better possession of his faculties, he receives information correctly, and yet his memory remains deeply affected. This reveals itself primarily in that the patient constantly asks the same questions and repeats the same stories. At first, during conversation with such a patient, it is difficult to note the presence of psychic disorder; the patient gives the impression of a person in complete possession of his faculties; he reasons about everything perfectly well, draws correct deductions from given premises, makes witty remarks, plays chess or game of cards, in a word, comports himself as a mentally sound person. Only after a long conversation with the patient, one may note that at times he utterly confuses events and that he remembers absolutely nothing of what goes on around him: he does not remember whether he had his dinner, whether he was out of bed. On occasion the patient forgets what happened to him just an instant ago: you came in, conversed with him, and stepped out for one minute; then you come in again and the patient has absolutely no recollection that you had already been with him. Patients of this type may read the same page over and again sometimes for hours, because they are absolutely unable to remember what they have read. In conversation they may repeat the same thing 20 times, remaining wholly unaware that they are repeating the same thing in absolutely stereotyped expressions. It often happens that the patient is unable to remember those persons whom he met only during the illness, for example, his attending physician or nurse, so that each time he sees them, even though seeing them constantly, he swears that he sees them for the first time.

With all this, the remarkable fact is that, forgetting all events which have just occurred, the patients usually remember quite accurately the past events which occurred long before the illness. What is forgotten usually proves to be everything that happened during the illness and a short time before the beginning of the illness. Such is the case in the more typical instances of the disease; in others, even the memory of remote events may also be disturbed.

It must be noted that in general, depending on the degree of the illness, that is, the depth of the affection, the amnestic manifestations vary. In milder degrees for example, there may be no complete abrogation of the memory of recent events, only the facts are remembered vaguely, unclearly. In some cases, the facts themselves are remembered, but not the time when they occurred. In other cases the forgetfulness affects chiefly the patients' own thought processes, and as a result they do not remember what they have said, and so they constantly repeat the same question. At times, all facts are remembered, yet to recover traces of these facts in their memory, to recall the forgotten, the patients need specially favorable conditions. Inversely, in very severe cases the amnesia is much more profound; here, not only memory of recent events is lost, but also that of the long past. In such cases it most frequently happens that present events disappear from the patients' memory instantly, and instead, some events of decades ago are recollected—as a result the patients confuse old recollections with the present impressions. Thus, they may believe themselves to be in the setting (or circumstances) in which they were some 30 years ago, and mistake persons who are around them now for people who were around them at that time but who are now perhaps even dead. In still more severe forms of amnesia, the memory of facts is completely lost, even the memory of words; the patient forgets his own name and instead of words utters broken sounds. In severe forms of amnesia the confusion of consciousness is greater, and in the extremely severe cases a state of complete unconsciousness may occur.

In this disease the amnesia is not stationary; it may wax and wane. These fluctuations in its degree depend sometimes on incidental circumstances such as the effort of attention, the degree of distress, and so forth. The memory often improves, yet with fatigue it again becomes worse. But of course, most frequently the intensity of the amnesia depends on the general course of the disease and on the depth of the affection, so that if the disease progresses toward improvement the amnesia diminishes and may entirely disappear; if the disease grows worse, however, the amnesia becomes deeper and deeper and the signs of profound confusion are added to the symptoms of amnesia.

In regard to the confusion, it must be noted that in this form of amnesia a slight degree of confusion is frequently present. This confusion does not involve that which the patient perceives at the present moment but affects only the recollection of the past events. Thus, when asked to tell how he has been spending his time, the patient would very frequently relate a story altogether different from that which actually occurred, for example, he would tell that yesterday he took a ride in town, whereas in fact he has been in bed for two months, or he would tell of conversations which have never occurred, and so forth. On occasion, such patients invent some fiction and constantly repeat it, so that a peculiar delirium develops, rooted in false recollections (pseudo-reminiscences). (qtd. in Victor & Yakovlev, 1955, pp. 397–399)

Acute symptoms of Wernicke-Korsakoff syndrome include gait imbalance, peripheral neuropathy, ocular disturbances, and confusion. The acute stages last 2 to 4 weeks. If appropriate vitamin therapy is provided, most symptoms other than a lasting anterograde and retrograde amnesia resolve. The anterograde amnesia is manifested as difficulty learning and retrieving new information. Korsakoff patients show normal learning in procedural motor tasks such as mirror tracing and normal long-term semantic memory in word retrieval. The retrograde amnesia often extends to a significant portion of their adult life and is characterized by a temporal gradient, with oldest memories, including childhood memories, preserved best (Bradshaw & Mattingley, 1995). The retrograde amnesia in Korsakoff syndrome is significantly longer than the 3- to 5-year retrograde amnesia that is common after electroconvulsive therapy (see below) and other amnesias (Heindel et al., 1991). This may be due to reduced learning during the 15 to 30 years of severe alcoholism that preceded the frank Korsakoff symptoms. Interestingly, some of the memory retrieval and problem-solving deficits seen in patients with Korsakoff syndrome are also seen in long-term chronic alcoholics without Korsakoff syndrome, demonstrating that the brain damage is progressive (Heindel et al., 1991).

General intelligence is relatively preserved in Korsakoff syndrome, although problem-solving and visuoperceptual deficits exist (Heindel

et al., 1991). Commonly reported features include (a) confabulations, often "plausible confabulations" or "honest lying," essentially inventing stories, particularly about the recent past, probably in an attempt to compensate for or cover up memory loss; (b) meager spontaneous conversation; (c) apathy, showing little interest in activities around them, including a lack of interest even in alcohol and an inability to formulate, organize, and initiate plans; and (d) poor insight into their memory deficit, often denying it.

Early Wernicke encephalopathy appears due to lesions of the brainstem and cerebellum. Chronic amnesia is due to damage of the dorsomedial nucleus of the thalamus and the mammillary bodies of the hypothalamus (Visser et al., 1999). Atrophy of the frontal lobes has also been found in patients with Korsakoff syndrome and is probably responsible for the cognitive, as well as some of the memory, deficits. Note that the regions of brain damage associated with amnesia are similar, whether the cause of the amnesia is alcoholism, stroke, or surgery: Diencephalic brain damage causes both anterograde and retrograde amnesia.

PSYCHOGENIC AMNESIA: DEPRESSION

The terms *psychogenic* and *functional* characterize disorders with no known organic, structural, or neurologic cause. For instance, schizophrenia, multiple personality disorder, and depression are considered psychogenic. Because no organic or structural cause is known, historically, explanations have relied on psychological notions such as "dissociation" and "repression" a opposed to specific locations of brain dysfunction. However, our current understanding of the role of neurochemistry and structural deficits in disorders such as schizophrenia has blurred many of the lines between organic and psychogenic disorders (e.g., Shenton et al., 2001). Depression and schizophrenia, classic psychogenic disorders, are now often described as neurochemical and/or structural disorders and treated pharmacologically.

Several psychogenic disorders present with amnesia as a primary symptom. These include situational amnesia, posttraumatic stress syndrome, and depressive amnesia (Mace & Trimble, 1991). The most common psychiatric disorder in the elderly is depression. Depression is one of the few psychiatric disorders that appear for the first time in late life. The prevalence of depression is difficult to determine, but is in the range of 6% to 18% throughout the life span and appears to be relatively consistent through old age. Depression may be equally prevalent throughout life, but it appears to take a greater toll in late life, as evidenced by the increase of suicide rates, which double from 12.5 per 100,000 in 17- to 24-year-olds to 22 per 100,000 in 75- to 84-year-olds (Gurland, 1976; Woodruf Pak, 1997).

The primary symptoms of depression are feelings of helplessness, despair, worthlessness, apathy, pessimism, and suicidal thoughts. Many depressed patients also complain of poor concentration and memory difficulty. Although it is clear that memory complaints rise significantly with depression, it is less clear how well these complaints reflect actual memory performance. Several studies have documented normal memory performance despite memory complaints (Derouesne, Labomblez, & Thibault, 1999; Feher, Larrabee, & Sudilovsky, 1994;), but other studies have documented memory decrements in depression, particularly in the area of verbal recall (Deptula, Singh, & Pomara, 1993; Golinkoff & Sweeney, 1989). If there is a memory problem in depressed individuals, it is typically in verbal recall. Immediate memory is generally normal, and difficulty performing on tests often appears due to carelessness, refusal to cooperate, and/or slow responses. Depressed patients are often critical of their own performance during testing and complain of fatigue, physical distress, and poor concentration despite relatively normal performance if encouraged to complete the tasks.

About 20% of elderly depressed patients do demonstrate significant memory and other cognitive deficits. This subpopulation of depressed elderly patients has been described with the terms *depressive pseudodementia* and *dementia syndrome of depression* (La Rue, 1992; Woodruff-Pak, 1997). It is not always clear whether these patients have cognitive impairment because of depression or if they are suffering from a combination of depression and dementia. Because dementia and depression are both frequent and of concern in older adults, it is important, if not easy, to distinguish the two. Depressive dementia has several features that are not present in dementia, including history of affective disorder, rapid onset, signs of depression, patient complaints of memory, other problems in excess of actual difficulties, and poor performance on cognitive tests is often by virtue of lack of participation and "don't know" responses (La Rue, 1992; Mace & Trimble, 1991; Woodruff Pak, 1997). With severe depression, recent memory, particularly in tasks of recall, can be severely impaired, whereas minimal problems are seen in tests of immediate and remote memory. Memory problems due to depression are generally more effectively treated than the memory problems due to an Alzheimer's-type dementia simply because there are more effective treatments available for depression than dementia. However, although many treatments are available to help relieve depression, some treatments for depression can cause memory problems (see below).

Electroconvulsive Therapy (ECT)

Electroconvulsive therapy (ECT) is the induction of grand mal seizures through electrical stimulation of the brain via electrodes placed on the scalp. It is a common and successful treatment for depression. It is used more often in elderly than young patients because depression in the elderly is more often severe, and the elderly are more likely to have undesirable side effects from antidepressant drugs due to age, other chronic diseases, and medication interactions (Albert & Moss, 1988; Jain, 2000). Over the past few decades, the ECT procedure has been refined in several ways to minimize discomfort and side effects. For instance, electrical stimulation is frequently given only to the nondominant (right) hemisphere rather than both hemispheres. Premedication, including muscle relaxants, reduces discomfort. However, because multiple treatments pose the largest risk and the procedure is typically repeated 6 to 10 times, it does pose a risk of memory loss.

Patients who have undergone ECT rate their memories as poor prior to ECT, improved 1 week later, and similar to healthy controls 2 months following ECT (e.g., Coleman & Sackheim, 1996). This suggests that patients' memories may actually improve following ECT. However, the positive self-reports may be due to the effectiveness of the treatment—as depression lifts, patients rate their memory more favorably, whether or not their memory actually improved. Objective measurements show that memory function decreases, at least for a time, following ECT. Squire and Slater (1975) tested ECT patients' remote memory using an ingenious task. Remote memory is usually tested by asking patients to recall events from their past. Obviously, past events differ from patient to patient, and all events are not created equal—some past events are mentioned repeatedly through the years, shown in photos and, therefore, are less likely to be forgotten than memories that are not practiced. Thus, asking patients about their past is a relatively uncontrolled and unreliable way to measure memory function. To determine how far back a retrograde amnesia extends after ECT, Squire and Slater asked questions about TV shows that had aired for only one season in each of the 17 years before testing. The results showed that untreated depressed patients and controls remembered the TV shows to the same extent: about 70% of the shows for the 3 years prior, 50% of the shows from 5 years prior to that, and less than 50% for shows that had aired more than 10 years prior to the investigation. The depressed group was then tested after ECT as well. Immediately (1 hour) after their fifth ECT treatment, the depressed group had difficulty remembering shows from the most recent 3 years but had no change in their memory for earlier shows. One to 2 weeks later, the amnesia had almost disappeared. This effect only happened for those who underwent bilateral treatment, not unilateral right treatment. These data show a retrograde amnesia immediately following ECT, with a temporal gradient in which the most recent 3 years are affected and the memory function returns within a few weeks.

Medication

Compared to young adults, older adults take more medication, are more sensitive to medication, and are at higher risk for inadvertent side effects (Sherwin, 2000). Most prominent on the list of medications that can cause memory and other cognitive problems are those that have anticholinergic properties, including some antidepressants, antiparkinsonian medications, and antipsychotics. Although it is important to realize that medications run the risk of causing unintentional memory problems, they can also relieve memory problems. For instance, medications that relieve depression can reduce the memory problems that often accompany depression; antipsychotic medications that treat thought disorders and psychosis can reduce attentional and information-processing deficits and thereby improve memory functions.

OTHER CAUSES OF MEMORY DEFICITS

Some causes of amnesia are less common in older than younger adults. Head injury, frequently associated with motor vehicle accidents, is a very common cause of memory deficits in younger adults but is relatively rare in older adults. Psychiatric disorders other than depression, such as multiple personality disorder, that may interfere with memory also decline in frequency with age. Brain infections, both bacterial such as anthrax and viral such as herpes, are not age related and can disrupt memory at any age. Some causes of memory loss such as brain tumors and neurosurgery to remove brain tumors or control epilepsy, increase somewhat with age but remain relatively rare causes of memory disorders.

The most common diseases that cause memory problems in older adults are dementia and Parkinson's disease. Because these disorders are so common and cause memory problems in the context of cognitive and motor disturbances, they are discussed in detail elsewhere (see Chapters 12 and 13).

DIAGNOSIS OF AMNESIA

The purpose of a diagnostic evaluation of memory function is to determine the type and extent of memory disorder. Memory can be informally and superficially assessed in conversation. Recent/episodic memory problems are revealed by the patients' orientation (do they know where they are and what time it is?) and memory for recent personal or public events (do they know what has happened to them or in the world over the past few days?). Remote memory is assessed by asking questions about childhood, schooling, work history, and world events from different decades. Informal testing is of limited use because the tester is usually not sufficiently familiar with the patient. Without detailed knowledge of the patient's life and prior level of knowledge about certain topics, it is difficult to verify errors related to personal history or current events.

There are more tests to assess memory than any other neuropsychological function (Lezak, 1995). Memory tests exist for each aspect (procedural vs. declarative), modality (verbal vs. visual), response type (recall vs. recognition), and time frame (immediate vs. working vs. recent vs. remote). More memory tests involve verbal than visual or tactile material, and that bias is reflected here. However, it is important to realize that visual and tactile information are an essential part of memory function and can be tested in similar formats, even if it is more complicated to develop such tests. This section includes examples of common and useful testing procedures for recent and remote memory. Immediate and working memory protocols, inherently linked to any evaluation of memory, are addressed in Chapter 9 in the discussion of attention and problem solving.

Recent Memory
(30 Seconds to Several Days)

Recent memory, also called new learning, is the focus of most memory testing. There are good reasons for this: The time frame coincides with the length of a typical diagnostic testing session, and it is the time frame that is crucial for initial consolidation and eventual learning of information. Tests of recent memory present the patient with new material and ask her or him to retrieve the information, often at several points, during the period of the evaluation. Retrieval is frequently tested in both recall and recognition formats. Testing retrieval at several points in time enables clinicians to determine, approximately, how long information can be retained.

Testing retrieval in both recall and recognition formats also allows clinicians to assess how well the information has been learned: Well-learned and easily retrieved information can be recalled without cues; less well-consolidated material, even though it may not be recalled, can be recognized and picked out of a list containing items that were presented and items that were not. Patients with difficulty learning new information will do poorly in both recall and retrieval. Patients with primarily retrieval deficits will do considerably better in recognition than recall because their impairment is in the ability to access their memories. Several testing procedures to assess recent memory are described here.

Word Lists

The examiner presents a list of 3 to 15 words and asks the patient to recall them (e.g., Delis, Kramer, Kaplan, & Ober, 1987; Morris et al., 1989; Wechsler, 1997b). Many protocols present the list several times and ask for recall after each presentation. Normally, people improve with successive presentations. To test retention of the word list, patients recall the list after 5 to 30 minutes of performing other, unrelated tasks. Retrieval is also tested in a recognition format by asking the patient to pick the words out of a longer list. One useful variation on this sort of test is to present semantically related words, as in a grocery list, to determine if patients can impose and use semantic organization to aid memory (Wingfield & Kahana, 2002).

Paired Associates (Verbal)

The examiner reads word pairs to the patient and then presents only the first word of each pair and asks the patient to recall the second. This task is similar to learning a word list, except that there are built-in cues. Most versions include pairs that are easy to remember because the words are semantically related (e.g., *rose-flower*) and pairs that are harder to remember because they have no inherent meaning relationships (e.g., *crush-dark*). The lists are usually presented several times, and recall is tested several times.

Story Recall

The examiner reads a one-paragraph story and asks the patient to repeat the story. This task is similar to what we are expected to do in the real world—recall verbal information in a meaningful context. However, the benefits gained in ecological validity are countered by difficulty scoring. Because patients seldom repeat the story verbatim, the examiner must decide which omissions are important and which are not and whether word changes alter the meaning versus capture the gist.

Visual Figure Memory

The examiner shows the patient abstract line drawings, and then either (a) the subject re-creates the drawings, analogous to recall in verbal tests, or (b) the subject picks the designs out of an array of drawings, in a recognition format. Like verbal counterparts, the stimuli are usually presented several times and recall and recognition probed over a period of time (Lezak, 1995; Sivan, 1992; Wechsler, 1997b).

Memory for Faces

The Benton test of facial recognition assesses complex visual perception. The patient sees a photograph of a face and must select the same face from a set of six other photographs. (Benton & Van Allen, 1968) (see Chapter 8, Figure 8.3). The sample and the target sometimes differ in the view (front vs. side) and lighting.

Complex Figures Task

The examiner shows the patient a single complex figure (see Chapter 7, Figure 7.6), and the subject is asked to copy the figure and then draw it from memory.

Hidden Objects

The clinician hides several objects in the room while the patient watches. Later, the patient is asked to find or point to the location where the objects are hidden (Lezak, 1995; Strub & Black, 2000).

Remote Memory
(A Few Days to Many Years)

Testing recall of old memories is difficult because the clinician, unless related to the patient or having a very thorough family history available, does not know what the patient knew many years ago. This makes it hard to formulate the questions and often precludes judging the veracity of the answer. Furthermore, a standardized test of remote memory is difficult to develop because it is hard to find information that any group of individuals has had equal exposure to and is equally knowledgeable about. Nevertheless, a few useful tests of remote memory function exist.

Autobiographical Memory

The examiner asks the patient specific questions about the past, including events sampling different stages of life, from elementary school through the present. The answers can be checked against common sense, available records, and family/caregiver interview. This has been developed into a formal questionnaire (Kopelman, Wilson, & Baddeley, 1989) to ensure some sort of uniformity with regard to the number of questions asked from each phase of life and scoring criteria.

Famous People

Some tests of remote memory capitalize on the fact that many adults have been exposed to certain people. One test focuses on recognition of famous people from many professions (Albert, Butters, & Brandt, 1981). Another test focuses on knowledge of U.S. presidents (Hamsher & Roberts, 1985). Both have the advantage of sampling many eras, and they can be expanded relatively easily as time elapses and new people become famous. Both tests can be administered in various formats: naming pictures, picking a picture from an array, providing information about the person, and so on. Both tests have the inherent flaw that it is hard to know precisely how familiar any famous individual was to a particular patient.

Memory Batteries

Many memory test batteries exist, but none has the wide distribution, norms, and reputation of the Wechsler Memory Scale–III (Wechsler, 1997b). This battery includes several measures of verbal and visual immediate span, working memory, and new learning. The only primary area missing is remote memory.

The Rivermead Behavioural Memory Test (Wilson, Cockburn, & Baddeley, 1985) was designed to assess memory in everyday circumstances. For instance, the battery includes finding objects placed at different locations in the testing room, recalling routes and errands, and learning to put a message into a computer (Wilson, 1987).

Memory questionnaires are also helpful. In these subjective assessment tools, patients answer questions or rate their memory function. Sample questions include "Do you find you forget why you went from one part of the house to the other?" and "Do you leave important letters unanswered for days?" The patient answers by circling how often these minor mistakes have happened to them in the past 6 months: very often, quite often, occasionally, very rarely, or never (Broadbent, Cooper, Fitzgerald, & Parkes, 1982). Although it is helpful to know how a patient perceives his or her memory function, these data must be interpreted cautiously because of how poorly memory complaints and self-assessment reflect memory performance.

TREATMENT OF AMNESIA

Treatment of memory deficits is tailored to the individual patient and is most beneficial when focused on memory problems in daily life. The patient's specific complaints, along with test data, identify at what point the memory process breaks down. If memory problems are caused by underlying deficits in attention as well as planning, these are treated directly (see Chapter 9).

Restorative Approach

This approach aims to restore memory function through direct teaching and practicing of specific strategies, many of which are used in typical learning. These processes may no longer be automatic or available to the patient. Some remedial strategies focus on the encoding stage, when the material is first encountered. The theory behind these exercises is that if material is more deeply analyzed at first, it is more likely to be consolidated into long-term memory, making it available for recall at a later time. Strategies to deepen the encoding process include the following:

Chunking/Organization (Harrell et al., 1992). Information is easier to recall if it is organized in a coherent way (Gianustos & Gianustos, 1979). Lists can be organized or chunked by any relevant parameters: Grocery store lists can be grouped by aisles or categories, names can be organized by first letter, and objects can be organized by size, shape, or color. We often spontaneously impose this sort of structure on complex information to facilitate encoding and recall. Patients can be taught to do so.

Visual associations, also called imagery mnemonics, include associating visual images with a verbal label or associating a name with a visual image (Crovitz, Harvey, & Horn, 1979; Lorayne & Lucas, 1974). Simple lists can be remembered by associating interactive images that link the words in the list. For example, the words *ROOF TOE KNIFE MOUTH BUTTON STREET* were remembered by one patient with amnesia by constructing the image "A ROOF fell on my TOE, I swallowed a KNIFE in my MOUTH . . . he threw a BUTTON across the STREET." Names can be remembered by associating the name with a prominent physical or other attribute of the person: To remember that a colleague's name is Daniel, a particular feature (e.g., that he has big ears) can be used by linking him to spaniel, a visual and rhyme association. (Bauer, 1993). Generally speaking, more bizarre associations are more memorable.

Spaced retrieval is a memory technique described and used by Camp and colleagues (e.g., Brush & Camp, 1998). The program has been used to teach elderly patients with memory problems due to dementia to remember names of objects, as well as to remember performing a future action and other information (e.g., Abrahams & Camp, 1993; Camp, Foss, O'Hanlon, & Stevens, 1996).

In this technique, a particular element is identified to learn, which could be remembering names of caregivers, locking the wheelchair brakes, getting dressed, and so forth. It begins by asking the patient to do something with no delay (e.g., "Today we are going to practice remembering my name. My name is Horace Fishfross. What is my name?"). The process is repeated with progressively longer delays, beginning with brief delays of 10 to 15 seconds and progressing to significant delays until the information is learned. The activity should remain relatively effortless for the patient, be relevant to the patient, and include as few errors as possible (with corrections as needed).

Rehearsal (Repetition). Patients remember more information accurately if they are prompted to recall it at several points during the minute just after they have heard it. The patient is therefore taught to repeat verbal information, either verbatim or in paraphrase. This is one of the simpler approaches because it does not involve much organization and visual imagery. Patients can often learn to do this without a therapist's prompting and thereby become independent quickly (Schacter, Rich, & Stampp, 1985).

The PQRST technique is an example of using a variety of strategies to deepen the encoding process and aid retrieval of verbal information. The acronym stands for Preview, Question, Read, State, and Test. A patient is presented with a text and goes through several steps to enhance memory of the material. First, the patient *previews* or skims the material. Second, the patient formulates *questions* about the theme and important topics in the material. Third, the patient *reads* the text with the aim of finding answers to the questions. Fourth, the answers are *stated* explicitly. Finally, there is frequent *testing* for retention of the material. This technique has been shown to improve retention of written material in patients with memory problems (Wilson, 1987).

Memory exercises for verbal information use word lists, sentences, and stories. Nonverbal memory uses visual images: Many games such as Concentration and Simon emphasize nonverbal memory. The patient's progress is shown by success with longer sequences and/or longer pauses between presentation and recall.

Specific Skills Training. Routine and complex skills can be learned by rote. Word processing on a computer, paying bills, or making a cup of tea are examples of common skills that require remembering and sequencing specific elements. These and other specific skills can be relearned by using any and all of the above-mentioned strategies. Although specific skill learning is not intended to generalize to other tasks, it is useful for accomplishing routine activities.

Compensatory Approach

The compensatory approach to memory rehabilitation introduces the patient to strategies and external devices that replace the automatic functions that usually help people remember.

The environment includes people, objects, and sounds, all of which can help or hinder memory. Strategies to optimize environmental support and minimize environmental distraction include the following:

- *Maintain eye contact during verbal interaction.* This increases focus and attention on the speaker. Use appropriate facial expression to supplement verbal expression to enhance encoding. Communicate face-to-face in well-lit rooms rather than, for example, talking from one room into another or in a car while one person is driving.
- *Eliminate distractions.* This includes external distractions such as irrelevant noise and internal distractions such as physical discomfort, intrusive thoughts, and emotions. Identify and attend to possible distractions prior to the activities that need to be remembered.
- *Use clear labels to enhance the likelihood of remembering specific information.* For example, one man frequently turned on the wrong burner on his stove until colored burner covers and color-coordinated knob stickers were used to remind him of which burner was associated with which knob.
- *Use clearly placed and legible written reminders.* For example, a list on the inside of the front door of the things to check before leaving the house relieves the burden of remembering each time to turn off the heat, lock the back door, and so on. Signs describing how to operate machines such as a video recorder or reminders to turn off lights are useful.

The colored stove labels and a list on the back of the front door mentioned above are examples of memory prostheses, devices that compensate for faulty memory. If cognition and memory permit, many external devices, from paper and pencil to sophisticated computers, can be very helpful. These include the following:

Schedules/Calendars. Schedules and calendars help prospective memory, that is, to remember future events. This is not unique to patients with memory impairments; calendars help many healthy people keep appointments. However, for patients with memory impairments, calendars also serve to remind them of recurring and routine activities that most healthy people do not have to write down, such as to check if appliances are off, go grocery shopping, exercise, and pay bills. Calendars are also a useful aid to memory consolidation and encoding after an event. By reviewing past activities on the calendar, the patient is reminded of, and therefore further encodes, those activities in recent memory. This further encoding and consolidation in memory should make those memories more readily retrievable for reminiscing and planning future events. An important supplement to a calendar is a regular schedule, doing the same activity at the same time each day. A predictable routine reduces the demands on planning and memory (Raskin & Mateer, 2000).

Lists. Lists are a useful tool for any busy person, but they become more important when your memory fails. Maintaining a things-to-do list and recording what on this list is accomplished increases the chance of remembering to do things, reduces the chances of doing the same thing twice (needlessly), and provides positive feedback and proof of having accomplished something. As with calendars, a review of the list, both of what was forgotten and what was remembered, aids consolidation of memory. A list or log of feelings may be less familiar to those without memory impairment but is very useful. Emotional experiences and expression often change with brain injury. A log of emotions can serve as an emotional outlet. Regular review of the emotion log can chart progress in recovery, including subtle emotional changes that might otherwise go unnoticed or forgotten. Review of the emotion log can also solidify memories of events that accompanied the emotions.

Telephone Book. An easy-to-use and complete address/phone book is very helpful. It can be annotated with information about individuals, from birthday to profession and even photographs to aid memory. These books should also contain important information about the patients themselves, including birth date and emergency contact information.

Therapy for patients with memory impairments frequently involves putting together and learning to use an individually tailored notebook containing a calendar and specific lists. Other frequently used aids include programmable telephones, a telephone message board kept in one location, a consistent location for keys and wallet, electronic signaling devices to find keys, programmable pillboxes that signal when it is time to take a pill, watches with built-in features such as timers, audio recorders for important conversations that must be reviewed, and a range of electronic devices to keep track of everything from the patient's own address to complex projects.

11

DEMENTIA

Chapter Preview

1. What is dementia?

Dementia involves multiple cognitive deficits, including memory impairment, that are due to brain dysfunction, interfere with work or social functioning, and are not due to delirium.

2. How is dementia different from healthy aging?

Age-associated cognitive impairment not due to dementia typically affects only one cognitive domain, does not progress, and is less severe than dementia.

3. What are the behavioral characteristics of dementia?

Prominent cognitive deficits include memory impairments, word-finding deficits, visuospatial problems, executive dysfunction, and apraxia. Dementia can be accompanied by delirium, personality change, and other noncognitive behavioral disturbances (see Chapter 12). Mood and behavioral disturbances associated with dementia include depression, anxiety, agitation, aggression, paranoia, wandering, and sleep disturbance.

4. What is the neuropathology of dementia?

There are many different causes of dementia, including Alzheimer's disease, stroke, and Parkinson's disease. Each cause has distinct neuropathological underpinnings.

5. How is dementia diagnosed?

Dementia is diagnosed by documenting deterioration in multiple areas of mental status.

6. How is dementia treated?

Medical treatments for dementia depend on the specific cause. Medical treatment can include drugs to restore neurologic function or prevent further decline. Behavioral treatments are often geared toward caregiver support but also include direct treatment to help maintain cognitive function and reduce disruptive behaviors.

What Is Dementia?

Dementia is characterized by persistent, multiple cognitive deficits in at least three spheres of mental function, including memory, language, visuospatial skills, abstraction, calculation, judgment, and emotional state/personality (Cummings & Mega, 2003; Reichman & Cummings, 1999). The cognitive impairments constitute a decrease in overall level of function from a previously higher level of functioning (i.e., they are acquired and not due to developmental delays). In addition, the deficits must be severe enough to interfere with work or social functioning (American Psychiatric Association, 2000). The cognitive impairment in dementia is not due to delirium, although the two can coexist (see Chapter 12). The onset is typically gradual and the course progressive, but in some cases, it can start abruptly and remain stable or even be reversed. In general, dementia is due to diffuse or multifocal brain dysfunction. This chapter describes the cognitive characteristics and neuropathology of the most common dementia in the elderly: Alzheimer's disease. Other common dementias in the elderly are characterized briefly.

How Is Dementia Different From Healthy Aging?

Many terms have been coined to describe the mild cognitive impairments that accompany aging: *aging-associated cognitive decline* (AACD), *age-related cognitive decline, mild cognitive disorder* (MCD), *age-consistent memory impairment, late-life forgetfulness,* and *age-associated memory impairment* (AAMI; see discussion in Chapter 10). The definitions of these diagnostic categories are typically vague:

> Individuals with [age-related cognitive decline] may report problems remembering names or appointments or may experience difficulty in solving complex problems. This [diagnosis] should be considered only after it has been determined that the cognitive impairment is not attributable to a specific mental disorder or neurological condition. (American Psychiatric Association, 2000, p. 740)

There is little agreement on what criteria should be used to distinguish cognitive decline that is mild enough to be considered "normal" or "age related" versus decline that qualifies as—or may develop into—dementia. One primary difference between AACD and dementia is that healthy older people are keenly aware of their deficits, whereas dementia patients are often unaware of their cognitive deficits and even deny them. Complaints of cognitive deficits do not correlate with objective measures (Schroder et al., 1998). Another main difference is that AACD often involves only one principal domain of cognition, whereas dementia requires deficits in at least two cognitive areas. Finally, and obviously, dementia is more severe and always interferes with work or social functioning, whereas AACD may not.

The prevalence of AACD is possibly as high as 27% (Hanninen & Koivisto, 1996; Schroder et al., 1998). AACD is associated with lower educational levels and lower socioeconomic status (Schroder et al., 1998). A key and as yet unanswered question is, Will individuals with AACD develop dementia? This is often difficult to determine, and accordingly, one of the common dementia diagnostic categories is "questionable dementia," pending further longitudinal evaluation (see section on diagnosis below). One study found that 50% of older participants diagnosed with AACD progressed to Alzheimer's disease (AD) over a 3-year period. This is significantly higher than the risk of AD in the general population (see below). However, with only 50% progressing over 3 years, AACD is still a poor predictor of dementia. Unfortunately, we have no better predictors at the moment (McKelvey et al., 1999).

Subtypes of Dementia: Incidence

The number of people with dementia is difficult to determine and estimates vary, so the numbers presented here may be disputed or even disproven, but they do give a sense of the overall incidence, distribution between subtypes, and expected growth patterns over the coming decades (see Kukull et al., 2002, for a discussion of some of these issues). Dementia affects about 5% of the population older than age 65 and is most frequent in those older than age 75 (Reichman & Cummings, 1999). One recent estimate suggests that the number of demented elderly worldwide will grow from approximately 25 million in 2000 to 63 million in 2030 (Wimo, Winblad, Aguers-Torres, & von Strauss, 2003). There are many causes of dementia and many ways to categorize the causes. They are often divided into the general categories of degenerative versus nondegenerative. Degenerative dementias cannot be stopped and include diseases affecting primarily the cortex (e.g., Alzheimer's disease) and those affecting primarily subcortical regions (e.g., Parkinson's and Huntington's diseases and Lewy body dementia). Nondegenerative dementias can often be stopped in their progression and/or reversed and include those caused by cerebrovascular infarctions, medication toxicity, alcoholism, normal-pressure hydrocephalus, head trauma, psychiatric disorders, brain infections, and metabolic disorders (brought on by many things, including vitamin deficiency, anemia, cirrhosis of the liver, and kidney malfunction).

Approximately half of all dementias are due to Alzheimer's disease, making it by far the greatest single cause of dementia (Kukull et al., 2002). Like dementia in general, the number of people with Alzheimer's disease is expected to grow dramatically. In the United States alone, the number of people with AD will increase from about 4.5 million in 2000 to 13.2 million in 2050 (Hebert, Scherr, Bienias, Bennett, & Evans, 2003). Vascular dementia and Lewy body dementia are the next most common types. Many individual patients suffer from more than one type of dementia, often a combination of Alzheimer's and vascular causes.

ALZHEIMER'S DISEASE

Definition and Course

Alzheimer's disease is characterized by a gradual onset of symptoms and slowly progressive cognitive impairments. The first symptoms are subtle and sometimes difficult to distinguish from the memory lapses and anomia that healthy older adults experience. Over the course of years, the initial symptoms worsen and new symptoms emerge, becoming unmistakably different from the mental slips of the healthy elderly. In the later stages of the disease, motor and sensory impairments appear, and patients finally have difficulty moving. Although Alzheimer's disease is often listed as an underlying cause of death (Hoyert & Rosenberg, 1997), the primary cause of death is typically the same as for the nondemented elderly: cardiovascular disease and/or pneumonia (Kammoun et al., 2000). The average life span from time of diagnosis is 8 years but is likely expanding due to improved medical and nursing care in the later stages, and some patients live 20 or more years with the disease.

Behavioral Characteristics

In 1907, a German neuropathologist named Alois Alzheimer described a 51-year-old woman with a "peculiar disease of the cerebral cortex" (Wilkins & Brody, 1969). Alzheimer's original narrative portrait of the woman's behavior (excepted below) captures most of the essential characteristics of the disease that are still used as criteria by the American Psychiatric Association (2000), including progressive deficits in memory, language, skilled movement, visuospatial recognition, and executive functioning.

> A woman, 51 years old, showed jealousy toward her husband as the first noticeable sign of the disease. Soon a rapidly increasing loss of memory could be noticed. She could not find her way around in her own apartment. She carried objects back and forth and hid them. At times she would think that someone wanted to kill her and would begin shrieking loudly.
>
> In the institution her entire behavior bore the stamp of utter perplexity. She was totally disoriented to time and place. Occasionally she stated that she could not understand and did not know her way around. At times she greeted the doctor like a visitor, and excused herself for not having finished her work; at times she shrieked loudly that he wanted to cut her, or she repulsed him with indignation, saying that she feared from him something against her chastity. Periodically she was totally delirious, dragged her bedding around, called her husband and her daughter, and seemed to have auditory hallucinations. Frequently, she shrieked with a dreadful voice for many hours.
>
> Because of her inability to comprehend the situation, she always cried out loudly as soon

as someone tried to examine her. Only through repeated attempts was it possible finally to ascertain anything.

Her ability to remember was severely disturbed. If one pointed to objects, she named most of them correctly, but immediately afterwards she would forget everything again. When reading, she went from one line into another, reading the letters or reading with a senseless emphasis. When writing, she repeated individual syllables several times, left out others, and quickly became stranded. When talking she frequently used perplexing phrases and some paraphrastic expressions (milk-pourer instead of cup). Sometimes one noticed her getting stuck. Some questions she obviously did not comprehend. She seemed no longer to understand the use of some objects. Her gait was not impaired. She could use both hands equally well. . . .

During her subsequent course, the phenomena that were interpreted as focal symptoms were at times more noticeable and at times less noticeable. But always they were only slight. The generalized dementia progressed however. After 4½ years of the disease, death occurred. At the end, the patient was completely stuporous; she lay in her bed with her legs drawn up under her, and in spite of all precautions she acquired decubitus ulcers. (Wilkins & Brody, 1969, p. 110)

The particular order, relative severity, and rate of progression of each deficit vary from patient to patient. Memory and/or language problems typically emerge early in the course. Face recognition and apraxic deficits typically arise later. Deficits in each major cognitive area are described below.

Memory

Alzheimer's dementia affects all the major divisions of memory—working, recent, and remote. The memory deficits in AD are similar in kind, although much more severe, to AAMI (see Chapter 10; Huppert, Brayne, & O'Connor, 1994). **Working memory deficits** are apparent in divided-attention tasks in which patients need to do two things at once during a very short period of time—less than 30 seconds—such as remembering a series of digits while listening to a sentence. **Recent memory deficits** are conspicuous from the early stages of the disease.

Recent memory describes the learning and retention of information over a period lasting from several minutes to several days. Even patients with AD who have mild impairments cannot recall what they ate for breakfast later the same day, the name of someone they have just met, or a list of items minutes after presentation. The deficit in learning new information applies to all types of material: words, faces, and locations where objects have been placed.

Prospective memory—that is, remembering to do something in the future while being distracted by doing something else—is the type of everyday memory task that combines divided attention, working, and recent memory functions. These are predictably impaired early in the disease. Real-world examples of prospective memory include remembering to turn off the stove or take something out of the oven while being distracted by getting something out of the refrigerator or remembering to call a doctor for an appointment at a particular time. Impairments in these aspects of memory are responsible for everything from minor inconveniences of a patient with Alzheimer's repeatedly asking the same question to potentially dangerous lapses such as forgetting to turn off an appliance.

Remote memory, the ability to recall older information and experiences, stays relatively intact, at least for a time. In contrast to marked deficits in recalling events that occurred earlier in the day, patients with AD often retain their ability to recall details of events that happened more than 20 years earlier. The oldest old memories are recalled more accurately than newer memories. Better memory for the oldest old than newer old memories is called a **temporal gradient,** and as the disease progresses, the gradient becomes more severe, with only very old, often childhood, memories remaining intact. We do not fully understand how older memories are lost. It is not likely due to a problem encoding new information because the older memories were learned long before the disease disrupted memory. Rather, the older memories were normally encoded and learned but then progressively lost by a weakening of associations between the remembered event and other contextual information. Older memories might be lost because they are no longer being associated with new information and are not being "practiced" by recall and reminiscing (Huppert et al., 1994). A functional consequence of impairment of remote memory is disorientation to situation and time. This precipitates patients' errors, which include thinking they are still at their childhood home living with (long-deceased) parents, going to work (when in the hospital), or misidentifying their daughters as their wives.

The origin of the working and recent memory deficits in AD is at least in part a problem with the initial processing of stimuli—the encoding phase of memory formation. This means that the memory of patients with AD for new information is poor because the information was never learned adequately in the first place. Information encoding may be impaired in several ways. For instance, when healthy people hear a list of words to remember, they cluster them into coherent categories (e.g., furniture, fruit). This seems to help in recall. Patients with AD do not seem to use the semantic structure of stimuli to help organize information they hear: Given a word list to remember, their responses are not clustered into semantic categories (Weingartner et al., 1981).

Patients with AD overall seem to engage in shallow initial processing, not making use of many contextual cues used to help encode information (Craik & Tulving, 1975; Nebes, 1992). One experiment showed patients with AD and healthy older adults pictures of familiar public figures from the 1940s and the 1980s and later tested their memory of these photos. Both the patients with AD and the healthy participants knew more about the people famous in the 1940s. Because the figures from the 1940s were more familiar to them, they should have been better remembered. This was true for the healthy adults. This was not true for the patients with AD, who apparently could not use the background familiarity with the pictured individuals to enrich or deepen their encoding of the stimuli (Backman & Herlitz, 1990).

One important lesson we have learned from memory experiments with patients with AD is that memory performance varies depending on how memory is measured. The more effortful the task, the worse the performance. A clear illustration of this is the difference between recall and recognition. If you ask a patient to recall a list of words, she or he may recall only half of the list. If you then give some cues (e.g., one was a color) or present the memory test in a multiple-choice format, the task becomes easier and performance will improve, at least in the earlier stages of the disease. This suggests that the patient is able to learn the information but not able to retrieve the information in certain tasks, particularly recall tasks. **Indirect methods of testing** memory involve no conscious attempts to learn, recall, or retrieve information and can be a powerful tool to assess how much learning is taking place and how much of the problem may lie in retrieval rather than encoding deficits. Indirect measures of learning allow us to test memory without conscious retrieval of information. Priming is one experimental technique that can be used to assess memory in an implicit manner. Repetition priming refers to the fact that participants react more quickly the second time they encounter a particular stimulus. For instance, when young participants, old participants, and patients with AD are asked to make lexical decisions ("Is it a word?"), all three groups show repetition priming—that is, they respond quicker the second time a word is seen (Nebes, 1992; Ober & Shenaut, 1995).

This suggests that patients with AD processed the word list similarly to the healthy young and older participants, even though the patients with AD would not have been able to recall the words nearly as well as the others. There is evidence that implicit and procedural memories are relatively well preserved in AD. For instance, Kuzis et al. (1999) found that patients with AD were impaired relative to healthy controls on tests of explicit learning but showed the same implicit learning as healthy controls (i.e., they improved over multiple trials). Specifically, patients with AD were significantly impaired compared to controls on the explicit tests in which they are asked to (a) recall a verbally presented word list across multiple trials and (b) recognize from previously seen geometric designs arrays of four designs. In contrast, patients with AD showed comparable implicit learning as healthy controls in several tasks demonstrated by (a) increasing speed across multiple trials of maze tracing and (b) a tendency to complete word stems with previously presented words despite brief exposure to the words and no explicit instructions to do so (see also Meiran & Jelicic, 1995). Although relatively preserved implicit memory does not compensate for the memory loss, it does suggest strategies for compensatory treatment: With repetition of routines or personnel, the patients will become familiar with caregivers and routines, which might very well translate into being more cooperative, even if they cannot explicitly recall much about their situation or caregivers. Although it is tempting to conclude that the memory deficit in AD is a by-product of explicit tasks and effortful recall paradigms, it is probably not the whole story. Some implicit tasks show intact performance, whereas others do not (e.g., Brandt, Spencer, McSorely, & Folstein, 1988; Nebes, 1992). Some patients with mild dementia show intact processing, but the patients with more severe impairments do not, suggesting that the type of memory problem changes with the progression of the disease. The take-home message: Memory is impaired in AD, but actual memory performance depends greatly on how memory is tested and the severity of dementia (Landrum & Radtke, 1990; MacDonald et al., 2001; Nebes, 1992).

Language

Patients with AD have trouble—sometimes severe trouble—finding words. Anomia can be the initial and most severe symptom, and it appears early in the course (e.g., Bayles & Kaszniak, 1987; Kempler, 1995; Nicholas, Obler, Albert, & Helm-Estabrooks, 1985; Ober, Dronkers, Koss, & Delis, 1986). Initially, patients with AD may have occasional word-finding hesitations and substitutions, calling a *fork* a *knife* or acting frustrated because they cannot think of the name of an object or a friend, substituting an empty word like *thing* or *him* for a name. As the disease progresses, the anomia worsens until many sentences are uninterpretable and totally empty. For instance, one patient, when asked what sorts of things she liked to do, responded, "If I have anything to do, I get something that has something doing, or I have some reason for being." Although awareness of the anomia is frustrating to the patient early on, awareness wanes as the disease progresses, and from then on, the anomia is frustrating

mostly to the listeners who cannot understand who or what the patient is talking about.

One interesting question about the anomia in Alzheimer's disease is whether it is similar to the normal word-retrieval problem called the tip-of-the-tongue phenomenon or whether patients with AD suffer from a more severe loss of word meaning. The tip-of-the-tongue phenomenon is typically brief, and the word or name is often recalled at some later point. Importantly, also during a normal tip-of-the-tongue episode, we can often recall bits of information about the to-be-recalled word, such as, *It is a plant, it starts with a 'k' sound, and it grows in the desert [cactus]*, demonstrating that our underlying knowledge of the word and concept is intact. But what happens in patients with Alzheimer's? Do they merely have difficulty retrieving words as we all do from time to time? Or have they lost the underlying semantic knowledge necessary and that is why they cannot recall the word? There is evidence for both a superficial retrieval deficit and a more severe impairment of semantic knowledge. It is likely that word-finding difficulty early in the disease is similar to normal word-retrieval deficits, but as the disease progresses, true semantic impairment emerges. Evidence for a superficial retrieval problem includes the facts that patients with AD perform much better on simple recognition tests of word meaning than they do in naming pictures, and their naming errors demonstrate intact knowledge. For instance, they can easily select a picture of a banana from an array of four unrelated pictures (a banana, a hammer, a chair, a shoe). But when asked to name a picture of a banana, they are likely to say something along the lines of, "It is a fruit, it's yellow, monkeys eat it, I can't remember the name" (e.g., Astell & Harley, 1996). If all patients with AD performed this way, we would say that they suffered from a relatively normal tip-of-the-tongue phenomenon, just more frequently than healthy adults. However, research indicates that for many patients, underlying semantic knowledge is disrupted and possibly lost. For instance, if we complicate a simple picture-pointing comprehension paradigm by showing four objects from the same semantic category, (a banana, an apple, a pineapple, and a pear), patients with AD will make more errors than if the foils are from four different categories. This suggests that patients with AD retain sufficient semantic information to differentiate a banana from a shoe but have lost the more detailed semantic information that differentiates a banana from other fruit. Other experiments involving direct probes of information (e.g., Is a saw sharp or dull?) show that patients with AD have difficulty answering information questions for just those items they cannot name, again suggesting that loss of semantics may underlie anomia (Chertkow, Bub, & Seidenberg, 1989).

Word-retrieval problems are the earliest and most prominent language disorder in patients with Alzheimer's disease. Problems with other components of language—sounds and sentences—are less obvious, if observed at all. By and large, patients with Alzheimer's disease, at least through the mild to moderate stages, speak with clear articulation and grammatically well-formed sentences. As the disease progresses, even after the semantic impairment is severe, their sentences are still well formed and, at least from a distance, sound perfectly normal. It is only when you are close enough to hear the words and try to make sense of them that the impairment is clear.

By the moderate stages, patients with AD have difficulty understanding spoken language. The sentence comprehension problems are likely due to memory deficits (e.g., Kempler, Almor, et al., 1998; Kempler et al., 1999; Small, Rabins, et al., 1997). We know, even for healthy older adults, as sentences become longer, the comprehension process requires more memory, and comprehension worsens (e.g., Light & Capps, 1986). The severity of the memory impairment in AD creates a problem understanding sentences of even moderate length. This becomes apparent in many sentence comprehension tests that require a patient to listen to a sentence and hold it in memory while looking at a set of pictures to select the picture that depicts the meaning. In this sort of test, patients with AD will make many errors. If the sentence is written, so that the patients do not have to remember the content while they look for the right picture, their performance improves (Grober & Bang, 1995).

Production and comprehension of discourse structures larger than the sentence is partly preserved in AD but also grossly impaired by the disease. On one hand, patients with AD take conversational turns appropriately; they speak when they are spoken to and use greetings ("Hi, how are you?") as well as leave-taking expressions ("See you later") at the right times. On the other hand, the content of their conversation is often repetitive, topics change with no notice, and they use pronouns and demonstratives (*he, they, here, there*) with no clear reference, often rendering their conversations hard, if not impossible, to follow (e.g., Ripich & Terrell, 1988).

Late in the course of the disease, speech and language worsen and are marked by paraphasias, repetition of others (echolalia), repetition of themselves (palilalia), and mutism (Cummings & Benson, 1983; Kempler, 1995).

Agnosia and Other Visuospatial Disorders

Visuospatial dysfunction is common in Alzheimer's disease (Filoteo, Delis, Massman, & Butters, 1994). In daily activities, visuospatial deficits are obvious: Patients get lost. Although it is hard to know exactly why they get lost, it is likely due to a combination of topographical agnosia, amnesia, and disorientation (Henderson, Mack, & Williams, 1989; see Chapter 8). Later in the disease, patients with AD have difficulty recognizing faces of family and friends (prosopagnosia), and by the severe stages, they cannot reliably even recognize their own face in a mirror, occasionally leading to talking to themselves in the mirror as if they were talking to another live person (Grewal, 1994). In specialized testing, many other visuospatial deficits can be elicited: constructional apraxia, dressing apraxia, poor performance on tasks of figure-ground and complex-form discrimination tasks, visual synthesis, and object recognition (Filoteo et al., 1994; Mendez, Turner, Gilmore, Remler, & Tomsak, 1990; Thaiss & De Bleser, 1992). Patients with AD do not typically demonstrate unilateral visual loss or neglect.

Problem Solving/Executive Functioning

As discussed in Chapter 9, problem solving involves attention, reasoning, and planning—sometimes collectively referred to as executive functions. Although most laboratory-based problem-solving tasks discussed in Chapter 9 are too complex for patients with AD, some tasks such as the Executive Interview (EXIT) (Royall et al., 1992; see Chapter 9) are simple enough to be tolerated by patients with dementia, and others have been simplified so that patients with AD can understand the instructions and attend sufficiently to perform them (e.g., Collette, Van der Linden, & Salmon, 1999). For instance, the Wisconsin Card Sorting Test was modified so that the patients with AD were told when a change of rule occurred (Paulsen & Salmon, 1995). Even in this simplified format, Paulsen and Salmon (1995) showed that a group of patients with AD was significantly impaired. Clock drawing is a simple procedure that involves executive functions of attention and planning. When a patient draws a clock and sets the time on a blank clock face, he or she chooses the clock's overall form, size, and elements; initiates and persists in drawing a sequence of constructions; and monitors progress, making corrections in placement as they occur (Royall, Cordes & Polk, 1998). Therefore, this test is very sensitive to executive dysfunction—and performance is impaired in AD. Nonliteral language interpretation is another indication of the ability to think abstractly and solve problems (see Chapter 9). The common format in which patients are asked to interpret an idiom (e.g., "What does it mean to say that people who live in glass houses shouldn't throw stones?") is too difficult for patients with AD. Their responses can be so semantically empty that it is hard to tell whether they misunderstood the instructions, the concept, or both. Kempler, Van Lancker, et al. (1988) used a simpler picture-pointing paradigm to compare comprehension of nonliteral phrases (e.g., "He is living high on the hog") and literal phrases (e.g., "He is sitting deep in the bubbles"). Patients with AD were significantly worse at understanding the nonliteral phrases. Because the nonliteral and literal phrases are matched in length, word frequency, and grammatical structure, and the picture-pointing task required the same amount of memory for both types of phrases, the authors concluded that the patients with AD had particular difficulty with the abstract meanings of

the idioms. Either patients with AD failed to recognize the fact that idioms must be understood as an integrated unit without literal analysis of the words, or they could not retrieve the abstract meanings associated with the nonliteral phrases.

Given the wealth of data that executive functions are impaired, it is not surprising that patients with AD have difficulty solving problems in everyday life. Although much of the evidence for everyday difficulties in problem solving is anecdotal, Willis and colleagues (1998) have shown problem-solving impairments in laboratory versions of everyday tasks. The Everyday Problems Test for the Cognitively Challenged Elderly uses printed materials that are found in everyday life (e.g., a phone bill, a medication label) and asks people to use the printed material to solve simple problems. For instance, given a chart of emergency telephone numbers and a friend who broke her hip, what number should you dial? Performance on this test correlates with dementia severity and independent laboratory tests of executive functions (e.g., trail making), demonstrating the impact of executive dysfunction in daily problem-solving activities (Willis et al., 1998).

Apraxia

Apraxia, the inability to carry out motor activities despite intact motor function (see Chapter 13), appears in drawing errors (constructional apraxia) and mistakes in pantomime (limb apraxia). Unless the patient is a particularly skilled artist or in the habit of using hand gestures, neither of these deficits is likely to interfere too obviously with daily activities. However, they both occur, sometimes early in the course of AD. Constructional apraxia is typically viewed as a visuospatial deficit because of the importance of visual recognition and analysis needed even to copy a drawing. To pantomime the use of an object, you must understand the relationship between the object, the typical action associated with the object, and the object(s) that it acts on (i.e., that a fork is held in the hand and is used to pick up food). Successful pantomime also involves information about sequencing of actions (you write a letter before putting it in an envelope, you put a stamp on the envelope before mailing it) and the spatial relationship between objects and actions (a fork is held with the tines facing toward the food and not the other way around). Coordination of these bits of knowledge about actions associated with objects breaks down in AD (e.g., Gonzalez-Rothi & Heilman, 1997; Kempler, 1988). The errors involve every aspect of action, including hand formation, movement direction, location, omission of elements, and substitution of inappropriate gestures. The errors are not due to primary motor weakness or inco-ordination because patients with AD have no problem performing routine, simple movements such as shaking hands or imitating gestures (e.g., Kempler, 1993). Kempler (1988, 1993) found a strong numerical correlation and many qualitative similarities between gesture and naming and errors by a group of patients with AD and suggested that conceptual semantic deficits underlie both gesture and language problems in this population.

Behavioral Disturbances

Early in the course of the disease, patients with Alzheimer's are relatively indifferent to their impairments and apathetic. In the moderate stages, patients often become agitated. This manifests itself in various ways, including wandering, pacing, and being verbally disruptive by interrupting, screaming, cursing, moaning, and repeating themselves (e.g., Cohen-Mansfield, Marx, & Rosenthal, 1989; Cummings et al., 1994). Agitated behaviors vary from person to person and moment to moment, and therefore it is difficult to quantify the incidence. However, using a nurses' rating questionnaire (Cohen-Mansfield, 1986), Cohen-Mansfield and colleagues documented that 93% of 408 nursing home residents were agitated at least once a week, with most showing agitated behaviors several times a week across different times of day. The most common agitated behaviors, in order of frequency, were restlessness, pacing, cursing, constant requests for attention, repetitive sentences or questions, complaining, and negativism. The rarest agitated behaviors, occurring in less than 5% of the residents at least once a week, were throwing things, intentional falling, eating

or drinking inappropriate substances, hurting oneself or others, biting, tearing things, verbal sexual advances, and physical sexual advances (Cohen-Mansfield et al., 1989).

The frequency of verbally disruptive behaviors is successfully diminished by several behavioral interventions, in order of effectiveness: engaging them in social interaction (56% decrease), having the patient watch a videotape of a family member talking to them (46% decrease), and listening to music (31% decrease), all significantly better than no intervention (Cohen-Mansfield & Werner, 1997).

Wandering occurs in up to 65% of patients with dementia at some point in the disease and appears related to the severity of cognitive impairment (Hope et al., 2001). Obviously, wandering creates possible danger to patients with dementia and concerns for the caregivers. Sleep disturbance is also common in patients with dementia and, along with wandering, creates a real hazard because patients will sometimes wander at night, posing further danger to the patients and exhaustion for caregivers (McCurry et al., 1999).

Delusions occur in up to 25% of patients in cross-sectional studies and in about half of the patients, taking into account the entire course of the disease. Delusions take many forms, from the relatively common paranoia regarding spousal infidelity and stolen property to Capgras syndrome, the delusion that a person (usually the spouse) has been replaced by an identical-appearing imposter (Cummings et al., 1987; Cummings & Mega, 2003; Wragg & Jeste, 1989). Although hallucinations are difficult to distinguish from delusions in patients with dementia, about 10% of patients with dementia have auditory and/or visual hallucinations. These neuropsychiatric symptoms appear to increase over the course of the disease. In longitudinal studies, these neuropsychiatric symptoms recur regularly over the period of 1 year, with prolonged episodes lasting variable amounts of time, from a month to 4 years (Levy et al., 1996).

Depressive symptoms such as apathy and feelings of hopelessness are very common in Alzheimer's disease but do not necessarily signal a true depressive episode. Clinically, it is sometimes hard to differentiate common affective

---

The Nun Study

David Snowdon of the University of Kentucky and his colleagues have conducted an ongoing study of 678 members of the School Sisters of Notre Dame in seven convents spread around the United States. Although the nuns may not fairly represent the average citizen, their homogeneity in background, diet, and lifestyle presents researchers with an ideal study group to investigate many crucial questions about Alzheimer's disease.

Ranging in age from 75 to 106, the sisters have participated in regular cognitive and physical testing and given the investigators a remarkable amount of access to their medical and personal histories. A majority of the sisters also agreed to donate their brains to the study after they die.

One of the more extraordinary findings of the study was reported by Susan Kemper of the University of Kansas. She found evidence that writing style early in life may predict who is likely to develop Alzheimer's later in life. Before entering the convent, each of the sisters wrote a short autobiography. Kemper and colleagues sorted through these and found that those sisters who demonstrated a greater complexity in their youthful writings were less likely to show signs of Alzheimer's later in life than those sisters with less complexity in their early writings. The team of researchers has also found that expression of positive emotion in the early autobiographies, an active intellectual life, and a college education may be associated with a decreased likelihood of developing Alzheimer's.

The Nun Study has also contributed to our understanding of the relationship between diet and Alzheimer's. The data indicate that a deficiency of folate in one's diet may increase the risk of Alzheimer's, whereas antioxidants such as vitamin E and vitamin C apparently have no significant effect either way. The nun data also suggest that mercury and aluminum—once considered possible causes of Alzheimer's—appear not to have any relationship to the disease. Finally, the study has solidified a suspected link between various types of brain damage and Alzheimer's: The autopsy data show a high association of stroke and head trauma in nuns who developed Alzheimer's disease.

To learn more, visit the official Web site of the study at www.mc.uky.edu/nunnet/.

---

symptoms such as apathy from true depression in the context of cognitive disorders. Ten to 20% of patients with AD meet the criteria for major depression and can be effectively treated. In some cases, depression is a precursor to dementia (Devanand et al., 1996; Jost & Grossberg, 1996). Depression is discussed in a broader context in Chapter 12.

There are probably many causes and immediate triggers of behavioral problems in dementia. The cognitive impairment of dementia, whether it is visual confusion, memory problems, or language comprehension deficits, can lead to confusion, disorientation, paranoia, restlessness, anxiety, and agitation. Some medications, particularly those with anticholinergic properties, including some antidepressants, antiparkinsonian medications, and antipsychotics, have side effects such as confusion and sleep disturbance.

Common medical illnesses, such as urinary tract infections, can also trigger confusion and other behavioral problems. The environment is very potent: The lack of appropriate stimulation (e.g., deprivation) or inappropriate stimulation (e.g., noise, interpersonal conflicts) can also set off restlessness, agitation, and other behavioral problems (see Teri, Logsdon, McCurry, 2002; Teri et al., 1992; Weiner et al., 2000).

Epidemiology/Risk Factors

The greatest risk factor for Alzheimer's is age. The prevalence of Alzheimer's is low until about age 65, when it is about 1%. It rises to between 3% and 10% for the decade between ages 65 and 74 and jumps about 19% for the decade between ages 75 and 84. At age 90, the prevalence is between 20% and 50% (American

Psychiatric Association, 2000; Geller & Reichel, 1998). About 4 million Americans currently suffer from Alzheimer's (Reichman & Cummings, 1999). Alzheimer's appears to be more common in women and those in the lower socioeconomic strata (Kawas, Gray, Brookmeyer, Fozard, & Zonderman, 2000). Some data suggest a history of head trauma may predispose one to Alzheimer's (Jellinger, Paulus, Wrocklage, & Litvan, 2001), although this may be a combined effect, making only patients with a genetic vulnerability for dementia more at risk due to head trauma (Mayeux et al., 1995). Patients with Alzheimer's tend also to have less education than age-matched controls without Alzheimer's (Jorm, 1997; Kukull et al., 2002). The reason behind the relationship between education and Alzheimer's disease is not clear. Education may confer a protective effect on the brains of older adults that makes them less susceptible to degenerative brain disorders. Or it may be that some individuals simply have greater cortical reserve than other individuals to begin with, and this, in turn, lends itself to both greater intellectual accomplishment, most often measured in terms of education, and greater ability to compensate for the disease. There is an interesting and related fact that people with simpler writing styles early in life appear to be at higher risk for AD when they age, suggesting that the crucial issue may not be the end result of education but rather the intellectual and, in particular, verbal ability relatively early on in life (Kemper, Greiner, Marquis, Prenovost, & Mitzner, 2001).

Alzheimer's is frequent in some families, and it often affects people with Down's syndrome. Both suggest genetic risk factors. There are several possible genetic contributors to Alzheimer's, including the presence of the apolipoprotein epsilon 4 (apoE4) allele on chromosome 19 and abnormalities of the presenilin 1 gene on chromosome 14, presenilin 2 gene on chromosome 1, the amyloid precursor protein (APP) gene on chromosome 21, and trisomy 21. The relationship between the genetic variants and AD is complex, and the extent of heritability is still unknown. For instance, apoE4, when present, conveys an additional risk of developing AD in a dose-dependent fashion, but not all persons with this allele will develop AD (Reichman & Cummings, 1999).

Neuropathology

The neuropathology of Alzheimer's includes the now classic signs of senile—or neuritic—plaques, neurofibrillary tangles, and neuronal loss, all described to some extent by Alzheimer in his original 1907 paper. Figure 11.1 shows visible areas of cerebral atrophy in the brain of a patient with Alzheimer's disease. Senile plaques are deposits of beta amyloid, a protein, between nerve cells. Neurofibrillary tangles are an abnormal formation of tau, a normal component of neurons, which forms a tangle within the nerve cells. Plaques and tangles are seen in healthy aging but occur in much greater density and in the context of significant brain atrophy in Alzheimer's. These structural abnormalities occur throughout the brain, but certain brain regions are affected more and earlier than other regions. The cerebral cortex tends to be more involved than subcortical regions, and within the cortex, hippocampal and lower frontal regions are affected severely even in the early stages. The damage appears to spread through the association areas of the neocortex, particularly the frontal, temporal, and parietal lobes, as the disease progresses. The occipital lobes and the primary motor and sensory areas remain relatively spared until late in the course (Gallo et al., 1998).

Since Alzheimer's (1907) publication, neurotransmitter abnormalities have been added to the list of pathological markers for the disease. A deficit of the cholinergic system is the most obvious, but this may not occur in the early stages. Deficits are also seen in norepinephrine, serotonin, somatostatin, and corticotrophin-releasing factor (Geller & Reichel, 1998).

Many other factors have been speculated to be associated with Alzheimer's, including exposure to aluminum from drinking water (Grant, Campbell, Itzhaki, & Savory, 2002; see Jorm, 1997, for discussion), hormone imbalance (Shumaker et al., 2003), oxidative stress (Anthony et al., 2003), inflammatory processes (Launer, 2003), and viruses (Dobson, Wozniak, & Itzhaki, 2003; Grant et al., 2002). However, to date, despite many associations with Alzheimer's, there is still no proof that these factors cause the disease or that alteration in them will alter the course of the disease (Launer, 2003; Shumaker et al., 2003). The cause remains unknown.

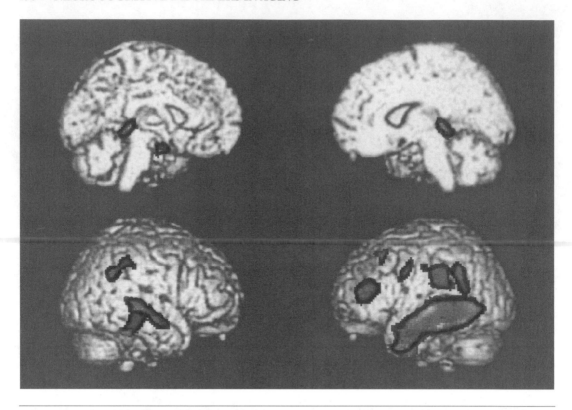

Figure 11.1 Four views of a brain showing the areas of statistically significant atrophy (outlined) in a patient with Alzheimer's disease. The images are derived from a magnetic resonance (MR) data set by subtracting the patient data from control group data. The control group consists of 12 age-matched healthy elderly subjects. In this case, there is substantial atrophy in both left and right temporal and parietal lobes and the left frontal cortex. The left hemisphere, pictured on the right side of the figure, appears more affected than the right hemisphere. (Courtesy of Murray Grossman, MD, School of Medicine, University of Pennsylvania, supported by grants AG15116 and AG17586 from the National Institutes of Health.)

Diagnosis of Alzheimer's Disease

Diagnosis of Alzheimer's proceeds in two stages. First, it must be determined if the patient has a dementia. Second, it is determined what the likely cause of the dementia is, with Alzheimer's disease being only one possible etiology. Diagnostic criteria for dementia laid out by the American Psychiatric Association (APA) include (a) an acquired impairment in memory and (b) deficits in at least one of the following domains: language, skilled motor movement, recognition, and executive functioning. In addition, the deficit(s) must (c) interfere with social or occupational functioning; (d) constitute a decline from a previous level of functioning; (e) have a gradual onset and progressive decline; (f) not be caused by any other medical, neurological, or psychiatric illness (e.g., neurosyphilis, HIV, CVA, Parkinson's disease,

depression, schizophrenia); and (g) not occur only in the course of a delirium (American Psychiatric Association, 2000, p. 157).

The diagnosis of Alzheimer's disease has been guided for two decades by a report from the NINCDS-ADRDA[1] work group (McKhann et al., 1984). Diagnosis of Alzheimer's falls into three general categories: *possible, probable,* and *definite.* Alzheimer's disease is diagnosed definitively by biopsy or autopsy, which shows the plaques and tangles. During life, without the aid of a brain biopsy, the diagnosis is either *possible AD* or *probable AD.* Criteria for probable, possible and definite Alzheimer's are summarized in Figure 11.2 (adapted from McKhann et al., 1984, p. 940, Table 1).

Many standard evaluation techniques ar used to rule out other possible causes of AD, including blood chemistry, urinalysis, and cerebrospinal

Probable Alzheimer's Disease

- Dementia
- Onset between 40 and 90 years of age
- Deficits in two or more areas of cognition
- Progressive worsening of memory and other cognitive functions
- No disturbance of consciousness
- Absence of systemic disorders or other brain disease that, in and of themselves, could account for the progressive deficits in memory and cognition

The diagnosis is supported by a number of other observations, including the following:

- progressive deterioration of specific cognitive functions such as language (aphasia), motor skills (apraxia), and perception (agnosia);
- impaired activities of daily living and altered patterns of behavior;
- family history of similar disorders;
- laboratory results of normal lumbar puncture, normal pattern or nonspecific changes in EEG, and evidence of cerebral atrophy on CT with progression documented by serial observation.

Other clinical features consistent with the diagnosis of probable AD, after exclusion of other causes, include the following:

- plateaus in the course of the illness;
- depression, insomnia, incontinence, delusions, illusions, hallucinations, sexual disorders, weight loss, and verbal, emotional, or physical outbursts;
- other neurologic abnormalities, especially with more advanced disease, including motor signs such as increased muscle tone and gait disorder;
- seizures in advanced disease;
- CT normal for age.

Features that make the diagnosis of probable AD uncertain or unlikely include the following:

- sudden, apoplectic onset;
- focal neurologic findings such as hemiparesis, sensory loss, visual field deficits, and motor incoordination early in the course of the illness;
- seizures or gait disturbances at the onset or very early in the course.

Possible Alzheimer's Disease

- May be made on the basis of dementia in the absence of other neurologic, psychiatric, or systemic disorders sufficient to cause dementia and in the presence of variations in the onset, in the presentation, or in the clinical course
- May be made in the presence of a second systemic or brain disorder sufficient to produce dementia, which is not considered to be *the* cause of the dementia

Definite Alzheimer's Disease

- Clinical criteria for probable AD
- Histopathologic evidence obtained from a biopsy or autopsy

Figure 11.2   Criteria for the diagnosis of Alzeirmer's disease

fluid examination to reveal toxic levels of drugs and hormones and conditions such as liver toxicity, kidney failure, and/or respiratory compromise that cause changes in mental status. Brain imaging (e.g., EEG, computed tomography [CT], and magnetic resonance imaging [MRI]) generally helps to rule in or rule out other brain disorders such as stroke, tumors, or focal degeneration but otherwise does not provide definitive information leading to a diagnosis of Alzheimer's; positron emission tomography (PET) scans might reveal temporoparietal hypoperfusion typical of AD (Colloby et al., 2002). Medication history, particularly those medications with known anticholinergic effects, can reveal potentially reversible causes of dementia. History of head injury; and cerebral, mental, or systemic diseases are other common causes of altered mental status; allergies and recent exposure to intense heat or cold or any potentially noxious substance are relevant because they can also prompt mental status changes (Lipowski, 1990). Although biochemical and genetic tests are available to ascertain the presence of, for example, apoE, they are not used for diagnosis because of the significant overlap between normal and abnormal levels; that is, they lack predictive power (e.g., Tsuang et al., 1999). These tests may indicate an increased risk, and once dementia is present, the presence or absence of the apoE4 allele(s) can help to determine if the AD is the likely cause. However, because healthy people who will not develop AD can have two copies of the apoE4 allele, it cannot be used to predict who will develop dementia and is inappropriate to use prior to a diagnosis of dementia (Kivipelto et al., 2002; Lange et al., 2002).

Neuropsychological evaluation provides evidence of cognitive changes and helps to distinguish AD from other diseases, including other dementias (e.g., Connor et al., 1998; Looi & Sachdev, 1999; Royall et al., 1992; see also below). Neuropsychological evaluation is particularly important early on when the cognitive changes are subtle and often the only sign predating, for example, brain atrophy that is seen in brain imaging. One of the most widely used neuropsychological batteries was developed by the Consortium to Establish a Registry for Alzheimer's Disease (CERAD) (Welsh et al., 1994). It combines a wide range of cognitive tests and has now been used across many different populations, providing relatively strong normative data. A clinical inventory developed by Cummings and Benson (1986) puts together the primary clinical features of Alzheimer's dementia into a short screening form that requires rating 10 specific areas of function (5 mental functions and 5 motor functions). The primary function of this instrument is to distinguish Alzheimer's dementia from other dementias. The higher the score, the more likely a diagnosis of Alzheimer's disease, with a score of 14 or greater correctly identifying 100% of the patients with Alzheimer's in their sample and 94% of the patients who do not have Alzheimer's (i.e., 2 patients with dementia due to other etiologies were misclassified as having Alzheimer's).

The areas of function and criteria used to rate and distinguish Alzheimer's from other dementias adapted from the Cummings and Benson (1986) inventory follows:

	0	*1*	*2*
Mental functions			
1. Memory	Normal forgetfulness that improves with cues	Recalls one or two of three words spontaneously without prompting	Disoriented; unable to learn three words in 3 minutes; not helped by prompting
2. Visuospatial	Normal or clumsy drawings; minimal distortions	Drawings with omissions and/or distortions	Disorganized drawings, unrecognizable copies from a model
3. Cognition	Normal or complex abstractions and calculations	Cannot abstract simple proverbs; trouble with mathematics problems	Fails to interpret even simple proverbs or idioms; acalculia
4. Personality	Disinhibition or depression	Appropriately concerned	Indifferent; can be irritable
5. Language	Normal	Anomia; mild comprehension deficits	Fluent aphasia with anomia; paraphasias; comprehension deficits

	0	*1*	*2*
Motor functions			
1. Speech	Mute, severely dysarthric	Slurred, amelodic, hypophonic	Normal
2. Psychomotor speed	Slow; long latency to response	Hesitant responses	Normal, prompt responses
3. Posture	Abnormal, flexed, extended or distorted	Stooped or mildly distorted	Normal, erect
4. Gait	Hemiparetic, ataxic, apractic, or hyperkinetic	Shuffling, dyskinetic	Normal
5. Movements	Tremor, akinesia, rigidity, or chorea	Imprecise, poorly coordinated	Normal

Even with all of the appropriate clinica information, only 75% to 80% of clinical diagnoses are confirmed at autopsy (Leech, 2001; Mendez, Mastri, & Sung, 1992). The remainder often have a combination of AD and vascular lesions or indications of Parkinson's disease (Lim et al., 1999).

Once a diagnosis is determined, the severity of the dementia is rated. Dementia severity is typically determined at the time of diagnosis and then at various points over the course of the disease. Dementia severity is gauged by performance on mental status tests and/or functional ability (e.g., Kashima, Tanemura, & Hasegawa, 2001; Reisberg, Ferris, de Leon, & Crook, 1982). Some authors propose as many as seven stages of decline (e.g., Reisberg et al., 1982), but most clinicians rely on a basic set of three: mild, moderate, and severe. The three basic stages are sometimes augmented by a category for very mild or questionable dementia, to avoid misdiagnosing healthy older adults when they are merely showing signs of age-related cognitive or memory impairment, and a category for profound dementia for patients who are no longer testable (Winograd & Jarvik, 1986). Various instruments are used to gauge severity of impairment. Neuropsychological batteries such as the CERAD do an

admirable job, but test batteries are most often used for diagnosis and determining severity at the time of diagnosis. Other shorter tests are typically used at various points in the course of the disease, including the 30-item Mini-Mental Status Examination (MMSE) (Folstein et al., 1975) and the Clinical Dementia Rating Scale (CDR) in which clinicians rate patients functioning in 7 areas (e.g., memory, personal care) on a 5-point scale (healthy, questionable dementia, mild, moderate, and severe dementia). (Morris, 1993).

Behavioral and functional disturbances are evaluated by various instruments, often relying on an informant report questionnaire that rates the frequency and severity of various behaviors. Logsdon et al. (1999) and Cohen-Mansfield et al. (1989) have both developed informant report questionnaires to rate agitated behavior. These inventories allow health care providers to rate different verbally disruptive behaviors such as shouting, complaining, cursing, and nonsense talk. Atleast one scale that has been shown to be reliable and valid with patients with dementia (Alexopoulos, Abrams, Young, & Shamoian, 1988). In addition, a few more general measures rate many different areas of behavior, perhaps the most widely used being the CERAD Behavior

Rating Scale for Dementia (Tariot, 1996). In addition, there are measures of function to help reveal how well the patient can carry out activities of daily living such as bathing, eating, money management, and so on (e.g., Spirrison & Pierce, 1992). Determining caregiver stress does not help to diagnose or gauge severity of dementia but is obviously an important adjunct to the diagnostic process because in most cases, both the patient and the caregivers need supportive measures.

Medical Treatment for Alzheimer's Disease

Medical treatments for Alzheimer's disease largely consist of administering drugs to improve the availability of acetylcholine in the brain (tacrine/Cognex® and donepezil/Aricept®) (Geller & Reichel, 1998). These medications temporarily stabilize or improve cognitive function in a small percentage of patients but have not prevented long-term decline. Other medical approaches include anti-inflammatory drugs, antioxidants, estrogen replacement (for women), and antidepressants, each aimed at slowing progression of the disease by mitigating factors thought to play a role in the development of the disease (reviewed by Jorm, 1997). Although some specific cholinesterase inhibitors such as donepezil (Aricept®), galantamine (Reminyl®), and rivastigmine (Exelon®) show some promise in slowing the progression of the disease, in general, they do not seem to help much past the moderate stage of dementia (e.g., Feldman et al., 2003). Although there has been much recent attention toward the role of estrogen in the development and progression of AD, it has not been shown to be an effective treatment. The role of estrogen in the prevention of dementia is still unclear (Shumaker et al., 2003).

Behavioral (Nonpharmacologic Treatment for Alzheimer's

For reversible dementias, the treatments are by and large medical, with little need for cognitive or behavioral rehabilitation. The patients often get better with the right medical treatment and never see a rehabilitation therapist. However, the vast majority of dementias are progressive, such as Alzheimer's, and the available medical treatments have modest benefits. The cognitive and behavioral interventions for Alzheimer's are geared toward maintaining function as well as possible. This is accomplished in great part by educating and supporting the caregivers. Direct cognitive training for patients with Alzheimer's has a small but increasing place in treatment (Brush & Camp, 1998; Davis, Massman, & Doody, 2001; Ham, 1999; Reichman & Cummings, 1999).

Areas of Concern

Impaired memory and judgment carry obvious safety risks. For instance, patients with visuospatial impairments and/or memory deficits get lost easily. In addition to the anxiety this causes in the patient and caregivers, it can lead to accidental injury. An identification bracelet with name, diagnosis, and address can help. Driving and even walking alone may have to be curtailed. If wandering and getting lost become serious concerns, locked doors may be necessary to maintain the patient's safety. Dangers also abound in the home. Any appliances at home that can cause injury if improperly used, such as gas stoves, may have to be disconnected or kept inaccessible. Although independence is often desirable, it comes with certain risks. Patients who spend much time alone can wear alarm devices that are used to call for help if they encounter trouble.

Poor health takes its toll on anyone. Poor physical health may have an even greater effect on patients with dementia given their low cognitive reserves. Responsibility for health management for a patient with dementia falls almost entirely to the caregiver. Therefore, caregivers must be vigilant about preventing, identifying, and treating health problems for the patient. For instance, hearing loss is a common problem in aging. Hearing loss in a patient with dementia will add to communication problems and increase social isolation, depression, and apathy. Therefore, early identification and treatment of hearing loss, which can be as simple as ear cleaning, can help to maintain psychological well-being (Palmer, Adams, Bourgeois, Durrant, & Rossi, 1999).

Malnutrition and dehydration are also common problems in older populations. Because these deplete the body of important resources and energy that underlie all physical and cognitive functions, it is crucial that patients with dementia be encouraged to eat and drink adequately. This may require altering foods, eating times, or both but is worthwhile. Some specific and helpful recommendations include the following: allow more time to eat, use prompts to help initiate eating, use finger foods, focus on one food at a time, directly feed, and, in the later stages when swallowing problems may arise, consider purees, thickened liquids, and/or tube feeding.

Acute illnesses, both physical and psychological, must be identified and treated before they become more stressful than they need to be. For instance, urinary tract infections in a person with dementia can cause behavioral and/or mental status changes (e.g., Teri et al., 2002). Chronic illnesses need to be managed aggressively to avoid controllable symptoms and unwanted side effects. For instance, untreated alcoholism will exacerbate paranoia and associated disruptive behaviors.

The caregiver burden in dementia is enormous. Therefore, much of the treatment in dementia is directed not toward the patient at all but rather toward the caregiver(s). This includes social support groups, education about the disease, respite care that gives the caregiver time away from the patient, help with estate planning, advanced directives and health care proxies, and direct psychological intervention to cope with changing domestic roles, setting realistic expectations, and making tough decisions about the extent of treatment and care for a loved one. The effectiveness of these treatments for the caregiver depends on many factors, including degree of caregiver stress and program type and intensity (Bourgeois, Schulz, & Burgio, 1996).

Principles of Alzheimer's disease management (adapted from Ham 1999):

- Early diagnosis is helpful.
- Teamwork is essential.
- Make function as good as possible.

- Use a preventive, anticipatory approach.
- Quality of life can be improved and joy maintained.
- Advance directives should be completed early.
- Patient safety is an early and continuing concern.
- Maintain the patient at home for as long as possible.
- Recognize and treat concurrent chronic and acute illness.
- Behavioral disturbances can be reduced or prevented.
- Psychotropic medications can be very valuable.
- All patients should be considered for cognitive medications.

Areas in which the caregiver can assist the patient:

- Memory aids (reminders, signage, computer-based reminder systems)
- Reminiscence enables satisfying access to retained brain function using photos, videos, audios, mementos
- Accessing medications for cognitive enhancement while avoiding unproven or unsafe medications
- Compliance with both drug and nondrug therapies
- Reducing apathy (e.g., by helping to initiate activities)
- Mood disorders (recognition and management of depression)
- Psychotic symptoms (reducing delusional thinking, coping with hallucinations)
- Orientation to person, place, and time
- Sleep phase disorders (early recognition and intervention)
- Concurrent illnesses, including alcoholism
- Environment (familiar, visuospatially friendly, reassuring)
- Safety maintenance (driving, cooking, fires, guns)
- Nutrition (reducing choices, spoon-feeding techniques)
- Exercise (preventing deconditioning, mobility maintenance)
- Facilitating socialization
- Relocation (including appropriate level of care and fiscal planning)

- Hospitalization (environment, companionship, discharge planning)
- Advanced directives and health care proxies
- Ethical decision making (such as appropriate intensity of treatment)
- Palliative care (recognizing terminality, avoiding inappropriate life support)

Services for the caregiver:

- Emotional and medical support
- Peer support
- Respite services, including day care
- Education
- Fiscal support (including care management to ensure optimal utilization of resources)
- Legal advice (such as advanced directives and living wills)

Services for the patient:

- Support groups for insightful patients in the early stages of the disease
- Nutritional programs
- Day care
- Activity programs to maintain physical and social function
- Specific living environments designed to accommodate symptoms such as wandering, disorientation, or visuospatial difficulties
- Home care services
- Palliative care and hospice services for the terminally ill (Ham, 1999)

General Environmental Recommendations

Books, pamphlets, and common sense provide a host of ideas to alter the built and human environment to maintain optimal function (e.g., Gruetzner, 1988; Ostuni & Santo-Pietro, 1986). These range from wearing hearing aids and eyeglasses to the construction of special care units with safe, enclosed courtyards and safe wandering paths. Many environmental factors can make a large difference in maintaining the patient's **orientation**—awareness of self in relation to one's surroundings. One primary goal of treatment for dementia is to minimize **disorientation**—confusion about time, location, and personal information, primarily

because disorientation often leads to disruptive behaviors, from verbal repetitions to violent outbreaks, wandering, and getting lost. One concrete and now very common technique to facilitate orientation to self and location in residential facilities is to mark patients' rooms with memory boxes that contain photos of themselves and family and other identifying memorabilia (McPherson, Furniss, & Sdogati, 2001). Environmental factors have proven very effective for promoting quality of life.

Common environmental recommendations to improve communication include using hearing aids and glasses when appropriate; maintaining eye contact; speaking in a simple, distinct, and calm manner; asking direct yes/no questions and avoiding open-ended *wh-* questions; orienting the patient regularly; and knowing when it is important to haggle over details and when not.

Physical and mental exercise within a regular schedule of structured activities is frequently recommended as a way to combat apathy, depression, wandering, physical deconditioning, sleep disturbance, and eating disorders. Regularly scheduled activities help the patient due to general stimulation and help the caregiver by access to social contacts and the good health and behavior of the patient.

Specific Treatments to Maintain or Improve Cognitive Function

The most frequent direct approach is cognitive stimulation, such as daily conversation, memory exercises, and problem-solving activities, led by a trained caregiver. Quayhagen, Quayhagen, Corbeil, Roth, and Rodgers (1995) compared patients who were involved in cognitively simulating activities for an hour a day with patients who were able to observe but not forced to participate in the activities. The patients involved in the active stimulation improved on cognitive measures during the study, whereas the uninvolved patients declined on the same measures. Nine months after the activity ceased, the stimulated group returned to baseline, but the uninvolved group declined below baseline.

Davis et al. (2001) attempted to train patients with Alzheimer's to associate staff members' faces with their names and relearn their own personal information (e.g., address, ZIP code, age). They used a combination of weekly direct teaching sessions led by a therapist and daily cognitive stimulation exercises led by caregivers. The authors compared the performance of this group with patients who received unstructured weekly clinic visits, during which they talked with an examiner, recited overlearned material (e.g., the alphabet), and watched videotapes about health. The patients who were explicitly taught personal information and face-name associations improved during the treatment: On average, they learned about half of the items they were taught. However, the intervention did not have any effect on untrained items or on measures of dementia severity, memory, motor speed, or caregiver ratings of the patient's quality of life.

Treatments to Eliminate Behaviors

Direct behavioral treatment is also used to eliminate irritating behaviors. For example, patients with Alzheimer's are often hard to follow in conversation and tend to repeat themselves, asking the same questions over and over. Behavioral treatments can aim to reduce these verbal behaviors. The treatments generally rely on external cues such as memory books, calendars, printed schedules, and index cards that contain the answers to frequently asked questions (e.g., Bourgeois, Burgio, Schulz, Beach, & Palmer, 1997). These interventions capitalize on the fact that patients with Alzheimer's can read well into the course of the disease. With enough training, the patients can learn to use a written cue to orient themselves and answer their own questions. This reduces their need to ask caregivers for information. In one such technique, caregivers told their spouse with dementia to find answers to their questions on an index card. After first presenting the information on a card, each subsequent request for that information was met with "Look at your card." Repetitive verbalizations diminished during this treatment. This provided caregivers some control over potentially upsetting behaviors.

Some other specific interventions for particular problems are suggested by Teri et al. (2002) and are listed below.

Depression

- Identify and increase enjoyable activities (e.g., being outside, listening to music, exercising, riding in the car).
- Redirect and focus patients by looking at familiar pictures and having pleasant conversations.
- Increase social activities, particularly ones that the patient once enjoyed but is no longer able to do alone.
- Eliminate sources of conflict (e.g., do not ask them to do things that they can no longer do successfully).
- Improve the caregiver's mood in whatever way possible.

Agitation

- Intervene early to prevent escalation and catastrophic reactions.
- Stay calm, use a gentle voice, avoid arguing, and use touch only if the patient finds it reassuring.
- Do not startle an agitated person. Approach slowly from the front and tell the patient what you are going to do. Stand or sit at their eye level.
- Redirect and focus by discussing something other than what is troubling the patient, changing activities and location.
- Get help.

Wandering

- Clearly label bathrooms and bedrooms to direct patients and use visual barriers (e.g., stop signs) to prevent entry into particular areas.
- Remove hats, coats, exit signs, and so on that suggest leaving.
- Have enjoyable seating areas that are inviting.
- Provide meaningful activities and social interactions to prevent boredom and loneliness.
- Use electronic alarms and transmitters to alert caregivers that someone is wandering.
- Use identification bracelets that provide contact information and state that the person is memory impaired.

Sleep Disturbance

- Encourage regular sleep time routines.
- Limit daytime napping.

- Limit alcohol and caffeine.
- Reduce light levels and nighttime noise.
- Compensate for changes in daily routine by having "quiet time" after unusual activities.

OTHER DEMENTIAS

Alzheimer's is the most common single cause of dementia in the elderly but not the only one. The differential diagnosis of dementia syndromes is often controversial because (a) there is frequent overlap in neuropathology and cognitive profiles of the different dementia syndromes, and (b) many individuals suffer from more than one dementia syndrome. In addition to complicating definitive diagnosis, these two facts make it difficult to estimate relative prevalence of the various dementia syndromes. The following sections briefly describe some of the most common non-Alzheimer dementia syndromes of the elderly.

Lewy Body Dementia (LBD)

This disease may be the second most common degenerative dementia in the elderly.

Lewy bodies are smooth, round protein lumps found in nerve cells, first described in 1912 by Frederich Heinrich Lewy, a contemporary of Alois Alzheimer. They are a characteristic of Parkinson's disease and are found in the brainstem and cortex (e.g., Cummings & Mega, 2003; Reichman & Cummings, 1999). They are also characteristic of what is now known as **Lewy body dementia (LBD).** The behavioral similarities between AD and LBD, as well as the finding of the typical Alzheimer pathology in the same individuals with Lewy bodies, suggest that this might be a variant of AD rather than a separate disease entity (Cummings & Mega, 2003).

LBD manifests as a progressive dementia with deficits in memory, clouding of consciousness, visual hallucinations, and disruption of executive functions. Rigidity, bradykinesia, and dystonia, common motor symptoms of Parkinson's disease, are also present in LBD and are distinct from AD. Decreased occipital blood flow and subcortical dopaminergic reductions are the unique imaging findings of LBD.

Medications used to treat parkinsonism (see Chapter 13) and those used to treat AD have both been used to treat LBD with some success. Consensus criteria for clinical diagnosis of probable and possible dementia with Lewy bodies are summarized as follows (McKeith et al., 1996):

1. A clinical diagnosis of probable and possible dementia with Lewy bodies requires evidence of progressive cognitive decline sufficient to interfere with normal social and/or occupational function. Memory impairment may not occur in the early stages but is evident with progression. Attention, frontal-subcortical, and visuospatial impairments may be prominent.

2. Two of the following three core features are essential for a diagnosis of probable LBD, and one is essential for possible LBD:
   a. Fluctuating cognition with pronounced variations in attention and alertness
   b. Recurrent visual hallucinations that are typically well formed and detailed
   c. Spontaneous motor features of parkinsonism

3. The following features support the diagnosis of LBD:
   a. Repeated falls
   b. Syncope
   c. Transient loss of consciousness
   d. Neuroleptic sensitivity
   e. Systematized delusions
   f. Hallucinations
   g. REM behavior disorder
   h. Depression

Frontotemporal Dementias

Frontotemporal dementia consists of three neurobehavioral syndromes resulting from progressive degeneration of the frontal and/or temporal cortices (e.g., Neary et al., 1998). It is also known as frontotemporal lobar degeneration. Some cases are diagnosed as Pick's disease, based on a particular anatomical finding called "Pick bodies," and some refer to this group of dementias as Pick complex (Kertesz, Davidson, McCabe, Takagi, & Munoz, 2003). The etiology of frontotemporal dementia is not known, but some cases appear to have a high familial incidence.

Mutations on chromosome 17 or 3 in some families suggest a genetic cause. It has a relatively early (presenile) onset and is associated with focal atrophy (gliosis and cell loss) of the frontal or anterior temporal lobes.

One variant of frontotemporal dementia is characterized by early disinhibition, known as a behavioral disorder with executive difficulty. The most common behavioral characteristics of this form include, early in the course, frontal lobe symptoms, including personality changes (e.g., tactlessness, violence), social disinhibition (e.g., sexual exposure), inertia, loss of volition, loss of insight, and deficits in attention, abstraction, planning, and problem solving. Memory and often language and spatial functions are relatively spared.

Two other variants affect primarily language early in the course, sometimes called **primary progressive aphasias** (see Grossman, 2002; Kertesz, 1997; Kertesz et al., 2003, for reviews, controversy, and discussion). A **progressive nonfluent aphasia** is associated with more frontal lobe involvement and manifests with anomia, effortful (nonfluent) spontaneous speech, agrammatism/grammatical errors, and phonemic paraphasias but preserved comprehension. Another variety, **semantic dementia,** is associated with more temporal lobe involvement. The language profile consists of a dominant semantic disorder throughout the course of the disease, characterized by grammatical, fluent, but semantically empty speech output with anomia and semantic paraphasias, alongside impaired word comprehension.

Vascular Dementia

Vascular dementia is characterized by cognitive decline due to multiple, usually small, strokes. Vascular dementia proceeds in a stepwise fashion, with cognitive impairments appearing abruptly, at the same time as stroke-like episodes, and often accompanied by focal neurologic signs. The course can be fluctuating, with periods of recovery, stability, and decline alternating over many years (e.g., Hershey, Modic, Jaffe, & Greenough, 1986). Vascular dementia is one of the most common dementias and often co-occurs with Alzheimer pathology (Nolan, Lino, Seligmann, & Blass, 1998). It can

be differentiated from Alzheimer-type dementia by use of a combination of instruments, including the Hachinski Ischemia Scale (Chin, Mack, Jackson, et al., 2000). This ischemia scale identifies signs of vascular disease not seen in pure Alzheimer dementias. The scale is a simple metric that assigns 2 points for each of four features if present (abrupt onset, history of stroke, focal neurological signs, and focal neurological symptoms) and 1 point for each of four other features, if present (stepwise deterioration, somatic complaints, emotional lability, and history of hypertension). Higher total scores are associated with a greater likelihood of vascular dementia (see Small, Rabins, et al., 1997).

The cognitive impairments of vascular dementia are variable and can include virtually all of the symptoms of cortical stroke discussed in previous chapters, as well as those associated with subcortical disease (slowness, depression, forgetfulness). The specific symptoms that each patient experiences depends on the location, size, and number of infarcts, which can be cortical, subcortical, or both. Patients with vascular dementia may show predominance of frontal- and subcortical-type symptoms, as noted above, and may have a more "spotty" memory deficit than in AD, with retrieval deficits/forgetfulness as in a subcortical pattern.

Noncognitive behavioral problems are common in vascular dementia. There is a slight tendency to see more emotional lability (emotional incontinence), psychosis, and depression in vascular dementia than in AD. Personality and insight are more commonly preserved in vascular dementia than in AD.

The neuropathology of vascular dementia is the same as stroke. MRIs reveal small subcortical infarctions, or lacunae, concentrated in the thalamus, basal ganglia, and internal capsule and/or cortical white matter lesions (Binswanger's disease).

The diagnosis of vascular dementia is made on the basis of cognitive criteria for dementia along with either focal neurological signs (e.g., extremity weakness, gait abnormalities) or laboratory evidence of cerebrovascular disease that could cause the cognitive disturbances. Brain scans are helpful in diagnosing vascular dementia because they may show areas of infarct. However, some brain scans, particularly

CTs, often do not show the small infarcts, so the diagnosis of vascular dementia can be made without imaging evidence of infarct. EEG studies may show focal slowing.

Risk factors for vascular dementia are the same as for stroke in general (see Chapter 3)—hypertension, diabetes, hyperlipidemia, cardiac arrhythmias, smoking and prior stroke (Small, Rabins, et al., 1997). The medical treatments for vascular dementia are aimed at controlling any conditions that might contribute to further infarcts. This includes control of hypertension and anticoagulation medication such as aspirin. Many cases of vascular dementia occur in conjunction with Alzheimer-type dementia, in which case the medical treatments designed for Alzheimer's disease can be used as well. The efficacy of medications in controlling the progression of vascular dementia is not clear (Small, Rabins, et al., 1997). Behavioral approaches combine the standard treatments designed to remediate stroke symptoms together with treatments for progressive dementias reviewed above.

Subcortical Degenerative Dementias

Several degenerative disorders affect the basal ganglia, thalamus, cerebellum, and/or brainstem and can cause cognitive impairments that result in subcortical dementia. Parkinson's disease, Wilson's disease, progressive supranuclear palsy, and Huntington's disease are the most common degenerative subcortical disorders that cause dementia. Less common causes of subcortical dementia include idiopathic basal ganglia calcification (Fahr's disease), multisystem atrophy, and thalamic dementia. These diseases typically have an insidious onset with slow progression, similar to Alzheimer's disease. However, unlike Alzheimer's disease, the early and primary symptoms are motor (Cummings & Benson, 1983, 1986).

Because these diseases primarily affect subcortical regions, the primary symptoms are motor. However, a fair number of these patients will also suffer from dementia. For instance, approximately 40% of patients with Parkinson's disease suffer from clear dementia, and up to 70% have some cognitive deficits. Subcortical

diseases tend not to cause aphasia, agnosia, and apraxia seen in cortical diseases but rather create deficits in attention, concentration, memory, and problem solving (Cummings & Benson, 1986). Patients with subcortical dementia process information very slowly and therefore respond slowly, a phenomenon called psychomotor retardation or psychomotor slowing. The patients often appear depressed and apathetic.

The epidemiology, neuropathology, diagnostic information, and treatment options for common subcortical diseases are further discussed in Chapter 13.

Toxic dementia can be caused by exposure to alcohol or numerous medications. The elderly are disproportionately at risk for toxic dementia because of the age-related changes in drug metabolism and excretion and the tendency toward polypharmacy. Fluctuating arousal, inattention, impaired memory, and disorientation characterize toxic dementias. Decreased exposure to the toxin can often resolve the dementia.

Hydrocephalus is ventricular enlargement caused by excessive cerebrospinal fluid (CSF). It is caused by either a blockage that prevents cerebrospinal fluid from being absorbed into the venous circulation (obstructive) or as a result of cerebral tissue loss with no change in CSF flow (nonobstructive). It can be idiopathic or triggered by head trauma, meningitis, hemorrhage, or brain tumor. The pressure on the brain tissue causes the triad of dementia, gait disturbance, and urinary incontinence. The dementia symptoms include psychomotor slowing, inattention, impaired memory, apathy, and concreteness, a subcortical dementia pattern. The symptoms come on slowly, over months or years, and some symptoms can be relieved by removal of the offending mass or shunting of the fluid. If not treated, the patient may lapse into a coma.

Neoplasms (brain tumors) put pressure on brain tissue by causing hydrocephalus or by the tumor growing into the brain tissue itself. Symptoms usually emerge over a period of weeks or months. Depending on the location, patients may experience headache, depression, ataxia (incoordination), incontinence, or features of dementia, including impaired concentration and memory deficits. Tumors are usually well visualized on brain scans and treated by a combination of surgery, radiation, and chemotherapy.

Traumatic dementia results from repeated blows to the head or a single serious head injury. The inferior frontal lobes and medial-temporal lobes are particularly susceptible, and the characteristic symptoms include memory deficits, aphasia, apraxia, and personality changes. Boxers who receive recurrent head trauma over many years can develop dementia pugilistica, a type of traumatic dementia, accompanied by ataxia and extrapyramidal symptoms.

Infection-related dementias originate from syphilis, Lyme disease, AIDS, and a host of other viral, bacterial, and fungal infections that can affect the brain. Jakob-Creutzfeldt disease and bovine spongiform encephalitis (mad cow disease) are rare but potentially transmissible through a poorly understood mechanism, an infectious protein called a prion. These two diseases are rapidly progressive, beginning with dementia and motor impairment and progressing to death, often within a few months.

NOTE

1. National Institute of Neurological and Communicative Disorders and Stroke (NINCDS) and the Alzheimer's Disease and Related Disorders Association (ADRDA).

12

DELIRIUM AND DEPRESSION

Chapter Preview

1. What are delirium and depression?

Delirium and depression are neuropsychiatric disorders that are frequently accompanied by cognitive deficits. Delirium is characterized by clouding of consciousness; depression is a mood disturbance characterized by persistent sadness, loneliness, and/or apathy.

2. How are delirium and depression different from healthy aging?

Delirium and depression can occur at any age but are relatively frequent in older adults. Delirium is particularly common in hospitalized elderly patients and those in nursing homes. Depression is the most common psychiatric disorder among the elderly and is one of the few psychiatric disorders that appears for the first time in later adulthood.

3. What are the behavioral characteristics of delirium and depression?

Cognitive impairment is present in patients with either delirium or depression. Patients with delirium often act confused, incoherent, forgetful, and/or disoriented. Patients with depression frequently express feelings of sadness, worthlessness, and guilt, and often display symptoms of fatigue, change in appetite, change in sleeping patterns, and loss of libido.

4. What are the neuropathology of delirium and depression?

Delirium is associated with structural brain damage, cognitive impairment, systemic infections, vision and hearing impairment, and various medications. A reduction in cerebral metabolism probably underlies delirium. Depression often occurs with, or is a result of, dementia, stroke, and Parkinson's disease, as well as real-life losses such as the death of a loved one. Depression is associated with alterations in brain neurochemistry.

5. How are delirium and depression diagnosed?

Both delirium and depression are diagnosed by observations of changes in functioning. Delirium is seen as fluctuations in a patient's level of arousal and ability to attend to stimuli and think clearly. Depression is usually diagnosed by psychiatric observations of mood and behavioral symptoms and measured by rating scales. There is no easily measured physiological or biological marker for depression.

(Continued)

(Continued)

6. How are delirium and depression treated?

Behavioral and medical treatments are common for delirium and depression. Treatment for delirium often involves medication to restore an adequate sleep-wake cycle and reduce agitation and hallucinations, as well as patient and family education, reorientation, and altering the physical environment to provide an appropriate amount of stimulation and close monitoring. Treatment for depression can involve a range of modalities, including individual and group psychotherapy, antidepressant medication, and electroconvulsive therapy.

DELIRIUM

Definition and Behavioral Characteristics

Delirium is also called **acute confusional state** or acute brain syndrome. Definitions of delirium have shared one particular feature for more than a century: They all refer to **clouding of consciousness** (Lipowski, 1990). Clouding of consciousness implies two different impairments: (a) alteration in **arousal,** reflected in decreased alertness or responsiveness, and (b) cognitive impairment. Cognitive impairment affects the content of consciousness and is globally impaired in delirium. This includes deficits in attention, learning, memory, and language. These cognitive functions are discussed at length in other chapters so are not discussed individually here.

The net result of combined alteration in arousal and cognitive impairment is that delirious patients appear confused and unable to relate in a meaningful way with their environment. Both patients and clinicians use the term **confusion** to describe delirious behavior. *Confusion* means the same thing in this medical context as it does in common usage: "a combination of incoherent thinking, difficulty in grasping the meaning of verbal and nonverbal stimuli, forgetfulness, bewilderment, and spatiotemporal disorientation" (Lipowski, 1990, p. 58).

In addition to clouded consciousness and cognitive impairment, delirious patients experience changes in sleep-wake cycles, changes in psychomotor activity, misinterpretations, illusions, and hallucinations. Disordered sleep-wake cycles include sleepiness during the daytime, agitation at night, and difficulty falling asleep. Psychomotor activity is a person's observable behavior. It includes verbal and nonverbal behavior, reaction time, speed of movement, flow of speech, involuntary movements, and even handwriting. Delirious patients may be either hyperactive or hypoactive and may shift from one to the other. *Hyperactivity* is an overall increase in movement, often accompanied by loud, frequent vocalizations. *Hypoactivity* is manifested as inertia, slow responses, and slow speech. Some experts reserve the term *delirium* for patients who are hyperactive and confused and use the term *acute confusional state* to describe patients who are hypoactive and confused (Jacobson, 1997). In this chapter, hyperactive and hypoactive confusion are both viewed as variants of delirium.

Other notable features of delirium are **misperceptions, illusions,** and **hallucinations.** Misperceptions include disturbances of body image and distortions of the size or stability of objects or the passage of time. For example, a delirious patient may think an object is bigger than it is or that he has not seen someone in a long time whom he has just visited. Illusions are misinterpretations of perceptions, such as mistaking a window for a door, a spot on the wall for an insect, or the sound of a falling object for a pistol shot. Hallucinations are similar to illusions insofar as they are inaccurate and vivid perceptual experiences, but hallucinations occur without the relevant sensory stimulus. For instance, a patient may insist there is another person in the room when there is not. Hallucinations occur in any sensory modality and in up to 75% of delirious patients. Delirious hallucinations include a great variety of objects, ranging in modality, size, complexity, and reality from colored spots to human figures to mythological and ghost-like apparitions to panoramic scenes (Lipowski, 1990).

Self-awareness of delirium varies. Mildly delirious patients may be aware of, and alarmed by, trouble directing their thoughts and recalling recent events. Naturally, this will cause anxiety and embarrassment. Some patients will admit to being confused. Other patients will try to conceal their confusion by denying it or covering it up with excuses. Severely delirious patients are not aware of their difficulty.

The clinical features of delirium have been concisely described by Jacobson (1997) and distinguish "core" from "associated" features. The core features include impairment in four areas of function:

1. *Consciousness:* clouding of consciousness, which may lessen with stimulation

2. *Attention:* difficulty maintaining or shifting attention

3. *Cognition:* disorientation, poor word list generation, impaired writing, poor imitation of nonrepresentational movements, perseveration, speech abnormalities, and abnormal thought content (delusions)

4. *Perception:* misinterpretations, illusions, and hallucinations

The associated features are described in five areas of dysfunction and, although not required for a diagnosis, frequently accompany delirium and therefore support a diagnosis, including abnormalities in the following:

1. *Sleep-wake cycle:* daytime sleepiness, night-time agitation, difficulty falling asleep, and reversal of sleep-wake cycle

2. *Psychomotor function:* slowness, slurred speech, tremors, myoclonus, seizures, ataxia, chorea, symmetric reflex changes, symmetrical tone changes, dysarthria, dysphagia, falls, and incontinence

3. *Affective function:* irritability, excitability, apprehension, fear, depression, lethargy, docility, jocularity, perplexity, and suicidal ideation

4. *Autonomic responses:* dilated pupils, tachycardia, fever, sweating, pallor or flushing, and constipation or diarrhea

5. *Neurophysiologic test results:* EEG slowing, increased latency of evoked potentials, low-voltage fast activity, and attenuation of amplitude

Course

Delirium is transient. It starts rapidly and resolves quickly, often within a week or so. Occasionally, it will progress to a permanent cognitive impairment, personality disorder, stupor, coma, or death (Lipowski, 1990). This is in contrast to chronic and progressive conditions such as schizophrenia and Alzheimer's disease, which are stable for long periods of time and have protracted courses.

The onset of delirium is acute (i.e., rapid), usually within a few hours or days, and often at night. In the prodromal stage, the patient may be restless, irritable, lethargic, and hypersensitive to light or noise; report difficulty concentrating; and have insomnia or vivid dreams. Older patients may be incontinent or refuse to walk. In mild delirium, patients may not be sure what day or month it is and mistake one location for another. They may not recognize familiar people (Lipowski, 1990).

If delirium progresses, patients become more distractible, either lethargic or agitated, and demonstrate the classic delirious symptoms of clouding of consciousness and cognitive impairment, misperceptions, hallucinations, disturbed sleep-wake cycle, and psychomotor changes. Severely delirious patients may just mutter, move involuntarily in tremor or jerks, not respond to verbal stimuli, and be incontinent.

Delirious patients display various behaviors, unpredictably. The fluctuations of arousal, cognitive impairment, and psychomotor activity occur over short periods of time, hours or days. Patients may be mute at one point and produce a constant flow of incoherent speech a short while later. Agitated and hallucinating patients may suddenly calm down and ask lucid questions about their surroundings. "The entire course of the illness may shift rapidly from states of overactivity with aggressiveness, crying, laughing, singing, dancing, and swearing to states of lethargy" (Lipowski, 1990, p. 95).

Confusion and other symptoms are typically worse at night, a phenomenon called **sundowning** (Jacobson, 1997). Sundowning may be due to physiological factors such as circadian rhythms, the cumulative stress of trying to make sense of a world when demented, or other psychological and/or environmental factors. Nighttime can be particularly difficult because of vivid dreams and hallucinations. Patients may wake up hallucinating, not know if they are awake or dreaming, and respond to the hallucinations as if they are real. When frightened by hallucinations, they may try to run away, particularly if they are in an unfamiliar place. The urge to run away may reflect a basic human urge to be in familiar surroundings when you do not feel well: "Every sick person craves ardently to be at home amidst relatives and friends; and in delirium the craving commonly takes the direction of an attempt to get away home by immediate escape from the room occupied at the time" (Fothergill, 1874, p. 404, qtd. in Lipowski, 1990, p. 57).

Epidemiology and Risk Factors

Delirium is most common in young children and older adults and very common in hospitalized elderly patients. Of the hospitalized elderly, 10% to 15% are delirious on admission, and 10% to 40% may be diagnosed with delirium while in the hospital. Up to 60% of nursing home residents age 75 years and older are delirious at any given time. Up to 80% of patients with terminal illness develop delirium near death (American Psychiatric Association, 2000; Inouye & Charpentier, 1996; Pompei, Foreman, Cassel, Alessi, & Cox, 1995).

Many factors bring on delirium. Delirium is most likely a threshold phenomenon, whereby systemic and cerebral insults accumulate and delirium is the final outcome. Delirium is associated with structural brain damage, vision and hearing impairment, unwanted responses to medications, and cognitive impairment (Jacobson, 1997). The typical causes of delirium change with age. Head trauma, epilepsy, drug intoxication, and systemic infections create delirium in all age groups, although the common drugs and infections change with age. Under age 16, common infections include measles, mumps, and meningitis, and the drugs are primarily recreational. In adulthood, from ages 17 to 64, the primary causes include infections such as pneumonia, HIV, encephalitis, and hepatitis, and the drugs include alcohol and sedatives, both in intoxication and withdrawal. In later adulthood, older than age 65, brain diseases associated with aging are a major risk factor for delirium (La Rue, 1992). Systemic infections, including pneumonia and urinary tract infections as well as prescription medications with anticholinergic effects are frequent causes in this age group. Common medications prescribed for older adults with anticholinergic effects include tricyclic antidepressants, sedatives (benzodiazepines), and antiparkinsonian and antihypertensive drugs (Jain, 2000; Lipowski, 1990). Fluid/electrolyte imbalance, metabolic imbalance, sensory and environmental disturbance, neoplasms, myocardial infarction, and cerebrovascular disease also join the list of probable causes of delirium in later adulthood (Francis, Martin, & Kapoor, 1990). In one study, the five precipitating factors for delirium identified for hospitalized patients age 70 years and older were the use of physical restraints, malnutrition, use of more than three medications, use of a bladder catheter, and any iatrogenic event (Inouye & Charpentier, 1996).

Neuropathology

Delirium is classified as an **organic mental syndrome**, meaning that it is the result of brain dysfunction. This contrasts with **functional mental disorders,** which are due to personality and learned behavioral or other mental states that are not caused by known brain impairments.

A reduction in cerebral metabolism generally is thought to underlie delirium. This is seen as diffuse and bilateral slowing of brain waves seen in EEG and reduced blood flow in functional imaging studies. Locally increased cortical function seen in fast EEG activity is associated with the hyperactive variant of delirium. Altered functions of the reticular activation system and thalamocortical projections are responsible for these cortical changes.

A study of stroke patients with focal brain damage and delirium sheds additional light on the relevant brain anatomy. Mori and Yamadori (1987) found that right middle cerebral artery stroke caused hypoactive delirium when the frontostriatal (striatum = caudate nucleus and putamen) regions were involved; hyperactive delirium was more likely to be associated with damage to the right middle temporal gyrus. Left posterior cerebral artery damage has also been known to cause hypoactive delirium (Devinsky, Bear, & Volpe, 1988).

Abnormal neurochemistry, particularly in the cholinergic neurotransmitter system, is also associated with delirium. The importance of the cholinergic neurotransmitter system is not surprising because anticholinergic drugs impair attention, memory, and information processing generally, and some anticholinergic medications cause mild confusion, if not frank delirium. More evidence that the cholinergic system is important in delirium is the fact that treatment with cholinesterase inhibitors such as physostigmine, which stop the breakdown of acetlycholine in the blood, reverses delirium caused by anticholinergic drugs (Lipowski, 1990). The cerebral hypometabolism associated with delirium and the anticholinergic effects are probably linked: A reduced rate of cerebral oxidative metabolism results in reduced acetylcholine synthesis.

Diagnosis

A diagnosis of delirium requires a clear idea of the patient's premorbid cognitive and functional levels and baseline emotional state. Against this background, changes in the patient's level of function are measured. Once it is determined that the symptoms are new and consistent with delirium (see below), (a) a physical examination, (b) a review of medication, and (c) history about recent activities will help to determine the cause(s). Physical examination includes vital signs, neurologic screening, and cardiac and pulmonary examinations (Jacobson, 1997). Laboratory tests can include blood chemistry, urinalysis, and cerebrospinal fluid examination, which are relevant for toxic levels of drugs and hormones and the presence of various conditions such as liver toxicity, kidney failure, and/or respiratory compromise that cause changes in mental status. EEG, computed tomography (CT), and magnetic resonance imaging (MRI) are done if there is some suspicion of neurological abnormalities on the physical screening. A complete medication history will help reveal if medication toxicity contributed to the delirium. Any medication with known anticholinergic effects should be identified. History of head injury or cerebral, mental, or systemic diseases can also reveal the underlying cause. Allergies and recent exposure to intense heat or cold are relevant because they can prompt mental status changes (Lipowski, 1990).

Because decreased arousal is a hallmark of delirium, it is important to determine how alert and how responsive a delirious patient is. Arousal is a continuum. Accordingly, delirious patients vary in the degree to which they are aware, awake, and interactive. Five commonly distinguished levels of arousal are defined as follows (see Strub & Black, 2000).

Alertness: Alert patients are awake and can interact in a meaningful way with the examiner and the environment.

Lethargy: Lethargic patients drift off to sleep when not actively stimulated. When awake, they have trouble focusing attention. Their conversation may be tangential or incoherent.

Obtundation: Obtunded patients are difficult to arouse. When aroused, they are confused and unable to cooperate in meaningful interaction.

Stupor: Stuporous patients respond only to vigorous stimulation and, when awake, only groan, mumble, or move restlessly in bed.

Coma: Comatose patients typically have their eyes closed and do not respond to any stimulation. Some comatose patients may respond reflexively, but they do not move purposefully.

Direct neuropsychological testing is difficult for the obvious reason that it is hard to get a confused, hallucinating, or agitated patient to sit still and answer questions. Therefore, measures for gauging the severity of delirium frequently rely on observation. Two such methods are described here.

The Confusion Assessment Method (CAM) was designed to help nonpsychiatric clinicians detect delirium quickly (Inouye et al., 1990). For this measure, four criteria from the third version of the *Diagnostic and Statistical Manual of Mental Disorders* (*DSM III-R*; American Psychiatric Association, 1987) were selected that have high agreement among professionals, are simple to detect, and have the least overlap with other disorders such as dementia. The ratings are based on observable behaviors and require minimal time and interpretation. The criteria are the presence of both (1) acute onset/ fluctuating course and (2) inattention and either (3) disorganized thinking or (4) altered level of consciousness. The criteria are satisfied by specific observations and/or responses, summarized as follows (from Inouye et al., 1990):

• *Acute onset and fluctuating course.* This information is usually obtained from a family member or nurse. It is shown by positive responses to the following questions: Is there evidence of an acute change in mental status from the patient's baseline? Did the (abnormal) behavior fluctuate during the day?

• *Inattention.* Evidence includes a positive response to the following questions: Did the patient have difficulty focusing attention? Was the patient easily distractible? Did the patient have difficulty keeping track of what was being said?

• *Disorganized thinking.* Evidence is a positive response to the following question: Was the patient's thinking disorganized or incoherent? Rambling or irrelevant conversation and unpredictable topic switching are the relevant data.

• *Altered level of consciousness.* This criterion is satisfied by an answer to the following multiple-choice question: How would you rate this patient's level of consciousness? Any answer other than "alert" is evidence of an altered level of consciousness. Possible answers include the following:

Alert (normal)

Vigilant (hyperalert)

Lethargic (drowsy, easily aroused)

Stupor (difficult to arouse)

Coma (unarousble)

The Delirium Rating Scale (DRS) and the Delirium Rating Scale–Revised-98 (DRS-R-98) (Trzepacz, Baker, & Greenhouse, 1988; Trzepacz et al., 2001) were created to provide a quantitative measure of delirium severity. The DRS rates 10 areas of function independently and results in a maximum score of 32, with higher scores indicating more severe delirium. The DRS-R-98 contains 3 items to confirm diagnosis and 13 items rated to establish severity of delirium, with a maximum of 46 points. The revised version improved on the earlier version by including specific items to assess attention, language, and hyperactivity versus hypoactivity independently. The DRS-R-98 distinguishes patients with delirium from those with dementia, schizophrenia, and depression, with delirious patients scoring above 15.25 (severity score) or 17.25 (total score) and the other groups scoring significantly below these cutoffs. Both the DRS and the DRS-R-98 have high interrater reliability and are simple to administer. The DRS includes items to assess sleep-wake cycle, delusions, lability of emotion, language, motor agitation, motor retardation, attention, short-term memory, long-term memory, and visuospatial ability. Each of the 13 items is scored from 0 to 3, and the total number indicates the delirium severity. Ratings are based on an examination of the patient and all other available sources of information (Trzepacz et al., 2001).

Examples of items and rating criteria include the following:

Perceptual Disturbances and Hallucinations (Item 2)

0. Not Present

1. Mild perceptual disturbances (e.g., feelings of derealization or depersonalization, or the patient may not be able to discriminate dreams from reality)

2. Illusions present

3. Hallucinations present

Thought Process Abnormalities (Item 6)

0. Normal thought processes

1. Tangential or circumstantial

2. Associations loosely connected occasionally but largely comprehensible

3. Associations loosely connected most of the time

Orientation (Item 9)

0. Oriented to person, place, and time

1. Disoriented to time (e.g., by more than 2 days or wrong month or wrong year) or to place (e.g., name of building, city, state) but not both

2. Disoriented to time and place

3. Disoriented to person

Depending on the severity of the delirium, several other tests are also helpful. If the patient can respond consistently, the Mini-Mental State Examination (Folstein et al., 1975) can estimate the extent of cognitive impairment and can be given repeatedly to gauge changes in mental state. For patients at the other end of the arousal spectrum (i.e., comatose), the Glasgow Coma Scale (GCS) can be helpful (Teasdale & Jennett, 1974). The GCS (Teasdale & Jennett, 1974) is an observational rating system that ranks eye opening (1–4), verbal responsiveness (1–5), and motor response (1–6) to yield a sum between 3 and 15, with 3 being the most impaired and 15 the least impaired. Note that a total score does not say anything about the individual components. The GCS is used primarily to rank patients who have sustained or are recovering from head injury. In that context, a score of 13 or higher correlates with a mild brain injury, 9 to 12 a moderate injury, and 8 or less a severe brain injury. The GCS can be used to rank the severity of coma in any patient. The three areas of function are listed as follows, followed by criteria and scores (in parentheses).

Eye Responses

No eye opening (1)

Eye opening to pain (2)

Eye opening to verbal command (3)

Eyes open spontaneously (4)

Verbal Responses

No verbal response (1)

Incomprehensible sounds (2)

Inappropriate words (3)

Confused (4)

Orientated (5)

Motor Responses

No motor response (1)

Extension to pain (2)

Flexion to pain (3)

Withdrawal from pain (4)

Localizes pain (5)

Obeys commands (6)

The most important differential diagnosis to make is between delirium and dementia. This can be difficult because they often co-occur. The temporal onset and course are the most helpful distinguishing characteristics. Delirium symptoms come on over hours or days, whereas dementia begins much more slowly. Delirium symptoms fluctuate greatly over a 24-hour period, whereas dementia symptoms typically do not (American Psychiatric Association, 2000).

Treatment of Delirium

Treatment for delirium is either definitive or palliative. Definitive treatment aims to control or reverse the physical conditions that caused the delirium. Palliative treatment controls the symptoms but not the underlying cause. Physicians guide definitive treatment. It generally involves tapering or discontinuing nonessential medications and close monitoring of vital signs. Supplemental oxygen for patients with cardiopulmonary disease and blood transfusion for patients with chronic anemia are examples of medical interventions that may correct the underlying pathophysiology of delirium. Restoring fluid, electrolyte balance, and nutrition also helps to restore normal mental function. Surgical intervention may be appropriate in cases of tumor and hematoma (Jacobson, 1997; Lipowski, 1990).

Palliative treatment for delirium often involves medication to restore an adequate sleep-wake cycle and reduce agitation and hallucinations. Occasionally, restraints will be necessary to avoid wandering and the patient pulling out intravenous lines and so forth. In addition, nursing staff, ancillary medical staff, and family and friends can provide helpful environmental interventions, including:

- *Patient and family education.* Delirium can be frightening to the patient and the family. Education and reassurance regarding the typically transient nature of delirium and the relationship between the underlying symptoms and causes are often comforting.
- *Frequent reorientation.* A clock and calendar placed in visible locations, as well as verbal reminders of the day, month, season, time, upcoming holidays, or relevant personal information, are helpful.
- *Personal environment.* Eyeglasses, hearing aids, and any other personal sensory devices that might help to retain accurate perception of the environment should be maintained. If the patient is not at home, personal photographs and belongings can be added to help maintain some sense of familiarity with the environment.
- *General environment.* Understimulation and overstimulation are both undesirable. Quiet rooms with adequate lighting, including a dim light at night, are helpful. A radio turned on in the evening might help minimize sundowning.
- *Close monitoring.* Because the symptoms of delirium change so quickly, close monitoring and frequent interaction are important. In this way, when symptoms begin to emerge, they may be better controlled by either environmental or timely medical management. This can help avoid the progression of symptoms.

The prognosis for recovery from delirium is typically good. Most patients have a full recovery, although the elderly have a poorer prognosis than others do. Up to 40% of hospitalized patients with delirium make a good recovery before discharge from the hospital. However, persistent cognitive deficits may linger even 6 months following hospital discharge, particularly in the elderly. The primary exception to good prognoses is elderly patients with significant medical illness. Elderly patients who develop delirium during a hospital stay have a 20% to 75% chance of dying during that hospitalization. Obviously, the type of illness, severity of illness, preexisting cognitive impairment, and age all contribute to the mortality rates (American Psychiatric Association, 2000).

DEPRESSION

Definition, Behavioral Characteristics, and Course

Depression (a.k.a. **major depression**) is a mood disturbance characterized by sadness, loneliness, and/or apathy that persist every day for at least 2 weeks and are not obviously related to bereavement (Bear et al., 2001). Most symptoms of depression can be seen as either psychological or somatic. Psychological symptoms include feelings of sadness, worthlessness, guilt, and so forth. Somatic signs and symptoms include fatigue, change in appetite, change in sleeping patterns, loss of libido, weight changes, and hypochondriasis. Depression is different from common, brief feelings of unhappiness, loss, or disappointment. When depression alternates with normal emotional states, it is called **unipolar depression.** When depression alternates with periods of overactivity, talkativeness, increased energy, and grandiosity, it is called either **manic depression** or **bipolar depression.** Other related mood disturbances include irritability, anxiety, **anhedonia** (inability to experience pleasure), **apathy** (reduced motivation and interest in all activities in the absence of sadness), **mania,** and **mood lability** (quick changes from one mood to another). **Dysthymia** describes mild depression with a chronic course, characterized by mild anhedonia, social withdrawal, and occasional sadness.

Patients with depression frequently complain of cognitive impairments, particularly poor concentration and memory loss. In most cases, the cognitive impairment is mild, although patients with severe depression can have significant cognitive impairments. In one study, about 20% of elderly patients with depression had serious cognitive impairments on standard neuropsychological tests. The most common cognitive impairment is memory deficit, particularly encoding and retrieval from episodic memory (Zakzanis, Leach, & Kaplan, 1998). Patients with depression also show decreased attention, visuospatial impairment, poor abstraction, and cognitive inflexibility. Depression that causes cognitive impairment in the elderly is called **dementia syndrome of depression.** It is sometimes difficult to distinguish between the cognitive impairment caused by depression and dementia caused by organic brain diseases such as Alzheimer's (e.g., Cummings & Mega, 2003). Treatment for depression improves the cognitive deficits for patients suffering from depression but may have more limited effects for those suffering from dementia and other neurological problems. This is due to cognitive limitations on their participation in psychotherapy and the underlying neurological problems, which are not generally improved by antidepressant and psychotherapeutic interventions.

Major depression is often chronic and recurrent. An episode of major depression without treatment may last for several months but rarely more than 2 years. Remission occurs in about 50% of people after 1 year. After recovery, relapse occurs in up to 85% of patients within 15 years. Depression is the main precipitating cause of suicide; approximately 80% of suicide victims are profoundly depressed (Parikh, Lam, & Group, 2001). Dysthymia, or mild chronic depression, seldom disappears spontaneously. The course of depression in patients with neurological impairments appears similar (Robinson, Bolduc, & Price, 1987).

Epidemiology and Risk Factors

Depression is the most common and serious mood disturbance. Approximately 6% to 20% of the U.S. population suffers from an incapacitating depressive episode at some point in their lives. Depression affects 5% of the population in a year (Boyd & Weisman, 1981; Cassens, Wolfe, & Zola, 1990; Rosenzweig, Leiman, & Breedlove, 1996).

About twice as many women as men suffer from major depression. Various explanations for the sex ratio have been proposed, including the following: Women seek health advice more than men; women suffer more social discrimination than men, which leads to low self-esteem

and depression; depression is linked to the x chromosome; depression is linked to female hormones; and depression is masked in men by their higher rates of alcohol use (Rosenzweig et al., 1996).

Although many people have the impression that depression is more common in older than younger adults, that is not true. In one large self-report study, adults older than 70 did not score higher on a depression scale than adults between ages 20 and 54 (Gatz, Kasl-Godley, & Karel, 1996). Several studies report that depression rates are higher in younger than older adults (Klerman, Lavori et al., 1985; Klerman & Weissman, 1994; Patten, 2000). Although the incidence of depression may not be higher in community-dwelling older adults than in younger adults, it is still the most common psychiatric disorder among the elderly (e.g., Blazer, 2002) and is one of the few psychiatric disorders that appears for the first time in later adulthood (Woodruff-Pak, 1997).

Although the elderly as a group may not be more frequently depressed than younger adults, certain groups of the elderly with neurological disorders are at an increased risk for depression. Depression often occurs with, or as a result of, dementia, stroke, and Parkinson's disease. Depressive symptoms occur in up to 40% of patients with dementia, 25% to 50% of patients following a stroke and about 50% of patients with Parkinson's disease. Interestingly, the cognitive impairments associated with major depression are similar whether the depression occurs with or without neurological disease. In all of these cases, patients with depression show impaired performance on delayed recall tests (Starkstein & Robinson, 1991).

Depression often follows a stroke. Depression following a stroke manifests with the same symptoms as idiopathic late-onset depression, with the exception that stroke patients show more psychomotor retardation (cited in Cummings & Mega, 2003, p. 206). Patients who have had a left hemisphere stroke are more likely to be depressed immediately after a stroke, but patients who have had a right hemisphere stroke are more likely to be depressed a year after the onset of the stroke. With cortical lesions, depression appears to be more severe the closer the lesion is to the frontal pole (e.g., Shimoda & Robinson, 1999; Starkstein & Robinson, 1991). With subcortical lesions, damage to the left caudate appears to cause more depression than damage to other subcortical areas. There is now recognition that many cases of depression in the elderly may be due to vascular causes other than overt stroke, including silent stroke, transient ischemic attack (TIA), subcortical white matter ischemia, and vascular risk factors such as hypertension (Provinciali & Coccia, 2002; Thomas et al., 2001). So-called **vascular depression** is similar to idiopathic depression but with poor insight, psychomotor retardation, and no family history (Cummings & Mega, 2003).

The relationship between dementia and depression is complex. The most common mood disturbance in patients with dementia is mild depression (Lyketsos, Treisman, Lipsey, Morris, & Robinson, 1998). In one study, 21% of patients with Alzheimer's disease (AD) showed significant depressive symptoms (tearfulness, sad affect, etc.), verified by a collateral source, and were recommended to have treatment (Rubin, Veiel, Kinscherf, Morris, & Storandt, 2001). Although many patients with AD have depressive symptoms, many fewer meet the criteria for major depression (Burke, Rubin, Morris, & Berg, 1988). The most consistent symptoms are depressed mood, fatigue, indecision, and social withdrawal. Depression in AD is associated with physical aggression, impaired activities of daily living (ADLs), and executive dysfunction (e.g., Lawlor & Ryan, 1994). With major depression, patients with dementia also experience disorders of sleep, eating, and libido and fatigue. Depression can also be a harbinger of AD: As many as 89% of elderly patients with a dementia syndrome of depression develop AD (Devanand et al., 1996; Kral & Emery, 1989). Depression appears more common in patients with vascular dementia than AD (Cummings et al., 1987).

Depression appears relatively common in disorders affecting subcortical brain regions, most notably Parkinson's disease (PD). Up to 50% of patients with PD will have depressive symptoms and/or frank depression. Prominent depressive symptoms in PD include dysphoria, pessimism, rapid cognitive decline, and relative impairment in ADLs (Cummings, 1992a, 1992b; Mayeux, Williams, Stern, & Cote, 1984).

Neuropathology of Depression

Functional depression is associated with real-life losses such as the death of a loved one and loss of physical health. Depression is also associated with alterations in brain neurochemistry. The brain chemistry of mood came to light by observing a series of drugs intended to treat other disorders—blood pressure and tuberculosis. One drug used to treat high blood pressure by depleting catecholamines (dopamine, norepinephrine, and epinephrine) and serotonin caused depression in a fair number of patients (Bear et al., 2001). Another drug used to treat tuberculosis inhibited monoamine oxidase (MAO), the enzyme that inactivates catecholamines and serotonin, and caused mood elevation. From these and other observations, we have learned that mood is very closely tied to the levels of norepinephrine and serotonin in the brain—most frequently to decreased levels of these important neurotransmitters. However, the story is more complex than that, involving genetic predisposition (mood disorders run in families), psychosocial stress, and other brain chemicals and receptors.

Positron emission tomography (PET) scans of depressed patients without brain damage show decreased activity of the caudate and increased blood flow in the frontal cortex when compared with healthy subjects (Posner & Raichle, 1994).

Depression associated with neurological disorders, including stroke and Parkinson's disease, also illuminates brain regions that are important in mood. Major poststroke depression is particularly associated with lesions in the left dorsolateral frontal cortex and left basal ganglia (e.g., Starkstein, Robinson, & Proce, 1987). Depressed patients with PD show *lower* metabolic activity in the head of the caudate and inferior frontal cortex than controls, as well as a significant correlation between degree of depression and metabolic activity in the inferior frontal cortex (the lower the metabolic activity, the more severe the depression) (Mayberg et al., 1990). Depressed patients with PD and stroke patients highlight the importance of the left hemisphere:

Depression appears more common immediately after left hemisphere stroke and in patients with PD with right-sided (i.e., left hemisphere) symptoms.

Putting together the data from depressed patients with and without brain damage yields a partially consistent and partially confusing picture. Both depressed patients without brain damage and depressed patients with PD show decreased activity of the caudate, suggesting it plays an important role. The role of the frontal lobe is less clear: Stroke data suggest that decreased frontal metabolism is associated with depression, whereas PET scans of depressed patients without brain damage show *increased* blood flow in the frontal cortex compared with healthy subjects (Posner & Raichle, 1994). Therefore, the frontal lobe appears important, but the particular regions of the frontal cortex and the manner in which frontal cortex interacts with depression are still not clear.

Diagnosis of Depression

The gold standard of depression diagnosis is a psychiatric interview, investigating depressed mood and somatic complaints. Despite great effort, there is still no easily measured physiological or biological marker for depression. One physiological measure that has met with some success is the dexamethasone suppression test. This test is based on the observation that hospitalized patients with depression showed high levels of cortisol, a naturally circulating corticosteroid, throughout the day and night. In nondepressed subjects, cortisol is typically high only in the morning. Dexamethasone is a synthetic corticoid that suppresses the early morning rise in cortisol in healthy subjects. However, in many patients with depression, dexamethasone does not suppress levels of circulating cortisol. Therefore, if dexamethasone fails to suppress cortisol, depression is a likely diagnosis. This procedure can be particularly helpful in determining the existence of treatable depression in patients with aphasia and comprehension deficits (Harvey & Black, 1996). However, false positives do occur: A failure to suppress cortisol (a positive finding) may be found in patients with AD and other diseases without depression, so it is not a foolproof diagnostic

test (Nierenberg & Feinstein, 1988). Depression can also be measured by observer or self-rating scales. Obviously, all mood/depression scales should be supplemented by evaluation for organic dysfunction and overall health status.

Depression in the context of neurological disorders necessarily complicates the diagnosis. First, the typical ways in which our mood is expressed and diagnosed, through words, intonation, and facial expression, may be unavailable to various patients with neurological impairments. Stroke patients with aphasia may have difficulty expressing their mood through words; patients with right hemisphere damage may be dysprosodic and not express their mood accurately through vocal intonation; patients with Parkinson's disease, because of the typical masked expression and slow movements, will likely appear depressed whether or not they feel depressed; and patients with pseudobulbar palsy often laugh and cry without the typical underlying mood associated with laughing and crying. Second, many symptoms of neurological disease overlap with symptoms of depression: Apathy, cognitive impairment, agitation, psychomotor slowing, and changes in appetite and sleep patterns are common symptoms of both dementia without depression and idiopathic depression. Therefore, evaluation of depression in patients with neurological disorders must be mindful of these confounds and proceed accordingly.

Four useful and common depression scales are briefly described here (see examples in Table 12.1). The Hamilton Rating Scale for Depression (HAM-D) (Hamilton, 1960) is a tool to help an interviewer objectively rate the degree of depression. It can be administered by any health care professional, but "its value depends entirely on the skill of the interviewer in eliciting the necessary information" (Hamilton, 1960, p. 56). On the basis of an interview, the examiner rates a patient on each of 17 variables, from 0 (*no depressive symptoms*) to 4 (*incapacitating level of symptoms*). The points are summed for a total score. In general, a total of 10 to 13 points indicates mild depression, 14 to 17 suggests mild to moderate depression, and more than 17 is associated with severe depression. The HAM-D was developed for people with no cognitive impairment and is not appropriate for patients with cognitive deficits. It has been criticized for its heavy reliance on somatic signs and symptoms that are frequent in the non-depressed elderly population.

The Beck Depression Inventory (BDI) (Beck, Ward, Mendelson, Mock, & Erbaugh, 1961) and the Beck Depression Inventory II (BDI-II) (Beck, Steer, & Brown, 1996) use the patients' own report to rate the degree of depression. They were developed for mixed-age populations. In both tests, patients read (or are read) 21 questions and choose 1 of the answers that best describes them. Each of the 21 answers is weighted from 0 (*not depressed*) to 3 (*severely depressed*), and the numbers are summed. In general, a total score of 0 to 4 indicates denial of depression, 5 to 9 is not depressed, 10 to 18 suggests mild to moderate depression, 19 to 29 suggests moderate to severe depression, and 30 to 63 indicates severe depression. A score of more than 40 may indicate an exaggeration of depressive symptoms.

The Geriatric Depression Scale (GDS) (Brink et al., 1982) is one of the few depression scales specifically designed for older adults. Physical complaints that are commonly associated with depression in younger adults, such as sleep and appetite disturbance, may be present in older adults for other reasons and do not necessarily indicate depression. They can be the result of healthy aging, other diseases, or medication. For this reason, self-rating scales that focus on somatic complaints may overestimate the number of elderly who are depressed. The GDS is a set of 30 yes/no questions that focus on non-somatic aspects of depression. For each question, either a yes or a no response (depending on the question) is associated with depression. The number of depression-associated responses is tallied, 1 point each, for a total from 0 to 30. Under 10 indicates no depression, 10 to 19 suggests mild depression, and above 20 implies severe depression.

The Cornell Scale for Depression in Dementia is unique insofar as it was developed for and validated with older patients with and without dementia (e.g., Alexopoulos et al., 1988). The Cornell scale consists of 19 questions that use information from both patients and their caregivers. It is sensitive to depression and is effective at distinguishing depression and other psychiatric disorders. (see Table 12.1 for examples from these four depression scales).

Treatment of Depression

An effective treatment for depression is conventionally seen as one that produces a 50% reduction in symptoms on a measure such as the Hamilton Depression Rating Scale (Kennedy, Lam, Cohen, et al., 2001). Effective treatment modalities include individual and group psychotherapy (Gallagher, 1986), antidepressant medication (Lyketsos et al., 1998), and electroconvulsive therapy (e.g., Datto, 2000). The treatments discussed below appear effective for treating young as well as elderly patients with depression.

In general, cognitive-behavioral psychotherapy has similar efficacy as antidepressant medication, and various methods of psychotherapy have similar levels of effectiveness as one another. Rates of improvement from psychotherapy are typically quoted in the 60% to 70% range (Segal, Whitney, & Lam, 2001). The chronicity and severity of depression, as well as the frequency of treatment, mitigate effectiveness. A study by Gallagher (1986) showed that short-term (4 months) individual psychotherapy, in which there is a clear focus on mutually defined goals, resolved depression in 52% of the patients. A year later, 57% of the patients were still not depressed, demonstrating lasting effects of short-term psychotherapy. Psychotherapy is also useful for depressed patients with early dementia and their families. In this context, treatment may involve introducing structured activities that give the patient pleasure and provide the caregiver with relaxation and training to solve problems.

Many antidepressant medications are effective for both the depressed elderly with no brain damage and depressed patients with dementia (Lyketsos et al., 1998). Tricyclic antidepressants block the reuptake of norepinephrine and serotonin. Selective serotonin reuptake inhibitors (SSRIs) act specifically on the serotonin receptors to keep serotonin available in the brain. Monoamine oxidase inhibitors (MAOIs) reduce the degradation of serotonin and norepinephrine in the brain. All of these drugs increase the

Table 12.1   Examples of Items From Different Instruments Used to Evaluate Depression

	Hamilton Rating Scale for Depression (Hamilton, 1960)	Beck Depression Inventory II (BDI-II) (Beck, Steer, & Brown, 1996)	Geriatric Depression Scale (Brink et al., 1982)	Cornell Scale for Depression in Dementia (Alexopoulos et al., 1988)
Format	The clinician rates 17 variables on a 5-point scale (0 = *no depressive symptom to* 4 = *incapacitating level of symptom*) based on a clinical interview.	The patient selects answers to 21 questions, assessing many areas of function on a 4-point scale (0 = *not depressed* to 3 = *severely depressed*). The ratings should reflect the answer that best describes how the patient has felt over the 2-week period just prior to filling out the ratings.	The patient selects answers to 30 yes/no questions about how he or she has felt over the past week.	The clinician rates 19 areas based on signs and symptoms observed or reported by the patient or the patient's caregiver during the week prior to the interview. Each area of function is rated on a 3-point scale (0 = *absent*, 1 = *mild or intermittent*, 2 = *severe*).
Example of items that assess interest in work and activities	Work and activities: 0 = No difficulty 1 = Thoughts and feelings of incapacity related to activities (work or hobbies) 2 = Loss of interest in activity (work or hobbies), either directly reported by patient or indirectly seen in listlessness, indecision, and vacillation (feels he or she has to push self to work or activities) 3 = Decrease in actual time spent in activities or decrease in productivity. In hospital, rate 3 if patient does not spend at least 3 hours a day in activities. 4 = Stopped working because of present illness. In hospital, rate 4 if patient engages in no activities except supervised ward chores.	Loss of interest: 0 = I have not lost interest in other people or activities. 1 = I am less interested in other people or things than before. 2 = I have lost most of my interest in other people or things. 3 = It's hard to get interested in anything.	Several questions get at the concept of interest in activities: 2. Have you dropped many of your activities & interests? 12. Do you prefer to stay at home, rather than going out and doing new things? 20. Is it hard for you to get started on new projects? 28. Do you prefer to avoid social gatherings?	Loss of interest: Has the patient been less involved in usual activities (score only if change occurred acutely, i.e., in less than 1 month).

Note: Example items were selected to illustrate similarities and differences between the instruments in the way they assess only one area of function that is important to any assessment of depression: interest in work and other activities.

215

levels of monoamine neurotransmitters in the brain and produce their therapeutic effect on mood in a period of 4 to 8 weeks. Side effects include sexual disturbance and weight gain, among others. The choice of medication is often made to minimize side effects. Patients generally stay on the medications for a minimum of 6 to 9 months and at least 6 months following full remission of symptoms. Some stay on medication longer. All major types of antidepressant medications are used to treat the elderly, although the choice of medication may differ for the elderly because of side effects. For instance, some medications have anticholinergic properties that can cause or exacerbate confusion.

Electroconvulsive therapy (ECT) induces seizure activity. In the mid-20th century, first chemicals, then electricity delivered through electrodes on the scalp, were used to induce seizures to treat schizophrenia. This treatment was not helpful for schizophrenia, but it did rapidly reverse depression and was subsequently used to treat depression. The practice was generally abandoned when antidepressant drugs became widely available and effective. However, ECT regained respect and use beginning in the 1980s primarily for two groups of patients: those who are not helped by antidepressant drugs and those who need a quick, effective treatment because they are at risk for suicide. The treatment has been modified since its inception to minimize adverse reactions and memory loss. Before the procedure, the patient is medically relaxed. The electrical stimulation is generally given only over one hemisphere, usually the nondominant hemisphere. Treatment can be given two to three times a week for up to 6 weeks, with maximum response usually reached after 2 to 4 weeks. The electrical dose is three to six times the seizure threshold for unilateral electrode placement. We do not understand how ECT works, but it can have dramatic, quick, and lasting effects, relieving depression in sometimes as little as one session. It is generally accepted as the most rapid and effective treatment for severe major depressive episodes, with a remission rate of 60% to 80%. The main problems with ECT are its image; minor side effects of nausea, headache, and muscle aches; and the more lasting side effects of transient retrograde amnesia. The amnesia lessens after time, resolving by 6 months following treatment, with the exception of persistent memory gaps for the time around the treatment (Datto, 2000; Kennedy et al., 2001). The elderly are often the best candidates for ECT because they are likely to have concurrent chronic diseases and take multiple medications, which make additional drug treatment less desirable. Without maintenance treatment, either with follow-up ECT or medication, relapse is more than 50% within 6 months.

Several other newer treatments for depression are being developed and assessed. Some of these are summarized here. For those who suffer from seasonal affective disorder, a specific type of depression, **light therapy,** exposure to a balanced spectrum that mimics bright sunlight via fluorescent lights for 30 minutes a day over a period of 2 to 3 weeks, can be very effective (Eastman, Young, Fogg, Liu, & Meaeden, 1998; Sher et al., 2001). Side effects include visual disturbances and headache, and most people suffer recurrence if the light therapy is stopped.

Based on the finding of abnormal sleep patterns in depressed patients, a regimen of **sleep deprivation** has the effect of resetting sleep patterns and relieving depressive symptoms for a sustained period of time in 15% of patients. There are different protocols, such as being kept awake for a single period of 40 hours or for a sequence of 36-hour periods with sleep recovery in between.

Several surgical procedures, referred to as **psychosurgery,** have been successful in relieving depression, although they are reserved for the most intractable depressives. Ablation procedures create small lesions in the limbic system, either in the area of the anterior cingulate or caudate; 30% to 60% of patients show good improvement after such procedures. Another surgical intervention implants an electrical stimulator wrapped around the vagus nerve. This procedure was developed for relieving epilepsy, but it has also proved to be effective in relieving severe depression in otherwise treatment resistant patients.

Transcranial magnetic stimulation is a procedure in which brief, repetitive, high-intensity magnetic fields are produced by an apparatus held near the scalp for about 30 minutes (Hasey,

2001). It is fast and easy, appears to have no effects on memory, and has quick antidepressant effects. Little is known about the long-term efficacy.

OTHER PSYCHIATRIC DISORDERS

Delirium and depression are typically considered part of the differential diagnosis when a patient presents with dementia. However, they are not the only psychiatric disorders encountered in an older population with or without neurological disorders. Although beyond the scope of this book to cover in much detail, two additional psychiatric disorders are briefly described here. The interested reader should refer to the work of Cummings for a review of these and other psychiatric phenomena in the context of brain damage (Cummings, 1992a, 1992b, 2000; Cummings & Mega, 2003; Cummings et al., 1987).

Mania

Mania refers to an elevated or euphoric mood, increased physical activity, irritability accelerated or pressured speech, distractibility, grandiosity, decreased need for sleep, poor judgment and poor insight, flight of ideas, and racing thoughts. Mania can occur idiopathically (primary mania) or as a result of medication or a neurological disorder (secondary mania). Precipitating causes include dopaminergic treatment for Parkinson's disease; stroke, particularly with right thalamic and right basal ganglia lesions; infections affecting the brain (e.g., neurosyphilis); brain tumors; head trauma; and frontotemporal dementia. Agitation, a symptom of mania, is one of the most frequent and difficult behavior problems associated with dementia (e.g., Cohen-Mansfield et al., 1989; Cohen-Mansfield & Werner, 1997). **Hypomania** refers to briefer and milder episodes that do not interfere with social function and work. **Bipolar disorders** consist of both depressive and manic episodes lasting longer than 1 week. Medication is the mainstay treatment for mania and bipolar disorders. ECT is helpful for many people who do not improve with pharmacotherapy.

Psychosis

Psychosis refers to a person's inability to accurately evaluate and draw inferences about his or her external reality. Primary symptoms include hallucinations, false perceptions, **delusions,** false beliefs that are sometimes based on hallucinations, and **confabulations** (made-up facts). Schizophrenia is an idiopathic psychosis with onset in young adulthood and a lifelong course. Very occasionally, schizophrenia will begin after age 40. It is characterized by delusions, hallucinations, and illogical thinking. With age, many schizophrenic symptoms become less severe and cognition declines. Late-onset psychosis is not likely to be due to schizophrenia but more likely secondary to neurological disorders, such as Alzheimer's and Parkinson's diseases, or metabolic disorders, such as hypothyroidism, vitamin B12 deficiency, or systemic lupus erythematosus. Paranoia and persecutory delusions are common psychotic symptoms in patients with dementia, occurring in up to 30% of patients with Alzheimer's and 40% of patients with vascular dementia. Pharmacologic treatment of psychotic symptoms can be successful in patients with neurological disorders, particularly if the underlying neurological disease can be well treated.

13

MOVEMENT DISORDERS

Chapter Preview

1. What are movement disorders?

Movement disorders are abnormalities in motor control. Common movement disorders in older adults include tremor, Parkinson's disease, paralysis, and apraxia.

2. How does movement change in healthy aging?

Movements become slower and less accurate in the course of healthy aging. Balance is often disrupted, frequently resulting in falls. There are many potential underlying causes and explanations for these changes, including slower reflexes, reduced strength, decreased attention, poor general health, poor vision, and instability.

3. What are the behavioral characteristics of movement disorders?

Movement disorders can create involuntary movements as with tremor, decrease muscle contraction as in paresis and paralysis, impair motor planning and control as in apraxia, or create a combination of abnormalities as in Parkinson's disease.

4. What is the neuropathology of movement disorders?

Movement disorders arise because of cortical and/or subcortical brain damage. For example, paralysis can result from a cortical stroke, while Parkinson's disease is due to a degenerative subcortical process. The neuropathology of other movement disorders, such as tremor, is not well understood.

5. How are movement disorders diagnosed?

A patient's medical history, observation of the patient at rest and patterns of movement errors help to differentiate one movement disorder from another.

6. How are movement disorders treated?

Movement disorders are treated with a wide range of modalities, including strength and flexibility training, compensatory strategies, medication, and surgery.

Types of Movement

Movements fall on a continuum between **reflex** and **voluntary.** Reflexes are rapid, involuntary, stereotyped movements. Examples include coughing when a foreign object enters the airway, withdrawing a hand from a hot surface, and the knee-jerk response elicited by striking the tendon just below the kneecap. At the other extreme of the movement continuum is voluntary movement, which is intentional, deliberate, and planned. Voluntary movements tend to be novel, and often complex actions such as opening a refrigerator, taking out a jar of peanut butter, and making a sandwich. The relatively simple division of movement into reflex versus voluntary is a useful teaching tool, but many movements are neither purely reflex nor voluntary and might be called an **automatic** or **semi-voluntary movement.** For instance, walking combines several types of movement: deliberate intention and planning where to go, semiautomatic aspects of starting and stopping and changing direction, and relatively reflexive, unconscious, and stereotyped actions of putting one foot in front of the other. To complicate matters further, movements can evolve from one end of the continuum to the other: What starts as a conscious, difficult movement can become automatic and, with practice, move toward the reflex end of the continuum. Typing and bicycle riding are good examples of this sort of evolution. As a movement changes in character along the voluntary → reflex continuum, so do the brain systems that control it.

Most reflexes are mediated at the brainstem and spinal levels. Some aspects of seemingly complex activities such as walking, which we do not ordinarily think of as reflexes, are also mediated at the brainstem and spinal levels: Even after cortical areas of experimental animal brains are sectioned, creating what is called a **decorticate state,** experimental nonhuman animals are able to stand up, walk, and run (e.g., Palisses, Pergesol, Viala, & Viala, 1988).

Voluntary actions are planned in the premotor regions of the frontal lobe(s), organized in the supplemental motor areas, executed by muscle control from the primary motor cortex, and involve, to different degrees, subcortical and cerebellar structures. Neural control of voluntary action is traditionally discussed as involving two semi-independent neurological systems, both originating in the frontal lobes and controlling muscle contractions through the spinal cord, but through different intermediate structures. The **corticospinal** (a.k.a. **pyramidal**) **system** controls movement quite directly from the cortex to the spinal cord via the internal capsule and the medulla. In contrast, the **extrapyramidal system** mediates movement through a more circuitous set of connections in the basal ganglia, cerebellum, and certain brainstem motor centers. These intermediate brain centers play complex roles in the modulation of movement. The basal ganglia, for instance, are involved in programming and initiating internally generated movements and complex motor strategies. The cerebellum plays an important role in producing smooth, sequenced movements. The cerebellum also coordinates posture and ongoing movement of the eyes, head, body, and limbs, as well as playing a role in learning new motor skills. The distinction between the pyramidal and extrapyramidal motor systems is appealing as a way to conceptualize the motor system, but as we learn more about control of movement, it is apparent that both systems, as well as feedback between them, are very well coordinated, and movement disorders often involve disruptions of both systems (Iyer, Mitz, & Winstein, 1999).

How Does Movement Change With Healthy Aging?

Movements become slower and less accurate in the course of healthy aging. Deterioration begins between ages 40 and 50 and continues from that point on (Ballard, Robin, Woodward, & Zimba, 2001; Kauranen & Vanharanta, 1996). This appears true for all body parts that have been assessed, quite literally from the head to foot. The movement of the lip, jaw, and larynx increases in variability and decreases in accuracy with aging. Arm movement, as in aimed pointing, becomes slower and jerkier, and often what are single arm movements for younger subjects are segmented into two movements by older subjects (Yan, 2000). Finger movement is slower in older adults (Carey, Bogard, King, & Suman, 1994; Li, McColgin, & Van Oteghen, 1998). In the lower extremities, foot movement, particularly stepping actions, significantly slow with advancing age (Berg & Blasi, 2000; Li et al., 1998).

Balance is another area in which subtle, well-coordinated movements are crucial and appear disrupted by the healthy aging process. Maintaining balance requires integrating signals from many parts of the body and making multiple, frequent, quick, and small compensatory movements with the head, arms, legs, and trunk to maintain balance. Quiet standing balance appears to be maintained well in aging, despite an increase of movements of the head and hip (i.e., more "sway") (Panzer, Bandinelli, & Hallett, 1995). However, in any difficult position, such as standing on one leg with eyes closed, balance is significantly impaired in aging (Kaye, Oken, Howieson, & Howieson, 1994). One recent screening study found that 21% of a group of adults older than 65 had sufficiently impaired balance to warrant balance training (Ness et al., 2003).

The most concerning functional change in movement seen in older adults is the increased incidence of falling. Older adults suffer more falls than younger adults, and the consequences of falling are more serious in older than in younger adults. The common causes of falls in the elderly include frailty, impaired balance, poor nutritional status, side effects of medications, polypharmacy, diabetes, sleep disturbance, and impaired vision (Baker & Harvey, 1985; Jain, 2000). The consequences of falls are also more dire for older than younger adults. Falls are a leading cause of hip fracture, depression, decreased independence, and death in older individuals (see Morley, 2002, for review). The financial impact of falls is significant, with one estimate of hospitalization costs following a fall being about $17,000 (Ellis & Trent, 2001).

There are many levels and types of explanations for the movement changes that result in, among other things, falls. These include slower reflexes; reduced strength; decreased attention; overall poor general health; decrease in visual acuity, which can lead to tripping over environmental hazards; diabetic neuropathy, which leads to loss of proprioception; an unstable gait; and instability. At a detailed level of explanation, movement changes are attributed to the loss of motor units or fibers in muscle, reduced firing rate, increased variability of firing rate, reduced diameter and force of contraction of fibers, or reduced nerve conduction velocities (Ballard et al., 2001). And of course, problems with movement may be the first signs of gross brain dysfunction associated with stroke or Parkinson's disease, topics to which we now turn.

CORTICAL MOVEMENT DISORDERS: PARALYSIS AND APRAXIA

Focal damage to the cortex can create two very distinct movement disorders: paralysis and apraxia. Patients who suffer cortical strokes in the frontal and/or parietal lobes, are most likely to demonstrate these disorders.

Cortical Paralysis

Definition and Behavioral Characteristics

Damage to the primary motor cortex of the left or right frontal lobes causes contralateral **paralysis** or **paresis** in the affected body part(s). *Paralysis* is defined as a muscle that does not contract sufficiently to produce joint movement or provide postural stability to the body segment (Ryerson & Levit, 1997). **Hemiplegia** is paralysis on one side of the body. Paralysis can affect individual muscles or groups of muscles. Paresis is sufficient muscle weakness to prevent muscle contraction for effective use. **Hemiparesis** is weakness on one side of the body. Muscle weakness can be manifested as a decrease in force, range of movement, or inability to sustain contraction long enough to perform a motor task. Immediately following a stroke, some patients experience paralysis of the affected side, whereas others only experience weakness. With recovery, paralysis can evolve into paresis.

Paralysis also involves changes in muscle tone. Muscle tone is the amount of tension in a muscle. Muscle tone in hemiplegia is measured subjectively by comparing the amount of resistance to passive lengthening on both sides. **Hypotonicity** describes lower than normal muscle tone; these muscles provide no resistance when moved. Hypotonic muscles are flaccid. They feel floppy and heavy and do not resist, follow, or assist with guided movements. **Hypertonicity** describes greater than normal muscle tension, stiffness, or rigidity; these muscles provide increased resistance to passive movement. Spasticity is an extreme type of hypertonicity in which increased muscle tension causes unnatural body and limb positions and impaired coordination. Most stroke patients first show hypotonicity on the affected side, followed in recovery by variations in tone and often hypertonicity. Parietal lesions are associated with hypotonia; severe head injury is associated with muscle spasticity. Tone can vary from muscle to muscle within an individual patient.

Paralysis is also accompanied by sensory changes, including a decrease in **sensory awareness**, impaired **sensory interpretation,** and poor **kinesthetic memory**, all of which affect movement. Poor sensory awareness describes the patient's inability to feel the involved side, which is associated with neglect of that side. Less severe deficits may cause numbness or tingling on the affected side. A deficit in sensory interpretation means that the patient may not be able to correctly perceive sensory stimuli, for instance, perceiving a therapist's light touch as painful. Kinesthetic memory refers to knowledge of what it feels like to move normally, including sequencing, timing, and speed of movements. With paralysis or paresis, patients may lose the muscle memory of what it should feel like performing activities of daily living, and these normal patterns of movement will have to be reestablished through repetitive guided movement practice.

Neuropathology

Brain damage that interrupts the motor system at any point can cause paralysis or paresis. Damage to the primary motor areas in the frontal lobes impairs movement of the corresponding body regions (see Figure 2.5 in Chapter 2). Because the fibers from this part of the cortex are almost fully crossed, focal injury to the motor strip on one side of the brain causes weakness or paralysis on the opposite side of the body (i.e., hemiplegia or hemiparesis). Because other cortical areas, the basal ganglia, cerebellum, thalamus, and internal capsule contribute to the control of movement, damage in these areas can also produce paresis and paralysis. Damage above the point of decussation causes contralateral muscle involvement except in the case of the cerebellum, which controls ipsilateral movement. Movements that involve the midline such as the jaw, throat, and larynx are often less affected than the limbs because they have input from both sides of the brain. Damage to the spinal cord causes paralysis but typically not unilaterally as with cortical damage. Damage to the lower spinal cord (below T1) paralyzes both legs, called **paraplegia.** Damage to the cervical level of the spinal cord paralyzes both arms and both legs, called **quadriplegia/tetraplegia.**

Diagnosis of Paralysis and Paresis

Physical therapists and physiatrists typically diagnose and treat paralysis and paresis. The goal of a diagnostic evaluation is to identify and understand functional limitations caused by the paralysis. A diagnostic examination will generally contain at least these three distinct elements (Ryerson & Levit, 1997):

- The clinician observes movement to see postural deviations and atypical movements. This includes observation of the patient sitting, standing, and performing specific movements such as putting on a shirt or climbing stairs, depending on the patient's degree of impairment. At this point in an evaluation, assistance is given only if the patient loses balance or other safety concerns arise.
- The clinician manually helps the patient with movements that cannot be accomplished independently. Thus, the clinician identifies potential therapeutic manipulations that help to

restore function. During this phase, the clinician also attempts to interfere with undesirable movements that the patient has developed that are inefficient or counterproductive.

- Using both observation and manual manipulation, the clinician assesses range of motion and abnormalities of tone, in addition to identifying which manipulations and movements cause the patient pain. Treatment goals incorporate all of this information and focus on the movement problems that are most relevant to the patient's functional goals.

Treatment of Paralysis and Paresis

Many modalities are used to treat paralyzed patients. **Movement reeducation** is one illustrative and systematic process of increasing the patient's ability to move independently in normal patterns of coordination for functional activities. Four stages are outlined by Ryerson and Levit (1997):

- **Sensory education** teaches the patient about the desired movement. The clinician moves the patient's body passively to establish kinesthetic perception of movement, the basis for muscle memory.
- In **assisted practice,** the patient actively assists the clinician-guided movements. This increases muscle strength and is complete when the patient can reproduce the movements with manual assistance.
- During the **independent movement** phase of reeducation, the clinician decreases physical assistance and encourages the patient to take greater control until able to produce the movement independently.
- **Functional movement reeducation and practice** requires the patient to practice the learned movements when not in therapy. Finally, the patient can be taught to combine learned movements to perform specific tasks, such as hitting tennis balls and cooking.

During the therapeutic process, the clinician also treats secondary impairments such as pain and swelling that interfere with movement control. Any of the steps of rehabilitation may involve the use of adaptive or compensatory devices and technology, including splints, wheelchairs, walkers, and smaller adaptive devices to help the patient get out of bed and get dressed. Patients learn to use one hand for tasks that in the past were performed with two hands, sometimes using trunk movements. Dogs, although used primarily to assist those with vision impairments, can be used to assist movement-impaired patients to perform activities such as opening doors and picking up and carrying objects (Modlin, 2001).

Apraxia

Definition and Behavioral Characteristics

The term **apraxia** comes from the Greek word for *action* (*praxis*). Apraxia literally means "no action." In reality, apraxia is more subtle and interesting than not being able to move. Apraxia is a disorder of voluntary, learned, or skilled movement that is not due to weakness, paralysis, poor comprehension, sensory loss, dementia, or poor motivation. Although apraxia is not caused by these other deficits, it can and often does accompany them, as in dementia, in which apraxia is one of the diagnostic criteria (see Chapter 11). Apraxia can be seen as a disorder of motor planning. Apraxic errors are distinctive. For example, when patients with apraxia affecting their hands are asked to perform specific actions with their hands, they understand what they are asked to do, want to comply, and try, but their actions contain errors of hand shape, hand location, and/or movement. For instance, a pantomime of combing hair might look like someone holding a comb but moving the hand in circles in front of the chest; saluting might look like the saluting movement but with a fist hand shape rather than a saluting hand shape. Sometimes, the pantomime or action will be recognizable but simply wrong, such as pretending to use a screwdriver when asked to demonstrate how to use a hammer. Complex actions that involve several steps may be simplified or the steps performed in the wrong order. For example, when asked to pantomime the sequence of cleaning a pipe, putting tobacco in it, lighting it, and smoking it, a patient with apraxia may first put tobacco in it and then clean it (Heilman & Gonzalez-Rothi, 1993). Pantomime to imitation is typically better than pantomime to command. Although imitation of actions is easier than pantomiming actions to command, it is typically not error free. If a patient errs on pantomime without actually holding an appropriate object, performance will usually improve if the real object is used as a prop; in fact, patients can typically perform these actions well in natural-istic contexts with all the props, contextual support, and motivation available. For instance, they can brush their teeth appropriately when at home, even if they cannot pretend to brush their teeth when asked to in the clinic. Patients with apraxia are sometimes aware when they have made an error and try to correct it.

Apraxia is described by what body part or parts are affected. **Limb apraxia** refers to impairment of volitional movement of the arms and hands. **Truncal apraxia** impairs the ability to perform body postures, such as standing like a boxer or bowing. **Oral apraxia,** sometimes called *buccofacial apraxia,* affects movement of the mouth in actions such as blowing out a match or sucking on a straw. **Verbal apraxia** or **apraxia of speech** affects the ability to articulate individual speech sounds and sound sequences. Apraxia of speech is one of the most disabling apraxias because it inter-feres with verbal communication. Patients with apraxia of speech typically produce clearly formed sounds, just the wrong sounds. Because they know what they want to say and can hear that they produced an error, they often try to self-correct, sometimes making many attempts at articulating a word without ever getting it right. Patients with apraxia of speech typically have more difficulty with sound sequences in longer than shorter words and phrases. Buccofacial apraxia and apraxia of speech often co-occur, but each can appear in isolation as well. Some authors suggest that the apraxias affecting the mouth may be points along a continuum, with speech most often affected because of the fine motor coordina-tion it requires and nonspeech tasks less often affected because they require relatively less fine motor control (Heilman & Gonzalez-Rothi, 1993).

There has long been a debate about the whether apraxia of speech and nonfluent Broca's aphasia are truly distinct disorders (see Chapter 4; Darley, Aronson, & Brown, 1975). In practice, they frequently co-occur, and it is sometimes difficult to identify which speech errors are due to a movement disorder versus a language disorder. But, at least in theory, and occasionally in the clinic, the two can be distinguished: It is clear that some nonfluent patients primarily have trouble with sound sequencing/motor planning, whereas others have little problem with motor planning but do have difficulty with word finding and sentence formulation. One distinguishing characteristic of apraxia of speech is the presence of articu-latory groping and multiple attempts, with the patient clearly aware of the difficulty and try-ing different tongue placements and mouth configurations prior to and during sound pro-duction. This phenomenon is not typical of aphasic nonfluency, in which case we are more likely to observe the silences without groping and frustration at not being able to produce the correct word ("Damn, what is that word?"). A predominance of sound substitutions is more consistent with apraxia of speech, whereas whole-word substitutions are more consistent with aphasia.

There can also be debate about whether to classify constructional apraxia and dressing apraxia (discussed in Chapter 8) as movement-based apraxias versus visuospatial disorders. Undoubtedly, both drawing and dressing would be and sometimes are compromised by limb apraxia, but it is likely that both functions are also frequently compromised by visuo-spatial impairment. Analysis of errors is the most helpful clue: Apraxic errors are likely to be accompanied by good recognition of errors and multiple attempts to produce the target. In contrast, patients with visuospatial disorders are often not aware of their errors and do not try to correct themselves. More purely spatial deficits can also sometimes be distinguished from apraxias because spatial deficits are more likely than apraxias to elicit impaired perfor-mance on tasks that require minimal volitional movement, such as perceptual and visuospatial tests of line orientation, shape discrimination, and face recognition (see Chapter 8; Benton et al., 1994).

Apraxia can be seen as a cognitive or a movement disorder. As a cognitive disorder, apraxia is an impairment in the manipulation of symbols. For instance, in apraxia of speech, the patient has difficulty producing linguistic symbols—meaningful speech sounds and words. Apraxia with hand gestures is seen as symbol based because most gestures have meanings (e.g., a particular communication, in the case of waving and tongue protrusion, or objects, in the case of pantomime) and therefore are symbols. The notion of apraxia as a disorder associated with symbols is supported by the frequent co-occurrence of apraxia and aphasia, a clear disorder of symbol manipulation: More than half of patients with aphasia are also apraxic. Finkelnburg (Duffy & Liles, 1979) originally proposed the term **asymbolia** to describe a broad range of impairments (in gesture, musical notation, and language) that are now known by separate names because he saw that they could be seen as sharing a common impairment in the use of symbols. In contrast, other authors view apraxia as a pure movement disorder—as a breakdown in the organization of complex movements and motor planning. In this theory, aphasia and apraxia may frequently co-occur either because (a) they are controlled by adjacent regions of the brain that share a regional blood supply and are concurrently damaged by single infarcts, or (b) both gesture and language involve complex movements, and in this view, nonfluent aphasias are recast as complex movement problems, not linguistic problems at all (Haaland & Yeo, 1989; Kimura & Archibald, 1974). This controversy has been lively for more than a hundred years and shows little sign of abating. No discussion, particularly any this brief, will resolve the issue. However, it is important to realize that it may not be obvious from observing behavior whether the underlying cause is a deficit of movement or thought. On an individual case basis, it is very helpful to ascribe proportions of impairment to movement versus cognitive deficits for the purpose of planning treatment approaches that can emphasize movement retraining, cognitive rehabilitation, or both.

Neuropathology

Apraxia, like aphasia, occurs most frequently after damage to the left cerebral cortex. Interestingly, apraxia of both hands is associated with left hemisphere lesions, suggesting that the motor control for these complex gestures lies not in the decussated fibers of the motor strips but rather elsewhere within the left hemisphere. On the basis of these types of data, Liepmann (1920), one of the earliest scholars of apraxia, proposed that the left hemisphere contained "movement formulas that control purposeful skilled movements" (Heilman & Gonzalez-Rothi, 1993, p. 146). The parietal and frontal lobes of the left hemisphere are important for control of complex movements, and disruption to either or both of them can create limb apraxia (see Figure 13.1). Damage to different brain regions is responsible for distinct apraxias. Patients suffering from apraxia of speech typically have lesions in the inferior frontal lobe, near those lesions that cause Broca's aphasia. Patients suffering from classic limb apraxia are more likely to have damage in the parietal lobe (Peigneux et al., 2001).

Diagnosis of Apraxia

Limb apraxia does not often disrupt daily functioning for obvious reasons: Most of us can avoid gesture in daily activities without causing a problem. A patient often does not even notice limb apraxia. Therefore, limb apraxia is most often identified by a clinician doing a full functional or neuropsychological exam. Apraxia of speech is much more obvious and disabling than limb apraxia, but because it often co-occurs with nonfluent Broca's-type aphasia, the speech disorder is often evaluated and treated alongside aphasia.

Assessment of apraxia typically includes elicitation of least three types of action (Goodglass et al., 2001; Heilman & Gonzalez-Rothi, 1993; Kertesz, 1982):

- Intransitive actions do not involve an object (e.g., waving, making the sign of the cross).
- Transitive actions involve an object (e.g., opening a door with a key, flipping a coin).

a

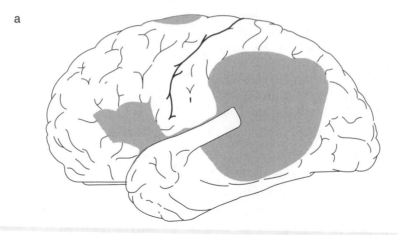

b

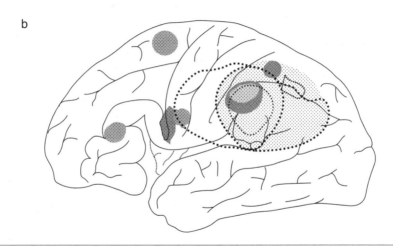

Figure 13.1   Typical distribution of lesions that produce (a) aphasia and (b) apraxia.

- Serial actions include several steps (e.g., folding a letter, putting it in an envelope, sealing it, putting a stamp on the envelope, and mailing it).

Some authors give different names to apraxic symptoms, depending on what type of action is impaired: **Ideomotor apraxia** refers to difficulty performing transitive movements, such as using a tool or instrument. **Ideational apraxia** has been used to describe patients who have difficulty carrying out "ideational plans," that is, sequencing acts in the proper order.

Actions Used to Elicit Apraxia

- Intransitive limb gestures (do not involve an object)
  - Wave goodbye
  - Hitchhike
  - Salute
  - Stop
  - Go

- Transitive limb gestures (involve an object)
  - Use a screwdriver
  - Flip a coin
  - Open a door
  - Use a hammer
  - Use scissors

- Sequential gestures
    Fold a letter, put it in an envelope, seal the envelope, and put a stamp on it
    Put tobacco in a pipe, light it, and smoke it

- Intransitive buccofacial (nonspeech) gestures
    Stick out your tongue
    Blow a kiss

- Transitive buccofacial gestures
    Blow out a match
    Suck on a straw

- Speech tasks involving repetition of increasingly long sequences of sounds
    zip-zipper-zippering
    thick-thicken-thickening
    jab-jabber-jabbering
    please-pleasing-pleasingly
    flat-flatter-flattering

Treatment of Apraxia

Treatment of apraxia, like aphasia, is determined by severity of the disorder and functional goals.

Compensatory approaches to apraxia of speech can involve the use of gesture, pointing boards, and computerized devices that use speech synthesis (e.g., Duffy, 1995; Lane & Samples, 1981) to communicate, which, of course, is difficult if limb apraxia is part of the clinical picture. Both external and internal cues can help elicit correct and/or well-sequenced actions. For instance, writing the first letter of a word will often cue the correct speech production. Ordered lists can be used as reminders when limb or body action sequences are the issue, as in performing activities of daily living (e.g., preparing food or performing nightly ablutions). Internal cues, such as talking oneself through the steps of brushing teeth, can be used either as a starting point or evolve if or when external cues are not necessary.

Restorative treatments include repetitive practice (drills) and feedback to facilitate motor learning. In apraxia of speech, this consists of multiple repetitions of sound sequences, progressing from simple (e.g., *papa*) to more complex (e.g., *Methodist Episcopal*), as tolerated.

The principle of repetitive motor drills can be used with any action, from speech to driving a car. Although some data indicate that behavioral therapy for apraxia of speech is beneficial, the data are relatively sparse and often confounded by the co-occurrence of aphasia and other problems (e.g., Duffy, 1995).

SUBCORTICAL MOVEMENT DISORDERS

The cortical disorders discussed above typically result from stroke, with abrupt onset and stable course. In contrast, movement disorders due to subcortical damage are often progressive and degenerative. Although stroke can does affect the basal ganglia and cerebellum and create symptoms such as those discussed below, this discussion focuses on the most frequent subcortical movement disorders in aging: essential tremor and Parkinson's disease.

Essential Tremor

Definition, Behavioral Characteristics, and Course

Essential tremor is an involuntary, rhythmic oscillation of one or more body parts. The tremor ranges between 4 and 12 cycles per second. It is called a **postural tremor** because it is pronounced when a person makes an effort to hold a limb in a certain position. It is also known as a **kinetic tremor** because it often becomes more pronounced during the active part of goal-directed movement. There are usually no other neurological signs or symptoms. Essential tremor most frequently affects the hands, often beginning in one hand and progressing to involve both. Hand tremors dramatically impair writing and eating. Essential tremor can also involve the head and neck, either in conjunction with the hand(s) or in isolation. Isolated tremors of the palate, neck, and larynx are also relatively common. Tremors that affect the larynx and throat, also called **voice tremors,** make the voice quiver and low in volume. Tremors of the tongue and palate can make speech slurred and eating difficult. The least frequently affected body parts are the legs and trunk. Tremors can become severe enough to interfere with work and can cause social embarrassment. Approximately 15% of people with essential tremor stop working because of the tremor (Koller & Busenbark, 1997).

Essential tremor usually stops during sleep. The tremor is exacerbated by fatigue, extreme temperatures, stimulants, and emotional and sexual arousal. It is decreased by alcohol. Essential tremor is slowly progressive. With time, the tremor increases in amplitude, decreases in frequency, and sometimes spreads to other body parts. Essential tremor usually begins after age 40. It is not associated with increased mortality and, for this reason, is sometimes called *benign essential tremor.*

Essential tremor may be the most common movement disorder, affecting approximately 5 million people older than age 40 in the United States and up to 10% of people older than age 65 (Koller & Busenbark, 1997; Louis et al., 1996). Age is the most potent risk factor. The strong association with aging is why it has sometimes been called **senile tremor.** Depending on the study, between 17% and 70% of the cases appear to run in families (Koller & Busenbark, 1997). The implicit genetic factor has prompted some to refer to this variant as **familial tremor.** However, the behavioral characteristics and treatment are the same for people of different ages and for those who do or do not have a family history, so all similar tremors are appropriately called *essential.*

Neuropathology of Tremor

The neuropathology of essential tremor is unknown. Postmortem studies do not show any gross anatomical changes in patients with essential tremor and thus are not helpful in identifying the brain abnormality behind this disorder. However, the brainstem, thalamus, and cerebellum are all raised as possible sites of origin for various reasons. For instance, thalamotomy, surgically created damage to the thalamus, can relieve the symptoms, suggesting that the thalamus or connected pathways are important (Pahwa, Lyons, & Koller, 2000). Hypometabolism in the brainstem (inferior olive) is seen during positron emission tomography (PET) scanning

with tremor activation, suggesting that the brainstem is involved. Hypermetabolism is seen in the cerebellum of patients with essential tremor, suggesting that the cerebellum is also involved (Koller & Busenbark, 1997).

Diagnosis of Tremor

Essential tremor is diagnosed by clinical observation and ruling out other possible causes such as stroke, an exacerbation of our natural physiological tremor from dietary stimulants, or the effects of various drugs (Manyam, 1997). The intensity and effects of essential tremor are rated by clinical rating scales, most often based on subjective judgments of severity on a range of parameters. Koller and Busenbark (1997, pp. 374–375) describe a tremor assessment based on a 5-point disability/abnormality/impairment rating scale (0 = *normal,* 1 = *slight,* 2 = *moderate,* 3 = *marked,* 4 = *severe*). The areas that are rated are those of functional importance and/or frequent impairment in tremor, including the following:

- Tremor (for the affected body part in resting postural and kinetic positions)
- Speaking phonation
- Feeding (other than liquids)
- Bringing liquids to mouth (drinking)
- Hygiene
- Dressing
- Writing
- Working
- Fine movements
- Embarrassment

Treatment of Tremor

Behavioral treatment, including psychotherapy, biofeedback, and hypnosis, is minimally helpful at reducing essential tremor and their benefits are short-lived. Medications, particularly Primidone® (an antiseizure medication) and propranolol (primarily an antihypertensive medication), are variably effective in minimizing the amplitude of the tremor, although not the frequency. Studies report some relief for 50% to 70% of patients using these medications. Many other drugs have also been used to treat essential tremor, with variable results (Koller & Busenbark, 1997). For patients with severe and asymmetric tremor, severe functional disability, and unsatisfactory response to medication, neurosurgery is an option. Stereotaxic thalamotomy, creating a small lesion in the ventral anterior or ventral intermediate nucleus of the thalamus on one side, the side opposite to the severe tremor, has had positive outcomes in 90% of cases, with no relapse (Pahwa et al., 2000). Neurosurgery is usually a last resort because it carries risks of hemiparesis, seizures, and speech impairment. Bilateral thalamotomy is rarely recommended because it carries risks of permanent cognitive and speech impairments, in addition to weakness on the both sides of the body. A reversible, effective, and potentially more controllable alternative to thalamotomy is thalamic stimulation, in which an electrode implanted in the thalamus delivers programmable amounts of electrical stimulation to the thalamus, mimicking the effect of thalamotomy without some of the irreversible risks.

Parkinson's Disease

Definition, Behavioral Characteristics, and Course

Parkinsonism is a general term for a clinical syndrome characterized by tremor, bradykinesia, rigidity, and postural instability. There are many causes, with some understood and treated better than others.

Idiopathic Parkinson's disease (IPD) is a distinct clinical and pathological entity and is currently the most common form of parkinsonism. IPD is characterized by tremor, rigidity, bradykinesia, postural instability, and a consistent beneficial response to levodopa (see below). The etiology of IPD is not known. Other causes of parkinsonism include brain tumor, toxin exposure, syphilis, and vascular disease. One of the more fascinating types of parkinsonism began during the worldwide epidemic of Von Economo's encephalitis, also called "sleeping sickness," between 1917 and 1927. This disease killed many people, but 80% of those who recovered developed a form of parkinsonism, called "postencephalic parkinsonism." A virus was presumed the cause but never proven.

A more limited and recent spate of parkinsonism occurred primarily in younger people in 1982 when several intravenous drug users developed severe parkinsonism after injecting a synthetic heroin (Langston, 1984). This section will focus on IPD because it is by far the most common cause of parkinsonism and the form that is linked to aging.

IPD usually begins between ages 50 and 60 years and progresses slowly over a 10- to 20-year period. Only 5% of cases begin before age 40. Early in the course of the disease, patients have nonspecific and often nonmotor symptoms: fatigue, malaise, and personality changes. The earliest motor symptoms can be weakness, clumsiness, incoordination, or difficulty writing. Some may experience pain or tension in certain muscles. IPD is difficult, if not impossible, to diagnose this early in the course, before the cardinal motor features of tremor, bradykinesia, rigidity, and postural instability emerge.

The tremor of IPD is a rest tremor, meaning it is present at rest and usually abates when the limb is used. It is the first motor symptom in 75% of patients, usually starting in one arm. The tremor is often called "pill rolling" because of the rhythmic oscillation of the opposed forefinger and thumb, and it is typically about three to five cycles per second. Over time, the tremor progresses to other limbs, as well as the head, but often remains asymmetrical. The tremor usually disappears during sleep. The tremor of IPD is different from essential tremor in that the IPD tremor is usually worse during rest and the early phase of a movement and does *not* get worse as the movement progresses, whereas essential tremor is in some ways the opposite: It is least notable at comfortable rest and worst during goal-directed movement (see Figure 13.2).

Movement in IPD is described by various terms, including *hypokinetic, bradykinetic,* and *akinetic*. These can be seen as points along a continuum from restricted movement to no movement. Early in the course of the disease, the movement is often described as **hypokinetic**—movements are restricted in range, falling short of their mark. This progresses to **bradykinesia,** slow movement, and finally to **akinesia,** lack of movement. Early in the

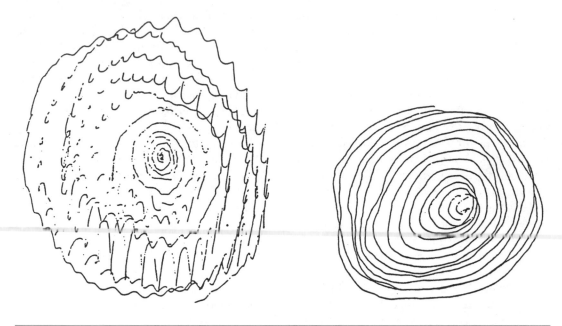

Figure 13.2   Spirals drawn by a patient with essential tremor (left) and a patient with Parkinson's disease tremor (right). Essential tremor can interfere with drawing a smooth spiral, as seen on the left. The patient with Parkinson's disease may have a tremor at rest that decreases upon action or writing; however, the spiral may be micrographic, as in the right panel. Reprinted from Fahn, Green, Ford, and Bressman (1998). Image courtesy of Seth Pullman, MD, Columbia-Presbyterian Medical Center, New York.

course, the difficulty is most obvious in small, complex, manual movements, particularly writing, which becomes micrographic (small) and illegible. As the disease progresses, other muscles are involved, and larger movements are affected. General slowing of movements will create dysarthric (slurred) speech, diminished facial expressions, short steps, shuffling gait, and diminished arm swing, and the patient may have difficulty rising from a chair. Akinesia becomes most obvious and most disruptive in the phenomenon known as *freezing:* IPD patients have difficulty initiating or continuing any movement and will appear totally frozen. This is common when starting to walk, attempting to turn, or approaching narrow places such as doorways and corners. It is often difficult to know whether these functional problems are due to bradykinesia or rigidity.

Rigidity, or stiffness, is caused by an involuntary increase in muscle tone, affecting all muscle groups. Initially, it may only affect fine finger movement, but then it progresses to involve larger muscles, including the neck and trunk. Rigidity also affects facial muscles and produces the characteristic "masked" appearance of the face. Rigidity of the neck muscles can produce headaches; rigidity of the chest causes poor posture and restricted breathing. Rigidity in the limbs is seen as increased resistance to passive movement. Limb rigidity is characterized by how the limb feels to the clinician holding and moving the patient's relaxed arm or leg: described as either "lead pipe" (smooth) or "cogwheel" (ratchety).

Postural instability, difficulty maintaining balance when standing or walking, usually appears late in the course of IPD but can be seriously disabling at any point. The earliest symptoms of instability are subtle, and patients can generally compensate well: They are unsteady when they first rise from a chair or make a sudden turn while walking. Possibly as a combination of rigidity, loss of muscle tone, and a fear of falling, patients develop a stooped posture and shuffling gait. Gait initiation and turning become very difficult. Once walking, loss of postural reflexes and stooped posture conspire to induce a **festinating gait**—increasingly fast shuffling, as the legs try to catch up with the body's forward momentum, contributing to a loss of balance. Patients with IPD eventually lose the ability to anticipate changes in their center of gravity, compensate for deviations in their center of gravity, and restore equilibrium or protect themselves as they lose balance. This often leads to falling. Patients with IPD tend to fall when bending forward to pick up something, walking backwards, or reaching up to grasp something.

In addition to the four cardinal motor features, there are other important behavioral manifestations of IPD, two of which will be mentioned here: oral motor and cognitive deficits.

As motor control over the mouth and throat become impaired, both speech and swallowing can be affected. Speech production in IPD is often dysarthric, characterized by low-volume, monotone, and slurred articulation. They make sound and syllable repetitions, similar to stuttering. The speech deficits are attributed to the weakness and incoordination of the mouth and throat, as well as the poor coordination of speech production with breathing (Sapir et al., 2001). As the motor control over the mouth and throat diminishes, **dysphagia,** a problem with chewing and swallowing, emerges. Dysphagia can be a minor nuisance, with food sticking in the mouth or throat, or can be life threatening because it can cause choking and aspiration. Swallowing problems late in the course of the disease put patients with IPD at great risk for pneumonia, which is often the ultimate cause of death in this disorder.

Many patients with IPD show mild to moderate cognitive deficits, including poor executive function, visuospatial impairment, and **bradyphrenia,** slowed thinking. Between 20% and 40% of patients with IPD develop dementia, making it a relatively common cause of dementia in the elderly (Mayeux et al., 1992; Tison et al., 1995). The dementia of IPD is often a subcortical type, characterized by bradyphrenia, psychomotor retardation, and memory deficits (Antonini, De Notaris, & Benti, 2001; see also discussion of Lewy body dementia in Chapter 11). However, some patients with IPD develop a cortical-type dementia indistinguishable from Alzheimer's.

Epidemiology/Risk Factors of Parkinson's Disease

Parkinson's disease is one of the most common neurological diseases. The incidence, the number of new cases occurring in a given time period for a specific location, ranges from 4.5 to 21 per 100,000 (Tanner, Hubble, & Chan, 1997). Prevalence, the total number of current cases in a population at a given time, ranges from 18 to 328 per 100,000, often estimated at about 200 per 100,000 in the United States (Fahn, Green, Ford, & Bressman, 1998). The great range of estimates in both incidence and prevalence is probably due to different diagnostic criteria and methods of collecting data. For example, some studies use data collected through referrals to an academic medical center, but others use information gathered in door-to-door surveys. The incidence and prevalence both increase with age. IPD is rare in those younger than age 50, and prevalence in some studies is as high as 3,055 per 100,000 in those older than age 80. IPD is slightly more common in men than women.

Although the cause of IPD is not known, possible causes have been identified by looking at factors that increase the risk of developing Parkinson's disease. The risk of developing IPD appears to increase with the following (Tanner et al., 1997):

- Older age
- Sex (men > women)
- Race (White > other) (see below)
- Family history of PD (see below)
- Trauma
- Emotional stress
- Personality characteristics (shyness and depression)
- Environmental exposures, including certain metals (manganese, iron), wood pulp mills, steel alloy industries, herbicides, and pesticides (see below)
- Infections
- Drinking well water
- Rural residence

The studies of epidemiology and genetics have been particularly fruitful in the search for the genetic and environmental cause(s) of IDP.

One of the more persistent theories about the cause of IDP stems from the connection between the chemical compound MPTP (pyridine 1-methyl-4-phenyl-1,2,3,6-tetrahydropyridine) known to cause parkinsonian symptoms in humans and primates. Similar compounds that are used in agriculture, wood pulp processing, and iron mining. A carefully done case control study in Canada found a particularly strong connection between these chemicals in certain herbicides, the rate of IPD in the local population, and postmortem brain tissue (Rajput et al., 1987).

The frequency of IPD appears to vary with race and is possibly linked to location: IPD is more frequent in Caucasians in Europe and North America than in Asians in Japan or China and Blacks in Africa. However, these differences in race and geography may be due to differences in reporting, health care availability, and perception of disease across cultures, as well as variations in genetic and environmental risk factors in different regions.

Parkinson's disease appears to run in some families but not others. The fact that 41% of patients with IPD had affected family members led Mjones (1949) to describe the genetic pattern associated with IPD as "autosomal dominant . . . with reduced penetrance" (p. 143). Others have found family history in only 10% of patients and suggested a multifactorial etiology combining a genetic predisposition and environmental factors to explain the familial patterns, although the environmental factors are rarely made explicit. Overall, having a first-degree relative with IPD increases one's risk of developing the disease and is higher if a sibling and a parent are both affected (e.g., Zorzon, Capus, & Pellegrino, 2002).

We understand much about the genetics of IPD from studies of several large families. These families appear to have a distinct form of the disease. For instance, one family had nine members in four generations with parkinsonism; all had an early onset at about 30 years of age and an atypically fast progression to death in 2 to 12 years. In other families, the pattern of parkinsonism has been more consistent with IPD and a very clear autosomal dominant pattern (Waters & Miller, 1994). Although these families suggest a genetic cause in at least some cases of IPD, twin studies, one of the best tools to study genetics, have shown no higher rate of concordance between monozygotic twins than would be expected in the general population (Ward et al., 1983). Because of the inconsistent data on genetic transmission of IPD, indirect models of inheritance have been proposed. For example, mitochondrial inheritance, a non-Mendelian transmission pattern, could explain the lack of concordance in monozygotic twins. With this mechanism, the disease is transmitted through a mitochondrial gene defect (Ward et al., 1983) rather than through the typical autosomal dominant gene pattern. Another approach explains the heritability of IPD as the result of environmental factors and aging in the context of genetically susceptible individuals (Barbeau et al., 1985). In this theory, some individuals inherit poor metabolism for particular enzymes that are responsible for degrading certain neurotoxins.

Neuropathology of Parkinson's Disease

Although the cause of IDP remains unknown, the neurochemistry and neuropathology associated with it are quite well understood (Wooten, 1997). IPD is associated with a progressive decline in the concentration of dopamine in the brain. The concentration of dopamine is significantly reduced in the caudate, putamen, and substantia nigra of patients with IPD. The most visible neuropathological abnormality is the loss of iron pigmentation in the substantia nigra. The brains of patients with IPD also show depigmentation and loss of neurons in the locus ceruleus, a major source of norepinephrine, although IPD brains do not show significant reductions of norepinephrine, suggesting that this is not a major cause of IPD symptoms (Wooten, 1997). Serotonin is also reduced in IPD, particularly in the striatum, substantia nigra, and hipppocampus.

Lewy bodies are smooth, round protein lumps that are found in the nerve cells of the substantia nigra, hypothalamus, locus ceruleus, the midbrain, pons, and spinal cord of patients with IPD. Lewy bodies accompany neuronal degeneration in IPD, although very little is know about the mechanisms that bring them into being (Defebvre et al., 1999).

Regional cerebral glucose utilization appears relatively normal in the cortex, caudate, and putamen. Interestingly, the globus pallidus shows increased glucose use, possibly in response to the decreased dopamine in the putamen and caudate (striatum) (Wooten & Collins, 1981). Using radiolabeled levodopa, PET scans can show the concentration of active dopamine neurons in the brain. These experiments show decreased uptake of dopamine in the putamen contralateral to the side of unilateral parkinsonian symptoms (Guttman et al., 1997).

Diagnosis of Parkinson's Disease

The diagnosis of IPD is based on history, clinical examination, and the absence of certain clinical, imaging, and laboratory findings. In addition to the cardinal clinical features of tremor, bradykinesia, rigidity, and postural instability, almost all patients with IPD respond positively to levodopa. The diagnosis is less likely if any of the following are found: a remitting course, neuroleptic use within the past year, repeated head trauma, early dementia, or evidence of cerebrovascular disease. No single feature ensures or excludes the diagnosis.

Rating scales measure the severity of disease symptoms, the progression of the disease, and the effectiveness of treatment. The Parkinson's Disease Disability Scale (Hoehn & Yahr, 1967) allows clinicians to categorize patients' disability into one of the five following stages based on associated clinical characteristics:

I. Unilateral involvement only, usually with minimal or no functional impairment.

II. Bilateral or midline involvement, without impairment of balance.

III. First sign of impaired righting reflexes. This is evident by unsteadiness as the patient turns or is demonstrated when pushed from a stable standing position with the feet together and eyes closed. Functionally, the patient is somewhat restricted in activities but may have some work potential depending on the type of employment. Patients are physically capable of leading independent lives, and their disability is mild to moderate.

IV. Fully developed, severely disabling disease; the patient is still able to walk and stand unassisted but is markedly impaired.

V. Confinement to bed or wheelchair unless aided.

Although very useful in describing general degree of impairment, this scale does not rate abilities with enough sensitivity to be useful for certain purposes. For instance, to judge the relative effectiveness of medications in controlling the severity of particular signs and symptoms or the overall rate of progression of the disease, we need rating scales with more detail. The Webster Rating Scale (Webster, 1968) and the Unified Parkinson's Disease Rating Scale (UPDRS) (Fahn & Elton, 1987) are both used to measure parkinsonian signs and symptoms in more detail than the scale devised by Hoehn and Yahr (1967). The Webster Rating Scale rates 10 areas of function on a 4-point scale, and the UPDRS rates 31 areas of function on a 5-point scale (see Table 13.1 for examples from each).

Overview of Treatment of Parkinson's Disease

The primary medications used to control the symptoms of IPD enhance dopamine or decrease acetylcholine. The mainstay of treatment for IPD, from 1961 through the present, is levodopa (L-dopa). L-dopa provides dopamine, replacing the dopamine that has decreased in IPD. Levodopa given by itself has two inherent problems: It has to be taken in large doses for adequate amounts to reach the brain, and it causes gastrointestinal distress. Therefore, it is typically given in combination with carbidopa, which increases the amount that crosses the blood-brain barrier and decreases side effects. The combination of levodopa and carbidopa is sold as Sinemet®. L-dopa generally works well, and a positive response is sometimes used as a diagnostic test. After 5 to 10 years of treatment, side effects related to L-dopa can appear, including motor fluctuations, when the medication unpredictably stops working for a time, and dyskinesias, abnormal involuntary movements. The pathophysiology of these side effects is not well understood, but they are probably related to dopamine receptor changes

Table 13.1   Summary of Areas Assessed by Two Parkinson's Disease Rating Scales

Webster Rating Scale (Webster, 1968)	Unified Parkinson's Disease Rating Scale (UPDRS) (Fahn & Elton, 1987)
Ten areas of function are rated on a 4-point scale (0 = *no involvement*, 1 = *detectable involvement*, 2 = *moderate involvement*, 3 = *severe symptoms*). The most severe impairment results in a score close to the maximum of 30 points.	Thirty-one areas of function are rated on a 5-point scale (0 = *normal function* to 4 = *severe impairment*). The most severely disabled patient could potentially be rated with the maximum of 108.
Bradykinesia of hands, including writing	Mentation
Rigidity	Thought disorder
Posture	Depression
Upper extremity swing	Motivation/initiative
Gait	Speech
Tremor	Salivation
Facies	Swallowing
Seborrhea	Handwriting
Speech	Cutting food
Self-care	Dressing
	Hygiene
	Turning in bed
	Falling
	Freezing
	Walking
	Tremor
	Sensory symptoms
	Speech
	Facial expression
	Tremor at rest (face, lips, chin, hands, feet)
	Action tremor (right/left)
	Rigidity (neck, arms, legs)
	Finger taps (right/left)
	Hand grips (right/left)
	Hand pronate/supinate (right/left)
	Leg agility (right/left)
	Arise from chair
	Posture
	Postural stability
	Gait
	Body bradykinesia

after chronic exposure to L-dopa. Slow-release formulations of the drug reduce some of these side effects.

Several other major categories of drugs are used in conjunction with levodopa therapy and with one another to reduce parkinsonian symptoms.

- Dopamine receptor agonists (e.g., bromocriptine) bind directly to postsynaptic dopamine receptors, effectively mimicking the action of dopamine rather than replacing it. These medications improve the effects of levodopa and help to decrease motor fluctuations. They are often useful in later stages of the disease when levodopa loses some of its effectiveness.

- Monoamine oxidase is the enzyme that metabolizes dopamine in the brain. MAO-B inhibitors (e.g., Selegiline®) block the degradation of dopamine, which in turn increases the length of time dopamine is circulating and available in the brain to coordinate and control movement.

- COMT is an enzyme that breaks down levodopa peripherally, before it even reaches the brain. COMT inhibitors (e.g., entacapone) inhibit peripheral levodopa metabolism, thereby optimizing the extent to which levodopa can reach the brain.
- Anticholinergic medications can decrease tremor and rigidity but can also cause cognitive impairment in the elderly, so their use is often reserved for younger and more mildly impaired patients.

When medical treatment is not effective in controlling symptoms of IPD, surgery is an increasingly available option, first pioneered in the 1960s (Cooper, 1981) and recently improved with modern techniques (Zesiewicz & Hauser, 2001). Surgical ablation of portions of the globus pallidus and/or thalamus can reduce motor symptoms, although it comes with the risk of infection, gait, and speech disorders. Deep brain stimulation can mimic destructive lesions of the globus pallidus, subthalamic nucleus, and thalamus in a more controllable and reversible procedure. This procedure has the advantage of reducing the likelihood of permanent neurological disability because the effects of the stimulator can be eliminated by turning it off. Electrodes are placed in the part of the thalamus and connected to a pacemaker placed in the chest at the location where cardiac pacemakers are placed. The pacemaker is then adjusted in voltage and frequency to produce the best effect. This strategy is very effective in controlling tremor, and the results appear to last a long time (Lyons, Koller, Wilkinson, & Pahwa, 2001). The use of growth factors and fetal cell transplants from lower primates and human embryos is evolving with clinical promise and spurring ethical debates, particularly related to abortion as the source of embryonic tissue (Zesiewicz & Hauser, 2001).

Behavioral Treatments

The cardinal symptoms of tremor, rigidity, bradykinesia, and postural instability affect virtually all activities of daily living, from walking to writing to eating. Medical and surgical treatments rarely, if ever, eliminate the symptoms completely. The progressive nature of the IPD also renders even most effective medical treatments less effective as the disease worsens. Therefore, behavioral treatments have an important place in treating IPD throughout its typically long course.

Physical therapy is often directed at maintaining gait, balance, and range of motion to maintain function and minimize the risk of falls. Treatment methods include education about appropriate environmental adaptations (see below), sensory feedback, strengthening, posture and balance training, stretching, and general conditioning. Assistive devices, including canes, walkers, and wheelchairs are sometimes beneficial. Like any behavioral therapy, physical therapy is tailored to specific problems of specific patients. In the case of IPD, it is likely to include getting in and out of beds and chairs, walking, and prevention of falls. Freezing is particularly frustrating to patients and caregivers alike and is the ultimate physical impediment. It can be successfully approached with some interesting and simple compensatory strategies. For instance, when movements such as taking a step may seem impossible, patients can often initiate voluntary movements through simple mental "tricks." One patient said he just has to imagine himself as John Wayne taking a big cowboy step to release himself from a freeze. Other visualization techniques such as marching in place, stepping over an imaginary object, or kicking through a wall of glass often allow patients to break out of a freeze. Actual visual cues such as a crack in the linoleum or sidewalk and auditory cues such as counting off a rhythmic cadence help. Patients can put lines in hallways or other plain floor surfaces to prevent freezing in those spaces. Canes can be equipped with a horizontal piece extending parallel to the floor to provide a horizontal line to step over with each step. Deep breathing and relaxation may help, as will distracting oneself from the frozen feet by focusing on arm or neck movement.

Because medical treatments are not very effective for balance problems, falls are often a focus of both physical therapy (PT) and occupational therapy (OT). Although PT may focus on physical conditioning, both OT and PT will train patients to perform certain activities safely and recommend assistive devices. OT often recommends a wide range of adaptations, home alterations, and assistive devices that enable patients to perform daily activities with greater ease and in a safer environment. This includes grab bars in a bathtub, arranging furniture and carpets to minimize the chance of tripping or head injury in the case of a fall, weighted eating utensils, and clothing with Velcro closures. Some basic adaptations to reduce the risk of falling include removing or securing throw rugs, covering lamp cords, limiting alcohol intake, and maintaining adequate vision and hearing.

Tremors are the focus of many interventions, including the following list compiled by the OT Department at the University of Southern California:

- Use both hands to lift a glass or cup.
- Use elbow as a pivot to raise a fork from a plate to mouth.
- If buttoning clothes becomes difficult, try using a buttonhook.
- If dressing becomes difficult, buy clothes with zippers or Velcro.
- Use elastic shoelaces.
- Squeeze a small rubber ball to reduce hand tremors.
- Weighted grips on handles (i.e., weighted utensils for feeding).
- 1-lb aerobic wrist weights.
- Lie on the floor, face down, and relax your body for 5 to 15 minutes.

Speech therapy focuses on issues of communication and swallowing. Speech intelligibility is compromised in IPD due to low vocal volume and imprecise articulation, both directly related to rigidity and bradykinesia of the speech musculature. Speech therapists improve intelligibility by physical exercise and increased attention to breathing and mouth movement. Speech therapists also evaluate and treat swallowing disorders in IPD. Swallowing is impaired in about 50% of patients with IPD, mostly due to slow and inefficient movement in the mouth and throat. Swallowing is important to evaluate and treat because the dysphagia associated with IPD can make it difficult to take medication and may lead to weight loss, choking, aspiration, and pneumonia. Treatment for dysphagia ranges from altering eating habits (eat more slowly, take smaller bites) and the consistency of food to make it easier to swallow, to tube feeding.

Mental health professionals and support groups can be of great help to patients with IPD and the families who all must deal with changing roles as a result of the disease. Stress makes all of the symptoms of IPD worse and slows the patient down even further. Given that the patient with IPD does everything more slowly, managing time is extremely important. The change in health and the effects on work, family, and self-esteem elicit important feelings, including fear, anger, and embarrassment. Patients who are still working will need support in dealing with colleagues and workplace accommodations. The disease also affects sleep and sexual functions, which add stress and need attention from medical as well as psychological perspectives. As mentioned earlier, a fair number of patients with IPD also have concentration, memory, and other intellectual impairments, which adds another layer of impaired function and stress that can be addressed both in terms of emotional adjustment and direct memory training and adaptations.

14

SUCCESSFUL COGNITIVE AND PHYSICAL AGING

MELISSA TABBARAH

TERESA E. SEEMAN

Chapter Preview

Many of us can identify an older individual who continues to maintain cognitive and physical functioning beyond the age of 70, 80, or even 100 years. These models of "successful aging" have heightened our curiosity and propelled our desire to understand the aging process. Of growing interest is how some reach these benchmarks of life with relatively minimal cognitive and physical dysfunction. What do they eat? Do they exercise? What form of exercise regimen do they follow? Were they born with superior genes? What are their attitudes like? Do they participate in social activities? Or did they find a "secret" elixir? What was it? If you stay apprized of any form of mainstream media, you will recognize that many are trying to sell us just that . . . a golden bullet. Simplifying the aging processes into a single formula for aging "successfully" is, however, shortsighted. Although we might assume that the aging trajectory is similar among individuals, a growing body of research shows that aging is heterogeneous, especially among those who age "successfully."

This chapter presents an overview of the concept of "successful aging": its various definitions, its relationship to cognitive functioning and physical functioning, and how one's sense of "creativity" might influence aging. A primary goal of this chapter is to highlight the fact that despite the considerable and needed attention that is devoted to the variety of health and functional problems commonly seen in older age groups, aging is not uniformly associated with significant disease and disability. A more positive trajectory of aging is possible, one that is characterized by the avoidance of many of the common age-related diseases and, more important, by the maintenance of relatively high levels of cognitive and physical functioning and a continued engagement in various life pursuits.

SUCCESSFUL AGING

In the past several decades, research on the health and functioning of older persons has focused on negative outcomes such as disability, dependency, morbidity, and mortality (Boult, Kane, Louis, Boult, & McCaffrey, 1994; Maddox & Clark, 1992; Nagi, 1976; Pinsky et al., 1985). Cicero, however, originally expressed a more optimistic view of aging more than 2,000 years ago in his famous essay "De Senectute" (Cicero, 44 B.C./1992). In his essay, Cicero argued that old age is not only a period of loss and decline but can offer opportunities for positive change and development, specifically in the realm of the mind.

Since the 1980s, there has been a growing appreciation for the fact that there is actually considerable heterogeneity within older age groups with respect to health and functioning— that there is, in fact, a trajectory that is characterized by avoidance of all, or many, of the common age-related diseases and maintenance of high levels of physical and cognitive functioning (Rowe & Kahn, 1987; Seeman, 1994). Perhaps the most commonly used term for this positive trajectory of aging has been *successful aging,* a concept first introduced by Rowe and Kahn (1987) in their seminal article titled "Human Aging: Usual and Successful." In their article, Rowe and Kahn argue that the aging process can be seen as being broadly characterized by three different trajectories: (a) "diseased/disabled," a trajectory characterized by the presence of pathology and/or disability; (b) "usual aging," a trajectory characterized by the absence of overt pathology but the presence of nonpathologic declines in some aspects of functioning (e.g., hearing, glucose tolerance, renal function), the types of declines that have traditionally been attributed to "normal" (i.e., nondiseased) aging; and (c) "successful aging," a trajectory characterized by a minimum (or none) of the physiologic losses seen in the "usual" aging group. As outlined in Figure 14.1 and elaborated in their book, *Successful Aging,* Rowe and Kahn (1998) argue that the salient characteristics of successful aging include avoiding common age-related diseases, maintaining relatively high levels of physical and cognitive functioning, and maintaining

Avoiding common age-related diseases
Maintaining higher levels of functioning in terms of
- Physical functioning
- Cognitive functioning
- Social functioning
- Psychological functioning

Figure 14.1 Characteristics of "Successful" Aging.

one's social and psychological engagement in life. Although various other terms have also been used to refer to the idea of more positive or "successful" aging (e.g., *productive aging, effective aging*), the common underlying theme is that aging is not inevitably or uniformly associated with heavy burdens of chronic disease or concomitant impairments in physical or cognitive functioning and that there are, in fact, many individuals who enjoy relatively high levels of health and functioning to quite old ages. Since the publication of the Rowe and Kahn article, some have argued that the avoidance of age-related diseases should not be considered a requisite for successful aging, as many older adults with chronic diseases continue to maintain high levels of functioning and could reasonably be considered to be aging "successfully." Regardless of the varied definitions that can be used to characterize "successful aging," the heart of the idea lies in the emphasis on the fact that much of what has traditionally been seen as unavoidable aspects of aging, including the onset of disease and disability, turns out to be much less inevitable than we thought. Many older adults do, in fact, manage not only to maintain high levels of functioning but also avoid many of the common age-related diseases, at least until well into their 70s, 80s, and even 90s. Our focus thus should be on understanding what factors contribute to their more positive trajectories of aging so that we can begin to develop policies and programs that will serve to promote such positive trajectories of aging for large proportions of our growing older population.

Successful cognitive aging is essential to successful aging as a whole (Teri, McCurry, & Logsdon, 1997). Cognitive health is multidimensional in that it encompasses an array of functions, including memory, language, intellectual ability, visuospatial skills, perception, and complex problem solving. There are several definitions of successful cognitive aging.

Although some use the upper most strata of cognitive functioning (i.e., scoring above an average value) (Albert et al., 1995; Garfein & Herzog, 1995), others define success as having minimal interruption of usual function (Blanchard-Fields & Chen, 1996; Brandstadter & Renner, 1990; Rudinger & Thomae, 1990; Schaie, 1996; Strawbridge, Cohen, Shema, & Kaplan, 1996). In addition, Teri et al. (1997) define successful aging as the "interplay between cognitive status and a person's ability to adapt, accommodate, and adjust to the environment" (p. 270).

Given the multidimensional nature of cognitive functioning, several large multivariate epidemiological studies have focused on the roles of physical, social, and psychological health in the maintenance of cognitive functioning with advancing age (Berkman et al., 1993; Garfein & Herzog, 1995; Poon et al., 1992; Schaie, 1990a, 1996; Seeman, McEwen, Singer, Albert, & Rowe, 1997; Seeman, Singer, Rowe, Horwitz, & McEwen, 1997). Although successful cognitive functioning was defined differently, five common themes emerge from these studies. The first theme specifies that age-related cognitive decline is variable. Analyses of data from the Seattle Longitudinal Study (Schaie, 1983, 1996), for example, have shown that few individuals decline globally on cognitive functioning. Instead, most participants of the study maintained or improved their level of performance in at least one cognitive domain (e.g., verbal meaning [recognition vocabulary], spatial orientation [the ability to rotate objects mentally in two-dimensional space], inductive reasoning [the ability to generate novel concepts or relationships], number skills [simple addition], and word fluency [verbal recent memory and word list generation from lexical categories]) well beyond 80 years of age (Schaie, 1990a). Furthermore, when participants began to decline in cognitive functioning, the age at which this occurred varied widely. Similarly, the Georgia Centenarian Study found that although everyday problem solving remained intact among older subjects, overall intellectual functioning was lower (Poon et al., 1992).

The second theme emerging from the epidemiological studies highlights the importance of education. Educational achievement predicts cognitive functioning in later life. Investigators have found that persons with higher educational levels show less age-related cognitive decline (Albert et al., 1995; Berkman et al., 1993; Farmer, Kittner, Rae, Bartko, & Regier, 1995; Leibovici, Ritchie, Ledesert, & Touchon, 1996; Nolan & Blass, 1992). Furthermore, educational experiences early in life also appear to exert some protection against the cognitive deterioration associated with dementing illnesses.

Perhaps unsurprisingly, the third theme that emerges is that physical health is correlated with cognitive functioning. In the Seattle Longitudinal Study, cardiovascular disease was the primary health-related variable predicting cognitive decline (Schaie, 1990b). Possible modifiable health factors, including strenuous physical activity, pulmonary function, and cardiovascular status, have also been identified as important factors in the maintenance of cognitive ability. For example, the Established Population for the Epidemiologic Study of the Elderly (EPESE)–MacArthur Foundation Research Network evaluated a sample of 4,030 persons ages 70 to 79 years from which 1,192 subjects were identified as "high functioning," based on brief assessments of physical and cognitive status (Berkman et al., 1993). These subjects were compared with age- and sex-matched subjects who were in the "medium-" or "low-functioning" groups. High-functioning subjects rated their health much higher, smoked fewer cigarettes, exercised more, and had better pulmonary function than medium- or low-functioning subjects. Furthermore, Dipietro, Seeman, Merrill, and Berkman (1996) showed that among a cohort of 1,189 healthy older adults (ages 70–79), higher levels of physical activity appear to be associated with some cognitive benefits.

The ability to adapt to stress, allostasis, has also been identified as important in the maintenance of cognitive functioning. During stressful situations, the production of cortisol increases for both men and women. Women, however, seem to react more strongly to this increased production. Among the participants of the MacArthur Studies of Successful Aging, both in cross section and over time (2.5 years), only women demonstrated poorer memory performance (Seeman, McEwen, et al., 1997). This effect, however, was not irreversible because declines in cortisol were associated with improvements in memory. A higher allostatic load, the wear and tear associated with excessive exposure to cortisol, was also associated with poorer cognitive (and physical) functioning among this same group of participants from the MacArthur Studies of Successful Aging (Seeman, McEwen, Rowe, & Singer, 2001; Seeman, Singer, et al., 1997).

The final theme of these studies focuses on the findings that psychological attributes are correlated with cognitive functioning. Self-efficacy (the belief that through one's actions, a person can produce a desired effect), depression, anxiety, and social support have each been significantly associated with cognition. For example, in the EPESE study, the high-functioning elders scored higher on scales of self-efficacy and mastery and reported fewer symptoms of anxiety and depression than lower functioning elders (Berkman et al., 1993). Among EPESE participants, those with lower self-efficacy declined significantly on their cognitive functions at follow-up 2.5 years later (Albert et al., 1995). Mental health was also significantly related to cognitive ability in the Georgia Centenarian Study (Poon et al., 1992), such that persons who had higher cognitive ability had lower levels of depression and anxiety. Social ties also promote better cognitive functioning (Bassuk, Glass, & Berkman, 1999). Furthermore, greater baseline emotional support has been shown to significantly predict better cognitive functioning at follow-up (7.5 years later) among high physical and cognitive functioning older adults (ages 70–79 years) (Seeman, Lusignolo, Albert, & Berkman, 2001).

SUCCESSFUL PHYSICAL AGING

Similar to the studies on successful cognitive aging, studies have shown that there is considerable heterogeneity within older age groups in terms of physical functioning, with some subgroups exhibiting levels comparable to those seen in younger age groups (Berkman et al., 1993; Seeman et al., 1994). Researchers have defined successful physical aging in various ways. For instance, the Alameda County studies defined successful physical aging as those persons in the top 20% on a scale of physical functioning, or "needing no assistance nor having difficulty in any of 13 activity/mobility measures plus little or no difficulty on five physical performance measures" (Guralnik & Kaplan, 1989, p. 704; Strawbridge et al., 1996, p. 136). Active life expectancy has been defined as the duration of life free of dependence in four basic activities of daily living (ADLs). Similarly, the MacArthur Studies of Successful Aging used performance-based measure to identify a high-functioning cohort of older Americans 70 to 79 years of age (Seeman et al., 1994). The physical performance tasks used in the MacArthur Studies include tasks that assess balance, gait speed, foot tapping, repeated chair stands, and manual dexterity.

Factors that have been found to predict successful physical functioning include younger age, higher income, lower relative weight, better lung functioning, absence of diabetes or hypertension, higher cognitive performance, and the absence of incident conditions or hospitalizations during the 2.5 years of follow-up (Seeman et al., 1994). Furthermore, in the past decade, epidemiological studies have shown that physical activity improves muscle strength, which improves mobility, which in turn decreases the risk of falls. For example, higher levels of physical activity are associated with greater muscular performance (Jonsson, Ringsberg, Josefsson, Johnell, & Birch-Jensen, 1992; Sandler, Burdett, Zaleskiewicz, Sprowls Repcheck, & Harwell, 1991; Tamai et al., 1993), better mobility (Hubert, Bloch, & Fries, 1993; LaCroix, Guralnik, Berkman, Wallace, & Satterfield, 1993; Wagner et al., 1992), and a lower risk of falls (Campbell, Borrie, & Spears, 1989; Nevitt, Cummings, Kidd, & Black, 1989; Sorock et al., 1988).

As with cognitive functioning, self-efficacy, depression, and social support also appear to influence physical functioning (Bruce, Seeman, Merrill, & Blazer, 1994; Seeman et al., 1995; Seeman, Unger, McAvay, & de Leon, 1999; Unger, McAvay, Bruce, Berkman, & Seeman, 1999). The findings from these studies all come from the MacArthur Studies of Successful

Aging. Independent of actual physical abilities, participants of the MacArthur studies with weaker instrumental self-efficacy (the self-efficacy required to manage one's daily activities) declined on their self-reported assessment of physical functioning over 2.5 years (Seeman et al., 1999). In terms of depression, participants with high depressive symptomatology were associated with an increased risk of onset of disability on the self-reported scale of activities of daily living (Bruce et al., 1994). Social support systems also seem to affect physical functioning. For instance, over a 7-year period, participants of the MacArthur studies with more social ties declined less on a reported measure of physical functioning (Unger et al., 1999). Furthermore, receiving more emotional support seems to also promote better physical functioning (Seeman et al., 1995). More specifically, those with greater emotional support from social networks, particularly among those reporting low frequency of instrumental support, had significantly better physical performance.

SUCCESSFUL AGING AND CREATIVITY

Another area of functioning valued by many societies is creativity. From the accomplished artisan struggling to express human emotion to the clever factory worker toiling to solve an industrial problem, creative solutions are frequently praised. Recently, researchers have begun to investigate the relationship between creativity and successful aging because one's ability to cope, adapt, and creatively solve potentially limiting cognitive or physical functioning may result in one's ability to age successfully.

Ryff (1989) identified the following criteria for aging successfully: (a) positive interactions with others, (b) a sense of purpose, (c) autonomy, (d) self-acceptance, (e) personal growth, and (f) environmental fit. Building on the work by Ryff (1989), Fisher (1992, 1995) found that older subjects also emphasized the importance of coping as a criterion to aging successfully. This notion of adaptability or coping has been discussed by others as central to well-being in later life (Brandstadter & Renner, 1992; Featherman, 1992). Adaptability and coping are also central to the creative process.

In a qualitative study, Fisher and colleagues (1999) interviewed 36 participants of a senior art exhibition (ages 60–93). Participants were generally asked about their understandings of successful aging and creativity, the factors viewed as necessary for each, and the benefits of creative activity and its relationship to successful aging. Their findings suggest that artistic creativity promotes successful aging by encouraging the development of problem-solving skills, motivation, and perceptions that translate into a practical creativity in the management of their everyday lives. When participants of this study were asked about the relationship between creativity and successful aging, three main ideas emerged as necessary components to successful aging: having a positive attitude, keeping active and involved, and staying open to opportunities that facilitate personal growth. Here are some excerpts that highlight these ideas:

A Positive Attitude

If you're going to age successfully, you're going to have challenges and how you meet those challenges is going to involve creativity and coping. Creativity involves everything you do—an emotional or mental coping. Life itself is a matter of creativity especially when you're older because you have the time to think about the challenges and come up with solutions. (Woman, 69)

Fisher et al. (1999, p. 468)

Keeping Active and Involved

Creativity keeps the mind active and adds to our life. Creativity keeps your brain and heart alive because you're involved with something meaningful to you. (Woman, 73)

Fisher et al. (1999, p. 468)

Personal Growth

You have more time in old age to create. You're not as busy. I don't think you can ever quit learning and it's nice to learn how others do different things, different techniques. It's a matter of letting that creativity out. You're freer to risk embarrassment and find things don't embarrass you as easily as when you were younger. (Woman, 66)

Fisher et al. (1999, p. 468)

CONCLUSION

Overall, the various studies discussed in this chapter provide support for the concept of "successful aging," indicating that there are older individuals who are characterized by physiologic and lifestyle profiles similar to those of much younger age groups. They also document the existence of considerable heterogeneity within older age groups in terms of such things as cognitive and physical functioning, with some individuals continuing to demonstrate high levels of performance in these various domains. Furthermore, data from perhaps the most direct studies of "successful aging," the MacArthur Studies of Successful Aging, show that even those functioning at relatively high cognitive and physical levels can show improvement. The importance of examining such patterns of change in addition to declines is suggested by a report on predictors of decline versus improvement in functional disability, which indicates that risk factors for these two patterns of change are quite different (Crimmins & Saito, 1993). In those analyses, sociodemographic and health status characteristics were associated with risks for decline but not for improvement, with the latter being most strongly predicted by higher levels of initial functioning (Crimmins & Saito, 1993).

From a behavioral perspective, research also indicates that lifestyle changes such as beginning regular physical activity can have beneficial effects even for individuals who make such changes at older ages. Data from the MacArthur Studies of Successful Aging show that those who did not report engaging in any regular physical activity at the beginning of the studies but who subsequently indicated that they had undertaken such activity during the next 2.5 years showed higher levels of functioning at the end of that period (Seeman, unpublished data). Furthermore, intervention programs for older adults have demonstrated benefits in terms of improved functioning as well as improvements in aerobic capacity and glucose metabolism (Centers for Disease Control and Prevention, 1989; Ehsani, Ogawa, Miller, Spiha, & Jilka, 1991; Hagberg, 1987; Holloszy, Shultz, Kusnierkiewicz, Hagberg, & Ehsani, 1986; Seals, Hagberg, Hurley, Ehsani, & Holloszy, 1984; Tipton, 1984). Notably, these data also indicate that the benefits from physical activity are seen to be generally comparable for those who engage in moderate rather than more strenuous activity, suggesting that programs for older adults can be tailored to their frequently expressed preference for moderately strenuous activities such as walking. Although these data are encouraging, the statistics on levels of physical activity among older adults are not. National statistics, for example, indicate that a large portion of the older U.S. population stands to benefit from such exercise programs, with more than 60% of men and more than 70% of women age 65 and older reporting that they do not get any regular physical exercise (Darnay, 1994).

Like exercise, social participation has also been shown to protect against poor health and mortality; the presence of close ties with friends and other relatives and participation in various group activities continue to confer significant health benefits at older ages. Although levels of social connection appear to be generally well maintained at older ages, factors such as retirement from regular employment and losses of friends and relatives as they age and experience greater mortality can and do result in lower levels of social integration for many older adults. Such losses in social contacts have been shown to result in increased health risks for older adults. Again, however, this is a factor that is potentially amenable to change. Several current efforts are under way to encourage continued social participation among older Americans and to evaluate the health benefits that are predicted to result from such social activity. Perhaps the most exciting of these efforts are those related to promoting opportunities for continued participation by older adults in various types of jobs. Due to a variety of factors, including the frequent financial disincentives to continued employment for older adults due to penalties from private pensions as well as previous Social Security provisions regarding earnings limits for beneficiaries, the vast bulk of older Americans retire relatively early from the workplace, frequently as young as age 55. These older Americans represent an untapped resource with extensive skills and knowledge; their reengagement in the U.S. economy not only could benefit American businesses but could also serve to promote their own continued social, psychological, and physical engagement in their communities, providing important support for more successful aging.

By pointing to the fact that aging is indeed a heterogeneous process and that more positive, successful trajectories of aging are possible, the "successful aging" concept provides a more optimistic view of the plasticity and potential for success inherent in the aging process. Such a perspective serves to highlight the possibility of developing effective interventions to increase the prevalence of "successful aging" within the general population so that many can enjoy greater success in maintaining or attaining higher levels of functioning as they age.

GLOSSARY

abstraction: the ability to identify common features between concepts.

action potential: the electrical impulse of a neuron.

acute confusional state: delirium.

affective prosody: variation in prosody related to a emotional state or mood of the speaker.

afferent: toward the center.

age-associated memory impairment (AAMI): age-related memory problems.

agnosia/mindblindness: the inability to recognize objects or people.

agrammatism: problems with morphological and syntactic (i.e., grammatical) aspects of language.

agraphia: acquired impairment of writing.

akinesia: lack of movement.

alertness: highest level of arousal, in which patients are awake and can interact in a meaningful way with the examiner and the environment.

alexia: acquired impairment of reading (aka acquired alexia).

alexia with agraphia: reading and writing disorder without significant aphasia.

alternating attention: shift in attention back and forth between relevant elements in the environment or task.

amusia: a deficit in musical ability.

anhedonia: the inability to experience pleasure.

anomia: inability to retrieve words and/or names.

anomic aphasia: aphasic syndrome marked by word finding problems.

anosognosia: lack of insight, awareness, and/or recognition of illness, often including denial of one's own deficits.

anterior: toward the front.

anterograde amnesia: a problem learning information and remembering events that occur after the onset of amnesia.

Anton's syndrome/cortical blindness: blindness due to bilateral damage to the visual cortex.

apathy: reduced motivation and interest in activities.

aphasia: impairment of language due to brain damage.

aphasic agraphia: writing problems parallel to and in the presence of aphasia.

aphasic alexia: reading problems parallel to and in the presence of aphasia.

aphemia: loss of articulate speech.

apoptosis: normal process of cell death.

apperception: the early stage of recognition, the perception of a sensory impression—piecing together of separate visual attributes into a whole.

apperceptive agnosia: agnosia attributed to perceptual deficits.

apraxia: a disorder of voluntary, learned, or skilled movement, not due to weakness, paralysis, poor comprehension, sensory loss, dementia, or poor motivation.

apraxic agraphia: writing deficits due to a motor planning impairment.

aprosodia: deficits in language production and/or comprehension, characterized by abnormalities in pitch, loudness, and/or timing.

arcuate fasciculus: fiber tracts connecting the superior and middle frontal gyri with the temporal lobe.

arousal: a continuum of alertness and responsiveness.

arterial occlusion: obstruction of blood flow to the brain.

arteriovenous malformation: congenitally and abnormally tangled arteries and veins.

association: a stage of recognition, linking the perception to a previous experience and thereby giving it meaning.

associative agnosia: agnosia attributed to a problem of memory or semantics, not deficits in perception.

astereognosis: see **tactile agnosia.**

asymbolia: a term originally proposed by Finkelnburg to describe a range of impairments using symbols (e.g., music and language).

atherosclerosis: narrowing of an artery by buildup of fatty or other deposits on the artery walls.

atrophy: shrinkage.

attention: several different capacities related to how people become receptive to certain stimuli.

auditory agnosia: failure to recognize auditory stimuli despite intact hearing.

auditory sound agnosia: auditory agnosia limited to nonverbal sounds.

autonomic nervous system: a subdivision of the peripheral nervous system that innervates the viscera, cardiac muscle, and the glands of the body.

axon: part of a neuron that carries impulses to other neurons.

basal ganglia: a group of subcortical structures, including the caudate nucleus, putamen, globus pallidus, substantia nigra, and the subthalamic nucleus.

bilateral: both sides.

bipolar depression: see **manic depression.**

bitemporal hemianopia: loss of vision in both temporal half-fields.

blindsight: blindness due to bilateral damage to the visual cortex in which a blind patient can still point to flashes of light in the blind visual field.

blood-brain barrier: limitation of movement of blood-borne substances through the walls of brain capillaries into the fluid of the brain.

body part agnosia/autotopagnosia: the inability to identify body parts.

body schema/body image: spatial representation of the body.

bradykinesia: slow movement.

bradyphrenia: slow thinking.

brain: the cerebrum (the cerebral cortex and subcortical structures), the cerebellum, and the brainstem.

brain attack: stroke.

brainstem: the medulla, pons, and midbrain.

Broca's aphasia: aphasic syndrome characterized by nonfluent speech output and good auditory comprehension.

Brodmann areas: brain regions characterized by their distinct cell patterns and referred to by distinct number.

carotid endarterectomy: surgical removal of carotid artery lesions.

cataract: a decrease in transparency of the lens of the eye.

caudal: below or toward the tail or, when applied to human beings, posterior.

central achromatopsia: loss of color vision due to brain damage.

central executive: the component of working memory that modulates and directs attention and other mental resources.

central nervous system (CNS): the brain and the spinal cord.

central sulcus/fissure of Rolando: the large sulcus separating the frontal and parietal lobes.

cerebellum: the structure posterior of the brainstem and part of the extrapyramidal system.

cerebral angiography: injection of dye into the cerebral arteries to visualize the nature of vascular lesions.

cerebral cortex/neocortex: outermost areas of the brain.

cerebral hemispheres: the left and right sides of the brain.

cerebrospinal fluid (CSF): a clear liquid that surrounds the brain and spinal cord and circulates within the ventricles.

cerebrovascular accident: stroke.

cerebrum: the cerebral cortex and subcortical structures.

circumlocution: talking around a word or topic.

clinical diagnosis: nature of a disease determined from the study of signs and symptoms.

clinical sign: an observed abnormality in behavior.

closed head injury: head trauma when the skull is not penetrated.

clouding of consciousness: decreased arousal and cognitive impairment, associated with delirium.

cohort: a group of people, defined by age, generation or other commonality.

cohort effect: the fact that different groups have different life experiences and therefore different knowledge and skills because their experiences.

color agnosia: failure to recognize previously known colors not due to color blindness.

coma: the lowest stage of arousal, in which patients typically have their eyes closed, do not respond to any stimulation, and do not make purposeful movements.

compensation for lost function: treatment aimed at developing the ability to accomplish a particular goal by a different means than prior to an injury.

computed tomography (CT): a method of visualizing body structures by passing an external beam of radiation through tissue and using a computer to measure the amount and distribution of X-rays that are absorbed versus deflected by the tissues.

concept formation: the process of identifying features and relationships between features to derive abstract categories; reasoning.

conduction aphasia: aphasic syndrome characterized by disproportionate difficulty with repetition.

confabulations: made-up "facts."

confusion: incoherent thinking and/or disorientation.

constructional apraxia: deficits in drawing structures building out of blocks or sticks, or similar problems with spatial behavior.

contralateral: opposite side.

contrecoup injury: injury to the brain on the side opposite of the impact.

cornea: the outer part of the eye, which refracts light onto the retina.

coronal: views based on the frontal plane.

corpus callosum: the fiber tract connecting the two cerebral hemispheres, divided into the genu (anterior portion), body (mid-portion), and splenium (posterior portion).

cortical blindness: see **Anton's syndrome.**

cortical deafness: a disorder in which the patient is not aware of sounds and has abnormally elevated auditory thresholds, due to cortical damage.

corticospinal (a.k.a. **pyramidal) system:** the part of the central nervous system that controls movement from the cortex to the spinal cord via the internal capsule and the medulla.

declarative memory: the ability to learn and remember information about events and the world.

decorticate state: a condition when higher cortical areas stop functioning, allowing brainstem and spinal cord functions to continue.

decussation: crossing of nerves at the level of the brain stem from one side of the brain to the other side of the body.

deductive reasoning: reasoning from the general to the specific.

deep agraphia: problems using grapheme-to-phoneme conversion rules for writing.

deep alexia: problems using grapheme-to-phoneme conversion rules for reading.

delirium: mental confusion with a sudden onset, impairing cognitive function and arousal.

delusions: false beliefs, sometimes based on hallucinations.

dementia syndrome of depression: dementia caused by depression.

dendrites: arms of the neuron that receive input from other neurons.

depression (a.k.a. **major depression**): a mood disturbance characterized by sadness, loneliness, and/or apathy that persists and is not obviously related to bereavement.

developmental aphasia: abnormal or interrupted language development in childhood.

diagnosis: the determination of the nature of a disease.

differential diagnosis: an educated guess of two or more diseases that fit a signs and patient's symptoms.

disability: deficit in performance that reduces the manner or range of activities that an individual would ordinarily be capable of accomplishing.

discourse structure: the structure of language units larger than a single sentence.

disorientation: confusion about time, location, and/or personal information.

divided attention: the ability to respond to more than one task at a time or to multiple elements within a task at the same time.

dorsal: toward the back.

dorsal visual system: the aspect of the visual system located in the dorsal occipital-parietal region, specialized to process spatial information, including the ability to reach toward visual targets and visual search, the "where" system.

dorsolateral frontal cortex: the brain regions at the most anterior reaches of the frontal lobes, also called the frontal convexity.

dressing apraxia: the inability to dress oneself generally due to visuospatial deficits.

dysfluency: slow and halting speech with excessive pauses and a notable absence of intonation.

dyslexia: difficulty learning to read (a.k.a. developmental dyslexia) or acquired reading problems.

dysphagia: problems with chewing and swallowing.

dysprosody: see **aprosodia**.

dysthymia: mild depression with a chronic course, characterized by anhedonia, social withdrawal, and occasional sadness.

echoic memory: short-term sensory information storage in the auditory system.

efferent: away from the center.

elderspeak: a speech register addressed to older adults, characterized by high pitch, slow speech rate, increased loudness, exaggerated intonation, simplified grammar, and elementary semantic content.

electroconvulsive therapy (ECT): the induction of grand mal seizures through electrical stimulation of the brain via electrodes placed on the scalp as a treatment for depression.

electroencephalography (EEG): a technique to measure electrical activity of the brain through electrodes placed on the skull.

embolism: an obstruction that moves inside a blood vessel until it becomes lodged and stops the flow of blood.

emotional prosody: see **affective prosody**.

encephalitis: inflammation of the central nervous system.

endarterectomy: see **carotid endarterectomy.**

epilepsy: uncontrolled electrical activity within the brain (a.k.a. seizures).

episodic memory: memory for specific events and personal experiences.

essential tremor: an involuntary, rhythmic oscillation of one or more body parts.

etiology: the cause of signs and symptoms of a disorder.

evaluation: the process of gathering the crucial information to decide what, if anything, is wrong.

evoked potentials (EPs): evoked response potentials (ERPs) a method of using EEGs to detect neural responses, time-locked to specific stimuli.

executive functions: those cognitive abilities that direct and organize behavior, including anticipation, goal selection, planning, initiation of activity, self-monitoring, and use of feedback.

extrapyramidal system: the part of the central nervous system that modulates movement through a set of connections in the cerebral cortex, basal ganglia, cerebellum, and certain brainstem motor centers.

familial tremor: essential tremor associated with family history of tremor.

festinating gait: increasingly fast shuffling, as the legs try to catch up with the body's forward momentum.

focal neurological damage: cell damage to a particular region of the brain.

forgetting: lapses in memory characterized by trouble recalling or recognizing information that one previously knew.

fovea: the center of the retina, an area dense in photoreceptor cells and used for high visual acuity.

frontal lobe: the anterior portion of the cerebral cortex.

frontotemporal dementia: a form of cortical dementia consisting of three neuro-behavioral syndromes resulting from progressive degeneration of the frontal and/or temporal cortices.

functional magnetic resonance imaging (fMRI): A method of measuring body function using MRI technology to determine changes in flow of oxygenated blood to specific regions.

functional mental disorder: a mental syndrome due to personality, learned behavior, or other mental states, not caused by known brain impairments.

ganglion (ganglia): group of neurons or nerve structures that work together as a unit.

geniculocalcarine tract (optic radiations): neurons originating in the thalamus that take visual information to the primary visual areas of the occipital lobes

glaucoma: the buildup of pressure within the eye, causing damage to the retina.

glia: nerve cells that serve to support neurons.

global aphasia: aphasic syndrome characterized by impairment affecting all modalities of language to a severe degree.

grapheme-to-phoneme conversion rules: phonics, the conventions that allow sounding out of words.

gray matter: neuron cell bodies, i.e., nonmyelinated parts of neurons.

gyrus/gyri: convolution(s) or ridge(s) of the brain's surface.

hallucination: an illusion in the absence of any relevant sensory stimulus.

handicap: social disadvantage caused by impairment and/or disability.

hematoma: the accumulation of blood.

hemiparesis: weakness on one side of the body.

hemiplegia: paralysis on one side of the body.

hemispheric specialization/lateralization of function: the notion that the two cerebral hemispheres control different cognitive and behavioral functions.

hemorrhage: bleeding.

holism: a philosophy about the brain that maintains that human mental and behavioral functions are distributed over many structures of the brain and that it is not possible to associate a specific behavior with a narrowly defined brain region.

homonymous hemianopia: loss of vision in the half-fields of each eye contralateral to a lesion.

homunculus: a representation of the body along the motor and sensory strips.

hydrocephalus: ventricular enlargement caused by excessive CSF that can present with clinical signs similar to subcortical dementias.

hyperfluency: fast speech without appropriate breaks.

hypertonicity: greater than normal muscle tone.

hypokinetic: restricted range of movements.

hypomania: brief and mild episodes of manic symptoms.

hypotonicity: lower than normal muscle tone.

iatrogenic: caused by medical intervention.

iconic memory: short-term sensory information storage in the visual system.

ideational apraxia: difficulty carrying out "ideational plans," that is, sequencing acts in the proper order, due to loss of the concept or idea.

ideomotor apraxia: a form of apraxia demonstrated by difficulty performing transitive movements, such as using a tool or instrument, due to loss of ability to organize the motor plans.

idiom: an example of nonliteral language in which a phrase has a conventional meaning that is not predictable based on the usual meaning of the words.

idiopathic: unclear cause.

illusion: the misinterpretation of perceptions.

immediate memory: an early stage of memory in which information can be repeated verbatim without rehearsal or manipulation.

implicit memory: information learned without conscious awareness and, once learned, typically recalled and used without awareness.

indirect request: an example of nonliteral language in which a person makes a statement or asks a question that is intended and interpreted as a request, such as, "Do you know what time it is?" as a request for the time.

inductive reasoning: reasoning from the particular to the general.

infarct: area of dead brain cells.

inferior: below.

inferior longitudinal fasciculus: fiber tracts connecting the occipital lobes with the temporal poles.

innervates: supplies with nerves.

insula: part of the temporal lobe inside the lateral fissure.

intracerebral/intraparenchymal hemorrhage: bleeding into brain tissue.

ipsilateral: same side.

irony/sarcasm: an example of nonliteral language in which words convey the opposite of their literal meaning.

ischemia: cell death due to oxygen deprivation.

ischemic penumbra: dysfunctional but not dead cells around an area of ischemia.

kana: Japanese symbols that represent syllables.

kanji: Chinese characters used in Japanese to represent words.

kinetic tremor: see **essential tremor.**

Korsakoff syndrome: a disorder caused by long-term chronic alcoholism and characterized by specific types of anterograde and retrograde amnesia.

lacunar infarct: small strokes, mostly in the subcortical regions.

lateral: toward the side.

lateral or Sylvian fissure: the large sulcus separating the temporal lobe from frontal and parietal lobes.

learning: the perception and acquisition of new information.

lens: part of the eye between the cornea and the retina that focuses light and images onto the retina.

lenticular nucleus: the putamen and globus pallidus.

lethargy: a state of arousal characterized by falling asleep when not actively stimulated, engaging in tangential conversation, and having a short attention span.

Lewy body dementia (LBD): a common form of dementia whose cognitive and behavioral symptoms include progressively worse hallucinations, clouding of consciousness, spontaneous extrapyramidal motor symptoms, and fluctuations in cognition.

limb apraxia: impairment of volitional movement of the arms and hands.

limbic lobe/limbic system: the subcortical regions that border the corpus callosum, including the hippocampus, amygdala, mammillary bodies, fornix, olfactory bulbs, and cingulate gyrus.

linguistic prosody: prosodic variation that distinguishes word meanings, the internal structure of utterances, and whether an utterance is a statement, question, or command.

localization of function: the idea that specific brain structures are responsible for specific aspects of behavior and silent for others.

logograph: a symbol that stands for a word.

long-term synaptic potentiation: the neurological theory of memory retention based on the fact that the temporary synaptic changes that accompany all events can become permanent by altering the structure of the synapse.

macula: the middle (of the retina).

macular degeneration: the most common cause of blindness in the elderly caused by degeneration of the central part of the retina, resulting in loss of or impaired central vision.

magnetic resonance imaging (MRI): a method of visualizing internal body structures by measuring energy released by a selected element (usually hydrogen atoms) in response to a large magnetic field.

malinger: to feign an illness.

mania: an elevated or euphoric mood, increased physical activity, irritability, accelerated or pressured speech, distractibility, grandiosity, decreased need for sleep, poor judgment and poor insight, flight of ideas, and/or racing thoughts.

manic depression: a condition when depression alternates with periods of overactivity, talkativeness, increased energy, and/or grandiosity.

medial: toward the center.

medial frontal cortex: the frontal lobe regions, including the anterior cingulate cortex, wrapping around the anterior portion (genu) of the corpus callosum.

meninges: layers of protection surrounding the brain, including (from the outside in) the dura mater, arachnoid, and pia mater.

misperception: a disturbance of body image, distortion of the size, or stability of objects or the passage of time.

mixed transcortical aphasia: also known as isolation of the speech area; global impairment of language except for the ability to repeat.

modularity of function: a philosophy of brain and behavior that maintains that certain specific brain structures are responsible for specific aspects of behavior and silent for others.

monocular blindness: loss of vision in both half-fields of one eye.

mood lability: quick changes from one mood to another.

motor end plate/myoneuronal junction: the point at which a neuron contacts voluntary muscle.

motor neurons: neurons that control movement.

motor strip: the portion of the precentral gyrus that controls voluntary movement of the body.

myelin: a fatty sheath of insulation around the axon of a nerve cell.

nasal half-field: the half of the visual field for each eye closest to the nose and to the center of the whole visual field.

nasal hemianopia: loss of vision in one or both nasal half-field(s).

neglect agraphia: difficulty writing due to visuospatial neglect.

neglect alexia: difficulty reading due to visuospatial neglect.

neologisms: nonwords.

neoplasm: an abnormal tissue growth that can induce dementing symptoms by putting pressure on brain tissue, by causing hydrocephalus, or by growing into the brain tissue itself.

neurofibrillary tangles: abnormal paired double helical filaments within the nerve cell bodies.

neurons: nerve cells that control movement, sensation, and cognition.

neurotransmitters: chemicals synthesized in the neuron, stored in the presynaptic vesicles, and released into the synapse to facilitate and inhibit cell contact.

nonfluent: language production that is generally characterized by slow and halting speech with excessive pauses and a lack of intonation.

nonliteral language: phrases and sentences that have an abstract meaning separate from the literal meanings of the words and sentence structure.

nucleus: cell body or group of neurons in the brain or spinal card.

obtundation: a difficult to arouse, confused and unable to cooperate in meaningful interaction when awake.

occipital lobe: the posterior portion of the cerebral cortex.

off-topic verbosity: the tendency to produce more speech and more tangential speech than is typical.

open head injury: head trauma when the skull is penetrated.

optic chiasm: the point at which the optic nerves from each eye partially cross.

optic nerves: the optic nerve fibers between the eye and the optic chiasm.

optic tracts: the optic nerve fibers between the optic chiasm and the visual centers of the thalamus.

oral apraxia (a.k.a. buccofacial apraxia): a disorder of the movement of the mouth in actions such as blowing out a match or sucking on a straw.

orbitofrontal cortex: the region of the brain just above the eye sockets.

organic mental syndrome: a mental disorder arising from a physical brain dysfunction.

orientation: awareness of self in relation to one's surroundings.

paragraphia: substitution errors made during writing.

paralexia: substitution errors made during reading.

paralysis: the condition when a muscle does not contract sufficiently to produce joint movement or provide postural stability to the body segment.

paraphasias: substitutions of one verbal production for another.

paraplegia: damage to the lower spinal cord (below T1) that paralyzes both legs.

paresis: sufficient muscle weakness to prevent muscle contraction for effective use.

parietal lobe: the middle-posterior and superior portion of the cerebral cortex.

pathological diagnosis: nature of a disease based on objective laboratory tests, such as blood tests or biopsy results.

perimetry: determination of the limits of the visual field.

peripheral nervous system: the 12 pairs of cranial nerves and 31 pairs of spinal nerves that control movement and sensation.

perseveration: the tendency for a response to persist after it is no longer appropriate.

phonagnosia: a deficit in recognizing familiar voices.

phoneme: one of a set of abstract units representing the sounds of a language that can be combined to create meaningful utterances (e.g., /b/ or /g/ in English).

phonological loop: component of working memory that allows for storage of speech material for about 2 seconds.

phrenologists: 19th-century scientists who associated skull shape and personal characteristics to arrive at maps of localization of brain function.

planning: the ability to develop a strategy to achieve a particular goal.

plasticity: the ability for the central nervous system to compensate for localized damage by creating alternative neural routes for functions normally controlled by the compromised regions.

polypharmacy: taking more over-the-counter and/or prescription medications than are needed.

positron emission tomography (PET): a method of visualizing the function of internal body structures by measuring which structures accumulate injected or inhaled radioactive substances.

postcentral gyrus: prominent gyrus in the parietal lobe, just posterior to the central sulcus, sometimes called the "sensory strip" due to its important role in processing sensory information.

posterior: toward the back.

postural instability: difficulty maintaining balance when standing or walking.

postural tremor: see **essential tremor.**

pragmatic prosody: prosodic variation that communicates emphasis and distinguishes literal from nonliteral meanings.

pragmatics: conventions for using language in context, including prosody, discourse structure, and nonliteral language.

precentral gyrus: prominent gyrus in the frontal lobe, just anterior to the central sulcus, sometimes called the "motor strip" due to its important role in controlling movement.

prefrontal cortex: the region toward the front of the brain anterior to the supplementary motor area.

presbycusis: age-related hearing loss.

presbyopia: the reduced ability of the older eye to adjust focus to see objects clearly.

primary aging: typical age-related decrements that are the usual and natural losses of function.

primary progressive aphasia: a variant of frontotemporal dementia that affects primarily language early in the course, sometimes further divided into two variants: semantic dementia and progressive nonfluent dementia.

procedural memory: the acquisition and retrieval of motor and cognitive skills that underlie specific procedures.

prognosis: likelihood of recovery from a disease.

progressive nonfluent aphasia: a dementing disorder associated with frontal lobe involvement that manifests with anomia, effortful speech production, and grammatical errors but preserved comprehension.

prosody: variation in pitch, loudness, and timing that creates the melody of speech.

prosopagnosia: a deficit in the ability to recognize previously familiar faces.

prospective memory: the process of remembering to do something in the future.

psychosis: a person's inability to accurately evaluate and draw inferences about his or her external reality.

psychosurgery: surgical procedures used to treat psychological syndromes.

pure agraphia: difficulty writing with preserved ability to read and no significant aphasia.

pure alexia: inability to read despite preserved ability to write and no significant aphasia.

pure word deafness: auditory agnosia that is limited to speech sounds.

quadranticanopia: the loss of vision in either the top or bottom of a visual half-field.

quadriplegia: damage to the cervical level of the spinal cord that paralyzes both arms and both legs.

radiation necrosis: cell death due to long-term exposure to radiation.

reasoning: the ability to draw inferences or conclusions from known or assumed facts.

recent memory: stage of memory in which information is consolidated and learned so that it lasts more than a few seconds.

redundancy: the notion that multiple brain areas can control the same behavioral function.

referential ambiguity: a noun or a pronoun in a discourse with an unclear referent.

reflex: rapid, involuntary, stereotyped movement (e.g., coughing).

rehabilitation: treatment to regain lost function.

remote memory: the ability to recall older information and experiences, including historical facts and childhood recollections.

restoration of function: treatment aimed at regaining the ability to accomplish a goal in the same way as before an injury.

retention: the process of storing information.

retina: the back of the eye, containing photoreceptor cells, rods, and cones, which transform light into nerve impulses to stimulate the optic nerve.

retrieval: the access of information stored in memory.

retrograde amnesia: difficulty recalling events that were experienced and known prior to the onset of memory problems.

right visual field: the area of vision on the right side of space for each eye.

rigidity: stiffness caused by involuntary increase in muscle tone.

rostral: toward the nose or toward the front.

sagittal: view of the body from the side.

scotoma: small blind spot caused by cortical lesions in the occipital lobe.

scripts: typical sequences of events involved in certain activities.

secondary aging: declines in function due to abuse, disuse, or disease that increase in risk or severity with age.

selective or immediate attention: focusing on one aspect of the environment more than others.

semantic dementia: a form of frontotemporal dementia associated with temporal lobe involvement and that manifests with fluent grammatical output but poor comprehension.

semantic memory: learning and recalling specific facts and general knowledge.

senile or neuritic plaques: deposits of the protein amyloid, surrounded by cellular debris between nerve cells.

senile tremor: essential tremor associated with aging.

sensitivity: the probability of a particular measurement accurately identifying patients with disease.

sensory stage (of memory): perception and recognition of the to-be-remembered object, information, or experience.

sensory strip: the postcentral gyrus where sensation of the body is represented.

set shifting: the ability to shift attention between categories.

silent stroke: a stroke that has no symptoms.

sleep deprivation: a treatment for depression in which the patient is prohibited from sleeping for extended periods of time followed by rest periods in an attempt to restore normal sleep rhythms.

spatial behavior: the use of vision and space to guide movement.

spatial cognition: the use of vision and space in thought.

specificity: the probability of a particular measurement accurately identifying patients without disease.

spinal cord: a cylinder of neurons running from the bottom of the brain to the level of the first lumbar vertebra.

split brain: reference to surgical separation of the cerebral hemispheres through the corpus callosum (callosectomy) to control seizures.

spontaneous/neurological recovery: rapid recovery of function during the first months after a neurological event, probably due to reduction of swelling and return of blood flow.

striate cortex: the primary visual areas of the occipital lobes (Brodmann area 17), having a characteristic horizontal stripe of white matter within the gray matter.

stroke: sudden onset of neurological deficits due to disruption of blood flow to the brain.

stupor: a state of arousal exhibited by patients who respond only to vigorous stimulation and, when awake, only groan, mumble, or move restlessly in bed.

subarachnoid hemorrhage: bleeding into the space between the brain and the arachnoid layer of the meninges.

sulcus/sulci: valley(s) of the brain's surface.

sundowning: symptoms of delirium appear to become worse at nighttime.

superior: above/on top.

superior longitudinal fasciculus: fiber tracts connecting the frontal and occipital lobes.

surface agraphia: problems using the whole-language route for writing.

surface alexia: problems using the whole-language route for reading.

sustained attention: focus on one aspect of the environment over time.

symptom: an abnormality described by a patient.

synapse: the contact zone between neurons.

syndrome: a group of signs and symptoms.

tactile agnosia: difficulty using touch, particularly with the hands, to identify shapes or objects, not attributed to basic sensory deficits, anomia, or dementia.

tangentiality: tendency for speech to be off-topic or contain digressions.

temporal gradient: different degrees of aphasia for older than newer old memories.

temporal half-field: the visual half-field for each eye farthest from the nose.

temporal lobe: the lateral, inferior portion of the cerebral cortex.

tetraplegia: another name for quadraplegia.

thalamus: a subcortical structure that receives input from many parts of the body and brain and projects output to many brain regions.

thematic coherence/macrostructure: the fact that sentences in a discourse are relevant and interpretable with respect to what came before and what follows.

theory of mind: a theory about the beliefs, knowledge, motivations, and intentions of another person.

thrombolysis: pharmacological treatment to dissolves blood clots.

thrombosis: a mechanism of occlusive stroke in which tissue narrows or occludes the lumen of a blood vessel.

topographic disorientation: inability to find one's way around familiar surroundings.

topographical agnosia: failure to recognize landmarks.

topographical amnesia: failure to recall relationships between landmarks in our visual or map schema.

tract: groups of nerve cells that arise in one area of the brain and end in another.

transcortical aphasias: aphasic syndromes characterized by the relative preservation of repetition.

transcortical motor aphasia: nonfluent aphasia characterized by reduced speech output, relatively good repetition, and good auditory comprehension.

transcortical sensory aphasia: fluent aphasia characterized by normal but paraphasic speech output, relatively good repetition, and poor auditory comprehension.

transcranial magnetic stimulation: a procedure in which brief, repetitive, high-intensity magnetic fields are produced by an apparatus and held near the scalp.

transient global amnesia (TGA): a syndrome of a sudden and brief period of antero-grade and retrograde amnesia.

transient ischemic attack: small strokes from which people recover within 24 hours.

traumatic dementia: dementia resulting from repeated blows to the head or a single serious head injury.

truncal apraxia: impaired ability to perform body postures, such as standing like a boxer or bowing.

tumor/neoplasm: a mass of tissue that grows independently of surrounding structures and has no physiological use.

unilateral body neglect: the inability to use information from one side of the body, as in failing to shave, dress, and so forth, on one side of the body.

unipolar depression: depression which alternates with normal emotional states.

vascular dementia: dementia caused by multiple small strokes that proceeds in a stepwise fashion, with cognitive impairments appearing abruptly, often accompanied by focal neurologic signs.

vascular depression: depression due to vascular causes, generally characterized by poor insight, psychomotor retardation, and no family history.

ventral: toward the front, or toward the underside of an animal.

ventral visual system: the aspect of the visual system in the occipital temporal regions, specialized to process and recognize objects, faces, and words, called the "what" system.

ventricle: a normal cavity, as in the brain.

verbal apraxia (a.k.a. **apraxia of speech**)**:** a disorder of the ability to articulate individual speech sounds and sound sequences.

visual agnosia: lack of recognition of visually presented material not due to problems in visual acuity, anomia, memory lapse, or general intellectual impairment.

visual field defect: partial or complete blindness.

visual half-field: vision in either the left or right side of space seen by each eye.

visual neglect/visual inattention: failure to respond to information usually on one side opposite, to brain lesion.

visuoconstructive deficit/apraxia: deficits in copying line drawings, drawing figures, or building constructions out of blocks or sticks.

visuoperceptual deficit: impaired visual scanning, poor depth perception, and/or localization of objects in space.

visuospatial deficit: a general term for many different problems in perceiving and responding to visual and/or spatial information.

visuospatial sketchpad: a component of working memory that allows for storage of visual information for about 2 seconds.

voice tremors: tremors that affect the larynx and throat and make the voice quiver and low in volume.

voluntary movement: intentional, deliberate movement.

Wernicke's aphasia: aphasic syndrome characterized by fluent speech output, paraphasias, and poor auditory comprehension.

white matter: the aspect of neurons covered with myelin (axons).

whole-language/whole-word reading: the process by which we access meaning from a written word without sounding it out.

working memory: initial stages of information processing and storage in memory, involving the capacity to simultaneously store and process information.

working memory deficits: a symptom apparent in divided-attention tasks in which patients need to do two things at once during a short period of time.

REFERENCES

Abrahams, J. P., & Camp, C. J. (1993). Maintenance and generalization of object naming training for anomia associated with degenerative dementia. *Clinical Gerontologist, 12,* 57–72.

Absher, J. R., & Cummings, J. L. (1995, March–April). Neurobehavioral examination of frontal lobe functions. *Aphasiaology, 9,* 181–192.

Albert, M. L., Sparks, R. W., & Helm, N. A. (1973). Melodic intonation therapy for aphasia. *Archives of Neurology, 29*(2), 130–131.

Albert, M. S., Butters, N., & Brandt, J. (1981). Patterns of remote memory in amnesic and demented patients. *Archives of Neurology, 38,* 495–500.

Albert, M. S., Jones, K., Savage, C. R., Berkman, L., Seeman, T., & Blazer, D. (1995). Predictors of cognitive change in older persons: MacArthur studies of successful aging. *Psychol. Aging, 10,* 578–589.

Albert, M. S., & Moss, M. B. (Eds.). (1988). *Geriatric neuropsychology.* New York: Guilford.

Alexopoulos, G. S., Abrams, R. C., Young, R. C., & Shamoian, C. A. (1988). Cornell Scale for Depression in Dementia. *Biological Psychiatry, 23,* 271–284.

Almli, C. R., & Finger, S. (1992). Brain injury and recovery of function: Theories and mechanisms of functional reorganization. *Journal of Head Trauma Rehabilitation, 7*(2), 70–77.

Alzheimer, F. (1907). Über eine eigenartige Erkrankung der Hirnrinde. *Allgemeine Zeitschrift für Psychiatrie und Psychisch-Gerichtlich Medicin, 64,* 146–148.

Amar, A. P., Heck, C. N., Levy, M. L., Smith, T., DeGiorgio, C. M., Oviedo, S., et al. (1998). An institutional experience with cervical vagus nerve trunk stimulation for medically refractory epilepsy: Rationale, technique, and outcome. *Neurosurgery, 43*(6), 1265–1276; discussion 1276–1280.

American Psychiatric Association. (1980). *Diagnostic and statistical manual of mental disorders* (3rd ed.). Washington, DC: Author.

American Psychiatric Association. (1987). *Diagnostic and statistical manual of mental disorders* (Rev. 3rd ed.). Washington, DC: Author.

American Psychiatric Association. (2000). *Diagnostic and statistical manual of mental disorders* (4th ed., text rev.). Washington, DC: Author.

Anderson, N. D., Craik, F. I. M., & Naveh-Benjamin, M. (1998). The attentional demands of encoding and retrieval in younger and older adults: 1. Evidence from divided attention costs. *Psychology and Aging, 13*(3), 405–423.

Andreasen, N. C., & Olsen, S. (1982). Negative v. positive schizophrenia: Definition and validation. *Archives of General Psychiatry, 39*(7), 789–794.

Anthony, S. G., Schipper, H. M., Tavares, R., Hovanesian, V., Cortez, S. C., Stopa, E. G., et al. (2003). Stress protein expression in the Alzheimer-related choroid plexus. *Journal of Alzheimer's Disease, 5*(3), 171–177.

Antonini, A., De Notaris, R., & Benti, R. (2001). Perfusion ECD/SPECT in the characterization of cognitive deficits in Parkinson's disease. *Neurological Sciences, 22*(1), 45–46.

Arbuckle, T. Y., & Gold, D. P. (1993). Aging, inhibition, and verbosity. *Journal of Gerontology, 48*(5), P225–P232.

Astell, A. J., & Harley, T. A. (1996). Tip-of-the-tongue states and lexical access in dementia. *Brain and Language, 54*(2), 196–215.

Babcock, R. L., & Salthouse, T. A. (1990). Effects of increased processing demands on age differences in working memory. *Psychology and Aging, 5*(3), 421–428.

Backman, K., & Hentinen, M. (1999). Model for the self-care of home-dwelling elderly. *Journal of Advanced Nursing, 30*(3), 564–573.

Backman, L. K., & Herlitz, A. (1990). The relationship between prior knowledge and face recognition memory in normal aging and Alzheimer's disease. *Journals of Gerontology: Psychological Sciences, 45,* P94–P100.f

Baddeley, A. (2000). Working memory: The interface between memory and cognition. In M. S. Gazzaniga (Ed.), *Cognitive neuroscience* (pp. 292–304). Malden, MA: Blackwell.

Baddeley, A. D., & Wilson, B. (1985). Phonological coding and short-term memory in patients without speech. *Journal of Memory and Language, 24,* 490–502.

Bahrick, H. P., Bahrick, P. O., & Wittlinger, R. P. (1975). Fifty years of memory for names and faces: A cross-sectional approach. *Journal of Experimental Psychology, 104,* 54–75.

Baker, S. P., & Harvey, A. H. (1985). Fall injuries in the elderly. *Clinical Geriatric Medicine, 1,* 501–512.

Ballard, K. J., Robin, D. A., Woodworth, G., & Zimba, L. D. (2001). Age-related changes in motor control during articulator visuomotor tracking. *Journal of Speech, Language, & Hearing Research, 44*(4), 763–777.

Barbeau, A., Cloutier, T., Roy, M., Plasse, L., Paris, S., & Poirier, J. (1985). Ecogenetics of Parkinson's disease: 4-hydroxylation of debrisoquine. *Lancet, 2*(8466), 1213–1216.

Barker, A., Jones, R., & Jennison, C. (1995). A prevalence study of age-associated memory impairment. *British Journal of Psychiatry: The Journal of Mental Science, 167*(5), 642–648.

Bartres-Faz, D., Junque, C., Lopez-Alomar, A., Valveny, N., Moral, P., Casamayor, R., et al. (2001). Neuropsychological and genetic differences between age-associated memory impairment and mild cognitive impairment entities. *Journal of the American Geriatrics Society, 49*(7), 985–990.

Basso, A., LeCours, A., Moraschini, S., & Vanier, M. (1985). Anatomicoclinical correlations of the aphasias as defined through computerized tomography: Exceptions. *Brain and Language, 26,* 201–229.

Bassuk, S. S., Glass, T. A., & Berkman, L. F. (1999). Social disengagement and incident cognitive decline in community-dwelling elderly persons. *Annals of Internal Medicine, 131,* 165–173.

Bates, E. (1996). Learning rediscovered. *Science, 274*(5294), 1849–1850.

Bates, E. (1999). Language and the infant brain. *Journal of Communication Disorders, 32*(4), 195–205.

Bates, E., & Carnevale, G. F. (1993). New directions in research on language development. *Developmental Review, 13*(4), 436–470.

Bates, E., Wulfeck, B., & MacWhinney, B. (1991). Cross-linguistic studies in aphasia: An overview. *Brain and Language, 41*(2), 123–148.

Bauer, R. M. (1993). Agnosia. In K. M. Heilman (Ed.), *Clinical neuropsychology* (3rd ed., pp. 215–278). New York: Oxford University Press.

Bayles, K. A., & Kaszniak, A. W. (1987). *Communication and cognition in normal aging and dementia.* Boston: Little, Brown.

Bear, M. F., Connors, B. W., & Paradiso, M. A. (2001). *Neuroscience: Exploring the brain.* Baltimore: Lippincott Williams & Wilkins.

Beaulieu, C. L. (2002). Rehabilitation and outcome following pediatric traumatic brain injury. *Surgical Clinics of North America, 82*(2), 393–408.

Beck, A. T., Steer, R. A., & Brown, G. K. (1996). *Manual for the Beck Depression Inventory* (2nd ed.). San Antonio, TX: The Psychological Corporation.

Beck, A. T., Ward, C. H., Mendelson, M., Mock, J., & Erbaugh, J. (1961). An inventory for measuring depression. *Archives of General Psychiatry, 4,* 561–571.

Becker, K. J. (1999). Thrombolysis for acute ischemic stroke. *Physical Medicine and Rehabilitation Clinics of North America, 10,* 773–786.

Behrens, S. J. (1988). The role of the right hemisphere in the production of linguistic stress. *Brain and Language, 33*(1), 104–127.

Bender, M. B., & Feldman, M. (1972). The so-called "visual agnosias." *Brain, 95*(1), 173–186.

Benson, D. F. (1979). Neurologic correlates of anomia. *Studies in Neurolinguistics, 4,* 293–328.

Benson, D. F. (1993). Aphasia. In K. M. Heilman & E. Valenstein (Eds.), *Clinical neuropsychology* (3rd ed., pp. 17–36). New York: Oxford University Press.

Benton, A., & Sivan, A. S. (1993). Disturbances of the body schema. In K. M. Heilman (Ed.), *Clinical neuropsychology* (3rd ed., pp. 123–140). New York: Oxford University Press.

Benton, A., & Tranel, D. (1993). Visuoperceptual, visuospatial, and visuoconstructive disorders. In K. M. Heilman (Ed.), *Clinical neuropsychology* (3rd ed., pp. 165–213). New York: Oxford University Press.

Benton, A. L. (1967). Constructional apraxia and the minor hemisphere. *Confinia Neurologica, 29*(1), 1–16.

Benton, A. L., Levin, H. S., & Van Allen, M. W. (1974). Geographic orientation in patients with unilateral cerebral disease. *Neuropsychologia, 12*(2), 183–191.

Benton, A. L., Sivan, A. B., Hamsher, K. D., Varney, N. R., & Spreen, O. (1994). *Contributions to neuropsychological assessment: A clinical manual* (2nd ed.). New York: Oxford University Press.

Benton, A. L., & Van Allen, M. W. (1968). Impairment in facial recogition in patients with cerebral disease. *Cortex, 4,* 344–358.

Berg, E. A. (1948). A simple objective treatment for measuring flexibility in thinking. *Journal of General Psychology, 39,* 15–22.

Berg, W. P., & Blasi, E. R. (2000). Stepping performance during obstacle clearance in women: Age differences and the association with lower extremity strength in older women. *Journal of the American Geriatrics Society, 48,* 1414–1423.

Berger, K. S. (1988). *The developing person through the life span* (2nd ed.). New York: Worth.

Berker, E. A., Berker, A. H., & Smith, A. (1986). Translation of Broca's 1865 report: Localization of speech in the third left frontal convolution. *Archives of Neurology, 43,* 1065–1072.

Berkman, L. F., Seeman, T. E., Albert, M., Blazer, D, Kahn, R., Mohs, R. et al. (1993). Successful, usual and impaired functioning in community-dwelling older men and women: Findings from the MacArthur Foundation Research Network on Successful Aging. *Journal of Clinical Epidemiology, 46,* 1129–1140.

Bisiach, E., Capitani, E., Luzzatti, C., & Perani, D. (1981). Brain and conscious representation of outside reality. *Neuropsychologia, 19*(4), 543–551.

Bisiach, E., & Luzzatti, C. (1978). Unilateral neglect of representational space. *Cortex, 14*(1), 129–133.

Blair, J. R., & Spreen, O. (1989). Predicting premorbid IQ: A revision of the National Adult Reading Test. *Clinical Neuropsychologist, 3*(2), 129–136.

Blanchard-Fields, F., & Chen, Y. (1996). Adaptive cognition and aging. *American Behavioral Scientists, 39,* 231–248.

Blazer, D. G. (2002). *Depression in late life* (3rd ed.). New York: Springer.

Boden, D., & Bielby, D. D. (1983). The past as resource: A conversational analysis of elderly talk. *Human Development, 26*(6), 308–319.

Bogen, J. E., & Bogen, G. M. (1976). Wernicke's region: Where is it? *Annals of the New York Academy of Sciences, 280,* 834–843.

Bolla, K. I., Lindgren, K. N., Bonaccorsy, C., & Bleeker, M. L. (1991). Memory complaints in older adults: Facts or fiction? *Archives of Neurology, 48,* 61–64.

Bornstein, B., Sroka, H., & Munitz, H. (1969). Prosopagnosia with animal face agnosia. *Cortex, 5*(2), 164–169.

Borod, J. C. (1993). Cerebral mechanisms underlying facial, prosodic, and lexical emotional expression: A review of neuropsychological studies and methodological issues. *Neuropsychology, 7*(4), 445–463.

Bosworth, H. B., Schaie, K. W., & Willis, S. L. (1999). Cognitive and sociodemographic risk factors for mortality in the Seattle Longitudinal Study. *Journal of Gerontology: Psychological Sciences, 54*(B), 273–282.

Botwinick, J. (1977). Intellectual abilities. In J. E. Birren & K. W. Schaie (Eds.), *Handbook of the psychology of aging* (pp. 580–605). New York: Van Nostrand Reinhold.

Boult, C., Kane, R. J., Louis, T. A., Boult, L., & McCaffrey, D. (1994). Chronic conditions that lead to functional limitations in the elderly. *Journal of Gerontology: Medical Sciences, 49,* M28–M36.

Bourgeois, M. S., Burgio, L. D., Schulz, R., Beach, S., & Palmer, B. (1997). Modifying repetitive verbalizations of community-dwelling patients with AD. *The Gerontologist, 37*(1), 30–39.

Bourgeois, M. S., Schulz, R., & Burgio, L. D. (1996). Interventions for caregivers of patients with Alzheimer's disease: A review and analysis of content, process, and outcomes. *International Journal of Aging & Human Development, 43*(1), 35–92.

Bowles, N. L., Obler, L. K., & Poon, L. W. (1989). Aging and word retrieval: Naturalistic, clinical, and laboratory data. In L. W. Poon, D. C. Rubin, & B. A. Wilson (Eds.), *Everyday cognition in adulthood and late life* (pp. 244–264). New York: Cambridge University Press.

Boyd, J. H., & Weisman, M. M. (1981). Epidemiology of affective disorders: A reexamination and future directions. *Archives of General Psychiatry, 38,* 1039–1046.

Bradshaw, J. L., & Mattingley, J. B. (1995). *Clinical neuropsychology: Behavioral and brain science.* San Diego: Academic Press.

Brandt, J., Spencer, M., McSorley, P., & Folstein, M. F. (1988). Semantic activation and implicit memory in Alzheimer disease. *Alzheimer Disease and Associated Disorders, 2,* 112–119.

Brandstadter, J., & Renner, G. (1990). Tenacious goal pursuit and flexible goal adjustment: Explication and age-related analysis of assimilative and accommodative strategies of coping. *Psychology and Aging, 5,* 58–67.

Brandtstadter, J., & Renner, G. (1992). Coping with discrepancies between aspirations and achievements in adult development: A dual-process model. In L. Montada, S. H. Filipp, & M. J. Lerner (Eds.), *Life crises and experience of loss in adulthood* (pp. 301–319). Hillsdale, NJ: Lawrence Erlbaum.

Brink, T. L., Yesavage, J. A., Lum, O., Heersema, P., Adey, M. B., & Rose, T. L. (1982). Screening tests for geriatric depression. *Clinical Gerontologist, 1,* 37–44.

Broadbent, D. E., Cooper, P. F., Fitzgerald, P., & Parkes, K. R. (1982). The Cognitive Failures Questionnaire (CFQ) and its correlates. *British Journal of Clinical Psychology, 21*(1), 1–16.

Broca, P. (1865). Sur le siege de la faculte de langage articule (On the attach of spoken language function). *Buletins de la Societe d'Anthropologie, 6,* 377–393.

Brookshire, R. H. (2003). *Introduction to neurogenic communication disorders* (6th ed.). St. Louis, MO: Mosby.

Brotons, M., Koger, S. M., & Pickett-Cooper, P. (1997). Music and dementias: A review of the literature. *Journal of Music Therapy, 34*(4), 204–245.

Brown, H., Prisuta, R., Jacobs, B., & Campbell, A. (2000). *Executive summary of literacy of older adults in America.* Retrieved from nces.ed.gov/pubs/ncesprograms/nals.html

Brown, J. W., Leader, B. J., & Blum, C. S. (1983). Hemiplegic writing in severe aphasia. *Brain and Language, 19*(2), 204–215.

Bruce, M. L., Seeman, T. E., Merrill, S. S., & Blazer, D. G. (1994). The impact of depressive symptomatology on physical disability: MacArthur Studies of Successful Aging. *American Journal of Public Health, 84*(11), 1796–1799.

Brush, J. A., & Camp, C. J. (1998). *A therapy technique on improving memory: Spaced retrieval.* Menorah Park, OH: Center for Senior Living.

Bub, D. (2002). The role of premorbid expertise on object identification in a patient with category-specific visual agnosia. *Cognitive Neuropsychology, 19*(5), 401–419.

Bub, D., Audet, T., & Lecours, A. R. (1990). Re-evaluating the effect of unilateral brain damage on simple reaction time to auditory stimulation. *Cortex, 26*(2), 227–237.

Burke, D. M., MacKay, D. G., Worthley, J. S., & Wade, E. (1991). On the tip of the tongue: What causes word finding failures in young and older adults? *Journal of Memory and Language, 30*(5), 542–579.

Burke, D. M., & Peters, L. (1986). Word associations in old age: Evidence for consistency in semantic encoding during adulthood. *Psychology and Aging, 1*(4), 283–291.

Burke, W. J., Rubin, E. H., Morris, J. C., & Berg, L. (1988). Symptoms of "depression" in dementia of the Alzheimer type. *Alzheimer Disease and Associated Disorders, 2,* 356–362.

Cacciari, C., & Tabossi, P. (Eds.). (1993). *Idioms: Processing, structure, and interpretation.* Hillsdale, NJ: Lawrence Erlbaum.

Camp, C. J., Foss, J. W., O'Hanlon, A. M., & Stevens, A. B. (1996). Memory interventions for persons with dementia. *Applied Cognitive Psychology, 10*(3), 193–210.

Campbell, A. J., Borrie, M. J., & Spears, G. F. (1989). Risk factors for falls in a community-based prospective study of people 70 years and older. *Journal of Gerontology, 44,* M112– M117.

Cancelliere, A. E., & Kertesz, A. (1990). Lesion localization in acquired deficits of emotional expression and comprehension. *Brain and Cognition, 13*(2), 133–147.

Caplan, D. (1994). Language and the brain. In M. Gernsbacher (Ed.), *Handbook of psycholinguistics* (pp. 1023–1053). New York: Academic Press.

Caplan, L. R. (2000). *Caplan's stroke: A clinical approach* (3rd ed.). Boston: Butterworth Heinemann.

Caporael, L. R. (1981). The paralanguage of caregiving: Baby talk to the institutionalized aged. *Journal of Personality and Social Psychology, 40*(5), 876–884.

Carey, J. R., Bogard, C. L., King, B. A., & Suman, V. J. (1994). Finger-movement tracking scores in healthy subjects. *Perceptual & Motor Skills, 79*(1, Pt. 2), 563–576.

Cassens, G., Wolfe, L., & Zola, M. (1990). The neuropsychology of depressions. *Journal of Neuropsychiatry and Clinical Neurosciences, 2,* 202–213.

Cattell, R. B. (1971). *Abilities: Their structure, growth, and action.* Boston: Houghton Mifflin.

Centers for Disease Control and Prevention. (1989). Surgeon General's workshop on health promotion and aging: Summary recommendations of the physical fitness and exercise working group. *Journal of the American Medical Association, 262,* 2507–2510.

Cerella, J. (1985). Information processing rates in the elderly. *Psychological Bulletin, 98*(1), 67–83.

Cerella, J. (1990). Pigeon pattern perception: Limits on perspective invariance. *Perception, 19,* 141–159.

Chabrier, S., Husson, B., Lasjaunias, P., Landrieu, P., & Tardieu, M. (2000). Stroke in childhood: Outcome and recurrence risk by mechanism in 59 patients. *Journal of Child Neurology, 15*(5), 290–294.

Channon, S., & Crawford, S. (1999). Problem-solving in real-life-type situations: The effects of anterior and posterior lesions on performance. *Neuropsychologia, 37*(7), 757–770.

Chavin, M. (2002). Music as communication. *Alzheimer's Care Quarterly, 3*(2), 145–156.

Chertkow, H., Bub, D., & Seidenberg, M. (1989). Priming and semantic memory loss in Alzheimer's disease. *Brain and Language, 36,* 420–446.

Chodosh, E. H., Foulkes, M. A., Kase, C. S., Wolf, P. A., Mohr, J. P., Hier, D. B., et al. (1988). Silent stroke in the NINCDS Stroke Data Bank. *Neurology, 38*(11), 1674–1679.

Chomsky, C. S. (1969). *The acquisition of syntax in children from 5 to 10.* Cambridge: MIT Press.

Christiansen, J. L., & Grzybowski, J. M. (1999). *Biology of aging.* New York: McGraw-Hill.

Chui, H. C., Mack, W., Jackson, J. E., Mungas, D., Reed, B. R., Tinklenberg, J., et al. (2000). Clinical criteria for the diagnosis of vascular dementia. *Archives of Neurology, 57,* 191–196.

Cicero, M. T. (1992). Cato maiaor, de senctute [On old age]. In G. P. Goold (Ed.), *Loeb classical library* (pp. 8–99). Cambridge, MA: Harvard University Press. (Original work published 44 B.C.)

Code, C. (1997). Can the right hemisphere speak? *Brain and Language, 57*(1), 38–59.

Cohen-Mansfield, J. (1986). Agitated behaviors in the elderly: II. Preliminary results in the cognitively deteriorated. *Journal of the American Geriatrics Society, 34,* 722–727.

Cohen-Mansfield, J., Marx, M. S., & Rosenthal, A. S. (1989). A description of agitation in a nursing home. *Journal of Gerontology: Medical Sciences, 44,* M77–M84.

Cohen-Mansfield, J., & Werner, P. (1997). Management of verbally disruptive behaviors in nursing home residents. *Journal of Gerontology, Biological Sciences, and Medical Sciences, 52*(6), M369–M377.

Coleman, E. A., & Sackeim, H. A. (1996). Subjective memory complaints prior to and following electroconvulsive therapy. *Biological Psychiatry, 39*(5), 346–356.

Collette, F., Van der Linden, M., & Salmon, E. (1999). Executive dysfunction in Alzheimer's disease. *Cortex, 35,* 57–72.

Colloby, S. J., Fenwick, J. D., Williams, D. E., Paling, S. M., Lobotesis, K., Ballard, C., et al. (2002). A comparison of [sup 99m] Tc-HMPAO SPECT changes in dementia with Lewy bodies and Alzheimer's disease using statistical parametric mapping. *European Journal of Nuclear Medicine & Molecular Imaging, 29*(5), 615–622.

Colsher, P. L., Cooper, W. E., & Graff Radford, N. R. (1987). Intonational variability in the speech of right-hemisphere damaged patients. *Brain and Language, 32*(2), 379–383.

Coltheart, M. (1998). Seven questions about pure alexia (letter-by-letter reading). *Cognitive Neuropsychology, 15*(1–2), 1–6.

Coltheart, M., Curtis, B., Atkins, P., & Haller, M. (1993). Models of reading aloud: Dual-route and parallel-distributed-processing approaches. *Psychological Review, 100*(4), 589–608.

Connor, D. J., Salmon, D. P., Sandy, T. J., Galasko, D., Hansen, L. A., & Thal, L. J. (1998). Cognitive profiles of autopsy-confirmed Lewy body variant versus pure Alzheimer's disease. *Archives of Neurology, 55,* 994–1000.

Cooper, I. S. (1981). *The vital probe: My life as a brain surgeon.* New York: W. W. Norton.

Corballis, M., & Morgan, M. (1978). On the biological basis of human laterality: 1. Evidence for a maturational left-right-gradient. *Behavioral and Brain Sciences, 1,* 261–269.

Cornelius, S. W., & Caspi, A. (1987). Everyday problem solving in adulthood and old age. *Psychology and Aging, 2*(2), 144–153.

Craik, F. I. M. (1977). Age differences in human memory. In J. E. Birren & K. W. Schaie (Eds.), *Handbook of the psychology of aging* (pp. 384–420). New York: Van Nostrand Reinhold.

Craik, F. I. M., & McDowd, J. M. (1987). Age differences in recall and recognition. *Journal of Experimental Psychology, Learning, Memory & Cognition, 13,* 479.

Craik, F. I. M., & Tulving, E. (1975). Depth of processing and the retention of words in episodic memory. *Journal of Experimental Psychology: General, 104,* 268–294.

Cramer, S. C. (1999). Stroke recovery: Lessons from functional MR imaging and other methods of human brain mapping. *Physical Medicine and Rehabilitation Clinics of North America, 10*(4), 875–886.

Crimmins, E. M., & Saito, Y. (1993). Getting better and getting worse: Transitions in functional status among older Americans. *Journal of Aging and Health, 5,* 3–36.

Critchley, M. (1965). Acquired anomalies of colour perception of central origin. *Brain, 88*(4), 711–724.

Crovitz, H. F., Harvey, M. T., & Horn, R. W. (1979). Problems in the acquisition of imagery mnemonics: Three brain-damaged cases. *Cortex, 17,* 273–278.

Crystal, D. (1994). *The Cambridge encyclopedia of language.* Cambridge, UK: Cambridge University Press.

Cummings, J., Miller, B., Hill, M. A., & Neshkes, R. (1987). Neuropsychiatric aspects of multi-infarct dementia and dementia of the Alzheimer type. *Archives of Neurology, 44,* 389–393.

Cummings, J. L. (1992a). Depression and Parkinson's disease: A review. *American Journal of Psychiatry, 149*(4), 443–454.

Cummings, J. L. (1992b). Psychosis in neurologic disease: Neurobiology and pathogenesis. *Neuropsychiatry, Neuropsychology, and Behavioral Neurology, 5,* 144–150.

Cummings, J. L. (2000). Cognitive and behavioral heterogeneity in Alzheimer's disease: Seeking the neurological basis. *Neurobiology of Aging, 21,* 845–861.

Cummings, J. L., & Benson, D. F. (1983). *Dementia: A clinical approach.* Boston: Butterworth.

Cummings, J. L., & Benson, D. F. (1986). Dementia of the Alzheimer type: An inventory of diagnostic clinical features. *Journal of the American Geriatrics Society, 34*(1), 12–19.

Cummings, J. L., & Mega, M. S. (2003). *Neuropsychiatry & behavioral neuroscience.* New York: Oxford University Press.

Cummings, J. L., Mega, M., Gray, K., Rosenberg-Thompson, S., Carusi, D. A., & Gornbein, J. (1994). The Neuropsychiatric Inventory: Comprehensive assessment of psychopathology in dementia. *Neurology, 44,* 2308–2314.

Cunningham, A. E., & Stanovich, K. E. (1997). Early reading acquisition and its relation to reading experience and ability ten years later. *Developmental Psychology, 33*(6), 934–945.

Curtiss, S. (1977). *Genie: A psycholinguistic study of a modern-day "wild child."* New York: Academic Press.

Damasio, A. R. (1989). Time-locked multiregional retroactivation: A systems-level proposal for the neural substrates of recall and recognition. *Cognition, 33*(1–2), 25–62.

Damasio, A. R., & Anderson, S. W. (1993). The frontal lobes. In K. M. Heilman (Ed.), *Clinical neuropsychology* (3rd ed., pp. 409–460). New York: Oxford University Press.

Damasio, A. R., & Damasio, H. (2000). Aphasia and the neural basis of language. In M.-M. Mesulam (Ed.), *Principles of behavioral and cognitive neurology* (2nd ed., pp. 294–315). Oxford, UK: Oxford University Press.

Damasio, A. R., Tranel, D., & Damasio, H. (1993). Similarity of structure and the profile of visual recognition defects: A comment on Gaffan and Heywood. *Journal of Cognitive Neuroscience, 5*(3), 371–372.

Damasio, A. R., Tranel, D., & Rizzo, M. (2000). Disorders of complex visual processing. In M.-M. Mesulam (Ed.), *Principles of behavioral and cognitive neurology* (2nd ed., pp. 332–372). New York: Oxford University Press.

Daneman, M., & Carpenter, P. A. (1980). Individual differences in working memory and reading. *Journal of Verbal Learning and Verbal Behavior, 19*(4), 450–466.

Daneman, M., & Carpenter, P. A. (1983). Individual differences in integrating information between and within sentences. *Journal of Experimental Psychology: Learning, Memory, and Cognition, 9*(4), 561–584.

Darley, F. L., Aronson, A. E., & Brown, J. R. (1975). *Motor speech disorders.* New York: W. B. Saunders.

Darnay, A. J. (Ed.). (1994). *Statistical record of older Americans.* Washington, DC: Gale Research.

Datto, C. (2000). Side effects of electroconvulsive therapy. *Depression & Anxiety, 12*(3), 130–134.

Davis, G., & Wilcox, J. (1985). *Adult aphasia rehabilitation: Applied pragmatics.* San Diego: College-Hill.

Davis, G. A., & Ball, H. E. (1989). Effects of age on comprehension of complex sentences in adulthood. *Journal of Speech & Hearing Research, 32*(1), 143–150.

Davis, R. N., Massman, P. J., & Doody, R. S. (2001). Cognitive intervention in Alzheimer disease: A randomized placebo-controlled study. *Alzheimer Disease and Associated Disorders, 15*(1), 1–9.

de Partz, M. P., Seron, X., & Van der Linden, M. (1992). Re-education of a surface dysgraphia with a visual imagery strategy. *Cognitive Neuropsychology, 9*(5), 369–401.

de Renzi, E. (1982). *Disorders of space exploration and cognition.* New York: John Wiley.

de Renzi, E., & Vignolo, L. A. (1962). The token test: A sensitive test to detect receptive disturbances in aphasia. *Brain, 85,* 665–678.

De Weerd, P., Peralta, M. R., III, Desimone, R., & Ungerleider, L. G. (1999). Loss of attentional stimulus selection after extrastriate cortical lesions in macaques. *Nature Neuroscience, 2*(8), 753–758.

Defebvre, L. J., Leduc, V., Duhamel, A., Lecouffe, P., Pasquier, F., Lamy-Lhullier, C., et al. (1999). Technetium HMPAO SPECT study in dementia with Lewy bodies, Alzheimer's disease and idiopathic Parkinson's disease. *Journal of Nuclear Medicine, 40*(6), 956–962.

Dehaene Lambertz, G., & Houston, D. (1998). Faster orientation latencies toward native language in two-month-old infants. *Language and Speech, 41*(1), 21–43.

Delaney, R. C., Wallace, J. D., & Egelko, S. (1980). Transient cerebral ischemic attacks and neuropsychological deficit. *Journal of Clinical Neuropsychology, 2,* 107–114.

Delis, D. C., Kramer, J. H., Kaplan, E., & Ober, B. A. (1987). *California Verbal Learning Test Manual.* New York: The Psychological Corporation.

Dennis, M. (2000). Developmental plasticity in children: The role of biological risk, development, time, and reserve. *Journal of Communication Disorders, 33*(4), 321–332.

Denny-Brown, D. (1958). The nature of apraxia. *Journal of Nervous and Mental Diseases, 126,* 9–32.

Deptula, D., Singh, R., & Pomara, N. (1993). Aging, emotional states, and memory. *American Journal of Psychiatry, 150*(3), 429–434.

Derouesne, C., Labomblez, L., & Thibault, S. (1999). Memory complaints in young and elderly subjects. *International Journal of Geriatric Psychiatry, 14*(4), 291–301.

Devanand, D. P., Sano, M., Tang, M. X., Taylor, S., Gurland, B. J., Wilder, D., et al. (1996). Depressed mood and the incidence of Alzheimer's disease in the elderly living in the community. *Archives of General Psychiatry, 53,* 175–182.

Devinsky, O., Bear, D., & Volpe, B. T. (1988). Confusional states following posterior cerebral artery infarction. *Archives of Neurology, 45,* 160–163.

Dick, A. O. (1974). Iconic memory and its relation to perceptual processes and other memory mechanisms. *Perception & Psychophysics, 16,* 575–596.

Dick, M. B., Teng, E. L., Kempler, D., Davis, D. S., & Taussig, I. M. (2002). The Cross-Cultural Neuropsychological Test Battery (CCNB): Effects of age, education, ethnicity, and cognitive status on performance. In F. R. Ferraro (Ed.), *Minority and cross-cultural aspects of neuropsychological assessment: Studies on neuropsychology, development, and cognition* (pp. 17–41). Bristol, PA: Swets & Zeitlinger.

Diehl, M., Willis, S. L., & Schaie, K. W. (1995). Everyday problem solving in older adults: Observational assessment and cognitive correlates. *Psychology and Aging, 10*(3), 478–491.

Diessel, H., & Tomasello, M. (2000). The development of relative clauses in spontaneous child speech. *Cognitive Linguistics, 11*(1–2), 131–151.

Digiovanna, A. G. (2000). *Human aging* (2nd ed.). Boston: McGraw-Hill.

Dimitrov, M. (1996). The effects of frontal lobe damage on everyday problem solving. *Cortex, 32*(2), 357–366.

Dipietro, L., Seeman, T. E., Merrill, S. S., & Berkman, L. F. (1996). Physical activity and measures of cognitive function in healthy older adults: The MacArthur Studies of Successful Aging. *Journal of Aging and Physical Activity, 4*(4), 362–376.

Dixon, M. J. (2000). A new paradigm for investigating category-specific agnosia in the new millennium. *Brain and Cognition, 42*(1), 142–145.

Dobson, C. B., Wozniak, M. A., & Itzhaki, R. F. (2003). Do infectious agents play a role in dementia? *Trends in Microbiology, 11*(7), 312–317.

Downton, J. H., & Andrews, K. (1991). Prevalence, characteristics and factors associated with falls among the elderly living at home. *Aging, 3,* 219–228.

Drewe, E. A. (1974). The effect of type and area of brain lesion on Wisconsin card sorting test performance. *Cortex, 10*(2), 159–170.

Drewe, E. A. (1975). An experimental investigation of Luria's theory on the effects of frontal lobe lesions in man. *Neuropsychologia, 13*(4), 421–429.

Duchek, J. M., Balota, D. A., & Thessing, V. C. (1998). Inhibition of visual and conceptual information during reading in healthy aging and Alzheimer's disease. *Aging, Neuropsychology, and Cognition, 5*(3), 169–181.

Duffy, J. R. (1995). *Motor speech disorders: Substrates, differential diagnosis, and management.* St. Louis, MO: Mosby.

Duffy, R. J., & Liles, B. Z. (1979). A translation of Finkelnburg's (1870) lecture on aphasia as 'asymbolia' with commentary. *Journal of Speech and Hearing Disorders, 44,* 156–168.

Eastman, C. I., Young, M. A., Fogg, L. P., Liu, L., & Meaeden, P. M. (1998). Bright light treatment of winter depression. *Archives of General Psychiatry, 55,* 883–889.

Ehsani, A. A., Ogawa, T., Miller, T. R., Spina, R. J., & Jilka, S. M. (1991). Exercise training improves left ventricular systolic function in older men. *Circulation, 83,* 96–103.

Eling, P. (1994). *Reader in the history of aphasia.* Amsterdam: John Benjamins.

Ellis, A. A., & Trent, R. B. (2001). Hospitalized fall injuries and race in California. *Injury Prevention: Journal of the International Society for Child and Adolescent Injury Prevention, 7*(4), 316–320.

Emmorey, K. D. (1987). The neurological substrates for prosodic aspects of speech. *Brain and Language, 30*(2), 305–320.

Eriksson, P. S., Perfilieva, E., Bjork-Eriksson, T., Alborn, A. M., Nordborg, C., Peterson, D. A., et al. (1998). Neurogenesis in the adult human hippocampus [see comments]. *Nature Medicine, 4*(11), 1313–1317.

Eslinger, P. J., & Damasio, A. R. (1985). Severe disturbance of higher cognition after bilateral frontal lobe ablation: patient EVR. *Neurology, 35,* 1731–1741.

Fahn, S., & Elton, R. (1987). Members of the UPDRS Committee Unified Parkinson's Disease Rating Scale. In S. Fahn, C. D. Mardsen, M. Goldstein & D. Calne (Eds.), *Recent developments in Parkinson's disease* (pp. 153–163). Florham, NJ: Macmillan Healthcare Information.

Fahn, S., Greene, P. E., Ford, B., & Bressman, S. B. (Eds.). (1998). *Handbook of movement disorders.* Malden, MA: Blackwell Science.

Farah, M. J. (1992). Agnosia. *Current Opinions in Neurobiology, 2*(2), 162–164.

Farah, M. J., Hammond, K. M., Mehta, Z., & Ratcliff, G. (1989). Category-specificity and modality-specificity in semantic memory. *Neuropsychologia, 27*(2), 193–200.

Farah, M. J., McMullen, P. A., & Meyer, M. M. (1991). Can recognition of living things be selectively impaired? *Neuropsychologia, 29*(2), 185–193.

Farmer, M. E., Kittner, S. J., Rae, D. S., Bartko, J. J., & Regier, D. A. (1995). Education and change in cognitive function: The Epidemiologic Catchment Area study. *Annals of Epidemiology, 5,* 1–7.

Farnsworth, D. (1957). *Farnsworth-Munsell 100 hue test for color vision.* Baltimore: Munsell Color Co.

Featherman, D. L. (1992). Development of reserves for adaptation to old age: Personal and societal agendas. In N. E. Cutler, D. W. Gregg, & M. P. Lawton (Eds.), *Aging, money, and life satisfaction: Aspects of financial gerontology* (pp. 135–168). New York: Springer.

Feher, E. P., Larrabee, G. J., & Sudilovsky, A. (1994). Memory self-report in Alzheimer's disease and in age-associated memory impairment. *Journal of Geriatric Psychiatry & Neurology, 7*(1), 58–65.

Feier, C., & Gerstman, L. (1980). Sentence comprehension abilities throughout the adult life span. *Journal of Gerontology, 35,* 722–728.

Feldman, H., Gauthier, S., Hecker, J., Vellas, B., Emir, B., Mastey, V., et al. (2003). Efficacy of donepezil on maintenance of activities of daily living in patients with moderate to severe Alzheimer's disease and the effect on caregiver burden. *Journal of the American Geriatrics Society, 51*(6), 737–744.

Fernandes, M. A., & Moscovitch, M. (2003). Interference effects from divided attention during retrieval in younger and older adults. *Psychology and Aging, 18*(2), 219–230.

Filley, C. M., & Cullum, C. M. (1994). Attention and vigilance functions in normal aging. *Applied Neuropsychology, 1*(1–2), 29–32.

Filoteo, J. V., Delis, D. C., Massman, P. J., & Butters, N. (1994). Visuospatial dysfunction in dementia and normal aging. In F. A. Huppert, C. Brayne, & D. W. O'Connor (Eds.), *Dementia and normal aging* (pp. 366–383). New York: Cambridge University Press.

Fisher, B. J. (1992). Successful aging and life satisfaction: A pilot study for conceptual clarification. *Journal of Aging Studies, 6,* 191–202.

Fisher, B. J. (1995). Successful aging, life satisfaction and generativity in later life. *International Journal of Aging and Human Development, 41,* 239–250.

Fitzgerald, L. K., McKelvey, J. R., & Szeligo, F. (2002). Mechanisms of dressing apraxia: A case study. *Neuropsychiatry, Neuropsychology, & Behavioral Neurology, 15*(2), 148–155.

Folstein, M. F., Folstein, S. E., & McHugh, P. R. (1975). Mini-mental state: A practical method for grading the cognitive state of patients for the clinician. *Journal of Psychiatric Research, 12*(3), 189–198.

Francis, J., Martin, D., & Kapoor, W. N. (1990). A prospective study of delirium in hospitalized elderly. *Journal of the American Medical Society, 263*(8), 1097–1101.

Freedman, M., Leach, L., Kaplan, E., Winocur, G., Shulman, K. I., & Delis, D. C. (1994). *Clock drawing: A neuropsychological analysis.* New York: Oxford University Press.

Freer, K. J. (1994). How the rural elderly view literacy in their lives. *Educational Gerontology, 20*(2), 157–169.

Freud, S. (1891a). On aphasia. In P. Eling (Ed.), *Reader in the history of aphasia* (pp. 181–196). Amsterdam: John Benjamins.

Freud, S. (1891b). *Zur Auffassung der Aphasien. Eine Kritische Studie* (On the concept of aphasia: A critical study). Vienna: Franz Deuticke.

Friedman, R. B., & Robinson, S. R. (1991). Whole-word training therapy in a stable surface alexic patient: It works. *Aphasiology, 5,* 1–7.

Friedman, R. F., Ween, J. E., & Albert, M. L. (1993). Alexia. In K. M. Heilman (Ed.), *Clinical neuropsychology* (3rd ed., pp. 37–62). New York: Oxford University Press.

Gallagher, D. (1986). The Beck Depression Inventory and older adults: A review of its development and utility. *Clinical Gerontologist, 5,* 149–163.

Gallo, J. J., Busby-Whitehead, J., Rabins, P. V., Silliman, R. A., Murphy, J. B., & Reichel, W. (Eds.). (1998). *Reichel's care of the elderly: Clinical aspects of aging* (5th ed.). Philadelphia: Lippincott Williams & Wilkins.

Garcia, L. J., & Orange, J. B. (1996). The analysis of conversational skills of older adults: Current research and clinical approaches. *Journal of Speech Language Pathology and Audiology, 20*(2), 123–135.

Gardner, H. (1974). *The shattered mind.* New York: Random House.

Gardner, H., Silverman, J., Denes, G., Semenza, C., & Rosenstiel, A. (1977). Sensitivity to musical denotation and connotation in organic patients. *Cortex, 13,* 243–256.

Garfein, A. J., & Herzog, A. R. (1995). Robust aging among the young-old, old-old, and oldest-old. *Journal of Gerontology: Social Sciences, 50B,* S77–S87.

Gatz, M., Kasl-Godley, J. E., & Karel, M. J. (1996). Aging and mental disorders. In J. E. Birren & K. W. Schaie (Eds.), *Handbook of the psychology of aging* (4th ed., pp. 365–382). San Diego: Academic Press.

Geller, L. N., & Reichel, W. (1998). Alzheimer's disease: Biologic aspects. In J. J. Gallo, J. Busby-Whitehead, P. V. Rabins, R. A. Silliman, J. B. Murphy, & W. Reichel (Eds.), *Reichel's care of the elderly: Clinical aspects of aging* (5th ed., pp. 229–240). Philadelphia: Lippincott Williams & Wilkins.

Gianustos, R., & Gianustos, J. (1979). Rehabilitating the verbal recall of brain-damaged patients by mnemonic training: An experimental demonstration using single-case methodology. *Journal of Clinical Neuropsychology, 1,* 117–135.

Gibbs, R. W., Jr. (2002). A new look at literal meaning in understanding what is said and implicated. *Journal of Pragmatics, 34*(4), 457–486.

Gillum, R. F. (1999). Stroke mortality in Blacks: Disturbing trends. *Stroke, 30*(8), 1711–1715.

Gilman, S., & Newman, S. W. (2003). *Manter and Gatz's essentials of clinical neuroanatomy and neuropsychology.* Philadelphia: F. A. Davis.

Glosser, G., & Goodglass, H. (1990). Disorders in executive control functions among aphasic and other brain-damaged patients. *Journal of Clinical & Experimental Neuropsychology, 12*(4), 485–501.

Goldman-Rakic, P. S. (1987). Circuitry of primate prefontal cortex and regulation of behavior by representational memory. In F. Plum (Ed.), *Handbook of physiology: The nervous system* (Vol. 5, pp. 373–417). Bethesda, MD: American Physiological Society.

Goldstein, K. (1944). The mental changes due to frontal lobe damage. *Journal of Psychology, 17,* 187–208.

Golinkoff, M., & Sweeney, J. A. (1989). Cognitive impairments in depression. *Journal of Affective Disorders, 17*(2), 105–112.

Gonzalez-Rothi, L. J., & Heilman, K. M. (1997). *Apraxia: The neuropsychology of action.* New York: Taylor & Francis.

Goodglass, H. (1993). *Understanding aphasia.* San Diego: Academic Press.

Goodglass, H., Kaplan, E., & Barresi, B. (2001). *The Boston Diagnostic Aphasia Examination* (3rd ed.). Baltimore: Lippincott Williams & Wilkins.

Goodglass, H., & Wingfield, A. (1997). *Anomia: Neuroanatomical and cognitive correlates.* San Diego: Academic Press.

Gordon-Salant, S., & Fitzgibbons, P. J. (1993). Temporal factors and speech recognition performance in young and elderly listeners. *Journal of Speech & Hearing Research, 36*(6), 1276–1285.

Gorelick, P. B., Rodin, M. B., Langenberg, P., Hier, D. B., & Costigan, J. (1989). Weekly alcohol consumption, cigarette smoking, and the risk of ischemic stroke: Results of a case-control study at three urban medical centers in Chicago, Illinois. *Neurology, 39*(3), 339–343.

Gorelick, P. B., Rodin, M. B., Langenberg, P., Hier, D. B., Costigan, J., Gomez, I., et al. (1987). Is acute alcohol ingestion a risk factor for ischemic stroke? Results of a controlled study in middle-aged and elderly stroke patients at three urban medical centers. *Stroke, 18*(2), 359–364.

Gorham, D. R. (1956). A proverbs test for clinical and experimental use. *Psychological Reports, 2*(Suppl. 1), 1–12.

Gould, S. J. (1985, June). The median isn't the message. *Discover,* pp. 40–42.

Grafman, J., Jonas, B., & Salazar, A. (1990). Wisconsin Card Sorting Test performance based on location and size of neuroanatomical lesion in Vietnam veterans with penetrating head injury. *Perceptual & Motor Skills, 71*(3, Pt. 2), 1120–1122.

Granger, L., & Granger, B. (1986). *The magic feather: The truth about "special education."* New York: E. P. Dutton.

Grant, D. A., & Berg, E. A. (1993). *Wisconsin Card Sorting Test.* Odessa, FL: Psychological Assessment Resources.

Grant, W. B., Campbell, A., Itzhaki, R. F., & Savory, J. (2002). The significance of environmental factors in the etiology of Alzheimer's disease. *Journal of Alzheimer's Disease, 4*(3), 179–189.

Gresham, G. E., Granger, C. V., Linn, R. T., & Kulas, M. A. (1999). Status of functional outcomes for stroke survivors. *Physical Medicine and Rehabilitation Clinics of North America, 10*(4), 957–966.

Gress, D. R., & Singh, V. (1999). Stroke prevention. *Physical Medicine and Rehabilitation Clinics of North America, 10*(4), 827–838.

Grewal, R. P. (1994). Self-recognition in dementia of the Alzheimer type. *Perceptual & Motor Skills, 79*(2), 1009–1010.

Grice, H. P. (1975). Logic and conversation. In P. Cole & J. Morgan (Eds.), *Speech acts, syntax and semantics* (Vol. 3, pp. 41–58). New York: Academic Press.

Grigoletto, F., Zappala, G., Anderson, D. W., & Lebowitz, B. D. (1999). Norms for the Mini-Mental State Examination in a healthy population. *Neurology, 53*(2), 315–320.

Grober, E., & Bang, S. (1995). Sentence comprehension in Alzheimer's disease. *Developmental Neuropsychology, 11,* 95–107.

Grodzinsky, Y. (1991). There is an entity called agrammatic aphasia. *Brain and Language, 41*(4), 555–564.

Grossman, M. (2002). Frontotemporal dementia: A review. *Journal of the International Neuropsychological Society, 8,* 566–583.

Gruetzner, H. (1988). *Alzheimer's: A caregiver's guide and sourcebook.* New York: John Wiley.

Grujic, Z., Mapstone, M., Gitelman, D. R., Johnson, N., Weintraub, S., Hays, A., et al. (1998). Dopamine agonists reorient visual exploration away from the neglected hemispace [see comments]. *Neurology, 51*(5), 1395–1398.

Gurland, B. J. (1976). The comparative frequency of depression in various adult age groups. *Journal of Gerontology, 31*(3), 283–292.

Guttman, M., Burkholder, J., Kish, S. J., Hussey, D., Wilson, A., DaSilva, J., et al. (1997). [11C]RTI-32 PET studies of the dopamine transporter in early dopa-naive Parkinson's disease: Implications for the symptomatic threshold. *Neurology, 48*(6), 1578–1583.

Haaland, K. Y., & Yeo, R. A. (1989). Neuropsychological and neuroanatomic aspects of complex motor control. In E. D. Bigler & R. A. Yeo (Eds.), *Neuropsychological function and brain imaging* (pp. 219–244). New York: Plenum.

Hagberg, J. M. (1987). Effects of training on the decline of VO2max with aging. *Federation Proceedings, 46,* 1830–1833.

Halle, P. A., de Boysson Bardies, B., & Vihman, M. M. (1991). Beginnings of prosodic organization: Intonation and duration patterns of disyllables produced by Japanese and French infants. *Language and Speech, 34*(4), 299–318.

Ham, R. J. (1999). Evolving standards in patient and caregiver support. *Alzheimer Disease and Associated Disorders, 13*(Suppl. 2), S27–S35.

Hamilton, M. (1960). A rating scale for depression. *Journal of Neurology, Neurosurgery and Psychiatry, 23,* 56–62.

Hamsher, K. D., & Roberts, R. J. (1985). Memory for recent U.S. presidents in patients with cerebral disease. *Journal of Clinical & Experimental Neuropsychology, 7*(1), 1–13.

Hanna, G., Schell, L. M., & Schreiner, R. (1977). *Nelson Reading Skills Test.* Itasca, IL: Riverside.

Hanninen, T., Hallikainen, M., Koivisto, K., Partanen, K., Laakso, M. P., Riekkinen, S. P. J., et al. (1997). Decline of frontal lobe functions in subjects with age-associated memory impairment. *Neurology, 48*(1), 148–153.

Hanninen, T., & Koivisto, K. (1996). Prevalence of ageing-associated cognitive decline in an elderly population. *Age & Ageing, 25*(3), 201–205.

Happé, F., Brownell, H. H., & Winner, E. (1999). Acquired "theory of mind" impairments following stroke. *Cognition, 70,* 211–240.

Harlow, J. M. (1848). Passage of an iron rod through the head. *Boston Medical and Surgical Journal, 39,* 389–393.

Harlow, J. M. (1868). Recovery from the passage of an iron bar through the head. *Publication of the Massachusetts Medical Society, 2,* 327–347.

Harper, C., Fornes, P., Duyckaerts, C., Lecomte, D., & Hauw, J. J. (1995). An international perspective on the prevalence of the Wernicke-Korsakoff syndrome. *Metabolic Brain Disease, 10*(1), 17–24.

Harrell, M., Parente, F., Bellingrath, E. G., & Lisicia, K. A. (1992). *Cognitive rehabilitation of memory: A practical guide.* Gaithersburg, MD: Aspen.

Harris, J. L., Rogers, W. A., & Qualls, C. D. (1998). Written language comprehension in younger and older adults. *Journal of Speech, Language, and Hearing Research, 41*(3), 603–617.

Hartley, A. A. (1992). Attention. In F. I. M. Craik & T. A. Salthouse (Eds.), *Handbook of aging and cognition* (pp. 3–49). Hillsdale, NJ: Lawrence Erlbaum.

Hartley, J. T., Stojack, C. C., Mushaney, T. J., & Kiku Annon, T. A. (1994). Reading speed and prose memory in older and younger adults. *Psychology and Aging, 9*(2), 216–223.

Hartman, M., Bolton, E., & Fehnel, S. E. (2001). Accounting for age differences on the Wisconsin Card Sorting Test: Decreased working memory, not inflexibility. *Psychology and Aging, 16*(3), 385–399.

Harvey, S. A., & Black, K. J. (1996). The dexamethasone supression test for diagnosing depression in stroke patients. *Annals of Clinical Psychiatry, 8*(1), 35–39.

Hasey, G. (2001). Transcranial magnetic stimulation in the treatment of mood disorder: A review and comparison with electroconvulsive therapy. *Canadian Journal of Psychiatry, 46,* 720–727.

Hasher, L., & Zacks, R. T. (1988). Working memory, comprehension, and aging: A review and a new view. In G. H. Bower (Ed.), *The psychology of learning and motivation: Advances in research and theory* (pp. 193–225). San Diego: Academic Press.

Hausmann, M., Waldie, K. E., & Corballis, M. C. (2003). Developmental changes in line bisection: A result of callosal maturation? *Neuropsychology, 17*(1), 155–160.

Hebb, D. O. (1949). *The organization of behavior: A neuropsychological theory.* New York: John Wiley.

Hebert, L. E., Scherr, P. A., Bienias, J. L., Bennett, D. A., & Evans, D. A. (2003). Alzheimer disease in the US population: Prevalence estimates using the 2000 census. *Archives of Neurology, 60*(8), 1119–1122.

Heilman, K. M., & Gonzalez-Rothi, L. J. (1993). Apraxia. In K. M. Heilman & E. Valenstein (Eds.), *Clinical neuropsychology* (3rd ed., pp. 215–235). Oxford, UK: Oxford University Press.

Heilman, K. M., & Van Den Abell, T. (1980). Right hemisphere dominance for attention: The mechanisms underlying hemispheric asymmetries of inattention (neglect). *Neurology, 30,* 327–330.

Heilman, K. M., Watson, R. T., & Valenstein, E. (1993). Neglect and related disorders. In K. M. Heilman & E. Valenstein (Eds.), *Clinical neuropsychology* (3rd ed., pp. 279–336). New York: Oxford University Press.

Heindel, W. C., Salmon, D. P., & Butters, N. (1991). The biasing of weight judgments in Alzheimer's and Huntington's disease: A priming or programming phenomenon. *Journal of Clinical & Experimental Neuropsychology, 13,* 189–203.

Helm-Estabrooks, N. (1997). Treatment of aphasic naming problems. In H. Goodglass & A. Wingfield (Eds.), *Anomia: Neuroanatomical and cognitive correlates* (pp. 189–202). San Diego: Academic Press.

Helm-Estabrooks, N., & Albert, M. (2004). *Manual of aphasia therapy.* Austin, TX: Pro-Ed.

Henderson, V. W., Mack, W., & Williams, B. W. (1989). Spatial disorientation in Alzheimer's disease. *Archives of Neurology, 46,* 391–394.

Hershey, L. A., Modic, L. T., Jaffe, D. F., & Greenough, P. G. (1986). Natural history of the vascular dementias: A prospective study of seven cases. *Canadian Journal of Neurological Sciences, 13*(Suppl. 4), 559–563.

Hilts, P. J. (1996). *Memory's ghost: The nature of memory and the strange tale of* Mr. M. Carmichael, CA: Touchstone.

Hoehn, H. M., & Yahr, M. D. (1967). Parkinsonism: Onset, progression and mortality. *Neurology, 17,* 427–442.

Hofer, S. M., & Sliwinski, M. S. (2001). Understanding ageing. *Gerontology, 47*(6), 341–352.

Hohl, C. M. (2001). Polypharmacy, adverse drug-related events, and potential adverse drug interactions in elderly patients presenting to an emergency department. *Annals of Emergency Medicine, 38*(6), 666–671.

Holland, A. (1989). Recovery in aphasia. In F. Boller & J. Graffman (Eds.), *Handbook of neuropsychology* (2nd ed., pp. 83–90). Amsterdam: Elsevier Science.

Holland, A., & Beeson, P. (1995). Aphasia therapy. In H. S. Kirshner (Ed.), *Handbook of neurological speech and language disorders* (pp. 445–464). New York: Marcel Dekker.

Holland, A., Frattali, C., & Fromm, D. (1999). *Communication activities of daily living.* Austin, TX: PRO-ED.

Hollander, M., Koudstaal, P. J., Bots, M. L., Grobbee, D. E., Hofman, A., & Breteler, M. M. (2003). Incidence, risk, and case fatality of first ever stroke in the elderly population: The Rotterdam Study. *Journal of Neurology, Neurosurgery, & Psychiatry, 74*(3), 317–321.

Holloszy, J. O., Schultz, J., Kusnierkiewicz, J., Hagberg, J. M., & Ehsani, A. A. (1986). Effects of exercise in glucose tolerance and insulin resistance. *Acta Medica Scandinavia, 711*(Suppl.), 55–65.

Honig, L. S., & Rosenberg, R. N. (2000). Apoptosis and neurologic disease. *American Journal of Medicine, 108*(4), 317–330.

Hooper, H. E. (1983). *The Hooper Visual Organization Test manual.* Los Angeles: Western Psychological Services.

Hope, T., Keene, J., McShane, R. H., Fairburn, C. G., Gedling, K., & Jacoby, R. (2001). Wandering in dementia: A longitudinal study. *International Psychogeriatrics, 13*(2), 137–147.

Horn, J. L. (1982). The theory of fluid and crystallized intelligence in relation to concepts of cognitive psychology and aging in adulthood. In F. I. M. Craik & S. Trehub (Eds.), *Aging and cognitive processes* (pp. 237–278). New York: Plenum.

Horn, J. L., & Cattell, R. (1967). Age differences in fluid and crystallized intelligence. *Acta Psychologica, 26,* 107–129.

Hornak, J. (1992). Ocular exploration in the dark by patients with visual neglect. *Neuropsychologia, 30*(6), 547–552.

Hough, M. S. (1990). Narrative comprehension in adults with right and left hemisphere brain-damage: Theme organization. *Brain and Language, 38*(2), 253–277.

House, A., Rowe, D., & Standen, P. J. (1987). Affective prosody in the reading voice of stroke patients. *Journal of Neurology, Neurosurgery and Psychiatry, 50*(7), 910–912.

Howard, G. (1999). Why do we have a stroke belt in the southeastern United States? A review of unlikely and uninvestigated potential causes. *American Journal of Medical Science, 317*(3), 160–167.

Howieson, D. B., Camicioli, R., Quinn, J., Silbert, L. C., Care, B., Moore, M. M., et al. (2003). Natural history of cognitive decline in the old old. *Neurology, 60*(1), 1489–1494.

Hoyert, D. L., & Rosenberg, H. M. (1997). Alzheimer's disease as a cause of death in the United States. *Public Health Reports, 112*(6), 497–505.

Huber, W., Willmes, K., Poeck, K., Van Vleymen, B., & Deberdt, W. (1997). Piracetam as an adjuvant to language therapy for aphasia: A randomized double-blind placebo-controlled pilot study. *Archives of Physical Medicine and Rehabilitation, 78*(3), 245–250.

Hubert, H. B., Bloch, D. A., & Fries, J. F. (1993). Risk factors for physical disability in an aging cohort: The NHANES I Epidemiologic Follow-Up Study. *Journal of Rheumatology, 20,* 480–488.

Hulicka, I. M., & Grossman, J. L. (1967). Age-group comparisons for the use of mediators in paired associate learning. *Journal of Gerontology, 22,* 46–51.

Humphreys, G. W., & Riddoch, M. J. (1987). *To see but not to see: A case study of visual agnosia.* London: Lawrence Erlbaum.

Huppert, F. A., Brayne, C., & O'Connor, D. W. (Eds.). (1994). *Dementia and normal aging.* New York: Cambridge University Press.

Inouye, S. K., & Charpentier, P. A. (1996). Precipitating factors for delirium in hospitalized elderly persons: Predictive model and interrelationship with baseline vulnerability. *Journal of the American Medical Association, 275*(11), 852–857.

Inouye, S. K., van Dyck, C. H., Alessi, C. A., Balkin, S., Siegal, A. P., & Horwitz, R. I. (1990). Clarifying confusion: The Confusion Assessment Method. *Annals of Internal Medicine, 113*(12), 941–948.

Ishihara, S. (1979). *Tests for blindness.* Tokyo: Kanehara Shuppan.

Iverson, G. L. (1995). Qualitative aspects of malingered memory deficits. *Brain Injury, 9*(1), 35–40.

Iyer, M. B., Mitz, A. R., & Winstein, C. (1999). Motor 1: Lower centers. In H. Cohen (Ed.), *Neuroscience for rehabilitation* (2nd ed., pp. 209–242). Philadelphia: Lippincott Williams & Wilkins.

Jackson, J. H. (1897). On affectation of speech from disease of the brain. In P. Eling (Ed.), *Reader in the history of aphasia* (pp. 145–167). Amsterdam: John Benjamins.

Jackson, J. H. (1915). On the nature of the duality of the brain. *Brain, 38,* 80–86.

Jacobson, S. A. (1997). Delirium in the elderly. *Psychiatric Clinics of North America, 20*(1), 91–110.

Jain, K. K. (2000). *Drug-induced neurological disorders.* Seattle: Hogrefe & Hubert.

James, L. E., Burke, D. M., Austin, A., & Hulme, E. (1998). Production and perception of "verbosity" in younger and older adults. *Psychology and Aging, 13*(3), 355–367.

Janowsky, J. S., Shimamura, A. P., Kritchevsky, M., & Squire, L. R. (1989). Cognitive impairment following frontal lobe damage and its relevance to human amnesia. *Behavioral Neuroscience, 103,* 548–560.

Jellinger, K. A., Paulus, W., Wrocklage, C., & Litvan, I. (2001). Effects of closed traumatic brain injury and genetic factors on the development of Alzheimer's disease. *European Journal of Neurology, 8*(6), 707–711.

Jenkins, J. J., Jimenez-Pabon, E., Shaw, R. E., & Sefer, J. W. (1975). *Schuell's aphasia in adults: Diagnosis, prognosis and treatment.* New York: Harper & Row.

Joanette, Y. (1989). Aphasia in left-handers and crossed aphasia. In H. Goodglass (Ed.), *Language, aphasia and related disorders* (Vol. 2, pp. 173–183). Amsterdam: Elsevier.

Joanette, Y., Goulet, P., Ska, B., & Nespoulous, J. L. (1986). Informative content of narrative discourse in right-brain-damaged right-handers. *Brain and Language, 29*(1), 81–105.

Jonsson, B., Ringsberg, K., Josefsson, P. O., Johnell, O., & Birch-Jensen, M. (1992). Effects of physical activity on bone mineral content and muscle strength in women: A cross-sectional study. *Bone, 13,* 191–195.

Jorgensen, H. S., Kammersgaard, L. P., Nakayama, H., Raaschou, H. O., Larsen, K., Hubbe, P., et al. (1999). Treatment and rehabilitation on a stroke unit improves 5-year survival: A community-based study. *Stroke, 30*(5), 930–933.

Jorgensen, H. S., Nakayama, H., Raaschou, H. O., & Olsen, T. S. (1999). Stroke: Neurologic and functional recovery. The Copenhagen Stroke Study. *Physical Medicine and Rehabilitation Clinics of North America, 10,* 887–906.

Jorm, A. F. (1997). Alzheimer's disease: Risk and protection. *Medical Journal of Australia, 167,* 443–447.

Jost, B. C., & Grossberg, G. T. (1996). The evolution of psychiatric symptoms in Alzheimer's disease: A natural history study. *Journal of the American Geriatrics Society, 44,* 1078–1081.

Kammoun, S., Gold, G., Bouras, C., Giannakopoulos, P., McGee, W., Herrmann, F., et al. (2000). Immediate causes of death of demented and non-demented elderly. *Acta Neurologica Scandinavica, 176,* 96–99.

Kannel, W. B. (1996). Blood pressure as a cardiovascular risk factor: Prevention and treatment. *Journal of the American Medical Association, 275,* 1571–1576.

Kaplan, E., Goodglass, H., & Weintraub, S. (1983). *Boston Naming Test.* Philadelphia: Lippincott Williams & Wilkins.

Kaplan, J. A., & Gardner, H. (1989). Artistry after unilateral brain disease. In H. Goodglass (Ed.), *Language, aphasia and related disorders* (Vol. 2, pp. 141–156). Amsterdam: Elsevier.

Kashima, H., Tanemura, J., & Hasegawa, T. (2001). Unidimensional scale for dementia. *Dementia & Geriatric Cognitive Disorders, 12*(5), 326–339.

Kauranen, K., & Vanharanta, H. (1996). Influences of aging, gender, and handedness on motor performance of upper and lower extremities. *Perceptual & Motor Skills, 82*(2), 515–525.

Kawachi, I., Colditz, G. A., Stampfer, M. J., Willett, W. C., Manson, J. E., Rosner, B., et al. (1993). Smoking cessation and decreased risk of stroke in women [see comments]. *Journal of the American Medical Association, 269*(2), 232–236.

Kawas, C., Gray, S., Brookmeyer, R., Fozard, J., & Zonderman, A. (2000). Age-specific incidence rates of Alzheimer's disease: The Baltimore Longitudinal Study of Aging. *Neurology, 54*(11), 2072–2077.

Kaye, J. A., Oken, B. S., Howieson, D. B., & Howieson, J. (1994). Neurologic evaluation of the optimally healthy oldest old. *Archives of Neurology, 51*(12), 1205–1211.

Kean, M. L. (1995). The elusive character of agrammatism. *Brain and Language, 50*(3), 369–384.

Kemper, S. (1987). Syntactic complexity and elderly adults' prose recall. *Experimental Aging Research, 13*(1–2), 47–52.

Kemper, S. (1990). Adults' diaries: Changes made to written narratives across the life span. *Discourse Processes, 13*(2), 207–223.

Kemper, S. (1992). Language and aging. In F. I. M. Craik (Ed.), *The handbook of aging and cognition* (pp. 213–270). Hillsdale, NJ: Lawrence Erlbaum.

Kemper, S. (1994). Elderspeak: Speech accommodations to older adults. *Aging, Neuropsychology, and Cognition, 1*(1), 17–28.

Kemper, S., Greiner, L. H., Marquis, J. G., Prenovost, K., & Mitzner, T. L. (2001). Language decline across the life span: Findings from the Nun Study. *Psychology & Aging, 16*(2), 227–239.

Kemper, S., Herman, R., & Lian, C. H. T. (2003). The costs of doing two things at once for young and older adults: Talking while walking, finger tapping, and ignoring speech or noise. *Psychology & Aging, 18*(2), 181–192.

Kemper, S., Othick, M., Warren, J., & Gubarchuk, J. (1996). Facilitating older adults' performance on a referential communication task through speech accommodations. *Aging, Neuropsychology, and Cognition, 3*(1), 37–55.

Kemper, S., Rash, S., Kynette, D., & Norman, S. (1990). Telling stories: The structure of adults' narratives. *European Journal of Cognitive Psychology, 2*(3), 205–228.

Kempler, D. (1988). Lexical and pantomime abilities in Alzheimer's disease. *Aphasiology, 2*(2), 147–159.

Kempler, D. (1993). Disorders of language and tool use: Neurological and cognitive links. In K. R. Gibson & T. Ingold (Eds.), *Tools, language and cognition in human evolution* (pp. 193–215). Cambridge, UK: Cambridge University Press.

Kempler, D. (1995). Language changes in dementia of the Alzheimer type. In R. Lubinski (Ed.), *Dementia and communication* (pp. 98–114). San Diego: Singular.

Kempler, D., Almor, A., Tyler, L. K., Andersen, E. S., & MacDonald, M. C. (1998). Sentence comprehension deficits in Alzheimer's disease: A comparison of off-line vs. on-line sentence processing. *Brain and Language, 64*(3), 297–316.

Kempler, D., Metter, E. J., Jackson, C. A., Hanson, W. R., Riege, W. H., Mazziotta, J. C., et al. (1988). Disconnection and cerebral metabolism: The case of conduction aphasia. *Archives of Neurology, 45,* 275–279.

Kempler, D., Teng, E. L., Dick, M., Taussig, I. M., & Davis, D. S. (1998). The effects of age, education, and ethnicity on verbal fluency. *Journal of the International Neuropsychological Society, 4*(6), 531–538.

Kempler, D., Van Lancker, D., Marchman, V., & Bates, E. (1999). Idiom comprehension in children and adults with unilateral brain damage. *Developmental Neuropsychology, 15*(3), 327–350.

Kempler, D., Van Lancker, D., & Read, S. (1988). Proverb and idiom comprehension in Alzheimer disease. *Alzheimer Disease and Associated Disorders, 2*(1), 38–49.

Kempler, D., & Van Lancker Sidtis, D. (1996). *Familiar and Novel Language Comprehension Test.* Unpublished manuscript.

Kempler, D., & Zelinski, E. M. (1994). Language function in dementia and normal aging. In F. A. Hupper, C. Brayne, & D. W. O'Connor (Eds.), *Dementia and normal aging* (pp. 331–365). Cambridge, UK: Cambridge University Press.

Kemtes, K. A., & Kemper, S. (1997). Younger and older adults' on-line processing of syntactically ambiguous sentences. *Psychology and Aging, 12*(2), 362–371.

Kennedy, S. H., Lam, R. W., Cohen, N. L., Ravindran, A. V., & The Canadian Depression Workgroup (2001). Medications and other biological treatments. *Canadian Journal of Psychiatry, 46*(5), 38S–58S.

Kertesz, A. (1979). *Aphasia and associated disorders.* New York: Grune & Stratton.

Kertesz, A. (1982). *Western Aphasia Battery.* New York: Grune & Stratton.

Kertesz, A., Davidson, W., McCabe, P., Takagi, K., & Munoz, D. (2003). Primary progressive aphasia: Diagnosis, varieties, evolution. *Journal of the International Neuropsychological Society, 9*(5), 710–719.

Kertesz, A., Harlock, W., & Coates, R. (1979). Computer tomographic localization, lesion size, and prognosis in aphasia and nonverbal impairment. *Brain and Language, 8*(1), 34–50.

Kimura, D., & Archibald, Y. (1974). Motor functions of the left hemisphere. *Brain, 97*(2), 337–350.

Kirshner, H. S. (1995a). Alexias. In H. S. Kirshner (Ed.), *Handbook of neurological speech and language disorders* (pp. 277–293). New York: Marcel Dekker.

Kirshner, H. S. (Ed.). (1995b). *Handbook of neurological speech and language disorders.* New York: Marcel Dekker.

Kivipelto, M., Helkala, E. L., Laasho, M. P., Hänninen, T., Hallikainen, N., & Alhainen, K. (2002). Apolipoprotein E epsilon4 allele, elevated midlife total cholesterol level, and high midlife systolic blood pressure are independent risk factors for late-life Alzheimer disease. *Annals of Internal Medicine, 137*(3), 149–155.

Kjelgaard, M. M., Titone, D. A., & Wingfield, A. (1999). The influence of prosodic structure on the interpretation of temporary syntactic ambiguity by young and elderly listeners. *Experimental Aging Research, 25*(3), 187–207.

Klein, R., & Harper, J. (1956). The problem of agnosia in the light of a case of pure word deafness. *Journal of Mental Science, 102,* 112–120.

Klerman, G. L., Lavori, P. W., Rice, J., Reich, T., Endicott, J., Andreasen, N. C., et al. (1985). Birth-cohort trends in rates of major depressive disorder among relatives of patients with affective disorder. *Archives of General Psychiatry, 42*(7), 689–693.

Klerman, G. L., & Weissman, M. M. (1994). Increasing rates of depression. *Journal of the American Medical Association, 261*(15), 2229–2235.

Koivisto, K., Reinikainen, K. J., Haenninen, M., Helkala, E.-L., Mykkaenen, L., Laasko, M., et al. (1995). Prevalence of age-associated memory impairment in a randomly selected population from eastern Finland, *Neurology, 45,* 741–747.

Kolb, B., & Whishaw, I. Q. (1990). *Fundamentals of human neuropsychology.* New York: Freeman.

Kolb, B., & Whishaw, I. Q. (2003). *Fundamentals of human neuropsychology* (5th ed.). New York: Worth.

Koller, W. C., & Busenbark, K. L. (1997). Essential tremor. In R. L. Watts & W. C. Koller (Eds.), *Movement disorders: Neurologic principles and practice* (pp. 365–385). New York: McGraw-Hill.

Kopelman, M. D., Wilson, B. A., & Baddeley, A. D. (1989). The autobiographical memory interview: A new assessment of autobiographical and personal semantic memory in amnesic patients. *Journal of Clinical and Experimental Neuropsychology, 11,* 724–744.

Kral, V. A., & Emery, O. B. (1989). Long term follow up of depressive pseudodementia of the aged. *Canadian Journal of Psychiatry, 34,* 445–446.

Kreisler, A., Godefroy, O., Delmaire, C., Debachy, B., Leclercq, M., Pruvo, J. P., et al. (2000). The anatomy of aphasia revisited. *Neurology, 54*(5), 1117–1123.

Kukull, W. A., Higdon, R., Bowen, J. D., McCormick, W. C., Teri, L., Schellenberg, G. D., et al. (2002). Dementia and Alzheimer disease incidence. *Archives of Neurology, 59,* 1737–1746.

Kuzis, G., Sabe, L., Tiberti, C., Merello, M., Leiguarda, R., & Starkstein, S. E. (1999). Explicit and implicit learning in patients with Alzheimer disease and Parkinson disease with dementia. *Neuropsychiatry, Neuropsychology, and Behavioral Neurology, 12*(4), 265–269.

Kwong See, S. T., & Ryan, E. B. (1996). Cognitive mediation of discourse processing in later life. *Journal of Speech Language Pathology and Audiology, 20*(2), 109–117.

Kynette, D., & Kemper, S. (1986). Aging and the loss of grammatical forms: A cross-sectional study of language performance. *Language and Communication, 6*(1–2), 65–72.

La Rue, A. (1992). *Aging and neuropsychological assessment.* New York: Plenum.

Laasko, M. P., Partanen, K., Soininen, H., Lehtovirta, M., Hallikainen, M., Hanninen, T., et al. (1996). MR T2 relaxometry in Alzheimer's disease and age-associated memory impairment. *Neurobiology of Aging, 17*(4), 535–540.

Labouvie-Vief, G., & Hakim Larson, J. (1989). Developmental shifts in adult thought. In S. Hunter (Ed.), *Midlife myths: Issues, findings, and practice implications* (pp. 69–96). Newbury Park, CA: Sage.

Labouvie-Vief, G., & Lawrence, R. (1985). Object knowledge, personal knowledge, and processes of equilibration in adult cognition. *Human Development, 28*(1), 25–39.

LaCroix, A. Z., Guralnik, J. M., Berkman, L. F., Wallace, R. B., & Satterfield, S. (1993). Maintaining mobility in late life II: Smoking, alcohol consumption, physical activity, and body mass index. *American Journal of Epidemiology, 137,* 858–869.

Landrum, R. E., & Radtke, R. C. (1990). Degree of cognitive impairment and the dissociation of implicit and explicit memory. *Journal of General Psychology, 117,* 187–196.

Lane, V. W., & Samples, J. M. (1981). Facilitating communication skills in adult apraxics: Application of Bliss symbols in a group setting. *Journal of Communication Disorders, 14,* 157–167.

Lange, K. L., Bondi, M. W., Salmon, D. P., Galasko, D., Delis, D. C., Thomas, R. G., et al. (2002). Decline in verbal memory during preclinical Alzheimer's disease: Examination of the effect of APOE genotype. *Journal of the International Neuropsychological Society, 8*(7), 943–955.

Langmore, S. E., & Canter, G. J. (1983). Written spelling deficit of Broca's aphasics. *Brain and Language, 18*(2), 293–314.

Langston, J. W. (1984). Parkinsonism induced by 1-methyl-4-phenyl-1,2,3,6-tetrahydropyridine (MPTP): Implications for treatment and the pathogenesis of Parkinson's disease. *Canadian Journal of Neurological Science, 11*(1, Suppl.), 160–165.

LaPointe, L., & Horner, J. (1998). *Reading comprehension battery for aphasia* (2nd ed.). Austin, TX: PRO-ED.

Larsen, P. D., & Martin, J. L. (1999). Polypharmacy and elderly patients. *AORN Journal, 69*(3), 619–622, 625, 627–628.

Lashley, K. S. (1950). In search of the engram. *Symposia of the Society for Experimental Biology, 4,* 454–482.

Launer, L. J. (2003). Nonsteroidal anti-inflammatory drug use and the risk for Alzheimer's disease: Dissecting the epidemiological evidence. *Drugs, 63*(8), 731–739.

Lawlor, B. A., & Ryan, T. M. (1994). Clinical symptoms associated with age at onset in Alzheimer's disease. *American Journal of Psychiatry, 151*(11), 1646–1649.

Lecours, A. R., & Joanette, Y. (1984). Francois Moutier or "From folds to folds." *Brain and Cognition, 3,* 198–230.

Leech, R. W. (2001). Dementia: The University of Oklahoma autopsy experience. *Journal of the Oklahoma State Medical Association, 94*(11), 507–511.

Leibovici, D., Ritchie, K., Ledesert, B., & Touchon, J. (1996). Does education level determine the course of cognitive decline? *Age and Ageing, 25,* 392–397.

Levelt, W. J. M. (1989). *Speaking: From intention to articulation.* Cambridge: MIT Press.

Levine, D. N. (1978). Prosopagnosia and visual object agnosia: A behavioral study. *Brain and Language, 5,* 431–465.

Levy, M. L., Cummings, J. L., Fairbanks, L. A., Bravi, D., Calvani, M., & Corta, A. (1996). Longitudinal assessment of symptoms of depression, agitation, and psychosis in 181 patients with Alzheimer's disease. *American Journal of Psychiatry, 153*(11), 1438–1443.

Lewis, R., Kelland, D. Z., & Kupke, T. (1990). A normative study of the Repeatable Cognitive-Perceptual Motor Battery. *Archives of Clinical Neuropsychology, 5,* 201.

Lezak, M. D. (1995). *Neuropsychological assessment* (3rd ed.). New York: Oxford University Press.

Li, Y., McColgin, C., & Van Oteghen, S. L. (1998). Comparison of psychomotor performance between the upper and lower extremities in three age groups. *Perceptual & Motor Skills, 87*(3, Pt. 1), 947–952.

Lichtheim, L. (1885). On aphasia. *Brain, 7,* 433–484.

Liepmann, H. (1920). Apraxie (Apraxia). In H. Brugsch (Ed.), *Ergebnisse der gesamten Medizin* (Results of general medicine) (pp. 516–543). Berlin: Urban & Schwarzenberg.

Light, L. L., & Capps, J. L. (1986). Comprehension of pronouns in young and older adults. *Developmental Psychology, 22*(4), 580–585.

Lim, A., Tsuang, D., Kukull, W., Nochlin, D,, Leverenz, J. B., McCormick, W., et al. (1999). Clinico-neuropathological correlation of Alzheimer's disease in a community-based case series. *Journal of the American Geriatrics Society, 47*(5), 564–569.

Lipowski, Z. J. (1990). *Delirium: Acute confusional states.* New York: Oxford University Press.

Lissauer, H. (1890). Ein Fall von Seelenblindheit nebst einem Beitrage zur Theorie derselben (A case of cortical blindness and implications to the theory itself). *Archives of Psychiatry, 21,* 222–270.

Logsdon, R. G., Teri, L., Weiner, M. F., Gibbons, L. E., Raskind, M., Peskind, E., et al. (1999). Assessment of agitation in Alzheimer's disease: The Agitated Behavior in Dementia Scale. Alzheimer's Disease Cooperative Study. *Journal of the American Geriatrics Society, 47*(11), 1354–1358.

Looi, J. C. L., & Sachdev, P. S. (1999). Differentiation of vascular dementia from AD on neuropsychological tests. *Neurology, 53,* 670–678.

Lorayne, H., & Lucas, J. (1974). *The memory book.* New York: Stein and Day.

Lott, S. N., & Friedman, R. B. (1999). Can treatment for pure alexia improve letter-by-letter reading speed without sacrificing accuracy? *Brain and Language, 67*(3), 188–201.

Louis, E. D., Marder, K., Cote, L., Wilder, D., Tang, M. X., Lantigua, R., et al. (1996). Prevalence of a history of shaking in persons 65 years of age and older: Diagnostic and functional correlates. *Movement Disorders: Official Journal of the Movement Disorder Society, 11*(1), 63–69.

Luria, A. R. (1966). *Higher cortical functions in man.* New York: Basic Books.

Luria, A. R. (1969). Frontal lobe syndromes. In P. J. Vinkin & G. W. Bruyn (Eds.), *Handbook of clinical neurology* (Vol. 2, pp. 725–757). Amsterdam: North-Holland.

Lyketsos, C. G., Treisman, G. J., Lipsey, J. R., Morris, P. L., & Robinson, R. G. (1998). Does stroke cause depression? *Journal of Neuropsychiatry and Clinical Neurosciences, 10*(1), 103–107.

Lynch, W. J. (1993). Update on a computer-based language prosthesis for aphasia therapy. *Journal of Head Trauma Rehabilitation, 8*(3), 107–109.

Lyons, K. E., Koller, W. C., Wilkinson, S. B., & Pahwa, R. (2001). Long term safety and efficacy of unilateral deep brain stimulation of the thalamus for parkinsonian tremor. *Journal of Neurology, Neurosurgery & Psychiatry, 71*(5), 682.

MacDonald, M. C., Almor, A., Henderson, V. W., Kempler, D., & Andersen, E. S. (2001). Assessing working memory and language comprehension in Alzheimer's disease. *Brain and Language, 78*(1), 17–42.

Mace, C. J., & Trimble, M. R. (1991). Psychosis following temporal lobe surgery: A report of six cases. *Journal of Neurology, Neurosurgery & Psychiatry, 54*(7), 639–644.

MacGinitie, W. H. (1978). *Gates-MacGinitie Reading Tests* (2nd ed.). Boston: Houghton Mifflin.

Macmillan, M. (1996). Phineas Gage: A case for all reasons. In C. Code (Ed.), *Classic cases in neuropsychology* (pp. 243–262). Hove, UK: Taylor & Francis.

MacPherson, S. E., Phillips, L. H., & Della Sala, S. (2002). Age, executive function, and social decision making: A dorsolateral prefrontal theory of cognitive aging. *Psychology & Aging, 17*(4), 598–609.

Maddox, G. L., & Clark, D. O. (1992). Trajectories of functional impairment in later life. *Journal of Health and Social Behavior, 33,* 114–125.

Manyam, B. V. (1997). Practical guidelines for management of Parkinson disease. *Journal of the American Board of Family Practitioners, 10,* 412.

Marie, P. (1906). The third left frontal convolution plays no special role in the function of language. In P. Eling (Ed.), *Reader in the history of aphasia* (pp. 231–241). Amsterdam: John Benjamins.

Marshall, R. C., Wertz, R. T., Weiss, D. G., Aten, J. L., Brookshire, R. H., Garcia-Bunuel, L., et al. (1989). Home treatment for aphasic patients by trained nonprofessionals. *Journal of Speech and Hearing Disorders, 54*(3), 462–470.

Marsiske, M., & Willis, S. L. (1998). Practical creativity in older adults' everyday problem solving: Life span perspectives. In C. Adams-Price (Ed.), *Creativity and successful aging* (pp. 73–113). New York: Springer.

Martin, A., Ungerleider, L. G., & Haxby, J. V. (2000). Category specificity and the brain: The sensory/motor model of semantic representation of objects. In M. S. Gazzaniga (Ed.), *The new cognitive neurosciences* (pp. 1023–1036). Cambridge: MIT Press.

Martin, F. N., Champlin, C. A., & McCreery, T. M. (2001). Strategies used in feigning hearing loss. *Journal of the American Academy of Audiology, 12*(2), 59–63.

Masterman, D. L., & Cummings, J. L. (1997). Frontal-subcortical circuits: The anatomic basis of executive, social and motivated behaviors. *Journal of Psychopharmacology, 11*(2), 107–114.

Mateer, C., & Kimura, D. (1977). Impairment of nonverbal oral movements in aphasia. *Brain and Language, 4*(2), 262–276.

Mayberg, H. S., Starkstein, S. E., Sadzot, B., Preziosi, T., Andrezejewski, P. L., Dannals, R. F., et al. (1990). Selective hypometabolism in the inferior frontal lobe in depressed patients with Parkinson's disease. *Annals of Neurology, 28*(1), 57–64.

Mayeux, R., Denaro, J., Hemenegildo, N., Marder, K., Tang, M. X., Cote, L. J., et al. (1992). A population-based investigation of Parkinson's disease with and without dementia: Relationship to age and gender. *Archives of Neurology, 49*(5), 492–497.

Mayeux, R., Ottman, R., Maestre, G., Ngai, C., Tang, M. X., Ginsberg, H., et al. (1995). Synergistic effects of traumatic brain injury and apolipoprotein-epsilon4 in patients with Alzheimer's disease. *Neurology, 142,* 1300–1305.

Mayeux, R., Williams, J. B., Stern, Y., & Cote, L. (1984). Depression and Parkinson's disease. *Advances in Neurology, 40,* 241–250.

Mazzocchi, F., & Vignolo, L. A. (1979). Localization of lesions in aphasia: Clinical-CT scan correlations in stroke patients. *Cortex, 15,* 627–654.

McCarthy, R. A., & Warrington, E. K. (1990). *Cognitive neuropsychology: A clinical introduction.* San Diego: Academic Press.

McCurry, S. M., Logsdon, R. G., Teri, L., Gibbons, L. E., Kukull, W., Bowen, J., et al. (1999). Characteristics of sleep disturbance in community-dwelling Alzheimer's disease patients. *Journal of Geriatric Psychiatry and Neurology, 12*(2), 53–59.

McDowd, J. M., & Shaw, R. J. (2000). Attention and aging: A functional perspective. In F. I. M. Craik & T. A. Salthouse (Eds.), *The handbook of aging and cognition* (pp. 221–292). Mahwah, NJ: Lawrence Erlbaum.

McFie, J., & Zangwill, O. L. (1960). Visual construction disabilities associated with lesions of the left cerebral hemisphere. *Brain, 83,* 243–260.

McKeith, I. G., Galasko, D., Viosaka, K., Perry, E. K., Dickson, D. W., Hansen, L. A., et al. (1996). Consensus guidelines for the clinical and pathologic diagnosis of dementia with Lewy bodies (DLB): Report of the consortium on DLB international workshop. *Neurology, 47,* 1113–1124.

McKelvey, R., Bergman, H., Stern, J., Rush, C., Zahirney, G., & Chertkow, H. (1999). Lack of prognostic significance of SPECT abnormalities in non-demented elderly subjects with memory loss. *Canadian Journal of Neurological Sciences, 26*(1), 23–28.

McKhann, G., Drachman, D. A., Folstein, M., Katzman, R., Price, D., & Stadlan, E. M. (1984). Clinical diagnosis of Alzheimer's disease: Report of the NINCDS-ADRDA Work Group under the auspices of the Department of Health and Human Services Task Force on Alzheimer's disease. *Neurology, 34,* 939–944.

McKhann, G. M., & Albert, M. (2002). *Keep your brain young: The complete guide to physical and emotional health and longevity.* New York: John Wiley.

McPherson, A., Furniss, F. G., & Sdogati, C. (2001). Effects of individualized memory aids on the conversation of persons with severe dementia: A pilot study. *Aging & Mental Health, 5*(3), 289–294.

Meiran, N., & Jelicic, M. (1995). Implicit memory in Alzheimer's disease: A meta-analysis. *Neuropsychology, 9*(3), 291–303.

Mendez, M. F., Mastri, A. R., & Sung, J. H. (1992). Clinically diagnosed Alzheimer disease: Neuropathologic findings in 650 cases. *Alzheimer Disease & Associated Disorders, 6*(1), 35–43.

Mendez, M. F., Turner, J., Gilmore, G. C., Remler, B., & Tomsak, R. L. (1990). Balint's syndrome in Alzheimer's disease: Visuospatial functions. *International Journal of Neuroscience, 54*(3–4), 339–346.

Mergler, N. L., Faust, M., & Goldstein, M. D. (1984). Storytelling as an age-dependent skill: Oral recall of orally presented stories. *International Journal of Aging and Human Development, 20*(3), 205–228.

Merzenich, M. M., Nelson, R. J., Stryker, M. P., Cynader, M. S., Schoppmann, A., & Zook, J. M. (1984). Somatosensory cortical map changes following digit amputation in adult monkeys. *Journal of Comparative Neurology, 224*(4), 591–605.

Mesulam, M. (1985). Attentional, confusional states, and neglect. In M.-M. Mesulam (Ed.), *Principles of behavioral neurology* (pp. 125–168). Philadelphia: F. A. Davis.

Mesulam, M.-M. (2000a). Attentional networks, confusional states and neglect syndromes. In M.-M. Mesulam (Ed.), *Principles of behavioral and cognitive neurology* (2nd ed., pp. 174–256). Oxford, UK: Oxford University Press.

Mesulam, M.-M. (2000b). Behavioral neuroanatomy. In M.-M. Mesulam (Ed.), *Principles of behavioral and cognitive neurology* (2nd ed., pp. 1–120). Oxford, UK: Oxford University Press.

Metter, E. J., Kempler, D., Jackson, C., Hanson, W. R., Mazziotta, J. C., & Phelps, M. E. (1989). Cerebral glucose metabolism in Wernicke's, Broca's, and conduction aphasia. *Archives of Neurology, 46*(1), 27–34.

Metter, E. J., Kempler, D., Jackson, C. A., Hanson, W. R., Riege, W. H., Camras, L. R., et al. (1987). Cerebellar glucose metabolism in chronic aphasia. *Neurology, 37*(10), 1599–1606.

Metter, E. J., Riege, W. H., Hanson, W. R., Jackson, C. A., Kempler, D., & Van Lancker, D. (1988). Subcortical structures in aphasia: An analysis based on (F-18)-fluorodeoxyglucose positron emission tomography and computed tomography. *Archives of Neurology, 45,* 1229–1234.

Meyer, B. J., Russo, C., & Talbot, A. (1995). Discourse comprehension and problem solving: Decisions about the treatment of breast cancer by women across the life span. *Psychology and Aging, 10*(1), 84–103.

Miller, J. W., Petersen, R. C., Metter, E. J., Millikan, C. H., & Yanagihara, T. (1987). Transient global amnesia: Clinical characteristics and prognosis. *Neurology, 37*(5), 733–737.

Mills, C. K. (1912). The cerebral mechanism of emotional expression. *Transactions of the College of Physicians of Philadelphia, 34,* 381–390.

Milner, B. (1971). Interhemispheric differences in the localization of psychological processes in man. *British Medical Bulletin, 27*(3), 272–277.

Mimura, M., Albert, M. L., & McNamara, P. (1995). Toward a pharmacotherapy for aphasia. In H. S. Kirshner (Ed.), *Handbook of neurological speech and language disorders* (pp. 465–482). New York: Marcel Dekker.

Mjones, H. (1949). *Paralysis agitans: A clinical and genetic study.* Copenhagen: Munksgaard.

Modlin, S. (2001). From puppy to service dog: Raising service dogs for the rehabilitation team. *Rehabilitation Nursing, 26*(1), 12–17.

Mohr, J. P., Watters, W. C., & Duncan, G. W. (1975). Thalamic hemorrhage and aphasia. *Brain and Language, 2*(1), 3–17.

Molloy, R., Brownell, H., & Gardner, H. (1990). Discourse comprehension by right-hemisphere stroke patients: Deficits of prediction and revision. In Y. Joanette & H. H. Brownell (Eds.), *Discourse ability and brain damage: Theoretical and empirical perspectives* (pp. 113–130). New York: Springer-Verlag.

Mori, E., & Yamadori, A. (1987). Acute confusional state and acute agitated delirium: Occurrence after infarction in the right middle cerebral artery territory. *Archives of Neurology, 44*(11), 1139–1143.

Morley, J. E. (2002). A fall is a major event in the life of an older person. *Journals of Gerontology, Series A, 57A*(8), M492–M495.

Morrell, C. H., Gordon-Salant, S., Pearson, J. D., Brant, L. J., & Fozard, J. L. (1996). Age- and gender-specific reference ranges for hearing level and longitudinal changes in hearing level. *Journal of the Acoustical Society of America, 100*(4, Pt. 1), 1949–1967.

Morris, J. C. (1993). The Clinical Dementia Rating (CDR): Current version and scoring rules. *Neurology, 43*(11), 2412–2414.

Morris, J. C., Heyman, A., Mohs, R. C., Hughes, J. P., van Belle, G., Fillenbaum, G., et al. (1989). CERAD Part I: Clinical and neuropsychological assessment of Alzheimer's disease. *Neurology, 39,* 1159–1165.

Moss, S. E., Gonzalez Rothi, L. J., & Fennell, E. B. (1991). Treating a case of surface dyslexia after closed head injury. *Archives of Clinical Neuropsychology, 6*(1–2), 35–47.

Munk, H. (1881). *Ueber die Functionen der Grosshirnrinde. Gesammelte Mittheilungenaus den Jahren 1877–80* (On the functions of the cortex: Collected treatments for the years 1877–1880). Berlin: Hirschwald.

Myers, P. S. (1999). *Right hemisphere damage: Disorders of communication and cognition.* San Diego: Singular.

Myerson, J., Emery, L., White, D. A., & Hale, S. (2003). Effects of age, domain, and processing demands of memory span: Evidence for differential decline. *Aging, Neuropsychology, & Cognition, 10*(1), 20–27.

Naeser, M. A., Alexander, M. P., Helm-Estabrooks, N., Levine, H. L., Laughlin, S. A., & Geschwind, N. (1982). Aphasia with predominantly subcortical lesion sites: Description of three capsular/putaminal aphasia syndromes. *Archives of Neurology, 39*(1), 2–14.

Nagi, S. Z. (1976). An epidemiology of disability among adults in the United States. *Milbank Quarterly, 54,* 439–467.

Nagy, W. E., & Herman, P. A. (1987). Breadth and depth of vocabulary knowledge: Implications for acquisition and instruction. In M. G. McKeown (Ed.), *The nature of vocabulary acquisition* (pp. 19–35). Hillsdale, NJ: Lawrence Erlbaum.

National Stroke Association. (2002). *National stroke.* Retrieved February 10, 2003, from www.stroke.org

Nauta, W. J. (1971). The problem of the frontal lobe: A reinterpretation. *Journal of Psychiatric Research, 8*(3), 167–187.

Neary, D., Snowden, J. S., Gustafson, M. D., Passant, M. D., Stuss, D., Black, S., et al. (1998). Frontotemporal lobar degeneration: A concensus on clinical diagnostic criteria. *Neurology, 51,* 1546–1554.

Nebes, R. D. (1992). Cognitive dysfunction in Alzheimer's disease. In F. I. M. Craik & T. A. Salthouse (Eds.), *The handbook of aging and cognition* (pp. 373–446). Boston: Lawrence Erlbaum.

Nelson, H. E. (1976). A modified card sorting test sensitive to frontal lobe defects. *Cortex, 12,* 313–324.

Ness, K. K., Gurney, J. G., & Ice, G. H. (2003). Screening, education, and associated responses to reduce risk for falls among people over age 65 years attending a community health fair. *Physical Therapy, 834*(7), 631–637.

Nevitt, M. C., Cummings, S. R., Kidd, S., & Black, D. (1989). Risk factors for recurrent nonsyncopal falls: A prospective study. *Journal of the American Medical Association, 261,* 2663–2668.

Nicholas, M. (2004). Computer alternative and augmentative communication approaches to aphasia. In N. Helm-Estabrooks & M. Albert (Eds.), *Manual of aphasia and aphasia therapy* (pp. 305–323). Austin, TX: Pro-Ed.

Nicholas, L. E., & Brookshire, R. H. (1986). Consistency of the effects of rate of speech on brain-damaged adults' comprehension of narrative discourse. *Journal of Speech & Hearing Research, 29*(4), 462–470.

Nicholas, L. E., MacLennan, D. L., & Brookshire, R. H. (1986). Validity of mulitple-sentence reading comprehension tests for aphasic adults. *Journal of Speech and Hearing Disorders, 52,* 358–366.

Nicholas, M., Barth, C., Obler, L. K., Au, R., & Albert, M. (1997). Naming in normal aging and dementia of the Alzheimer type. In H. Goodglass & A. Wingfield (Eds.), *Anomia: Neuroanatomical and cognitive correlates* (pp. 166–191). San Diego: Academic Press.

Nicholas, M., Obler, L. K., Albert, M. L., & Helm-Estabrooks, N. (1985). Empty speech in Alzheimer's disease and fluent aphasia. *Journal of Speech and Hearing Research, 28,* 405–410.

Nierenberg, A. A., & Feinstein, A. R. (1988). How to evaluate a diagnostic marker test: Lessons from the rise and fall of dexamethasone suppression test. *Journal of the American Medical Association, 259*(11), 1699–1702.

Nies, K. J., & Sweet, J. J. (1994). Neuropsychological assessment and malingering: A critical review of past and present strategies. *Archives of Clinical Neuropsychology, 9*(6), 501–552.

Nippold, M. A., & Haq, F. S. (1996). Proverb comprehension in youth: The role of concreteness and familiarity. *Journal of Speech and Hearing Research, 39*(1), 166–176.

Nippold, M. A., Uhden, L. D., & Schwarz, I. E. (1997). Proverb explanation through the lifespan: A developmental study of adolescents and adults. *Journal of Speech, Language, and Hearing Research, 40*(2), 245–253.

Nolan, K. A., & Blass, J. P. (1992). Preventing cognitive decline. *Clinical Geriatric Medicine, 8,* 19–34.

Nolan, K. A., Lino, M. M., Seligmann, A. W., & Blass, J. P. (1998). Absence of vascular dementia in an autopsy series from a dementia clinic. *Journal of the American Geriatrics Society, 46*(5), 597–604.

Norman, S., Kemper, S., Kynette, D., Cheung, H. T., & Anagnopoulos, C. (1991). Syntactic complexity and adults' running memory span. *Journal of Gerontology, 46*(6), 346–351.

Ober, B. A., Dronkers, N. F., Koss, E., & Delis, D. C. (1986). Processes of verbal memory failure in Alzheimer-type dementia. *Journal of Clinical and Experimental Neuropsychology, 8,* 75–92.

Ober, B. A., & Shenaut, G. K. (1995). Semantic priming in Alzheimer's disease: Meta-analysis and theoretical evaluation. In P. Allen & T. R. Bashore (Eds.), *Age differences in word and language processing* (pp. 247–271). London: Elsevier.

Obler, L. K., Nicholas, M., Albert, M. L., & Woodward, S. (1985). On comprehension across the adult lifespan. *Cortex, 21*(2), 273–280.

Odderson, I. R. (1999). The National Institutes of Health Stroke Scale and its importance in acute stroke management. *Physical Medicine and Rehabilitation Clinics of North America, 10*(4), 787–800.

Ojemann, G., Ojemann, J., Lettich, E., & Berger, M. (1989). Cortical language localization in left, dominant hemisphere: An electrical stimulation mapping investigation in 117 patients. *Journal of Neurosurgery, 71*(3), 316–326.

Orange, J. B., Ryna, E. B., Meredith, S. D., & MacLean, M. J. (1995). Application of the communication enhancement model for long-term care residents with Alzheimer's disease. *Topics in Language Disorders, 15*(2), 20–35.

Osterrieth, P. A. (1944). Le test de copie d'une figure complexe (The Complex Figure Copying Test). *Archives de Psychologie, 30,* 206–356.

Ostuni, M. J., & Santo-Pietro, E. (1986). *Getting through: Communicating when someone you know has Alzheimer's disease.* Princeton, NJ: The Speech Bin.

Pahwa, R., Lyons, K., & Koller, W. C. (2000). Surgical treatment of essential tremor. *Neurology, 54*(11, Suppl. 4), S39–S44.

Palisses, R., Pergesol, D., Viala, D., & Viala, G. (1988). Reflex modulation of phrenic activity through hindlimb passive motion in decorticate and spinal rabbit preparation. *Neuroscience, 24*(2), 719–728.

Palmer, C. V., Adams, S. W., Bourgeois, M. S., Durrant, J., & Rossi, M. (1999). Reduction in caregiver-identified problem behaviors in patients with Alzheimer disease post-hearing-aid fitting. *Journal of Speech, Language & Hearing Research, 42*(2), 312–328.

Palumbo, B., Parnetti, L., Nocentini, G., Cardinali, L., Brancorsini, S., & Riccardi, C. (1997). Apolipoprotein-E genotype in normal aging, age-associated memory impairment, Alzheimer's disease and vascular dementia patients. *Neuroscience Letters, 231*(1), 59–61.

Panzer, V. P., Bandinelli, S., & Hallett, M. (1995). Biomechanical assessment of quiet standing and changes associated with aging. *Archives of Physical Medicine & Rehabilitation, 76, 2,* 151–157.

Papousek, M., Bornstein, M. H., Nuzzo, C., Papousek, H., & Symmes, D. (2000). Infant responses to prototypical melodic contours in parental speech. In D. Muir (Ed.), *Infant development: The essential readings* (pp. 261–267). Malden, MA: Blackwell.

Parasuraman, R., Nestor, P., & Greenwood, P. (1989). Sustained-attention capacity in young and older adults. *Psychology and Aging, 4*(3), 339–345.

Parikh, S. V., Lam, R. W., & Group, C. D. W. (2001). Clinical guidelines for the treatment of depressive disorders: I. Definitions, prevalence, and health burden. *Canadian Journal of Psychiatry, 46*(Suppl. 1), 13S–20S.

Parkin, A. J. (1996). H.M.: The medial temporal lobes and memory. In C. Code & C. W. Wallesch (Eds.), *Classic cases in neuropsychology* (pp. 337–347). Oxford, UK: Psychology/Lawrence Erlbaum.

Parnell, M. M., & Amerman, J. D. (1987). Perception of oral diadochokinetic performances in elderly adults. *Journal of Communication Disorders, 20*(4), 339–352.

Parnetti, L., Lowenthal, D. T., Presciutti, O., Pelliccioli, G. P., Palumbo, R., Gobbi, G., et al. (1996). 1H-MRS, MRI-based hippocampal volumetry, and 99mTc-HMPAO-ASPECT in normal aging, age-associated memory impairment, and probably Alzheimer's disease. *Journal of the American Geriatrics Society, 44,* 133–138.

Patten, S. B. (2000). Incidence of major depression in Canada. *Canadian Medical Association Journal, 164*(6), 714–775.

Patterson, A., & Zangwill, O. L. (1944). Disorders of visual space perception associated with lesions of the right cerebral hemisphere. *Brain, 67,* 331–358.

Paulsen, J. S., & Salmon, D. P. (1995). Discrimination of cortical from subcortical dementias on the basis of memory and problem-solving. *Journal of Clinical Psychology, 51*(1), 48–58.

Pehoski, C. (1970). *Analysis of perceptual dysfunction and dressing in adult hemiplegics.* Unpublished master's thesis, Boston University.

Peigneux, P., Salmon, E., Garraux, G., Laureys, S., Willems, S., Dujardin, K., et al. (2001). Neural and cognitive bases of upper limb apraxia in corticobasal degeneration. *Neurology, 57*(7), 1259–1268.

Pell, M. D., & Baum, S. R. (1997a). The ability to perceive and comprehend intonation in linguistic and affective contexts by brain-damaged adults. *Brain and Language, 57*(1), 80–99.

Pell, M. D., & Baum, S. R. (1997b). Unilateral brain damage, prosodic comprehension deficits, and the acoustic cues to prosody. *Brain and Language, 57*(2), 195–214.

Penfield, W., & Roberts, L. (1959). *Speech and brain mechanisms.* New York: Freeman.

Peterson, L. R., & Peterson, M. J. (1959). Short-term retention of individual verbal items. *Journal of Experimental Psychology, 58,* 193–198.

Pinker, S. (1994). *The language instinct.* New York: Morrow.

Pinsky, J. L., Branch, L. G., Jette, A. M., Haynes, S. G., Femleib, M., Cornoni-Huntley, J. C., et al. (1985). Framingham disability study: Relationship of disability to cardiovascular risk factors among persons free of diagnosed cardiovascular disease. *American Journal of Epidemiology, 122*(4), 644–656.

Poeck, K., Huber, W., & Willmes, K. (1989). Outcome of intensive language treatment in aphasia. *Journal of Speech and Hearing Disorders, 54*(3), 471–479.

Poizner, H., Bellugi, U., & Klima, E. S. (1989). Sign-language aphasia. In H. Goodglass (Ed.), *Language, aphasia and related disorders* (Vol. 2, pp. 157–172). Amsterdam: Elsevier.

Pompei, P., Foreman, M., Cassel, C., Alessi, C., & Cox, D. (1995). Detecting delirium among hospitalized older patients. *Archives of Internal Medicine, 13*(155), 301–307.

Poon, L. W., Martin, P., Clayton, G. M., Messner, S., Noble, C. A., & Johnson, M. A. (1992). The influences of cognitive resources on adaptation and old age. *International Journal of Aging and Human Development, 34,* 31–46.

Porteus, S. D. (1959). *The Maze Test and clinical psychology.* Palo Alto, CA: Pacific Books.

Porteus, S. D. (1965). *Porteus Maze Test: Fifty years' application.* New York: The Psychological Corporation.

Posner, M. I., & Raichle, M. E. (1994). *Images of mind.* New York: Scientific American Library.

Prather, E. M., Hedrick, D. L., & Kern, C. A. (1975). Articulation development in children aged two to four years. *Journal of Speech and Hearing Disorders, 40*(2), 179–191.

Pratt, M. W., Boyes, C., Robins, S., & Manchester, J. (1989). Telling tales: Aging, working memory, and the narrative cohesion of story retellings. *Developmental Psychology, 25*(4), 628–635.

Pratt, M. W., & Robins, S. L. (1991). That's the way it was: Age differences in the structure and quality of adults' personal narratives. *Discourse Processes, 14*(1), 73–85.

Provinciali, L., & Coccia, M. (2002). Post-stroke and vascular depression: A critical review. *Neurological Sciences, 22*(6), 417–428.

Quayhagen, M. P., Quayhagen, M., Corbeil, R., Roth, P., & Rodgers, J. (1995). A dyadic remediation program for care recipients with dementia. *Nursing Research, 44,* 153–159.

Radanovic, M., & Scaff, M. (2003). Speech and language disturbances due to subcortical lesions. *Brain and Language, 84*(3), 337–352.

Rajput, A. H., Uitti, R. J., Stern, W., Laverty, W., O'Donnell, K., O'Donnell, D., et al. (1987). Geography, drinking water chemistry, pesticides and herbicides and the etiology of Parkinson's disease. *Canadian Journal of Neurological Sciences, 14*(Suppl. 3), 414–418.

Rascol, O., Goetz, C., Koller, W., Poewe, W., & Sampaio, C. (2002). Treatment interventions for Parkinson's disease: An evidence based assessment. *Lancet, 359*(9317), 1589–1599.

Raskin, S. A., & Mateer, C. A. (2000). *Neuropsychological management of mild traumatic brain injury.* Oxford, UK: Oxford University Press.

Raven, J. C. (1960). *Guide to the standard progresive matrices.* London: H. K. Lewis.

Recanati, F. (1995). The alleged priority of literal interpretation. *Cognitive Science, 19*(2), 207–232.

Recanzone, G. H. (2000). Cerebral cortical plasticity: Perception and skill acquisition. In M. S. Gazzaniga (Ed.), *The new cognitive neurosciences* (2nd ed., pp. 237–247). Cambridge: MIT Press.

Rechtman, E., Ciulla, T. A., Criswell, M. H., Pollack, A., & Harris, A. (2002). An update on photodynamic therapy in age-related macular degeneration. *Expert Opinion on Pharmacotherapy, 3*(7), 931–938.

Reeves, S., Bench, C., & Howard, R. (2002). Ageing and the nigrostriatal dopaminergic system. *International Journal of Geriatric Psychiatry, 17*(4), 359–370.

Rehak, A. (1992). Sensitivity to conversational deviance in right-hemisphere-damaged patients. *Brain and Language, 42*(2), 203–217.

Reichman, W. E., & Cummings, J. L. (1999). Dementia. In E. H. Duthie & P. R. Katz (Eds.), *Practice of geriatrics* (3rd ed., pp. 295–304). Philadelphia: W. B. Saunders.

Reilly, J. S., Bates, E. A., & Marchman, V. A. (1998). Narrative discourse in children with early focal brain injury. *Brain and Language, 61*(3), 335–375.

Reisberg, B., Ferris, S. H., de Leon, M. J., & Crook, T. (1982). The Global Deterioration Scale for assessment of primary degenerative dementia. *American Journal of Psychiatry, 139,* 1136–1139.

Reitan, D. (1958). Validity of the Trail Making Test as an indicator of organic brain damage. *Perceptual and Motor Skills, 8,* 271–276.

Rey, A., & Osterrieth, P. A. (1993). Translations of excerpts from Andre Rey's Psychological examination of traumatic encephalopathy and P.A. Osterrieth's The Complex Figure Copy Test. *The Clinical Psychologist, 7*(1), 4–21.

Riddoch, M. J., & Humphreys, G. W. (1987a). Perceptual and action systems in unilateral visual neglect. In M. Jeannerod (Ed.), *Neurophysiological and neuropsychological aspects of spatial neglect* (pp. 151–181). Amsterdam: Elsevier Science.

Riddoch, M. J., & Humphreys, G. W. (1987b). Picture naming. In G. W. Humphreys (Ed.), *Visual object processing: A cognitive neuropsychological approach* (pp. 107–143). Hove, UK: Lawrence Erlbaum.

Riddoch, M. J., & Humphreys, G. W. (1987c). Visual object processing in optic aphasia: A case of semantic access agnosia. *Cognitive Neuropsychology, 4*(2), 131–185.

Rieben, L., & Perfetti, C. A. (1991). *Learning to read: Basic research and its implications.* Hillsdale, NJ: Lawrence Erlbaum.

Ripich, D. N., & Terrell, B. Y. (1988). Cohesion and coherence in Alzheimer's disease. *Journal of Speech and Hearing Disorders, 53,* 8–14.

Robertson, I., Ward, T., & Ridgeway, V. (1996). *The Test of Everyday Attention.* Gaylord, MI: Northern Speech Services.

Robinson, R. G., Bolduc, P. L., & Price, T. R. (1987). Two-year longitudinal study of post-stroke mood disorder: Diagnosis and outcome at one and two years. *Stroke, 18,* 837–843.

Rosenzweig, M. R., Leiman, A. L., & Breedlove, S. M. (1996). *Biological psychology.* Sunderland, MA: Sinauer Associates, Inc.

Rosin, A. J. H., & Van Dijk, Y. M. (1980). Subdural hematoma: A clinical approach. *Journal of the American Geriatrics Society, 28*(4), 180–183.

Ross, E. D., & Mesulam, M. M. (1979). Dominant language functions of the right hemisphere? Prosody and emotional gesturing. *Archives of Neurology, 36*(3), 144–148.

Rossi, P. W., Kheyfets, S., & Reding, M. J. (1990). Fresnel prisms improve visual perception in stroke patients with homonymous hemianopia or unilateral visual neglect. *Neurology, 40*(10), 1597–1599.

Rousseau, G. K., Lamson, N., & Rogers, W. A. (1998). Designing warnings to compensate for age-related changes in perceptual and cognitive abilities. *Psychology and Marketing, 15*(7), 643–662.

Rowe, J. W., & Besdine, R. W. (Eds.). (1988). *Geriatric medicine* (2nd ed.). Boston: Little, Brown.

Rowe, J. W., & Kahn, R. L. (1987). Human aging: Usual and successful. *Science, 237,* 143–149.

Rowe, J. W., & Kahn, R. L. (1988). *Successful aging.* New York: Pantheon.

Royall, D. R., Cordes, J. A., & Polk, M. (1998). CLOX: An executive clock drawing task. *Journal of Neurology, Neurosurgery, & Psychiatry, 64,* 588–594.

Royall, D. R., Mahurin, R. K., & Gray, K. F. (1992). Bedside assessment of executive cognitive impairment: The executive interview. *Journal of the American Geriatrics Society, 40*(12), 1221–1226.

Rubens, A. B. (1985). Caloric stimulation and unilateral visual neglect. *Neurology, 35*(7), 1019–1024.

Rubens, A. B., & Benson, D. F. (1971). Associative visual agnosia. *Archives of Neurology, 24,* 305–316.

Rubin, E. H., Veiel, L. L., Kinscherf, D. A., Morris, J. C., & Storandt, M. (2001). Clinically significant depressive symptoms and very mild to mild dementia of the Alzheimer type. *International Journal of Geriatric Psychiatry, 16*(7), 694–701.

Rudinger, G., & Thomae, H. (1990). The Bonn Longitudinal Study of Aging: Coping, life adjustment, and life satisfaction. In P. B. Baltes & M. M. Baltes (Eds.), *Successful aging: Perspectives from the behavioral sciences* (pp. 265–295). Cambridge, MA: Cambridge University Press.

Ryan, E. B. (1992). Beliefs about memory changes across the adult life span. *Journal of Gerontology, 47,* 41–46.

Ryan, E. B. (1996). Psychosocial perspectives on discourse and hearing differences among older adults. *Journal of Speech Language Pathology and Audiology, 20*(2), 95–100.

Ryan, E. B., Maclean, M., & Orange, J. B. (1994). Inappropriate accommodation in communication to elders: Inferences about nonverbal correlates. *International Journal of Aging and Human Development, 39*(4), 273–291.

Ryerson, S., & Levit, K. (1997). *Functional motor reeducation*. London: Churchill Livingstone.

Ryff, C. D. (1989). Beyond Ponce de Leon and life satisfaction: New directions in quest of successful aging. *International Journal of Behavioral Development, 12,* 35–55.

Sacco, R. L., Elkind, M., Boden-Albala, B., Lin, I. F., Kargman, D. E., Hauser, W. A., et al. (1999). The protective effect of moderate alcohol consumption on ischemic stroke. *Journal of the American Medical Association, 281*(1), 53–60.

Sacks, O. (1990). *The man who mistook his wife for a hat*. New York: HarperCollins.

Saint-Cyr, J. A., & Taylor, A. E. (1992). The mobilization of procedural learning: The "key signature" of the basal ganglia. In L. Squire & N. Butters (Eds.), *Neuropsychology of memory* (2nd ed., pp. 188–202). New York: Guilford.

Salas-Provance, M. B., Erickson, J. G., & Reed, J. (2002). Disabilities as viewed by four generations of one Hispanic family. *American Journal of Speech-Language Pathology, 11*(2), 151–162.

Salthouse, T. (1988). Effects of aging on verbal abilities: Examination of the psychometric literature. In L. L. Light & D. M. Burke (Eds.), *Language, memory, and aging* (pp. 17–35). Cambridge, UK: Cambridge University Press.

Salthouse, T. A. (1985). Tests of the neural noise hypothesis of age-related cognitive change. *Journal of Gerontology, 40*(4), 443–450.

Salthouse, T. A. (1990). Working memory as a processing resource in cognitive aging. *Developmental Review, 10,* 101–124.

Salthouse, T. A. (1991). Mediation of adult age differences in cognition by reductions in working memory and speed of processing. *Psychological Science, 2*(3), 179–183.

Salthouse, T. A. (1992). What do adult age differences in the digit symbol substitution test reflect? *Journal of Gerontology and Psychologic Sciences, 47,* P121–P28.

Salthouse, T. A. (1994). The aging of working memory. *Neuropsychology, 8*(4), 535–543.

Salthouse, T. A. (1996). The processing-speed theory of adult age differences in cognition. *Psychological Review, 103*(3), 403–428.

Salthouse, T. A., & Babcock, R. L. (1991). Decomposing adult age differences in working memory. *Developmental Psychology, 27*(5), 763–776.

Salthouse, T. A., Babcock, R. L., & Shaw, R. J. (1991). Effects of adult age on structural and operational capacities in working memory. *Psychology and Aging, 6*(1), 118–127.

Sandler, R. B., Burdett, R., Zaleskiewicz, M., Sprowls-Repcheck, C., & Harwell, M. (1991). Muscle strength as an indicator of the habitual level of physical activity. *Medicine and Science in Sports and Exercise, 23,* 1375–1381.

Sands, L. P., Terry, H., & Meredith, W. (1989). Change and stability in adult intellectual functioning assessed by Wechsler item responses. *Psychology and Aging, 4,* 79–87.

Sapir, S., Pawlas, A. A., Ramig, L. O., Countryman, S., O'Brien, C., Hoehn, M. M., et al. (2001). Voice and speech abnormalities in Parkinson disease: Relation to severity of motor impairment, duration of disease, medication, depression, gender, and age. *Journal of Medical Speech-Language Pathology, 9*(4), 213–226.

Saumier, D., Arguin, M., Lefebvre, C., & Lassonde, M. (2002). Visual object agnosia as a problem in integrating parts and part relations. *Brain and Cognition, 48*(2–3), 531–537.

Saygin, A. P., Dick, F., & Bates, E. (2001). Linguistic and non-linguistic auditory processing in aphasia. *Brain and Language, 79*(1), 143–145.

Schacter, D. L., Rich, S. A., & Stampp, M. S. (1985). Remediation of memory disorders: Experimental evaluation of the spaced retrieval technique. *Journal of Clinical and Experimental Neuropsychology, 7,* 79–96.

Schaie, K. W. (1983). The Seattle Longitudinal Study: A 21-year exploration of psychometric intelligence in adulthood. In K. W. Schaie (Ed.), *Longitudinal studies of adult psychological development* (pp. 64–135). New York: Guilford.

Schaie, K. W. (1989). The hazards of cognitive aging. *The Gerontologist, 29,* 484–493.

Schaie, K. W. (1990a). Intellectual development in adulthood. In J. E. Birren & K. W. Schaie (Eds.), *Handbook of the psychology of aging* (3rd ed., pp. 291–309). New York: Academic Press.

Schaie, K. W. (1990b). Optimization of cognitive functioning. In P. M. Baltes & M. M. Baltes (Eds.), *Successful aging: Perspectives from the behavioral sciences* (pp. 94–117). Cambridge, MA: Cambridge University Press.

Schaie, K. W. (1994). The course of adult intellectual development. *American Psychologist, 49,* 304–313.

Schaie, K. W. (1996). *Intellectual development in adulthood: The Seattle longitudinal study.* New York: Cambridge University Press.

Schaie, K. W. (2000). The impact of longitudinal studies on understanding development from young adulthood to old age. *International Journal of Behavioral Development, 24,* 257–266.

Schaie, K. W., & Willis, S. L. (2002). *Adult development and aging.* Upper Saddle River, NJ: Prentice Hall.

Schegloff, E. A. (1998). Reflections on studying prosody in talk-in-interaction. *Language and Speech, 41*(3–4), 235–263.

Schmand, B., Geerlings, M. M. I., Jonker, C., & Lindeboom, J. (1998). Reading ability as an estimator of premorbid intelligence: Does it remain stable in emergent dementia? *Journal of Clinical & Experimental Neuropsychology, 20*(1), 42–51.

Schonfield, D., & Robertson, B. A. (1966). Memory storage and aging. *Canadian Journal of Psychology, 20,* 228–236.

Schroder, J., Kratz, B., Pantel, J., Minnemann, E., Lehr, U., & Sauer, H. (1998). Prevalence of mild cognitive impairment in an elderly community sample. *Journal of Neural Transmission, 54,* 51–59.

Schuell, H. (1965). *Minnesota Test for Differential Diagnosis of Aphasia.* Minneapolis: University of Minnesota.

Seals, D. R., Hagberg, J. M., Hurley, B. F., Ehsani, A. A., & Holloszy, J. O. (1984). Effects of endurance training on glucose tolerance and plasma lipid levels in older men and women. *Journal of the American Medical Association, 252,* 645–649.

Seashore, C. E., Lewis, D., & Saetveit, D. L. (1960). *Seashore Measures of Musical Talent.* New York: The Psychological Corporation.

Seeman, T. E. (1994). Successful aging: Reconceptualizing the aging process from a more positive perspective. *Facts and Research in Gerontology, 8,* 3–15.

Seeman, T. E., Berkman, L. F., Charpentier, P., Blazer, D., Albert, M., & Tinetti, M. (1995). Behavioral and psychosocial predictors of physical performance: MacArthur Studies of Successful Aging. *Journal of Gerontology: Medical Science, 50A,* M177–M183.

Seeman, T. E., Charpentier, P. A., Berkman, L. F., Tinetti, M. E., Guralnik, J. M., Albert, M., et al. (1994). Predicting changes in physical performance in a high functioning elderly cohort: MacArthur Studies of Successful Aging. *Journal of Gerontology, 49,* M97–M108.

Seeman, T. E., Lusignolo, T. M., Albert, M., & Berkman, L. (2001). Social relationships, social support, and patterns of cognitive aging in healthy, high-functioning older adults: MacArthur Studies of Successful Aging. *Health Psychology, 20*(4), 243–255.

Seeman, T. E., McEwen, B. S., Rowe, J. W., & Singer, B. H. (2001). Allostatic load as a marker of cumulative biological risk: MacArthur Studies of Successful Aging. *Proceedings of the National Academy of Sciences of the United States of America, 98*(8), 4770–4775.

Seeman, T. E., McEwen, B. S., Singer, B. H., Albert, M. S., & Rowe, J. W. (1997). Increase in urinary cortisol excretion and memory declines: The MacArthur Studies of Successful Aging. *Journal of Clinical Endocrinology & Metabolism, 82*(2), 2458–2465.

Seeman, T. E., Singer, B. H., Rowe, J. W., Horwitz, R. I., & McEwen, B. S. (1997). Price of adaptation: Allostatic load and its health consequences: MacArthur Studies of Successful Aging. *Archives of Internal Medicine, 157*(19), 2259–2268.

Seeman, T. E., Unger, J. B., McAvay, G., & de Leon, C. F. M. (1999). Self-efficacy beliefs and perceived declines in functional ability: MacArthur Studies of Successful Aging. *Journals of Gerontology: Psychological Sciences and Social Sciences, 54*(4), P214–P222.

Segal, Z. V., Whitney, D. K., & Lam, R. W. (2001). Clinical guidelines for the treatment of depressive disorders. *Canadian Journal of Psychiatry, 46*(Suppl. 1), 29S–37S.

Seki, K., Yajima, M., & Sugishita, M. (1995). The efficacy of kinesthetic reading treatment for pure alexia. *Neuropsychologia, 33*(5), 595–609.

Shallice, T. (1982). Specific impairments of planning. *Philosophical Transactions of the Royal Society of Biological Sciences, 298,* 199–209.

Shapiro, B. E., & Danly, M. (1985). The role of the right hemisphere in the control of speech prosody in propositional and affective contexts. *Brain and Language, 25*(1), 19–36.

Sharps, M. J., & Gollin, E. S. (1988). Aging and free recall for objects located in space. *Journal of Gerontology, 43*(1), 8–11.

Shenton, M. E., Frumin, M., McCarley, R. W., Maier, S. E., Westin, C. F., Fischer, I. A., et al. (2001). Morphometic magnetic resonance imaging studies: Findings in schizophrenia. In D. D. Dougherty & S. L. Rauch (Eds.), *Psychiatric neuroimaging research: Contemporary strategies* (pp. 1–60). Washington, DC: American Psychiatric Publishing.

Sher, L., Matthews, J. R., Turner, E. H., Postolache, T. T., Katz, K. S., & Rosenthal, N. E. (2001). Early response to light therapy partially predicts long-term antidepressant effects in patients with seasonal affective disorder. *Journal of Psychiatry & Neuroscience, 26*(4), 336–338.

Sherwin, B. B. (2000). Mild cognitive impairment: Potential pharmacological treatment options. *Journal of the American Geriatrics Society, 48*(4), 431–441.

Shiffrin, R. M., & Schneider, W. (1977). Controlled and automatic human information processing: II. Perceptual learning, automatic attending and a general theory. *Psychological Review, 84*(2), 127–190.

Shimoda, K., & Robinson, R. G. (1999). The relationship between poststroke depression and lesion location in long-term follow-up. *Biological Psychiatry, 45*(2), 187–192.

Shumaker, S. A., Legault, C., Thal, L., Wallace, R. B., Ockene, J. K., Hendrix, S. L., et al. (2003). Estrogen plus progestin and the incidence of dementia and mild cognitive impairment in postmenopausal women: The Women's Health Initiative Memory Study: A randomized controlled study. *Journal of the American Medical Society, 289*(20), 2651–2662.

Sivan, A. B. (1992). *Benton Visual Retention Test Manual* (5th ed.). San Antonio, TX: Psychological Corporation, Harcourt Brace & Company.

Ska, B., & Joanette, Y. (1996). Discourse in older adults: Influence of text, task, and participant characteristics. *Journal of Speech Language Pathology and Audiology, 20*(2), 101–108.

Slavin, M. J., Phillips, J. G., & Bradshaw, J. L. (1996). Visual cues and the handwriting of older adults: A kinematic analysis. *Psychology and Aging, 11*(3), 521–526.

Small, G. W., Chen, S. T., Komo, S., Ercoli, L., Bookheimer, S., Miller, K., et al. (1999). Memory self-appraisal in middle-aged and older adults with the apolipoprotein E-4 allele. *American Journal of Psychiatry, 156*(7), 1035–1038.

Small, G. W., Rabins, P. V., Barry, P. P., Buckholtz, N. S., DeKosky, S. T., Ferris, S. H., et al. (1997). Diagnosis and treatment of Alzheimer disease and related disorders: Consensus statement of the American Association for Geriatric Psychiatry, the Alzheimer's Association, and the American Geriatrics Society. *Journal of the American Medical Society, 278*(16), 1363–1371.

Small, J. A., Andersen, E. S., & Kempler, D. (1997). Effects of working memory capacity on understanding rate-altered speech. *Aging, Neuropsychology, and Cognition, 4*(2), 126–139.

Small, J. A., Kemper, S., & Lyons, K. (1997). Sentence comprehension in Alzheimer's disease: Effects of grammatical complexity, speech rate, and repetition. *Psychology and Aging, 12*(1), 3–11.

Smith, A., & Sugar, O. (1975). Development of above normal language and intelligence 21 years after left hemispherectomy. *Neurology, 25*(9), 813–818.

Smith, A. D. (1996). Memory. In J. E. Birren & K. W. Schaie (Eds.), *Handbook of the psychology of aging* (pp. 236–250). San Diego: Academic Press.

Snow, C. E., & Ferguson, C. (1977). *Talking to children.* Cambridge, UK: Cambridge University Press.

Sohlberg, M. M., & Mateer, C. A. (1989). *Introduction to cognitive rehabilitation: Theory and practice.* New York: Guilford.

Sorock, G. S., Bush, T. L., Golden, A. L., Fried, L. P., Breuer, B., & Hale, W. E. (1988). Physical activity and fracture risk in a free-living elderly cohort. *Journal of Gerontology, 43,* 134–139.

Spina, E., & Scordo, M. G. (2002). Clinically significant drug interactions with antidepressants in the elderly. *Drugs & Aging, 19*(4), 299–320.

Spirrison, C. L., & Pierce, P. S. (1992). Psychometric characteristics of the Adult Functional Adaptive Behavior Scale (AFABS). *The Gerontologist, 32,* 234–239.

Spreen, O., Benton, A. L., & Fincham, R. (1965). Auditory agnosia without aphasia. *Archives of Neurology, 13,* 84–92.

Springer, S. P., & Deutsch, G. (1993). *Left brain, right brain* (4th ed.). New York: Freeman.

Squire, L. R., Cohen, N. J., & Nadel, L. (1984). The medial temporal region and memory consolidation: A new hypothesis. In H. Weingartner & E. Parkers (Eds.), *Memory consolidation* (pp. 185–210). Hillsdale, NJ: Lawrence Erlbaum.

Squire, L. R., & Slater, P. C. (1975). Retrograde amnesia: Temporal gradient in very long term memory following electroconvulsive therapy. *Science, 187*(4171), 77–79.

Starkstein, S. E., & Robinson, R. G. (1991). Dementia of depression in Parkinson's disease and stroke. *Journal of Nervous and Mental Disease, 179*(10), 593–601.

Starkstein, S. E., Robinson, R. G., & Proce, T. R. (1987). Comparison of cortical and subcortical lesions in the production of poststroke mood disorders. *Brain, 110,* 1045–1059.

Stein, D. G. (2000). Brain injury and theories of recovery. In A. L. Christensen (Ed.), *International handbook of neuropsychological rehabilitation* (pp. 9–32). Dordrecht, the Netherlands: Kluwer Academic.

Strawbridge, W. J., Cohen, R. D., Shema, S. J., & Kaplan, G. A. (1996). Successful aging: Predictors and associated activities. *American Journal of Epidemiology, 144,* 135–141.

Streifler, J. Y., Benavente, O. R., Harbison, J. W., Wliasziw, M., Hachinski, V. C., & Barnett, H. J. (1992). Prognostic implications of retinal versus hemispheric TIA in patients with high grade carotid stenosis: Observations from NASCET. *Stroke, 23,* 159.

Strub, R. L., & Black, F. W. (1988). *Neurobehavioral disorders: A clinical approach.* Philadelphia: F. A. Davis.

Strub, R. L., & Black, F. W. (2000). *The mental status examination in neurology* (4th ed.). Philadelphia: F. A. Davis.

Stuss, D. T. (1992). Biological and psychological development of executive functions. *Brain and Cognition, 20*(1), 8–23.

Stuss, D. T., & Benson, D. F. (1987). The frontal lobes and control of cognition and memory. In E. Perecman (Ed.), *The frontal lobes revisited* (pp. 141–158). New York: IRBN Press.

Stuss, D. T., Stethem, L. L., & Poirier, C. A. (1987). Comparison of three tests of attention and rapid information processing across six age groups. *The Clinical Neuropsychologist, 1,* 139–152.

Svennerholm, L., Bostrom, K., & Jungbjer, B. (1997). Changes in weight and compositions of major membrane components of human brain during the span of adult human life of Swedes. *Acta Neuropathologica (Berlin), 94*(4), 345–352.

Tamai, M., Kubota, M., Ikeda, M., Nagao, K., Irikura, N., Sugiyama, M., et al. (1993). Usefulness of anaerobic threshold for evaluating daily life activity and prescribing exercise to the healthy subjects and patients. *Journal of Medical Systems, 17,* 219–225.

Tanaka, J. W., & Curran, T. (2001). A neural basis for expert object recognition. *Psychological Science, 12*(1), 43–47.

Tanaka, Y., Miyazaki, M., & Albert, M. L. (1997). Effects of increased cholinergic activity on naming in aphasia. *Lancet, 350*(9071), 116–117.

Tanner, C. M., Hubble, J. P., & Chan, P. I. U. (1997). Epidemiology and genetics of Parkinson's disease. In R. L. Watts & W. C. Koller (Eds.), *Movement disorders: Neurologic principles and practice* (pp. 137–152). New York: McGraw-Hill.

Tariot, P. N. (1996). CERAD Behavior Rating Scale for dementia. *International Psychogeriatrics, 8*(Suppl. 3), 317–320, 514–515.

Taylor, A. E., Saint-Cyr, J. A., & Lang, A. E. (1986). Frontal lobe dysfunction in Parkinson's disease: The cortical focus of neostriatal outflow. *Brain, 109*(Pt. 5), 845–883.

Teasdale, G., & Jennett, B. (1974). Assessment of coma and impaired consciousness: A practical scale. *Lancet, 2*(7872), 81–84.

Tekin, S., & Cummings, J. L. (2002). Frontal-subcortical neuronal circuits and clinical neuropsychiatry: An update. *Journal of Psychosomatic Research, 53*(2), 647–654.

Teri, L., Logsdon, R. G., & McCurry, S. M. (2002). Nonpharmacologic treatment of behavioral disturbance in dementia. *The Medical Clinics of North America, 86,* 641–656.

Teri, L., McCurry, S. M., & Logsdon, R. G. (1997). Memory, thinking and aging: What we know about what we know. *Western Journal of Medicine, 167,* 269–275.

Teri, L., Rabins, P., Whitehouse, P., Berg, L., Reisberg, B., Sunderland, T., et al. (1992). Management of behavior disturbance in Alzheimer disease: Current knowledge and future directions. *Alzheimer Disease and Associated Disorders, 6,* 77–88.

Terman, L. M. (1921). Intelligence and its measurement. *Journal of Educational Psyuchology, 12,* 430–443.

Terman, L. M., & Merrill, M. A. (1973). *Stanford-Binet Intelligence Scale: Manual for the third revision Form L-M.* Boston: Houghton Mifflin.

Teuber, H. L. (1964). The riddle of frontal lobe function in man. In J. M. Warren & K. Akert (Eds.), *The frontal granular cortex and behavior* (pp. 410–441). New York: McGraw-Hill.

Teuber, H. L. (1968). Alteration of perception and memory in man. In L. Weiskrantz (Ed.), *Analysis of behavioral change* (pp. 274–328). New York: Harper & Row.

Teuber, H. L., Battersby, W. S., & Bender, M. B. (1951). Performance on complex visual tasks after cerebral lesion. *Journal of Nervous and Mental Disease, 114,* 413–429.

Thaiss, L., & De Bleser, R. (1992). Visual agnosia: A case of reduced attentional "spotlight"? *Cortex, 28*(4), 601–621.

Thomas, A. J., Ferrier, I. N., Kalaria, R. N., Perry, R. H., Brown, A., & O'Brien, J. T. (2001). A neuropathological study of vascular factors in late-life depression. *Journal of Neurology, Neurosurgery & Psychiatry, 70*(1), 83–87.

Thompson, C. K., & Shapiro, L. P. (1995). Training sentence production in agrammatism: implications for normal and disordered language. *Brain and Language, 50*(2), 201–224.

Tipton, C. M. (1984). Exercise, training and hypertension. *Exercise Sport Science Review, 12,* 245–306.

Tison, F., Dartigues, J. F., Auriacombe, S., Letenneur, L., Boller, F., & Alpérovitch, A. (1995). Dementia in Parkinson's disease: A population-based study in ambulatory and institutionalized individuals. *Neurology, 45*(4), 705–708.

Tompkins, C. A., Boada, R., & McGarry, K. (1992). The access and processing of familiar idioms by brain-damaged and normally aging adults. *Journal of Speech and Hearing Research, 35*(3), 626–637.

Tranel, D., Damasio, H., & Damasio, A. R. (1997a). A neural basis for the retrieval of conceptual knowledge. *Neuropsychologia, 35*(10), 1319–1327.

Tranel, D., Damasio, H., & Damasio, A. R. (1997b). On the neurology of naming. In H. Goodglass & A. Wingfield (Eds.), *Anomia: Neuroanatomical and cognitive correlates* (pp. 65–90). San Diego: Academic Press.

Tranel, D., Logan, C. G., Frank, R. J., & Damasio, A. R. (1997). Explaining category-related effects in the retrieval of conceptual and lexical knowledge for concrete entities: Operationalization and analysis of factors. *Neuropsychologia, 35*(10), 1329–1339.

Trzepacz, P. T., Baker, R. W., & Greenhouse, J. (1988). A symptom rating scale for delirium. *Psychiatry Research, 23*(1), 89–97.

Trzepacz, P. T., Mittal, D., Torres, R., Kanary, K., Norton, J., & Jimerson, N. (2001). Validation of the Delirium Rating Scale–Revised-98: Comparison with the Delirium Rating Scale and the Cognitive Test for Delirium. *Journal of Neuropsychiatry and Clinical Neurosciences, 13*(2), 229–242.

Tsuang, D., Larson, E. B., Bowen, J., McCormick, W., Teri, L., Nochlin, D., et al. (1999). The utility of apolipoprotein E genotyping in the diagnosis of Alzheimer disease in a community-based case series. *Archives of Neurology, 56*(12), 1489–1495.

Tucker, D. M., Watson, R. T., & Heilman, K. M. (1977). Discrimination and evocation of affectively intoned speech in patients with right parietal disease. *Neurology, 27*(10), 947–958.

Tun, P. A. (1998). Fast noisy speech: Age differences in processing rapid speech with background noise. *Psychology and Aging, 13*(3), 424–434.

Tun, P. A., Wingfield, A., Stine, E. A., & Mescas, C. (1992). Rapid speech processing and divided attention: Processing rate versus processing resources as an explanation of age effects. *Psychology and Aging, 7*(4), 546–550.

Tyler, H. R. (1968). Abnormalities of perception with defective eye movements (Balint's syndrome). *Cortex, 4*(2), 154–171.

Ulatowska, H. K., Hayashi, M. M., Cannito, M. P., & Fleming, S. G. (1986). Disruption of reference in aging. *Brain and Language, 28*(1), 24–41.

Unger, J. B., McAvay, G., Bruce, M. L., Berkman, L., & Seeman, T. E. (1999). Variation in the impact of social network characteristics on physical functioning in elderly persons: MacArthur Studies of Successful Aging. *Journals of Gerontology: Psychological Sciences and Social Sciences, 54*(5), S245–S251.

U.S. Bureau of the Census. (2000). *The older population in the United States: March 1999* (No. P20–532). Washington, DC: Government Printing Office.

U.S. Department of Labor. (2001). *Employment characteristics of families in 2000.* Washington, DC: Author.

Vallar, G. (1993). The anatomical basis of spatial hemineglect in humans. In I. H. Robertson (Ed.), *Unilateral neglect: Clinical and experimental studies* (pp. 27–59). Hove, UK: Lawrence Erlbaum.

Van Lancker, D. (1980). Cerebral lateralization of pitch cues in the linguistic signal. *International Journal of Human Communication, 13*(2), 201–277.

Van Lancker, D. (1987). Nonpropositional speech: Neurolinguistic studies. In A. W. Ellis (Ed.), *Progress in the psychology of language* (pp. 49–118). London: Lawrence Erlbaum.

Van Lancker, D. (1991). Personal relevance and the human right hemisphere. *Brain and Cognition, 17*(1), 64–92.

Van Lancker, D., Canter, G. J., & Terbeek, D. (1981). Disambiguation of ditropic sentences: Acoustic and phonetic cues. *Journal of Speech and Hearing Research, 24*(3), 330–335.

Van Lancker, D., & Klein, K. (1990). Preserved recognition of familiar personal names in global aphasia. *Brain and Language, 39*(4), 511–529.

Van Lancker, D., & Sidtis, J. J. (1992). The identification of affective-prosodic stimuli by left- and right-hemisphere-damaged subjects: All errors are not created equal. *Journal of Speech and Hearing Research, 35*(5), 963–970.

Van Lancker, D. R., & Kempler, D. (1987). Comprehension of familiar phrases by left- but not by right-hemisphere damaged patients. *Brain and Language, 32*(2), 265–277.

Van Lancker, D. R., Kreiman, J., & Cummings, J. (1989). Voice perception deficits: Neuroanatomical correlates of phonagnosia. *Journal of Clinical and Experimental Neuropsychology, 11*(5), 665–674.

Vargha Khadem, F., Carr, L. J., Isaacs, E., & Brett, E. (1997). Onset of speech after left hemispherectomy in a nine-year-old boy. *Brain, 120*(1), 159–182.

Verhaeghen, P., & Vandenbroucke, A. (1998). Growing slower and less accurate: Adult age differences in time-accuracy functions for recall and recognition from episodic memory. *Experimental Aging Research, 24*(1), 3–19.

Victor, M., & Yakovlev, P. I. (1955). Korsakoff's psychic disorder in conjunction with peripheral neuritis: A translation of Korsakoff's original article with brief comments on the author and his contribution to clinical medicine. *Neurology, 5,* 394–406.

Villardita, C. (1985). Raven's colored Progressive Matrices and intellectual impairment in patients with focal brain damage. *Cortex, 21*(4), 627–634.

Visser, P. J., Scheltens, P., Verhey, F. R., Schmand, B., Launer, L. J., Jolles, J., et al. (1999). Medial temporal lobe atrophy and memory dysfunction as predictors for dementia in subjects with mild cognitive impairment. *Journal of Neurology, 246*(6), 477–485.

Von Monakow, C. (1914). *Die Lokalisation im Grosshirn und der Abbau der Funktion durch Kortikale Herde* (Brain localization and the distribution of function across cortical centers). Wiesbaden, Germany: J. F. Bergman.

Wada, J., & Rasmussen, T. (1960). Intracarotid injection of sodium amytal for the localization of cerebral speech dominance. *Journal of Neurosurgery, 17,* 266–282.

Walker, A. E., Robins, M., & Weinfeld, F. D. (1985). Epidemiology of brain tumors: The National Survey of Intracranial Neoplasms. *Neurology, 35*(2), 219–226.

Walsh, K. W., & Darby, D. (1999). *Neuropsychology: A clinical approach* (4th ed.). Edinburgh, UK: Churchill Livingstone.

Ward, C. D., Duvoisin, R. C., Ince, S. E., Nutt, J. D., Eldridge, R., & Calbe, D. B. (1983). Parkinson's disease in 65 pairs of twins and in a set of quadruplets. *Neurology, 33,* 815–824.

Warren, C. J. (2002). Emergent cardiovascular risk factor: Homocysteine. *Progress in Cardiovascular Nursing, 17*(1), 35–41.

Warrington, E. (1985). Agnosia: The impairment of object recognition. In P. J. Vinken, G. W. Gruyn, & H. L. Klawans (Eds.), *Handbook of clinical neurology* (pp. 333–349). Amsterdam: Elsevier.

Warrington, E. K., & McCarthy, R. A. (1987). Categories of knowledge: Further fractionation and an attempted integration. *Brain, 110,* 1273–1296.

Warrington, E. K., & McCarthy, R. A. (1994). Multiple meaning systems in the brain: A case for visual semantics. *Neuropsychologia, 32*(12), 1465–1473.

Waters, C. H., & Miller, C. A. (1994). Autosomal dominant Lewy body parkinsonism in a four-generation family. *Annals of Neurology, 35*(1), 59–64.

Waters, G. S., & Caplan, D. (1996). The capacity theory of sentence comprehension: Critique of Just and Carpenter (1992). *Psychological Review, 103,* 761–772.

Waters, G. S., & Caplan, D. (2001). Age, working memory, and on-line syntactic processing in sentence comprehension. *Psychology and Aging, 16*(1), 128–144.

Webster, D. D. (1968, March). Critical analysis of the disability in Parkinson's disease. *Modern Treatment,* pp. 257–282.

Wechsler, D. (1944). *The measurement of intelligence* (3rd ed.). Baltimore: Williams & Wilkins.

Wechsler, D. (1997a). *Wechsler Adult Intelligence Scale* (3rd ed.). San Antonio, TX: The Psychological Corporation, Harcourt Brace & Company.

Wechsler, D. (1997b). *Wechsler Memory Scale–III.* San Antonio, TX: The Psychological Corporation.

Weiner, M. F., Tractenberg, R., Teri, L., Logsdon, R. G., Thomas, R. G., Gamst, A., et al. (2000). Quantifying behavioral disturbance in Alzheimer's disease patients. *Journal of Psychiatric Research, 34*(2), 163–167.

Weingartner, H., Kaye, W., Smallberg, S. A., Ebert, M. H., Gillin, J. C., & Sitaram, N. (1981). Memory failures in progressive idiopathic dementia. *Journal of Abnormal Psychology, 90,* 187–196.

Weintraub, S., Mesulam, M.-M., & Kramer, L. (1981). Disturbances in prosody. A right-hemisphere contribution to language. *Archives of Neurology, 38*(12), 742–744.

Welsh, K. A., Butters, N., Mohs, R. C., Beekly, D., Edland, S., Fillenbaum, G., et al. (1994). The Consortium to Establish a Registry for Alzheimer's Disease (CERAD): Part V. A normative study of the neuropsychological battery. *Neurology, 44*(4), 609–614.

Wernicke, C. (1874). *Der Aphasische Symptomencomplex* (The aphasia symptom complex). Breslau: Cohn and Weigert.

Wertz, R. T., Henschel, C. R., Auther, L. L., Ashford, J. R., & Kirshner, H. S. (1998). Affective prosodic disturbance subsequent to right hemisphere stroke: A clinical application. *Journal of Neurolinguistics, 11*(1–2), 89–102.

Whisnant, J. P., Homer, D., Ingall, T. J., Baker, H. L., Jr., O'Fallon, W. M., & Wievers, D. O. (1990). Duration of cigarette smoking is the strongest predictor of severe extracranial carotid artery atherosclerosis. *Stroke, 21*(5), 707–714.

White, L. D., & Barone, J., S. (2001). Qualitative and quantitative estimates of apoptosis from birth to senescence in the rat brain. *Cell Death and Differentiation, 8,* 345–356.

Whitehouse, P. J. (1999). Alzheimer's disease: Past, present, and future. *European Archives of Psychiatry & Clinical Neuroscience, 249*(Suppl. 3), 43–45.

Wilkins, R. H., & Brody, I. A. (1969). Alzheimer's disease. *Archives of Neurology, 21,* 109–110.

Wilkinson, I. M. S. (1993). *Essential neurology* (2nd ed.). Oxford, UK: Blackwell Scientific.

Williams, G. R., Jiang, J. G., Matchar, D. B., & Samsa, G. P. (1999). Incidence and occurrence of total (first-ever and recurrent) stroke. *Stroke, 30*(12), 2523–2528.

Willis, S. L. (1996). Everyday problem solving. In J. E. Birren (Ed.), *Handbook of the psychology of aging* (4th ed., pp. 287–307). San Diego: Academic Press.

Willis, S. L., Allen-Burge, R., Dolan, M. M., Bertrand, R. M., Yesavage, J., & Taylor, J. L. (1998). Everyday problem solving among individuals with Alzheimer's disease. *The Gerontologist, 5,* 569–577.

Wilson, B. (1987). *Rehabilitation of memory.* New York: Guilford.

Wilson, B. A., Alderman, N., Burgess, P., Emslie, H., & Evans, J. (1996). *Behavioral assessment of dysexecutive syndrome.* Gaylord, MI: Northern Speech Services.

Wilson, B. A., Cockburn, J., & Baddeley, A. D. (1985). *The Rivermead Behavioural Memory Test.* Thurston, UK: Thames Valley Test Company.

Wimo, A., Winblad, B., Aguers-Torres, H., & von Strauss, E. (2003). The magnitude of dementia occurrence in the world. *Alzheimer Disease & Associated Disorders, 17*(2), 63–67.

Wingfield, A., & Kahana, M. J. (2002). The dynamics of memory retrieval in older adulthood. *Canadian Journal of Experimental Psychology, 56*(3), 187–199.

Wingfield, A., Poon, L. W., Lombardi, L., & Lowe, D. (1985). Speed of processing in normal aging: Effects of speech rate, linguistic structure, and processing time. *Journal of Gerontology, 40*(5), 579–585.

Wingfield, A., Stine, E. A., Lahar, C. J., & Aberdeen, J. S. (1988). Does the capacity of working memory change with age? *Experimental Aging Research, 14*(2–3), 103–107.

Wingfield, A., Tun, P. A., Koh, C., & Rosen, M. J. (1999). Regaining lost time: Adult aging and the effect of time restoration of recall of time-compressed speech. *Psychology and Aging, 14*(3), 380–389.

Wingfield, A., Waters, G. S., & Tun, P. (1997). Does working memory work in language comprehension? Evidence from cognitive neuroscience. In N. Raz (Ed.), *The other side of the error term: Aging and development as model systems in cognitive neuroscience* (pp. 319–394). New York: North-Holland.

Winner, E., Rosenstiel, A. K., & Gardner, H. (1977). Language development: Metaphoric understanding. *Journal of Learning Disabilities, 10*(3), 147–149.

Winograd, C. H., & Jarvik, L. F. (1986). Physician management of the demented patient. *Journal of the American Geriatrics Society, 34*(4), 295–308.

Woodruff Pak, D. S. (1997). *The neuropsychology of aging.* Cambridge, MA: Blackwell.

Woods, B. T. (1995). Acquired childhood aphasia. In H. S. Kirshner (Ed.), *Handbook of neurological speech and language disorders* (pp. 415–430). New York: Marcel Dekker.

Wooldridge, D. E. (1963). *The machinery of the brain.* New York: McGraw-Hill.

Wooten, G. F. (1997). Functional, anatomical, and behavioral consequences of dopamine receptor stimulation. *Annals of the New York Academy of Sciences, 835,* 153–156.

Wooten, G. F., & Collins, R. C. (1981). Metabolic effects of unilateral lesion of the substantia nigra. *Journal of Neuroscience: The Official Journal of the Society for Neuroscience, 1*(3), 285–291.

World Health Organization. (1990). *International classification of impairments, disabilities, and handicaps: A manual of classification relating to consequences of disease.* Geneva, Switzerland: Author.

World Health Organization. (2000). *Healthy ageing: Adults with intellectual disabilities: Summative report.* Geneva, Switzerland: Author.

Wragg, R. E., & Jeste, D. V. (1989). Overview of depression and psychosis in Alzheimer's disease. *American Journal of Psychiatry, 146*(5), 577–587.

Yan, J. H. (2000). Effects of aging on linear and curvilinear aiming arm movements. *Experimental Aging Research, 26*(4), 393–408.

Yanagihara, T. (1991). Metabolic derangement and cell damage in cerebral ischemia with emphasis on protein and nucleic acid metabolism. In H. Takeshima, B. K. Siesjoe, & J. D. Miller (Eds.), *Advances in brain resuscitation* (pp. 77–98). Tokyo: Springer-Verlag.

Zacks, R. T., Hasher, L., & Li, K. Z. H. (2000). Human memory. In T. A. Salthouse & F. I. M. Craik (Eds.), *Handbook of aging & cognition* (2nd ed., pp. 293–357). Mahwah, NJ: Lawrence Erlbaum.

Zaidel, E. (1978). Auditory language comprehension in the right hemisphere following cerebral commissurotomy and hemispherectomy: A comparison with child language and aphasia. In A. Caramazza & E. Zurif (Eds.), *Language acquisition and language breakdown* (pp. 229–275). Baltimore: Johns Hopkins University Press.

Zakzanis, K. K., Leach, L., & Kaplan, E. (1998). On the nature and pattern of neurocognitive function in major depressive disorder. *Neuropsychiatry, Neuropsychology, and Behavioral Neurology, 3,* 111–119.

Zatorre, R. J. (1984). Musical perception and cerebral function: A critical review. *Music Perception, 2,* 196–221.

Zelinski, E. M., Gilewski, M. J., & Thompson, L. W. (1980). Do laboratory tasks relate to self-assessment of memory in young and old? In L. W. Poon, J. L. Fozzard, L. S. Cermak, D. Arenberg, & L. W. Thompson (Eds.), *New directions in memory and aging: Proceedings of the George Talland Memorial Conference.* Hillsdale, NJ: Lawrence Erlbaum.

Zesiewicz, T. A., & Hauser, R. A. (2001). Neurosurgery for Parkinson's disease. *Seminars in Neurology, 21*(1), 91–101.

Zoltan, B., & Siev, E. (1996). *Vision, perception, and cognition: A manual for the evaluation and treatment of the neurologically impaired adult* (3rd ed.). Thorofare, NJ: SLACK, Inc.

Zorzon, M., Capus, L., & Pellegrino, A. (2002). Familial and environmental risk factors in Parkinson's disease: A case-control study in north-east Italy. *Acta Neurologica Scandinavica, 105*(2), 77–82.

SOURCES OF ILLUSTRATIONS

Table 2.1:   From *Fundamentals of Human Neuropsychology* by Bryan Kolb & Ian Q. Whishaw. Copryight © 1980, 1985, 1990, 1996 by W.H. Freeman and Company. Used with permission.

Figure 2.10: From "Disconnection and cerebral metabolism: The case of conduction aphasia," *Archives of Neurology, 45,* 275–279, by Kempler, D., Metter, E. J., Jackson, C. A., Hanson, W. R., Riege, W. H., Mazziotta, J. C., et al. Copyright © 1988 American Medical Association. All rights reserved.

Figure 2.11: From " Cognitive aging," by Naftali Raz, in *Encyclopedia of the Human Brain, Vol. 1,* edited by Ramachandran, V. S. Copyright © 2004. Used with permission from Elsevier/Academic Press.

Figure 3.1:   From "Incidence and occurrence of total (first-ever and recurrent) stroke," by Williams, G. R., Jiang, J. G., Matchar, D. B., & Samsa, G. P. in *Stroke, 30*(12), 2523–2528. Reprinted with permission from Lippincott Williams & Wilkins.

Figure 4.1:   From "The effects of age, education, and ethnicity on verbal fluency," by Kempler, D., Teng, E. L., Dick, M., Taussig, I. M., & Davis, D. S. in *Journal of the International Neuropsychological Society, 4,* pp. 531–538. Copyright © 1998. Reprinted with the permission of Cambridge University Press.

Table 4.2:   From *Fundamentals of Human Neuropsychology* by Bryan Kolb & Ian Q. Whishaw. Copryight © 1980, 1985, 1990, 1996 by W. H. Freeman and Company. Used with permission.

Figure 4.3:   From *Boston Diagnostic Aphasia Examination, 3rd edition* by Goodglass, H., Kaplan, E., & Barresi, B. Copyright © 2000. Reprinted with permission from Lippincott Williams & Wilkins.

Figure 5.3:   From *Right Hemisphere Damage: Disorders of Communication and Cognition, 1st Edition* by Myers, P. S. Copyright © 1999. Reprinted with permission of Delmar Learning, a division of Thomson Learning: www.thomsonrights.com. Fax: 800–730–2215.

Figure 5.4:   From *Reading Comprehension Battery for Aphasia, 2nd edition* by LaPointe, L., & Horner, J. Copyright © 1998. Reprinted with permission of Pro-Ed, Inc.
Excerpts from *The Nelson Reading Skills Test:* Copyright © 1977 by the Riverside Publishing Company. Reproduced from *The Nelson Reading Skills Test,* with permission of the publisher. All rights reserved. No Part of this work may be reproduced or transmitted in any form or by any means, electronic or mechanical, including photocopying and recorded, or any information storage or retrieval system without prior written permission of The Riverside Publishing Company, unless such copying is expressly permitted by federal copyright law. Address inquiries to Permissions, The Riverside Publishing Company, 425 Spring Lake Drive, Itasca, IL 60143.

Author Index

SUBJECT INDEX

ABOUT THE AUTHOR

Daniel Kempler earned master's and Ph.D. degrees in Linguistics and obtained clinical training and a certificate of clinical competence in Speech-Language Pathology.

Since 2002, he has been Professor and Chair of the Department of Communication Sciences and Disorders at Emerson College in Boston. Prior to this, he held (simultaneously) positions as Professor in the School of Medicine (Department of Otolaryngology) and School of Gerontology at the University of Southern California and Director of the Speech and Hearing Clinics at the Los Angeles County + USC Medical Center.

Dr. Kempler's research has centered on the theme of understanding the neurological and psychological processes underlying speech and language abilities by studying communication disorders due to brain injury. Within this area, he has pursued research on several topics, including language deficits in Alzheimer's disease and aphasia, how understanding of idioms and proverbs is affected by brain damage, and speech impairments in Parkinson's disease. In collaboration with colleagues, he has developed several tests that are used to assess understanding of idioms and proverbs, nonverbal reasoning, and sentence comprehension as well as a battery to assess dementia in several cultural and language groups. He has written or coauthored more than 100 journal publications and book chapters. He provides professional and community service in many areas, from initiating and coordinating a support group for Parkinsonians and their families to serving as an Associate Editor for the *Journal of Speech-Language Hearing Research* and a member of the Board of Governors of the Academy of Aphasia.

When not at work, he enjoys gardening, swimming, and being outdoors.

ABOUT THE CONTRIBUTORS

Teresa E. Seeman, Ph.D., is a Professor of Medicine & Epidemiology in the UCLA Schools of Medicine and Public Health. Previously, she was on the faculty at the Department of Epidemiology in the Yale School of Public Health from 1985 to 1995 and then spent 2 years on the faculty at the Andrus School of Gerontology at USC. She joined the faculty at UCLA in January 1998 with joint appointments in the Schools of Medicine and Public Health. Her research interests focus on the role of sociocultural factors in health and aging, with specific interest in understanding the biological pathways through which these factors influence health and aging. A major focus of her research relates to understanding how aspects of the social environment, particularly social ties, influence health and aging. She was a member of the MacArthur Research Network on Successful Aging (1985–1995) and has published numerous articles examining psychosocial, behavioral, and biological predictors of more successful aging. Most recently, in collaboration with Drs. Bruce McEwen and Burton Singer, she has taken a lead in empirical research on the new concept of allostatic load.

Melissa Tabbarah, **Ph.D., M.P.H.,** received her B.S. in Biology (Ecology) at the University of California–Riverside and trained at the UCLA School of Public Health, where she received her M.P.H. She subsequently trained as a gerontologist, receiving a Ph.D. in Gerontology from the University of Southern California in 2000. As a predoctoral Fellow of the National Institute on Aging and a postdoctoral Fellow of the Agency for Healthcare Research Quality, her research focused on housing and disability issues specific to older Americans. She currently works as a Research Associate in the Department of Family Medicine at the University of Pittsburgh.